VANGUARD

AICHI SENDOU TOSHIKI KAI MISAKI TOKURA KAMUI KATSURAGI

TEAM Q4

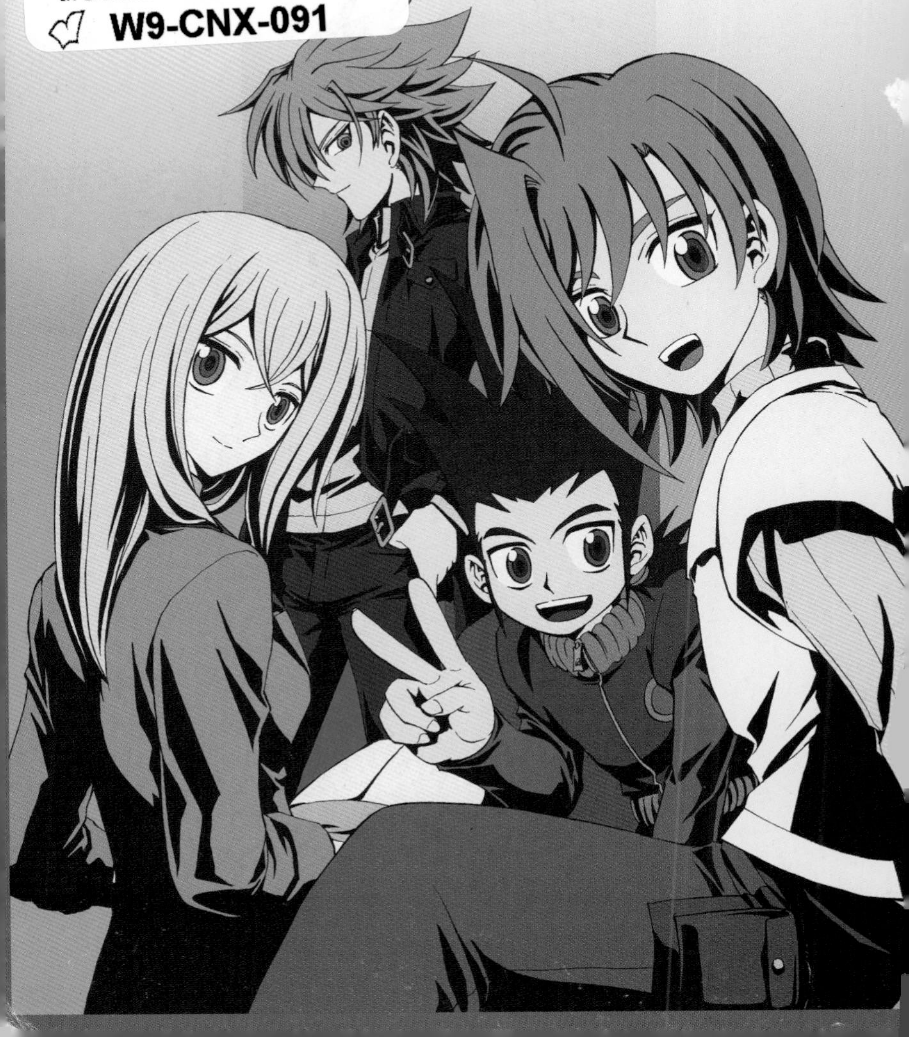

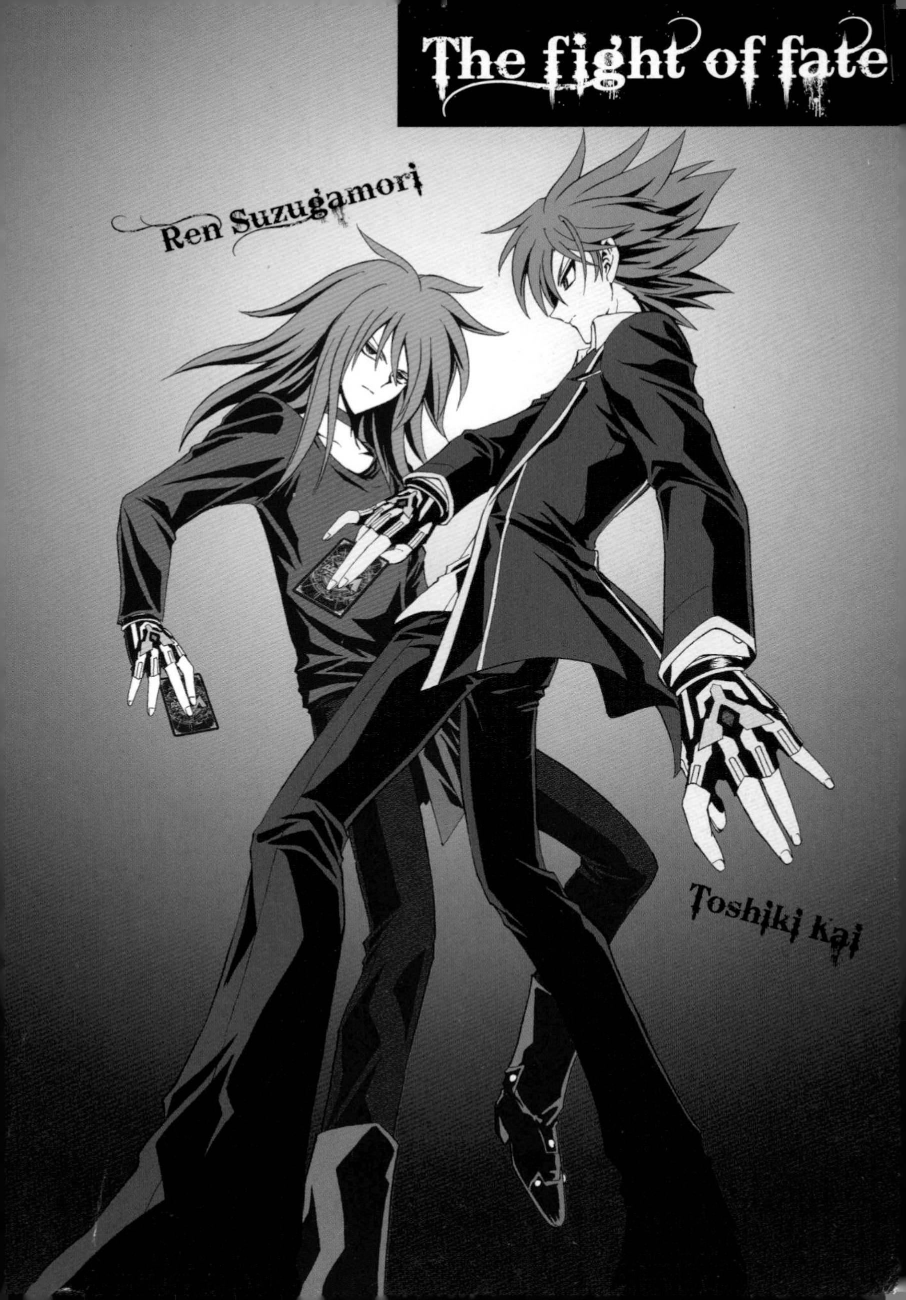
The fight of fate
Ren Suzugamori
Toshiki Kai

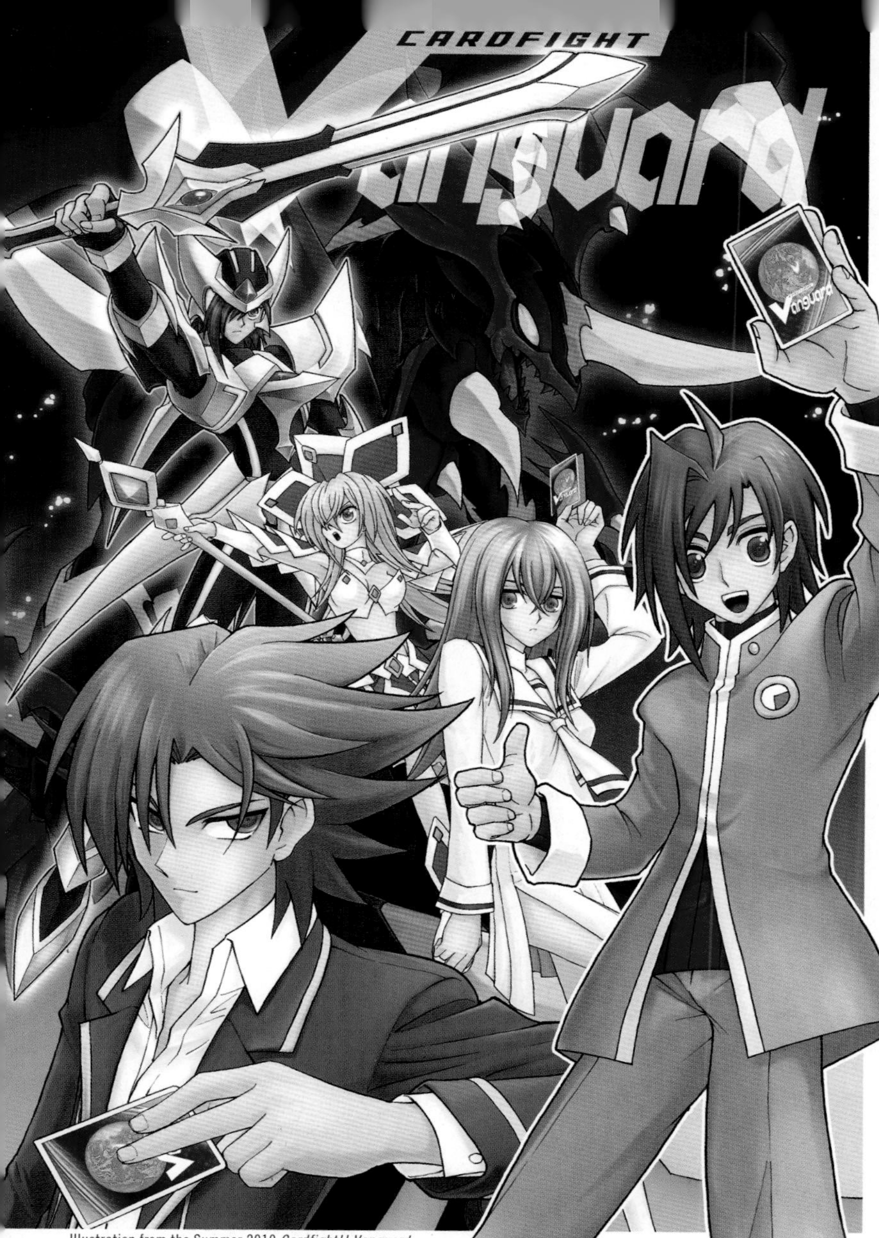
CARDFIGHT
Vanguard

Illustration from the Summer 2010 *Cardfight!! Vanguard* production announcement.

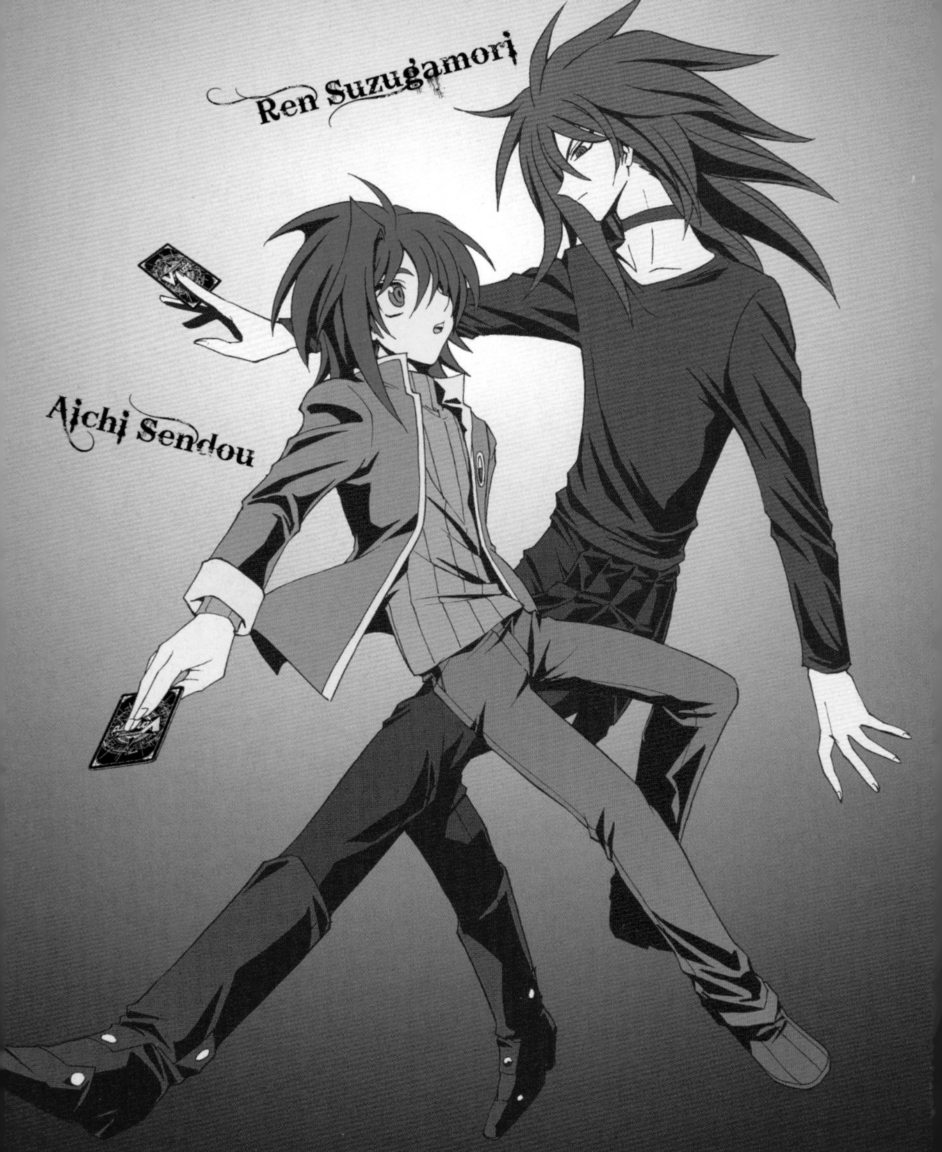
Ren Suzugamori
Aichi Sendou

The fight of PSY.qualia

HI, TETSU.

WHAT IS THE MEANING OF THIS,

KAI?

DIDN'T THINK YOU'D VENTURE IN HERE ...

GEEZ, YOU ARE SUCH A...

ALL THESE FOO FIGHTERS LOITERING ABOUT RIGHT UNDER MY NOSE IS ANNOYING!

THE HEAD OF FOO FIGHTER...

SORRY YOU CAME ALL THIS WAY, BUT NO FIGHTER HERE CAN SATISFY YOU, OTHER THAN

REN SUZU-GAMORI-SAMA!

6

SO HE'S TOSHIKI KAI, THE GUY REN WAS LOOKING FOR!

THAT'S **REN-SAMA** TO YOU!

FOO FIGHTER— SUCH A FEEBLE GANG!

AFTER FIGHTING HIM, I REALIZED

HE'S ABNORMALLY STRONG.

CAN DEFEAT HIM!

TOSHIKI KAI... ONLY REN-SAMA

DAMN... I COULDN'T STOP HIM!

CLENCH

IT'S LIKE HE'S REVERTED TO THE WAY HE WAS WHEN HE HUNG OUT WITH FOO FIGHTER.

KAI'S AIRS...

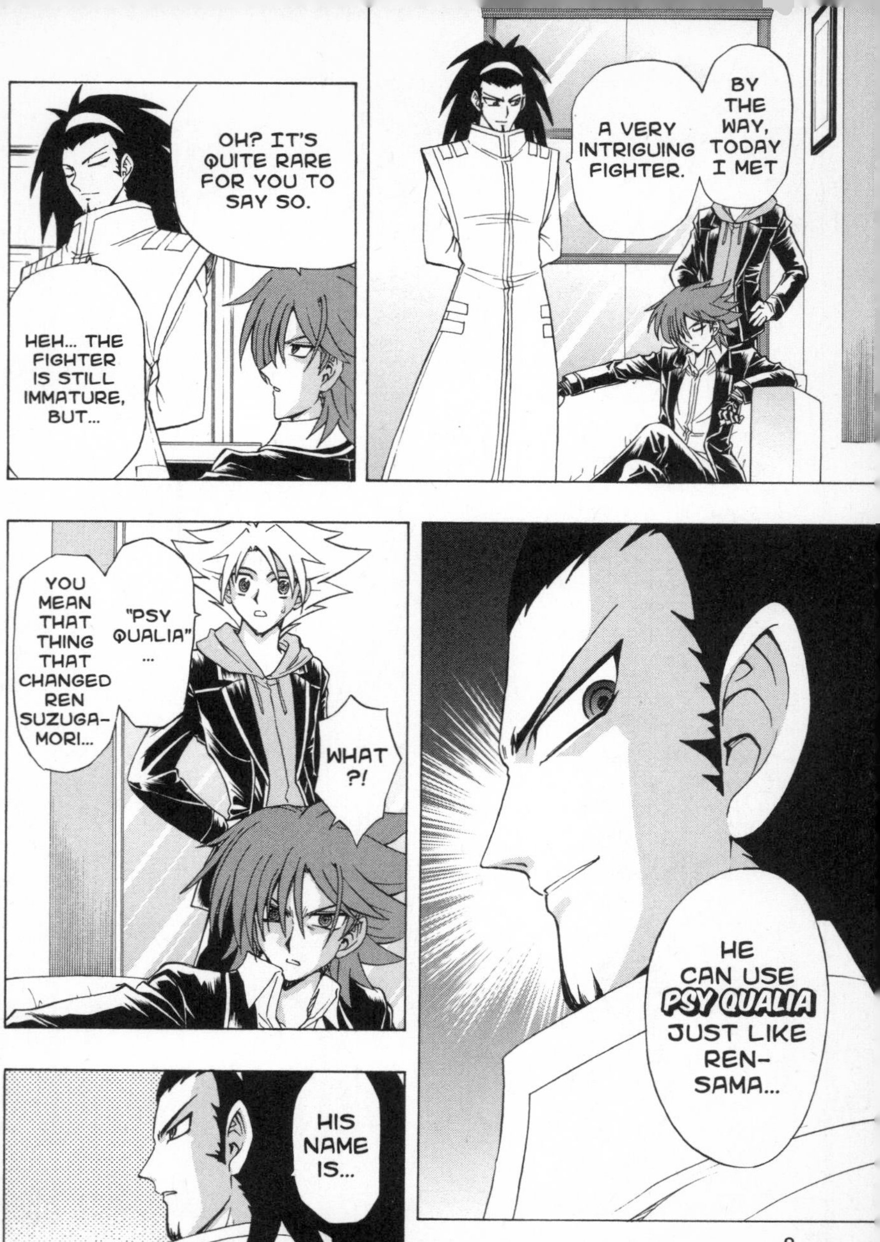
BY THE WAY, TODAY I MET
A VERY INTRIGUING FIGHTER.
OH? IT'S QUITE RARE FOR YOU TO SAY SO.
HEH... THE FIGHTER IS STILL IMMATURE, BUT...
HE CAN USE PSY QUALIA JUST LIKE REN-SAMA...
"PSY QUALIA" ...
YOU MEAN THAT THING THAT CHANGED REN SUZUGA-MORI...
WHAT?!
HIS NAME IS...

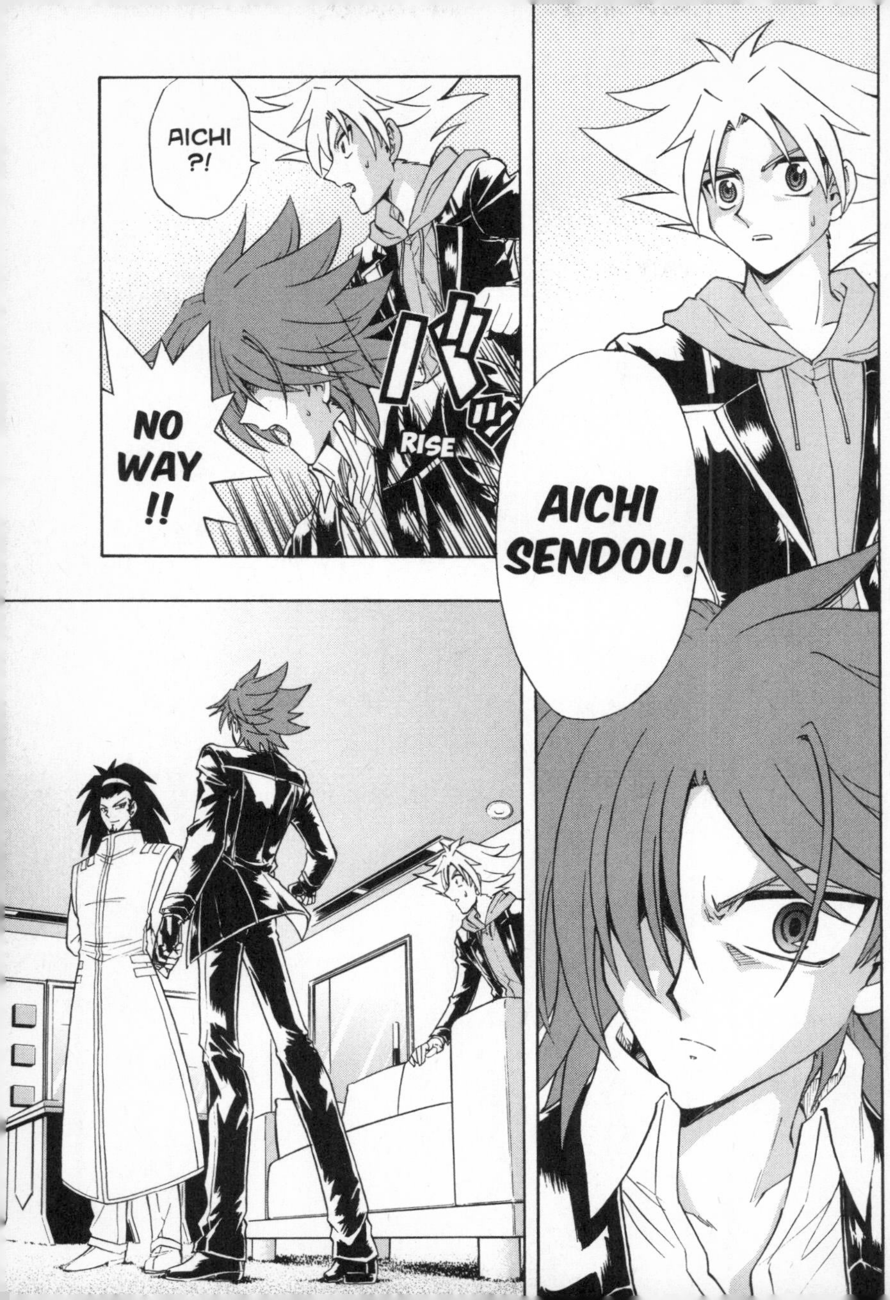
AICHI SENDOU.
AICHI ?!
NO WAY !!
RISE

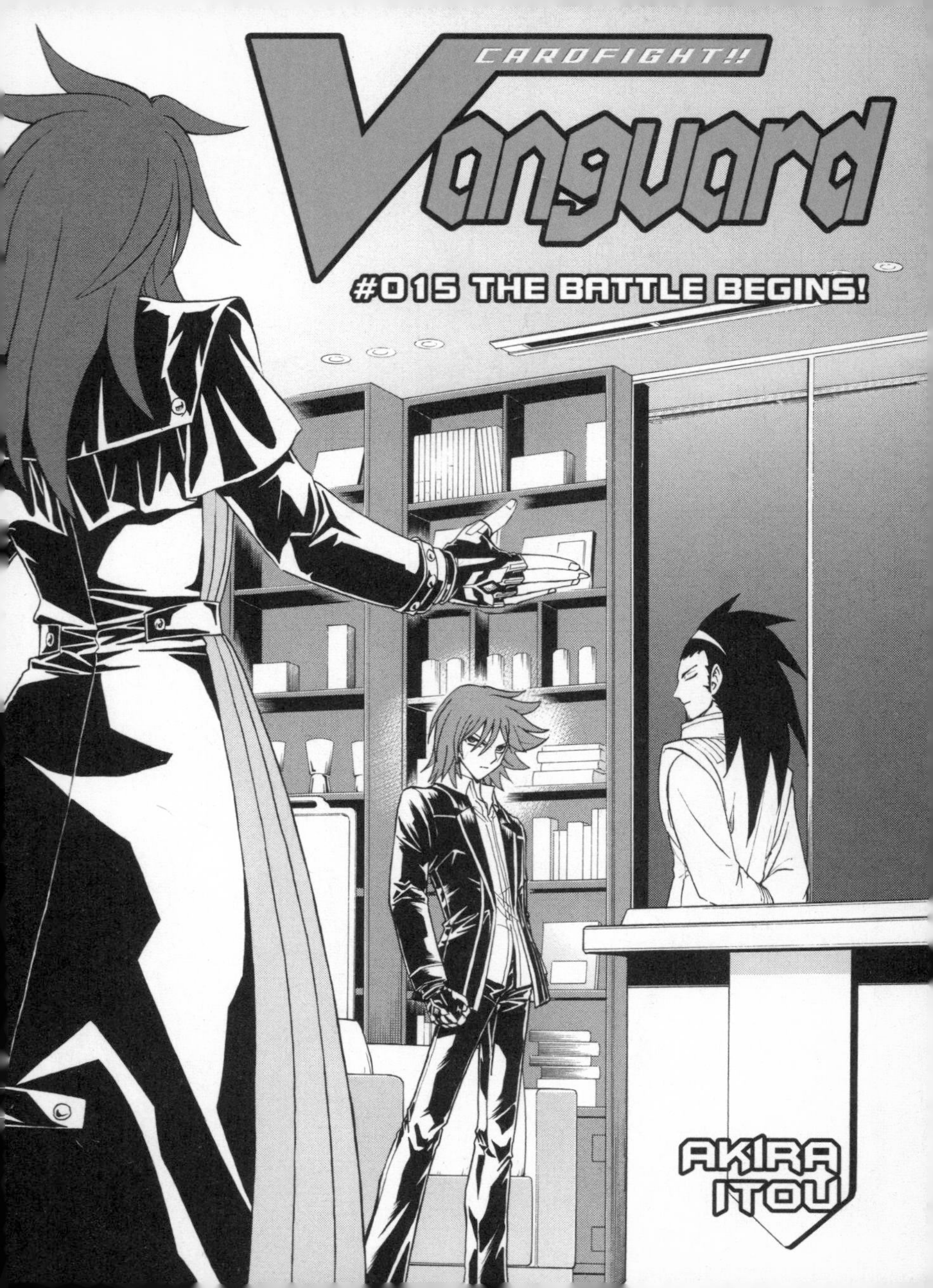
CARDFIGHT!!
Vanguard
#015 THE BATTLE BEGINS!
AKIRA ITOU

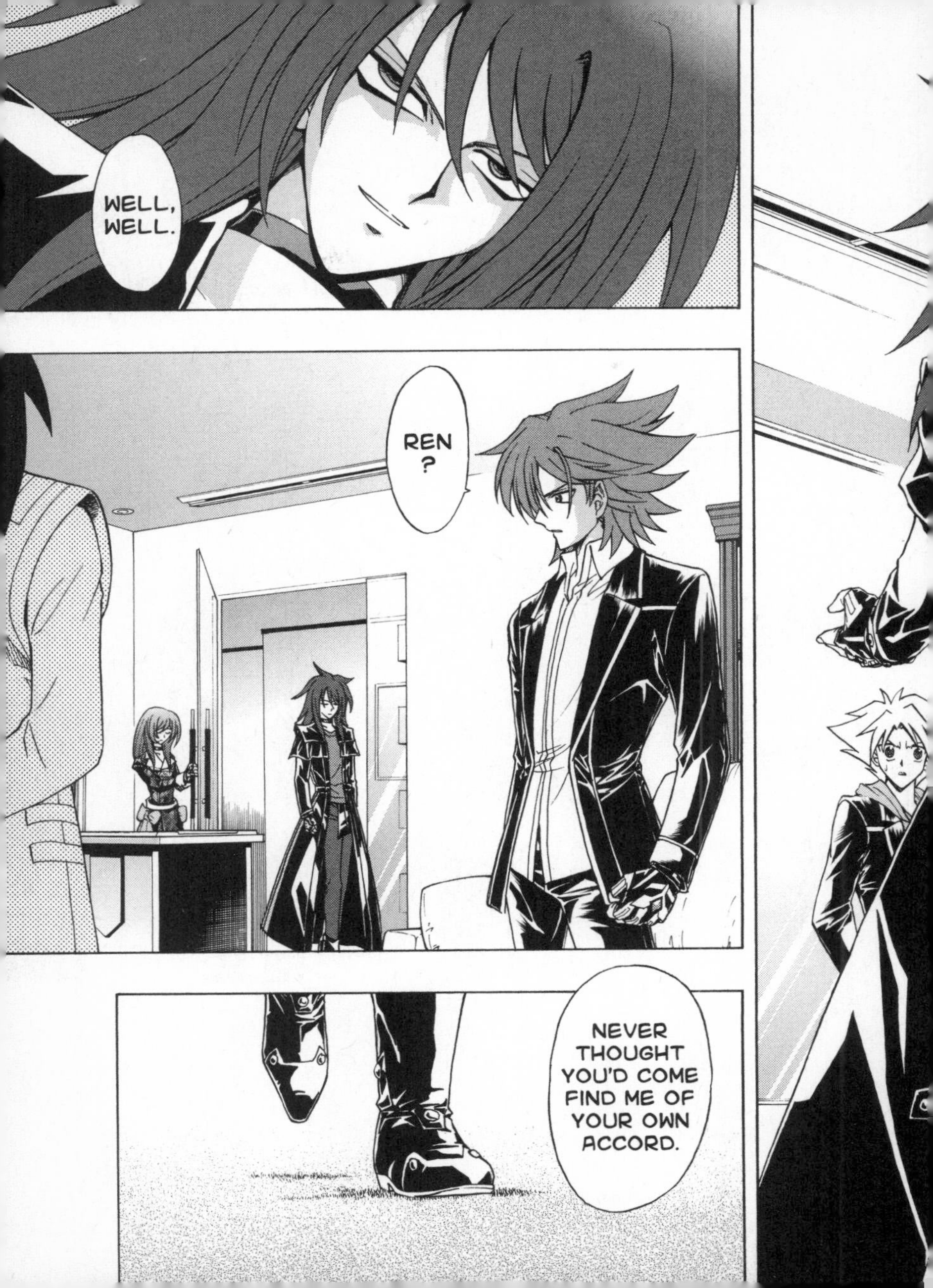
WELL, WELL.
REN?
NEVER THOUGHT YOU'D COME FIND ME OF YOUR OWN ACCORD.

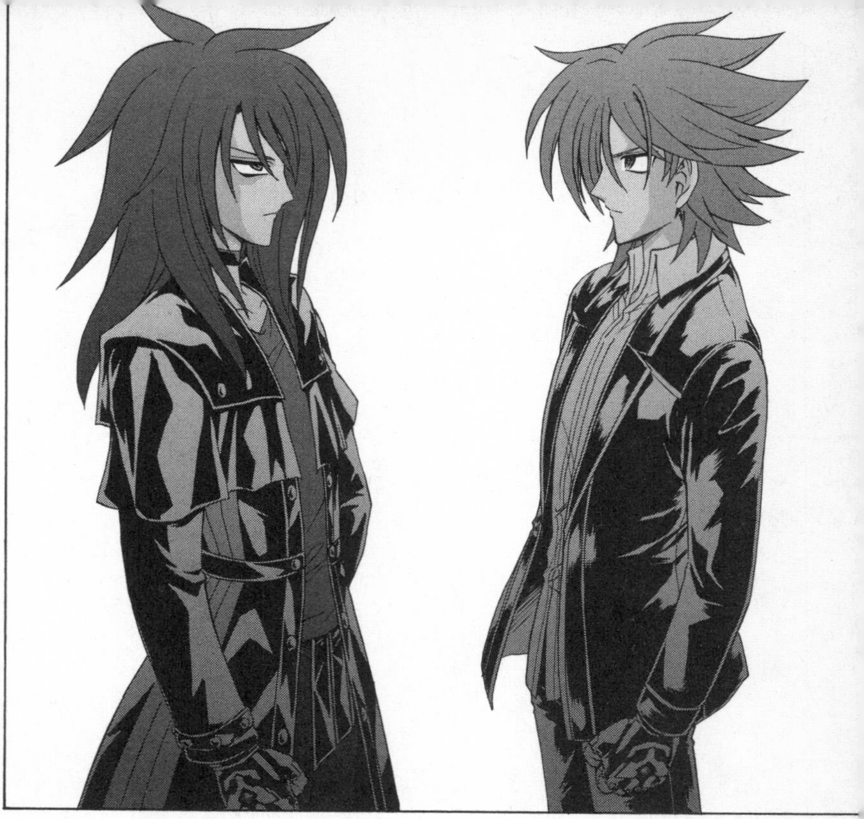
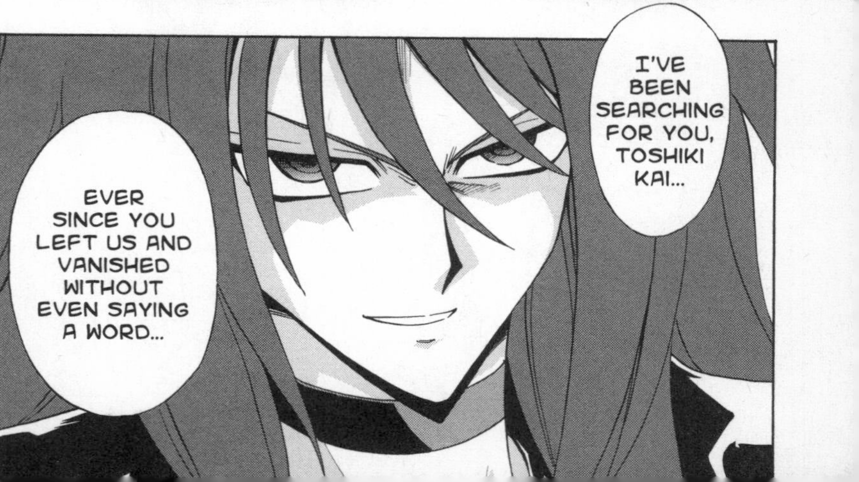
I'VE BEEN SEARCHING FOR YOU, TOSHIKI KAI...
EVER SINCE YOU LEFT US AND VANISHED WITHOUT EVEN SAYING A WORD...

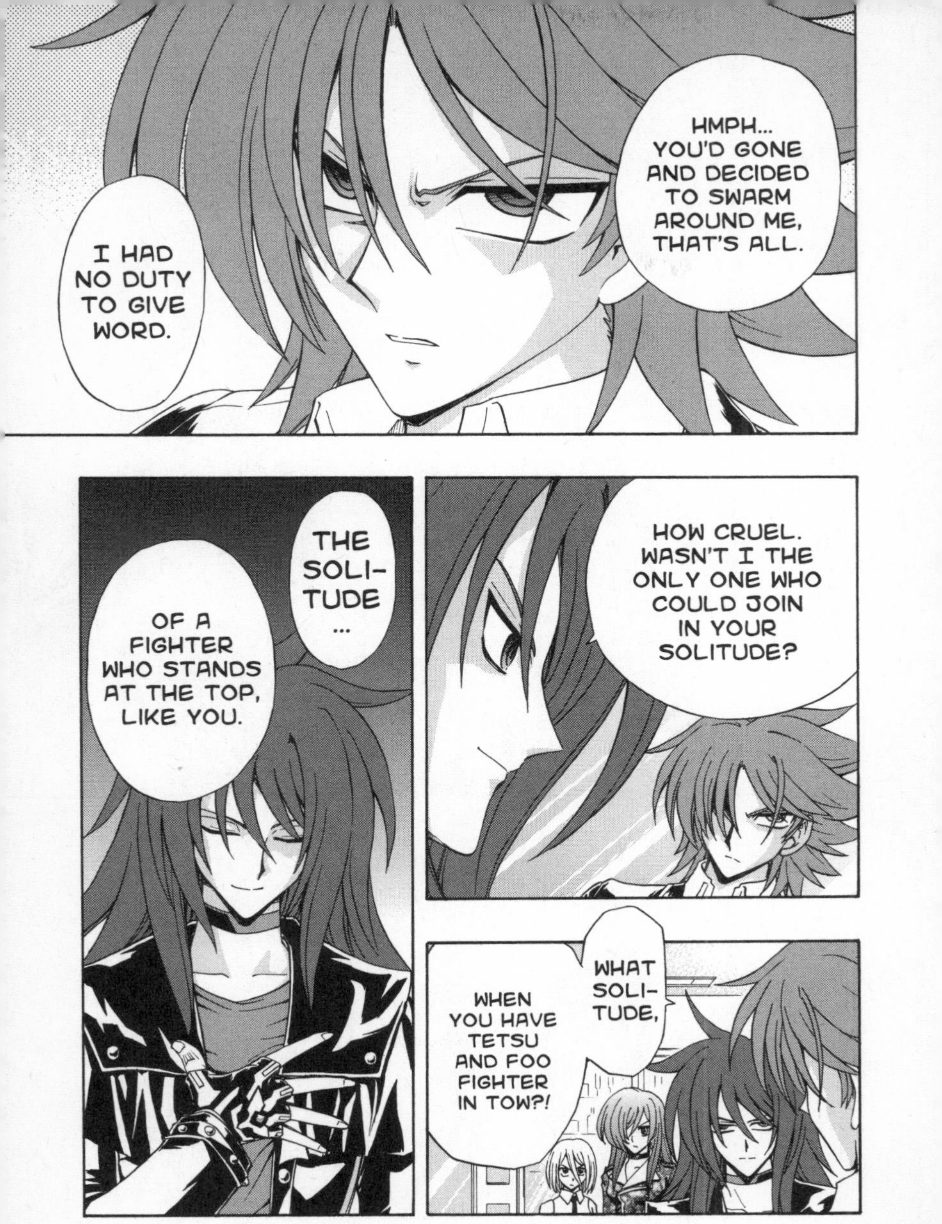
HMPH... YOU'D GONE AND DECIDED TO SWARM AROUND ME, THAT'S ALL.
I HAD NO DUTY TO GIVE WORD.
HOW CRUEL. WASN'T I THE ONLY ONE WHO COULD JOIN IN YOUR SOLITUDE?
WHAT SOLI-TUDE,
WHEN YOU HAVE TETSU AND FOO FIGHTER IN TOW?!
THE SOLI-TUDE ...
OF A FIGHTER WHO STANDS AT THE TOP, LIKE YOU.

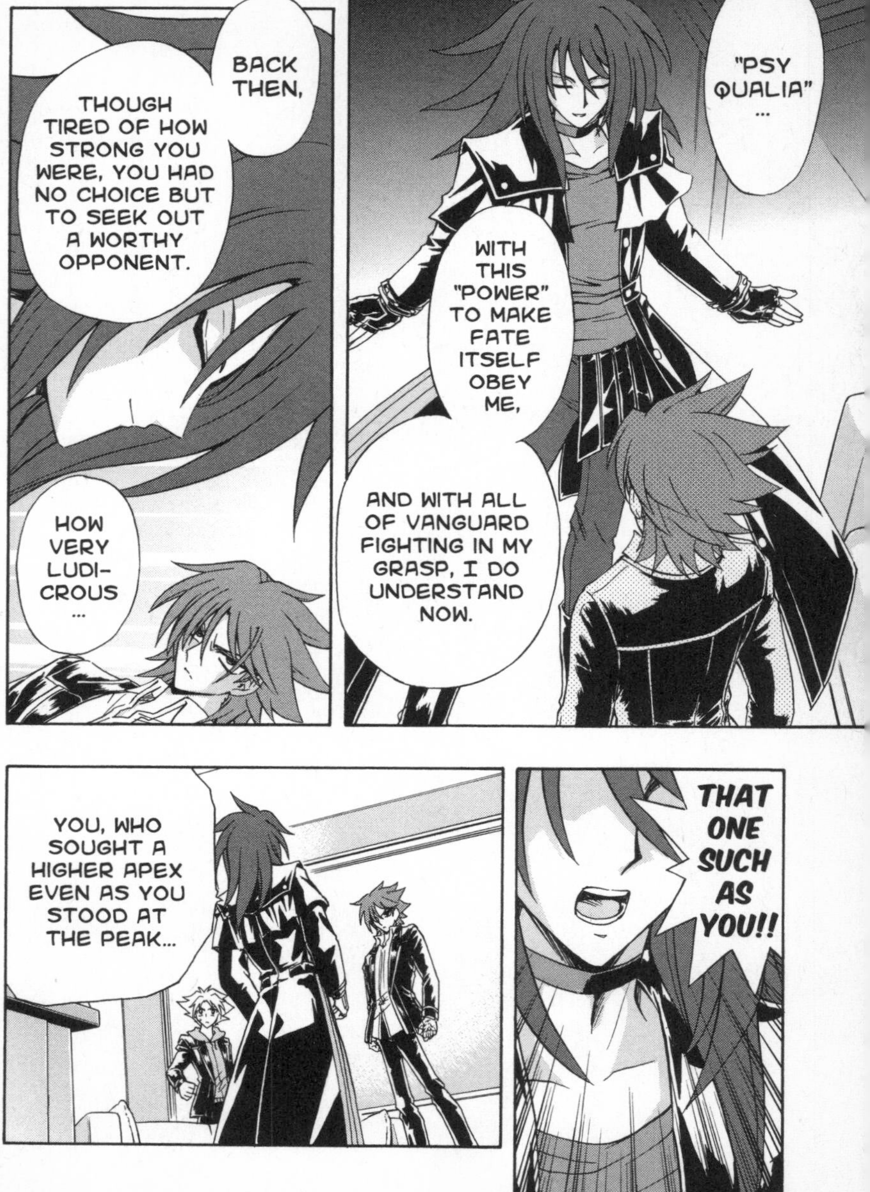
"PSY QUALIA" ...
WITH THIS "POWER" TO MAKE FATE ITSELF OBEY ME,
AND WITH ALL OF VANGUARD FIGHTING IN MY GRASP, I DO UNDERSTAND NOW.
BACK THEN,
THOUGH TIRED OF HOW STRONG YOU WERE, YOU HAD NO CHOICE BUT TO SEEK OUT A WORTHY OPPONENT.
HOW VERY LUDI- CROUS ...
THAT ONE SUCH AS YOU!!
YOU, WHO SOUGHT A HIGHER APEX EVEN AS YOU STOOD AT THE PEAK...

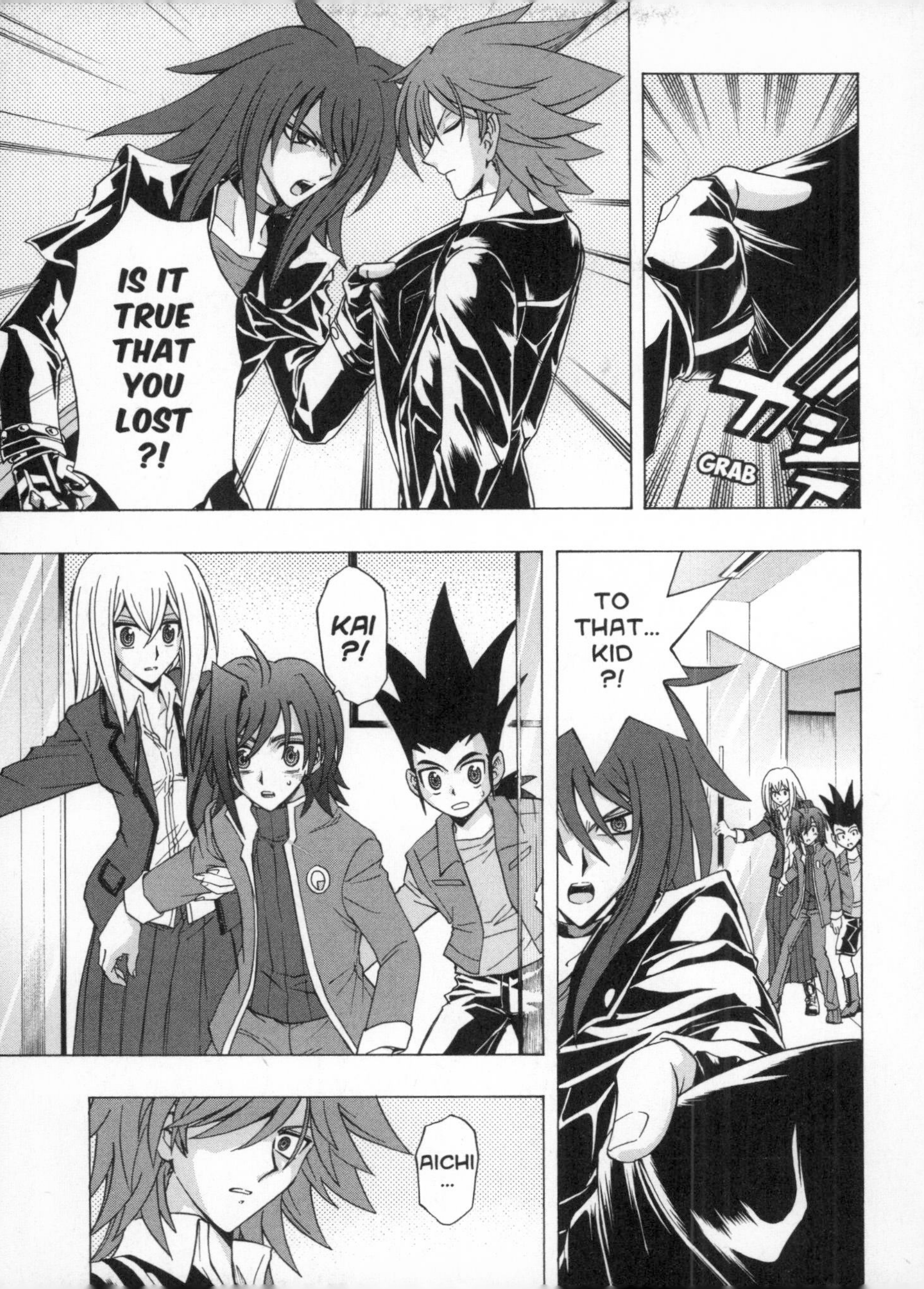
GRAB
IS IT TRUE THAT YOU LOST ?!
TO THAT... KID ?!
KAI ?!
AICHI ...

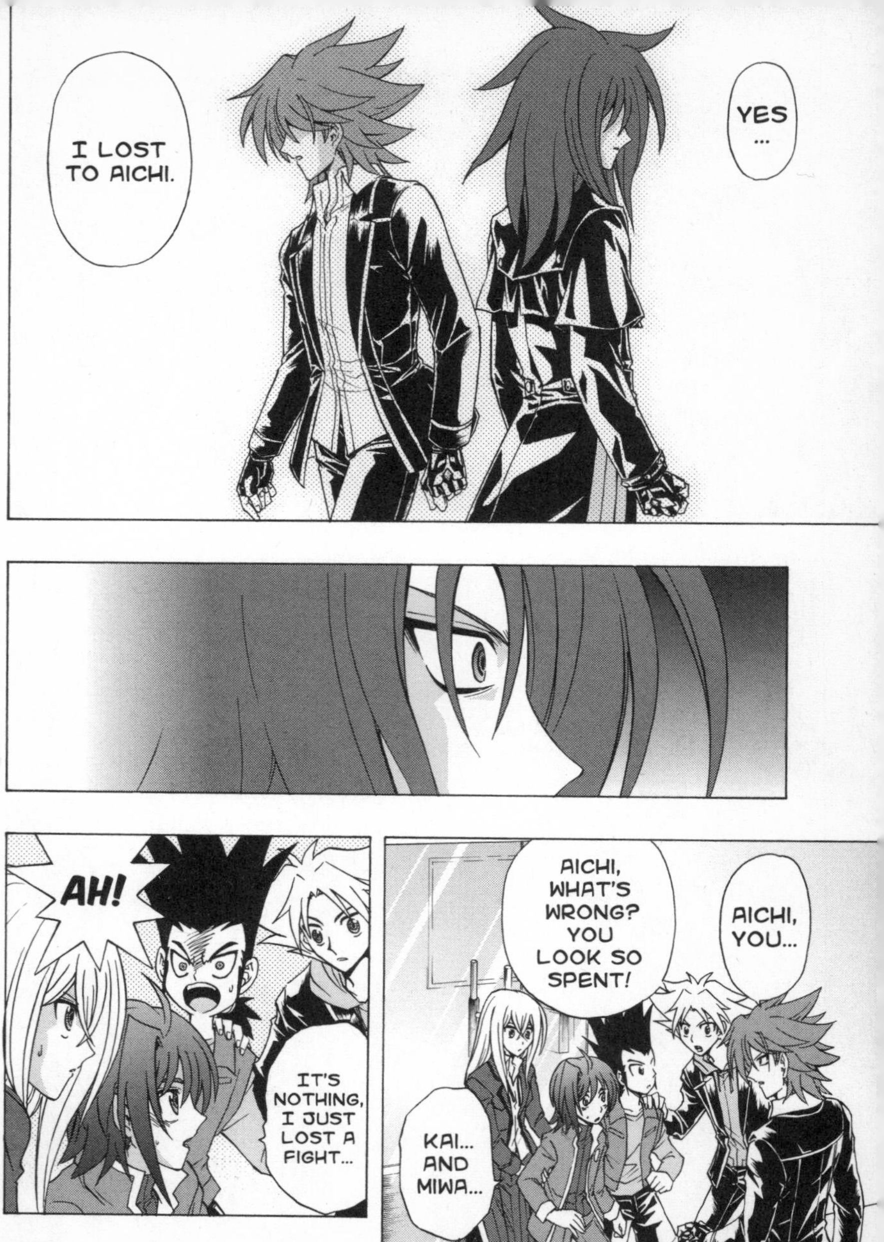
YES ...
I LOST TO AICHI.
AICHI, YOU...
AICHI, WHAT'S WRONG? YOU LOOK SO SPENT!
KAI... AND MIWA...
AH!
IT'S NOTHING, I JUST LOST A FIGHT...

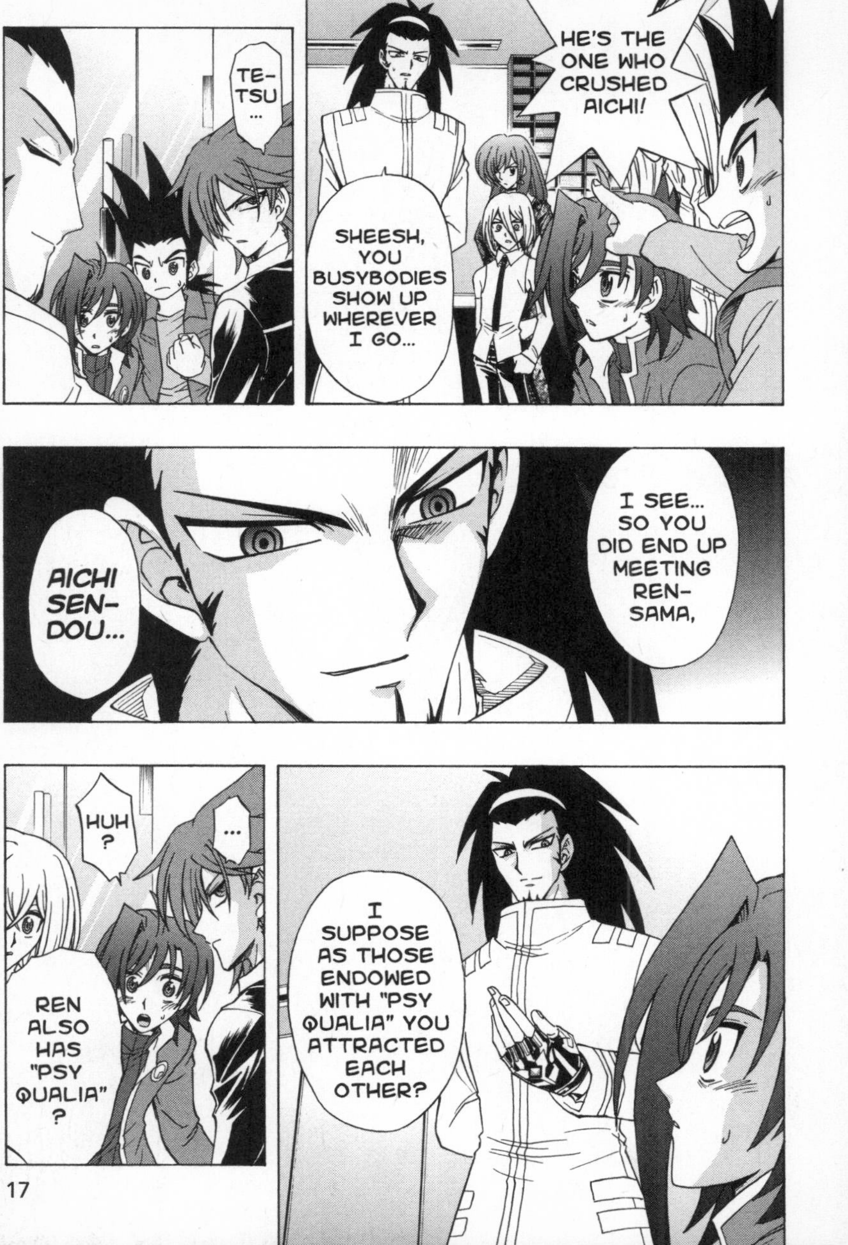
HE'S THE ONE WHO CRUSHED AICHI!
SHEESH, YOU BUSYBODIES SHOW UP WHEREVER I GO...
TE-TSU ...
I SEE... SO YOU DID END UP MEETING REN-SAMA,
AICHI SEN-DOU...
I SUPPOSE AS THOSE ENDOWED WITH "PSY QUALIA" YOU ATTRACTED EACH OTHER?
...
HUH ?
REN ALSO HAS "PSY QUALIA" ?

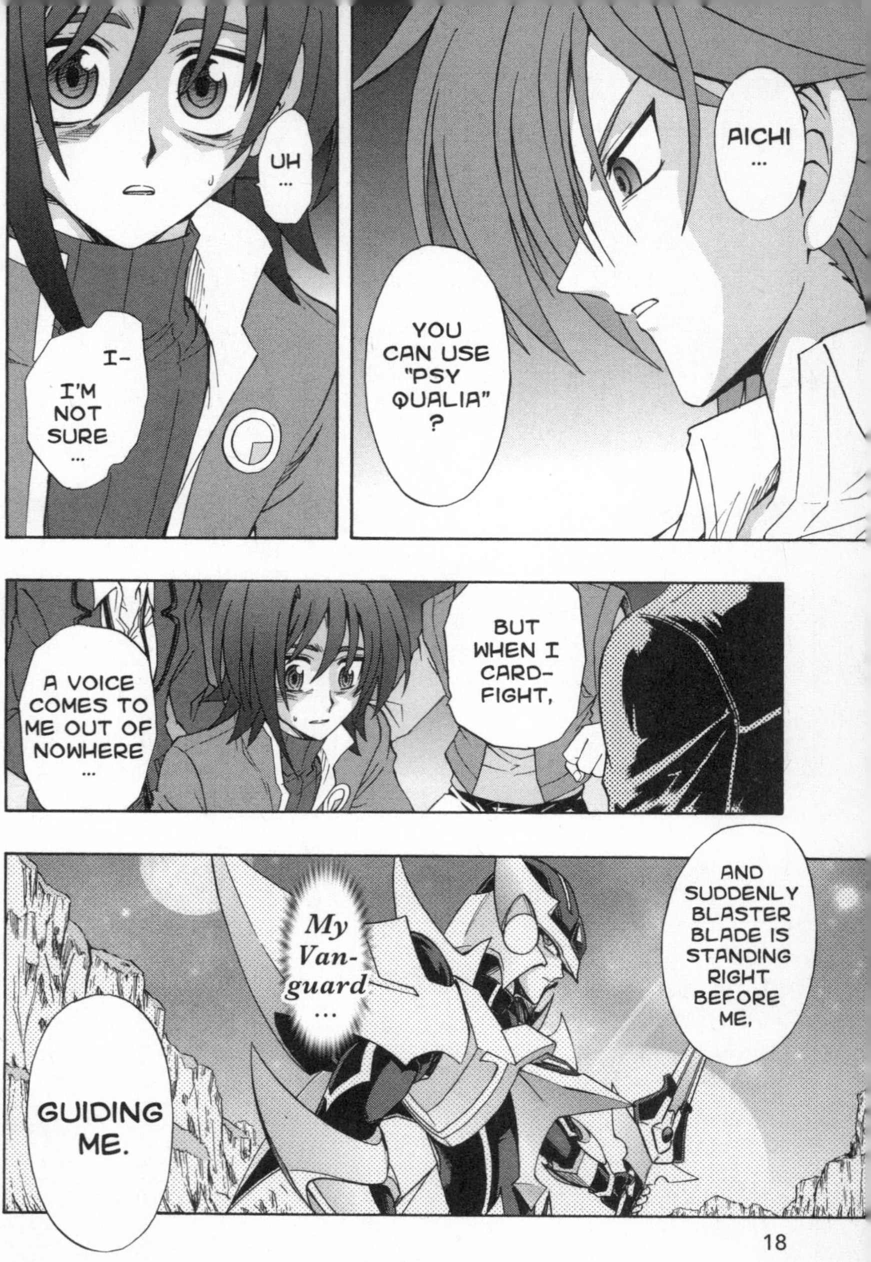
AICHI ...
YOU CAN USE "PSY QUALIA"?
UH ...
I- I'M NOT SURE ...
BUT WHEN I CARD-FIGHT,
A VOICE COMES TO ME OUT OF NOWHERE ...
AND SUDDENLY BLASTER BLADE IS STANDING RIGHT BEFORE ME,
My Van-guard ...
GUIDING ME.

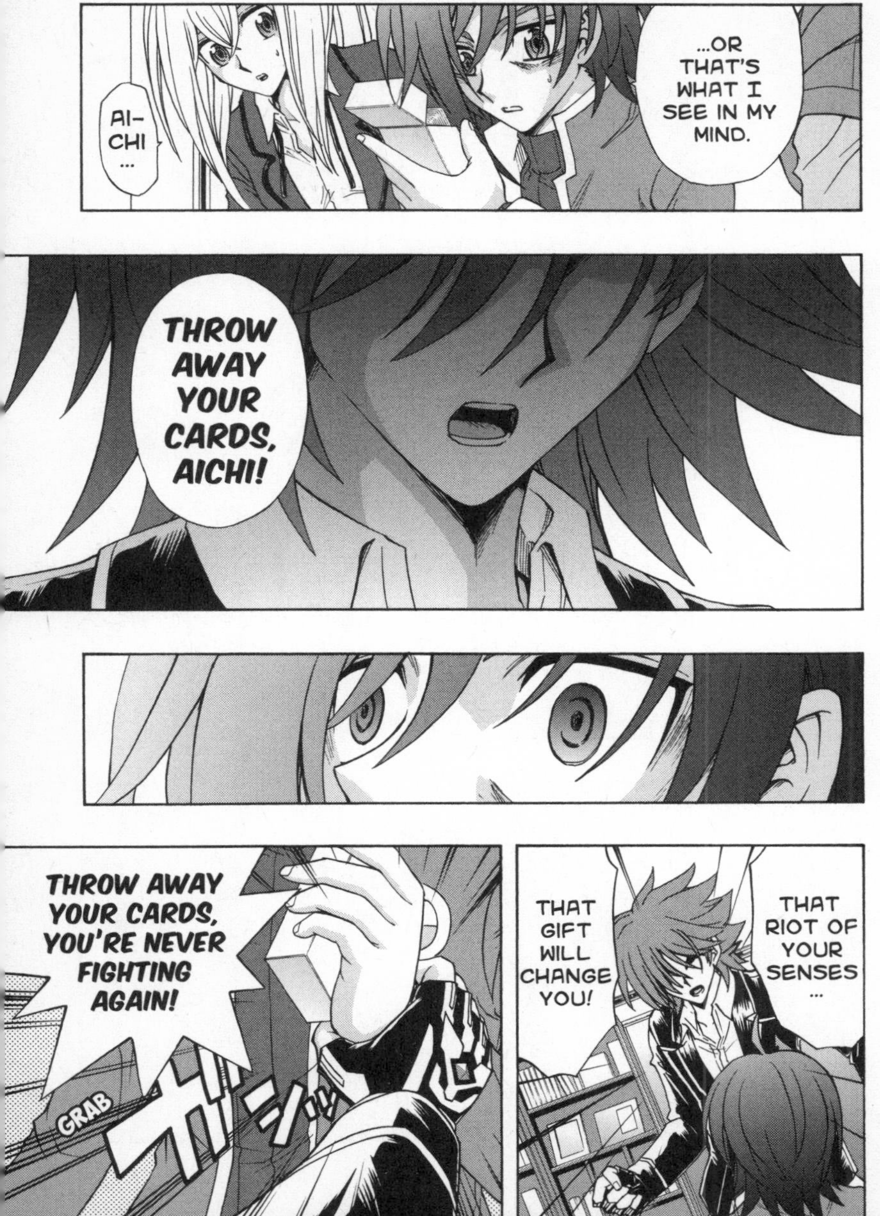
...OR THAT'S WHAT I SEE IN MY MIND.
AI-CHI ...
THROW AWAY YOUR CARDS, AICHI!
THAT RIOT OF YOUR SENSES ...
THAT GIFT WILL CHANGE YOU!
THROW AWAY YOUR CARDS, YOU'RE NEVER FIGHTING AGAIN!
GRAB

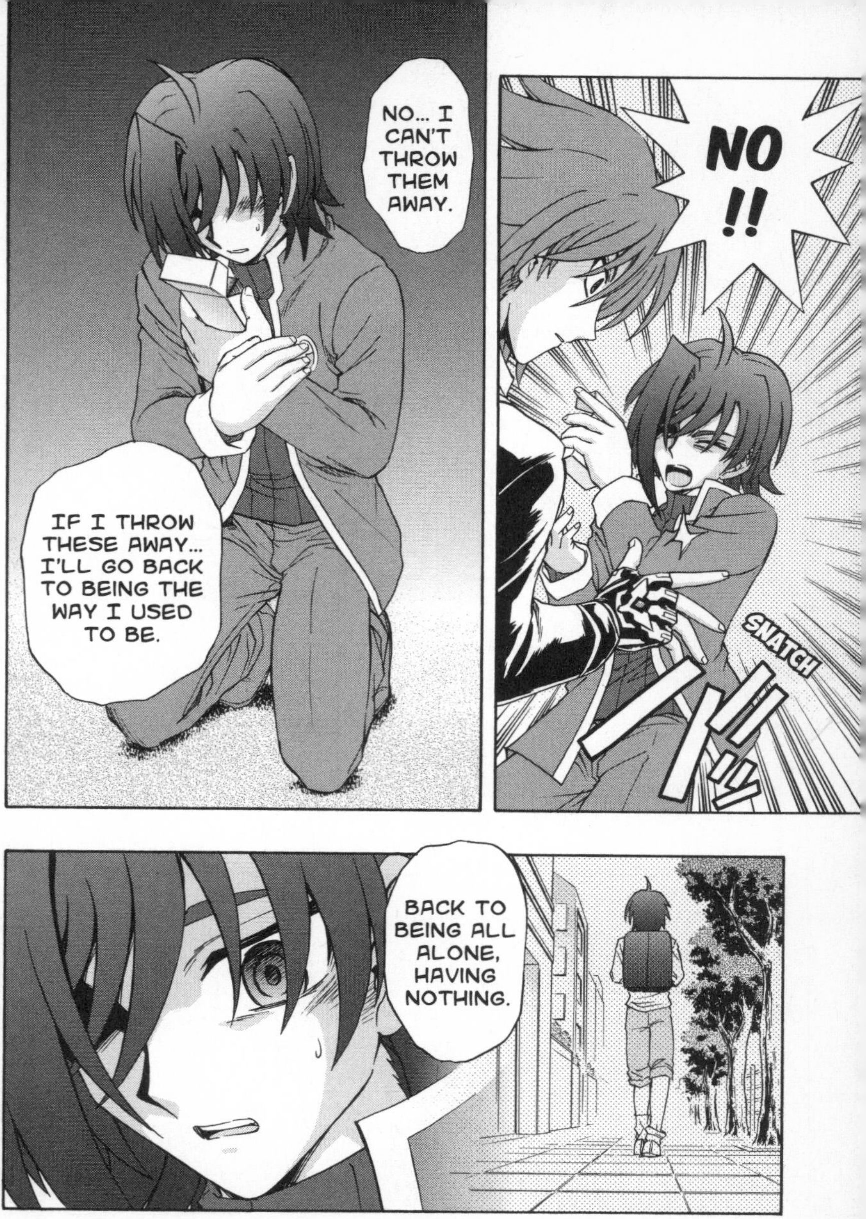
NO !!
SNATCH
NO... I CAN'T THROW THEM AWAY.
IF I THROW THESE AWAY... I'LL GO BACK TO BEING THE WAY I USED TO BE.
BACK TO BEING ALL ALONE, HAVING NOTHING.

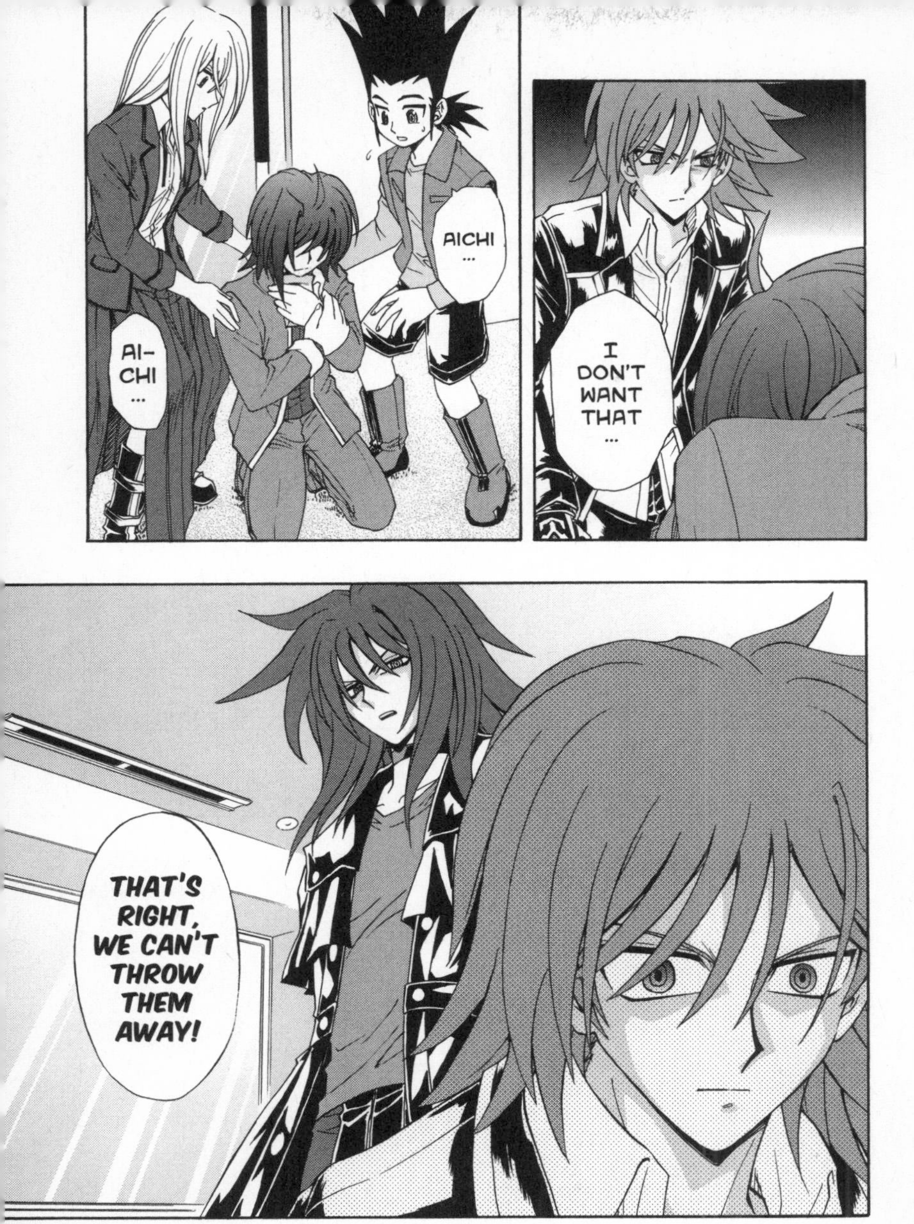
I DON'T WANT THAT ...
AICHI ...
AI-CHI ...
THAT'S RIGHT, WE CAN'T THROW THEM AWAY!

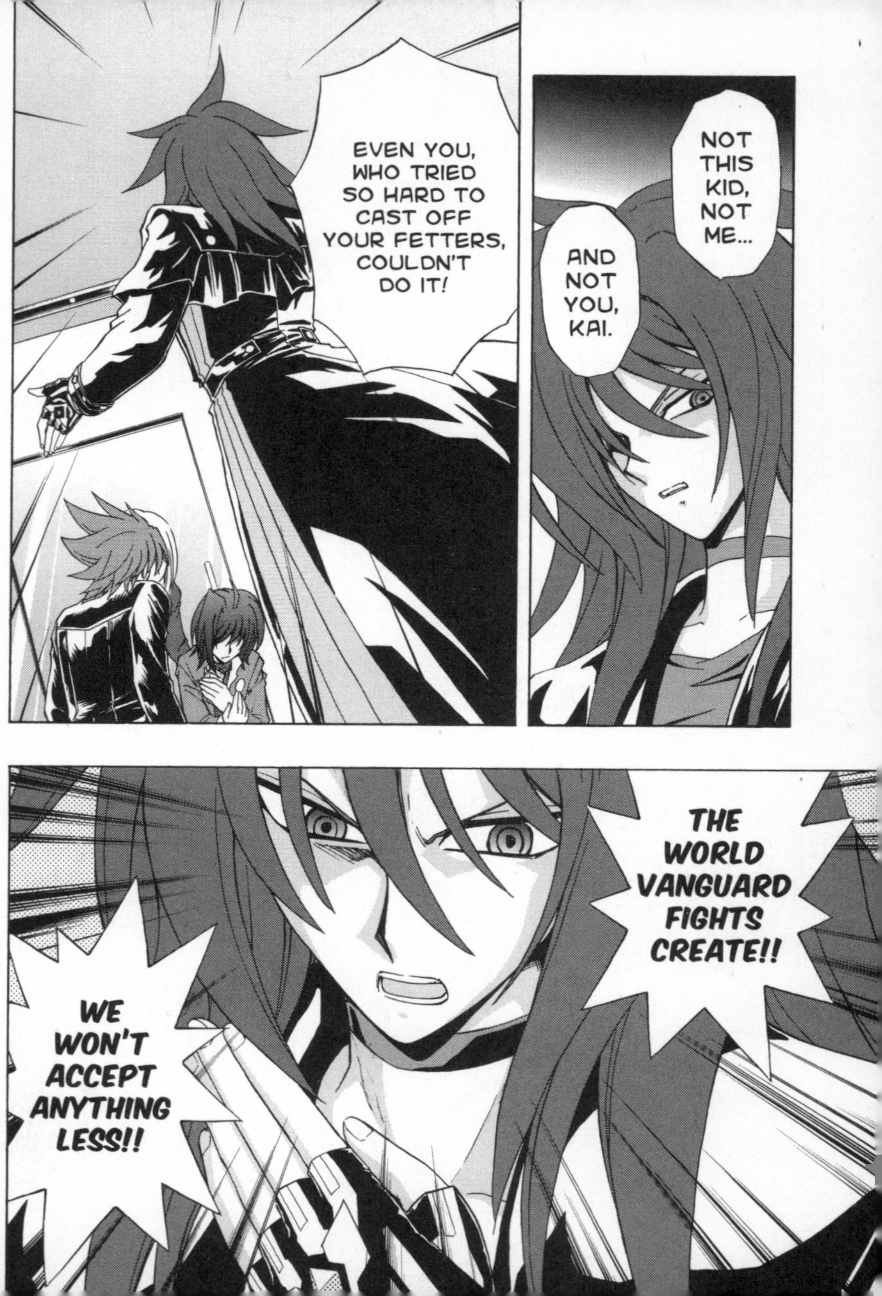
NOT THIS KID, NOT ME...
AND NOT YOU, KAI.
EVEN YOU, WHO TRIED SO HARD TO CAST OFF YOUR FETTERS, COULDN'T DO IT!
THE WORLD VANGUARD FIGHTS CREATE!!
WE WON'T ACCEPT ANYTHING LESS!!

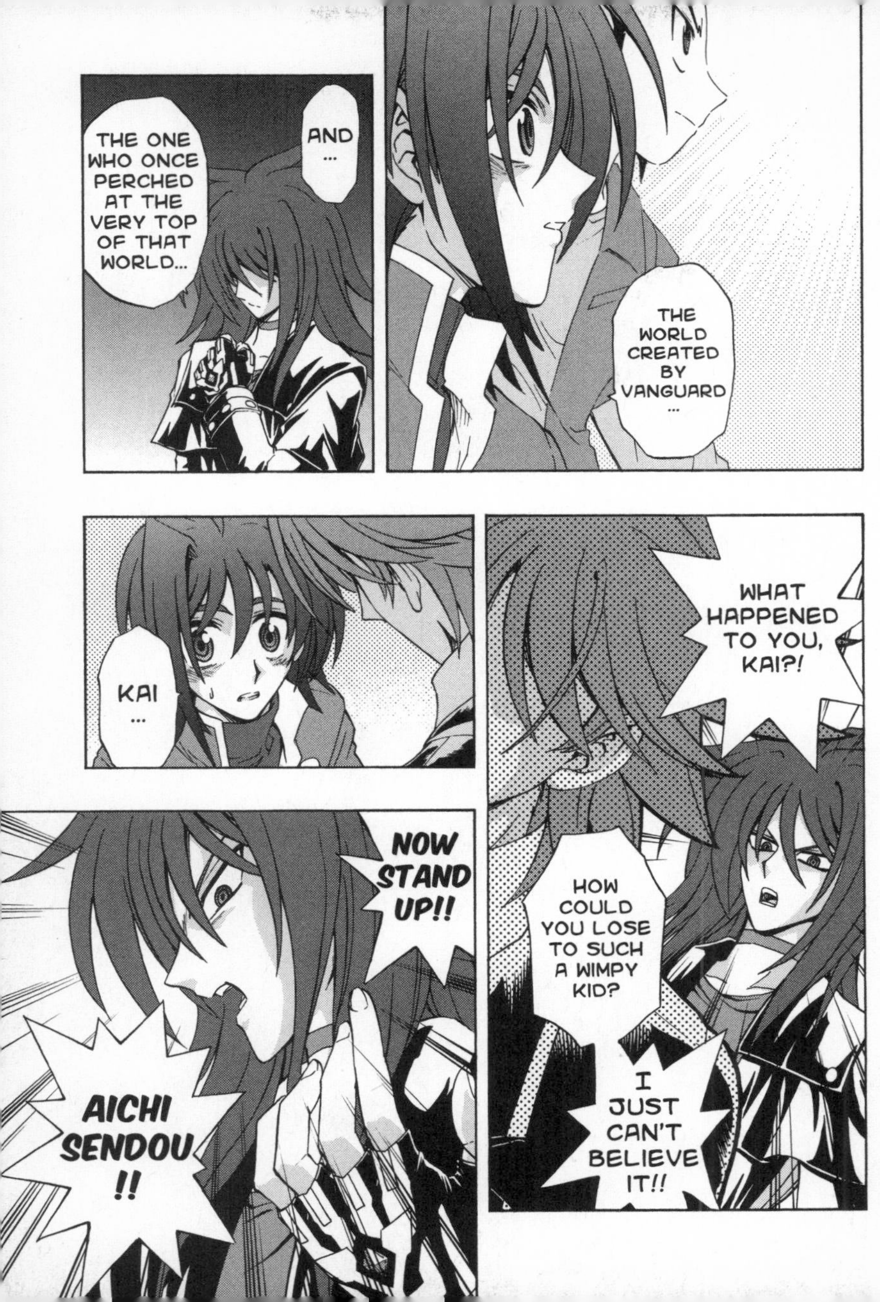
THE WORLD CREATED BY VANGUARD ...
AND ...
THE ONE WHO ONCE PERCHED AT THE VERY TOP OF THAT WORLD...
WHAT HAPPENED TO YOU, KAI?!
HOW COULD YOU LOSE TO SUCH A WIMPY KID?
I JUST CAN'T BELIEVE IT!!
KAI ...
NOW STAND UP!!
AICHI SENDOU !!

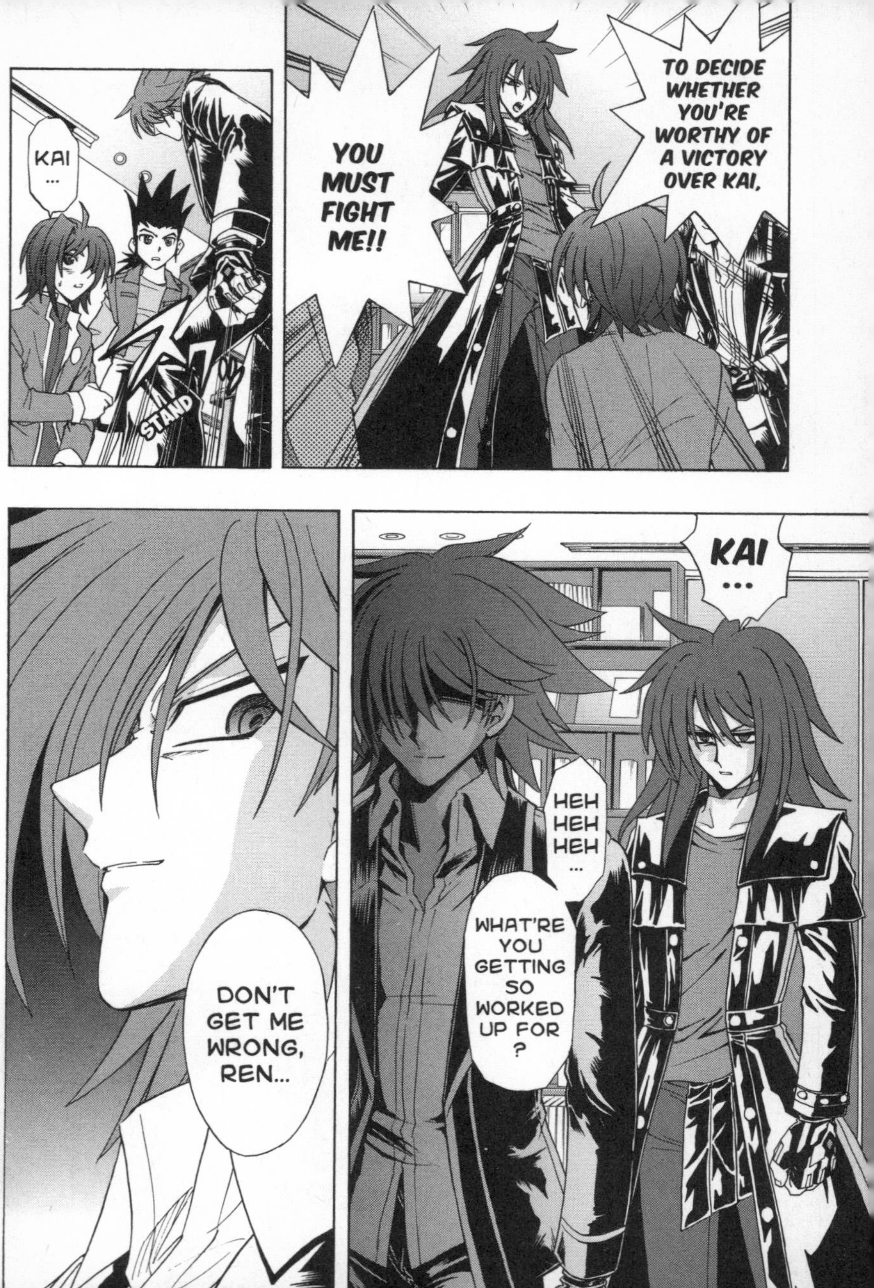
TO DECIDE WHETHER YOU'RE WORTHY OF A VICTORY OVER KAI,
YOU MUST FIGHT ME!!
KAI ...
STAND
KAI ...
HEH HEH HEH ...
WHAT'RE YOU GETTING SO WORKED UP FOR ?
DON'T GET ME WRONG, REN...

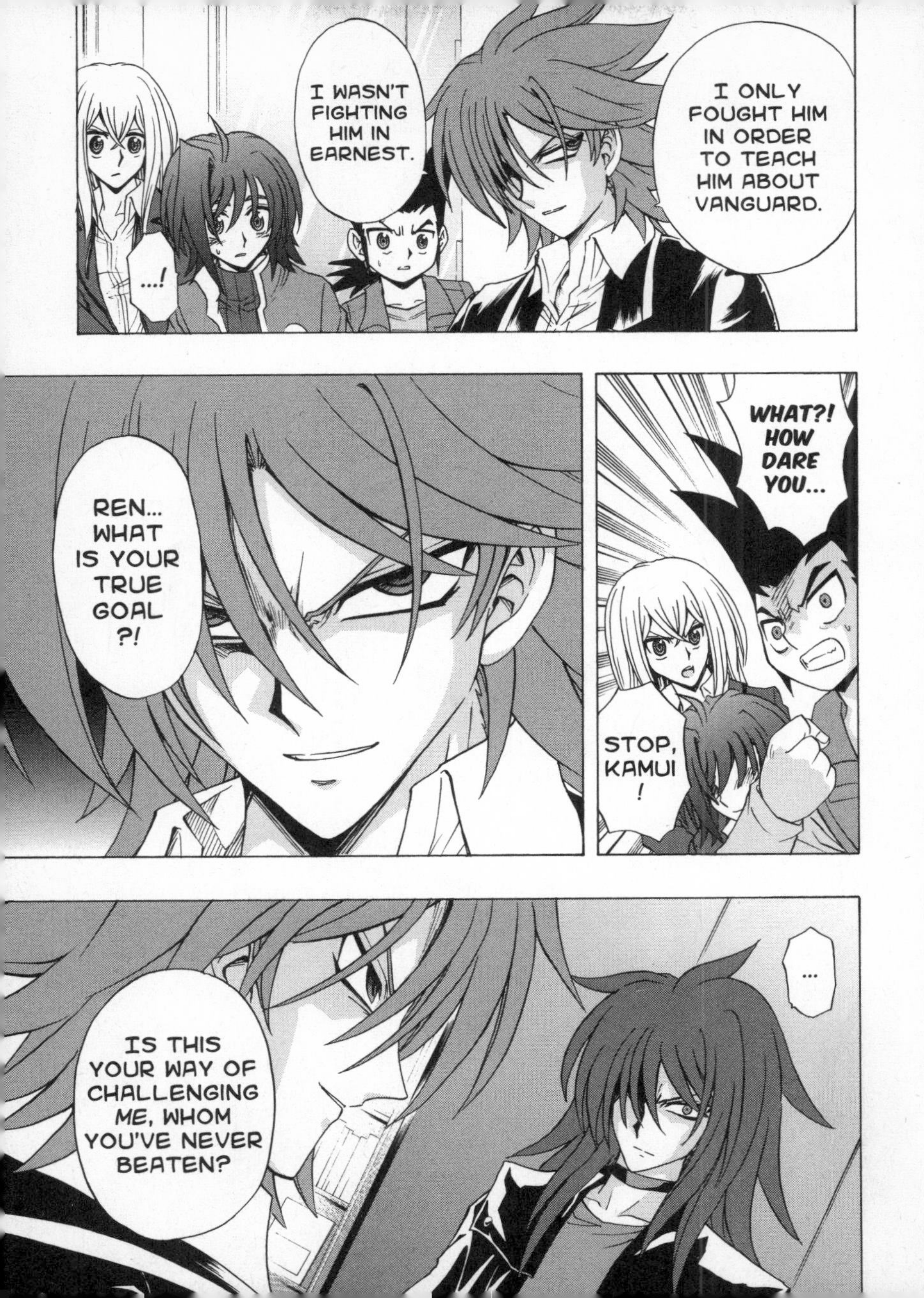
I ONLY FOUGHT HIM IN ORDER TO TEACH HIM ABOUT VANGUARD.
I WASN'T FIGHTING HIM IN EARNEST.
...!
WHAT?! HOW DARE YOU...
STOP, KAMUI!
REN... WHAT IS YOUR TRUE GOAL?!
...
IS THIS YOUR WAY OF CHALLENGING ME, WHOM YOU'VE NEVER BEATEN?

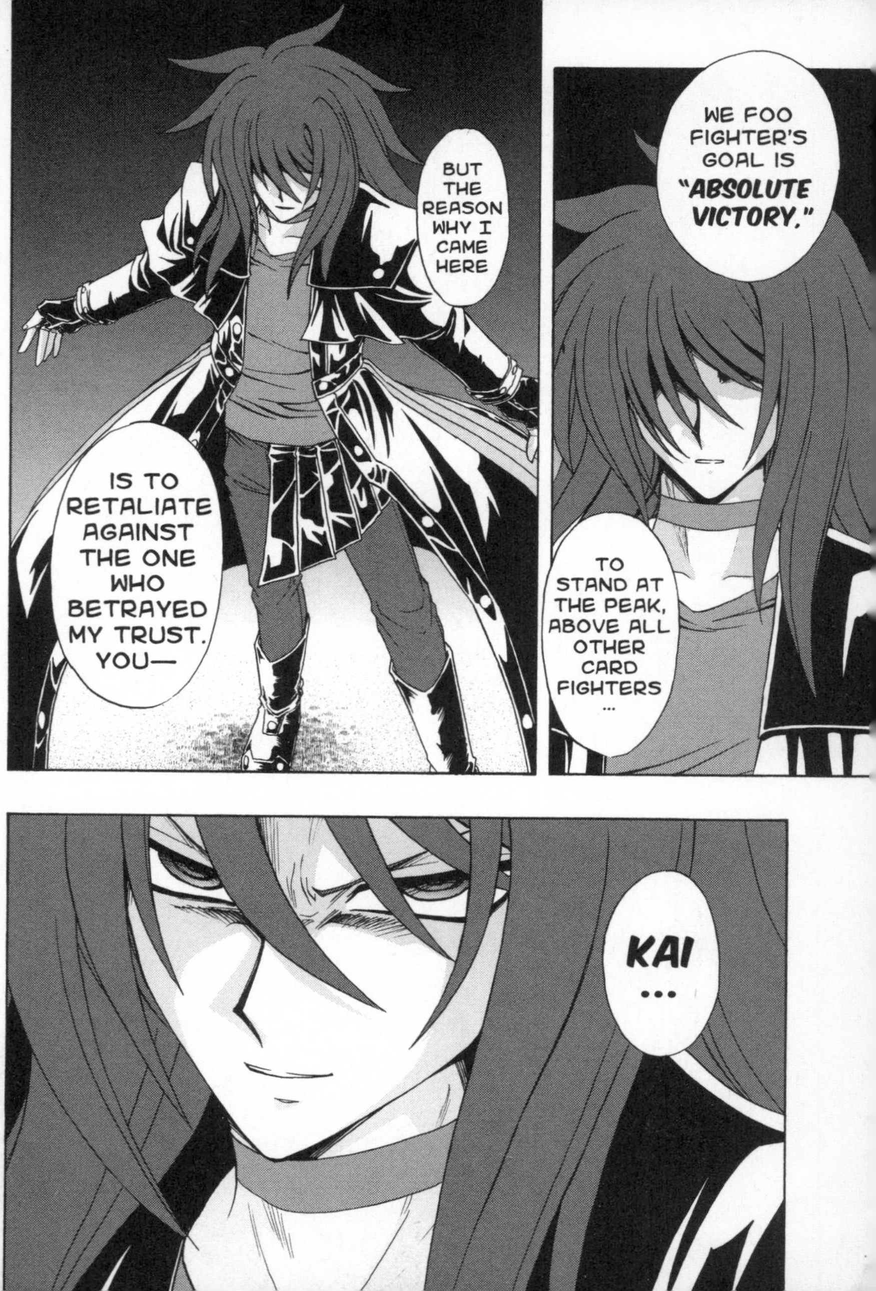
WE FOO FIGHTER'S GOAL IS "ABSOLUTE VICTORY."
TO STAND AT THE PEAK, ABOVE ALL OTHER CARD FIGHTERS ...
BUT THE REASON WHY I CAME HERE
IS TO RETALIATE AGAINST THE ONE WHO BETRAYED MY TRUST. YOU—
KAI ...

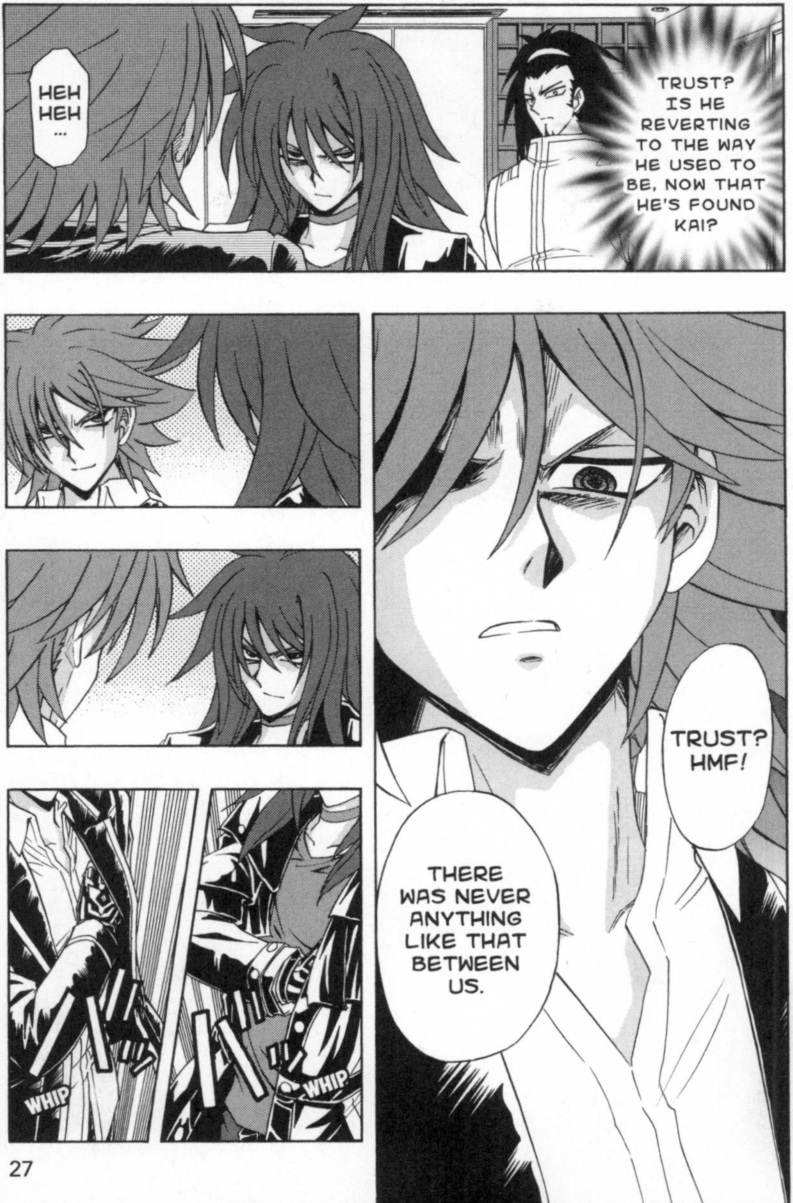
TRUST? IS HE REVERTING TO THE WAY HE USED TO BE, NOW THAT HE'S FOUND KAI?
HEH HEH ...
TRUST? HMF!
THERE WAS NEVER ANYTHING LIKE THAT BETWEEN US.
WHIP
WHIP

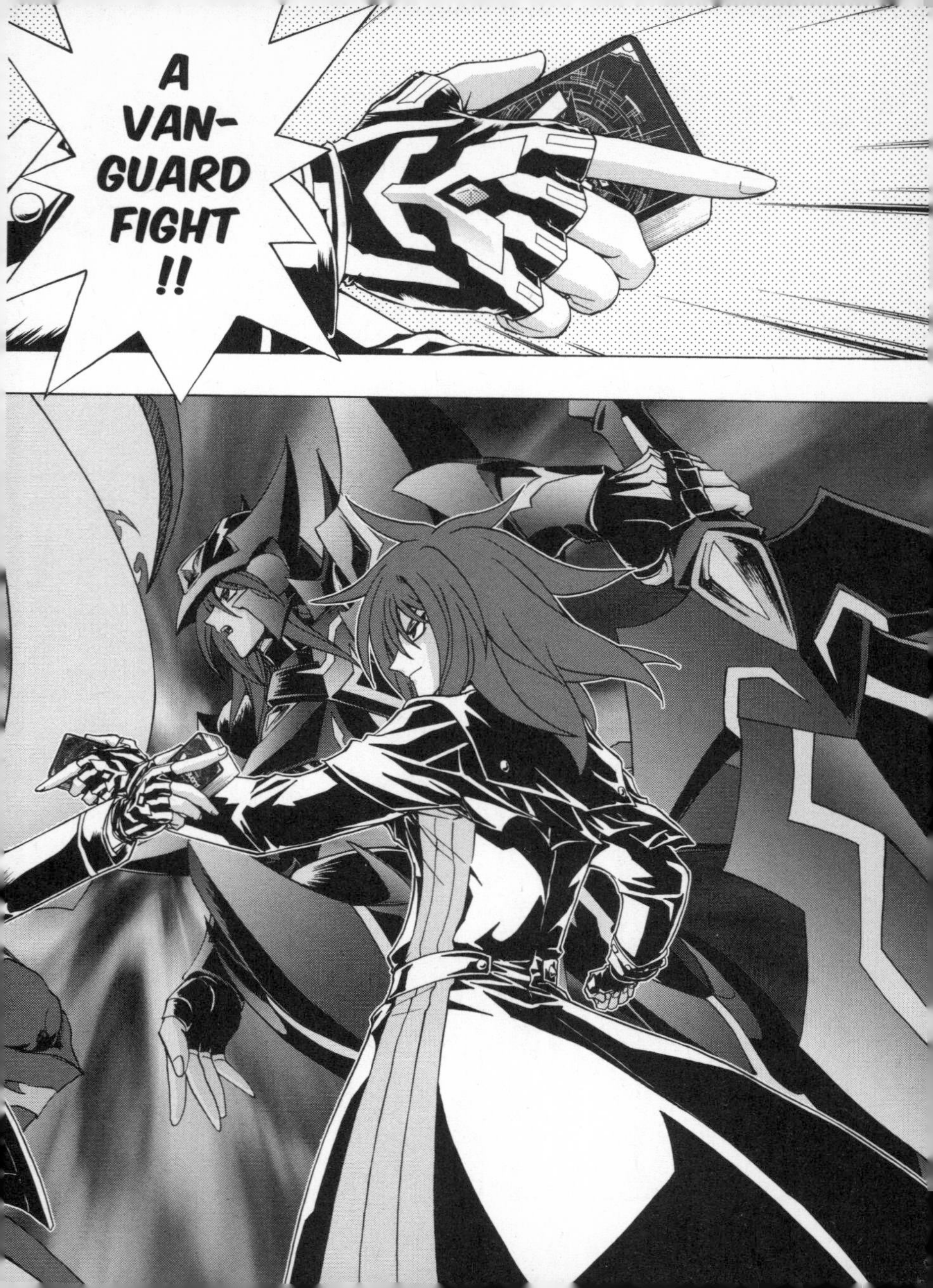
A VAN-GUARD FIGHT !!

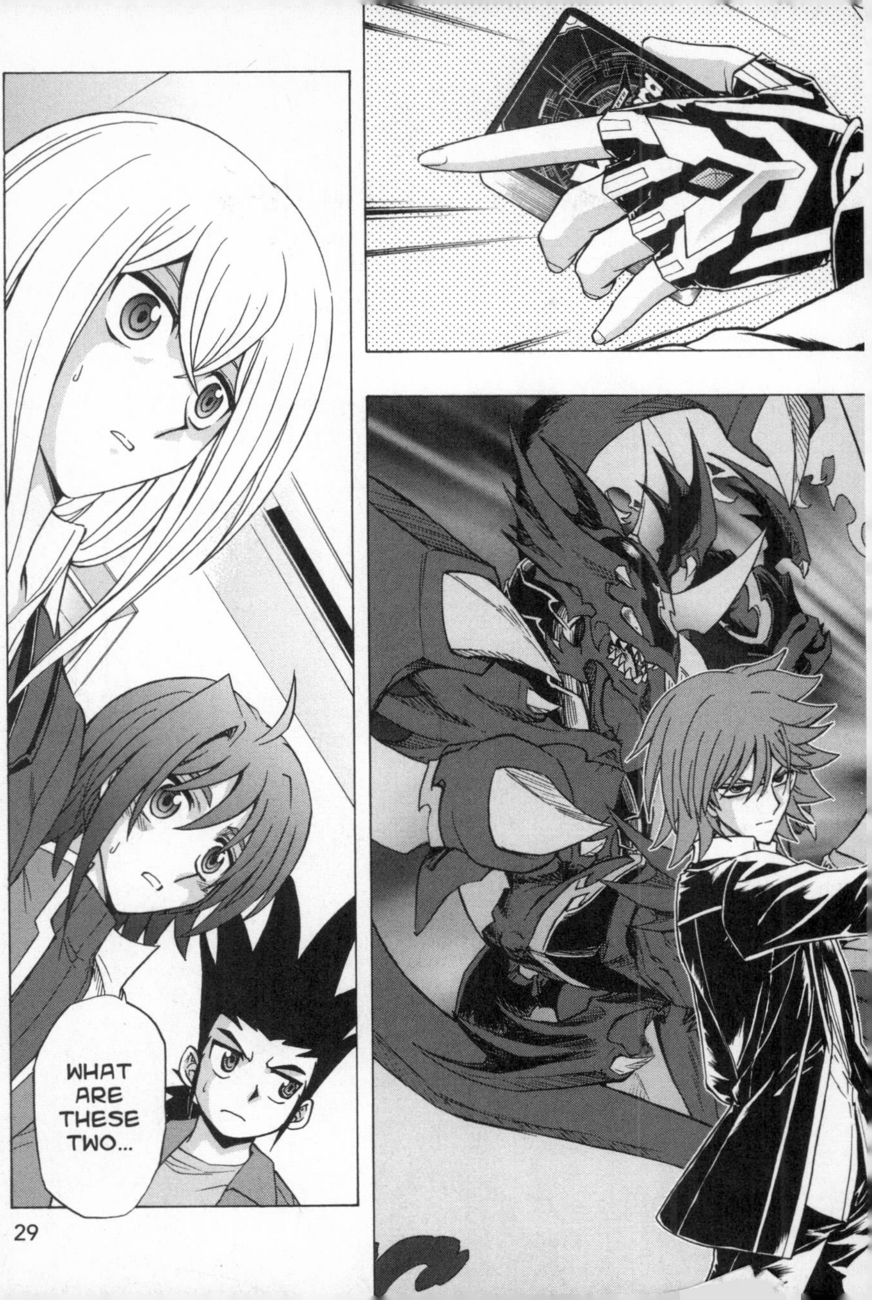
WHAT ARE THESE TWO...

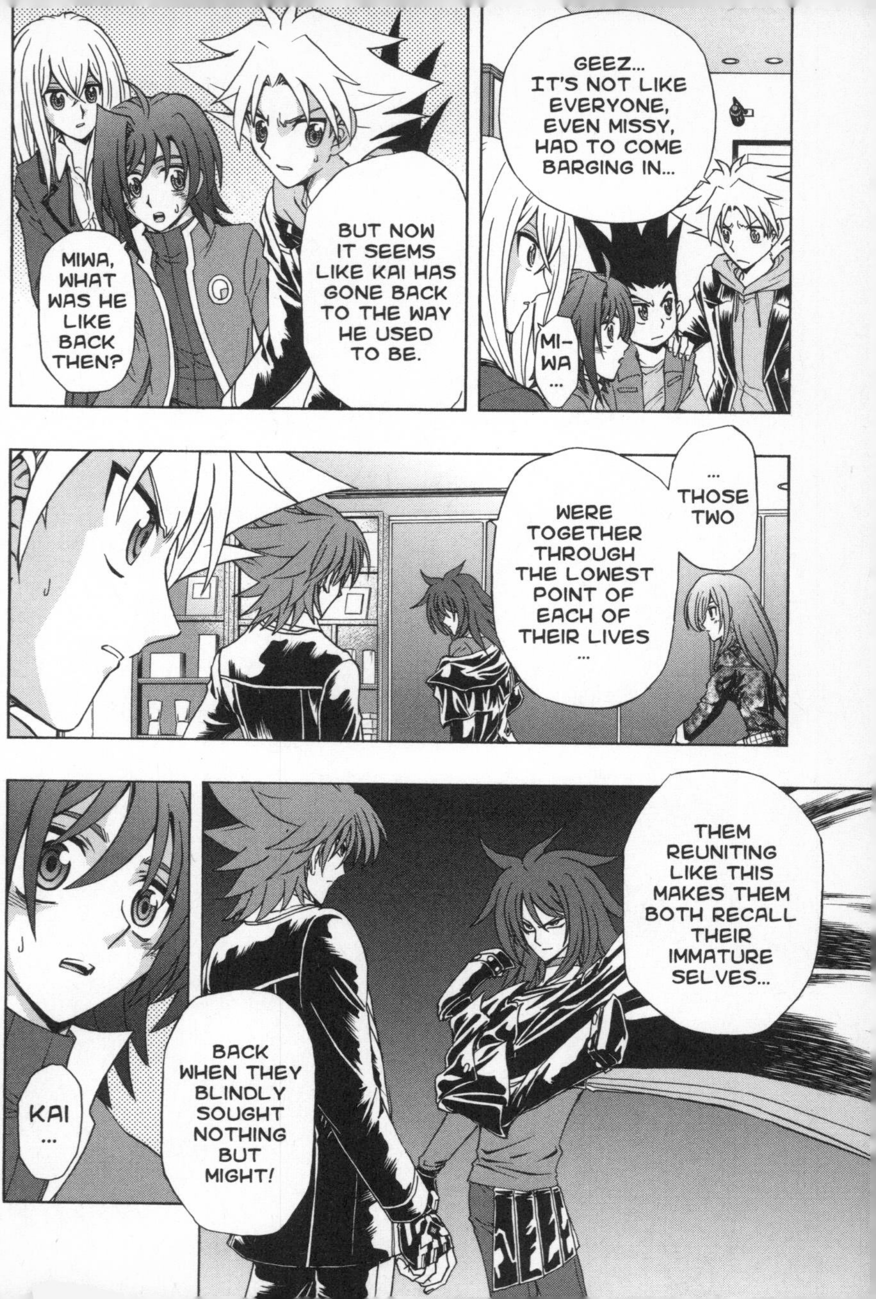
GEEZ... IT'S NOT LIKE EVERYONE, EVEN MISSY, HAD TO COME BARGING IN...
MI- WA ...
BUT NOW IT SEEMS LIKE KAI HAS GONE BACK TO THE WAY HE USED TO BE.
MIWA, WHAT WAS HE LIKE BACK THEN?
... THOSE TWO
WERE TOGETHER THROUGH THE LOWEST POINT OF EACH OF THEIR LIVES ...
THEM REUNITING LIKE THIS MAKES THEM BOTH RECALL THEIR IMMATURE SELVES...
BACK WHEN THEY BLINDLY SOUGHT NOTHING BUT MIGHT!
KAI ...

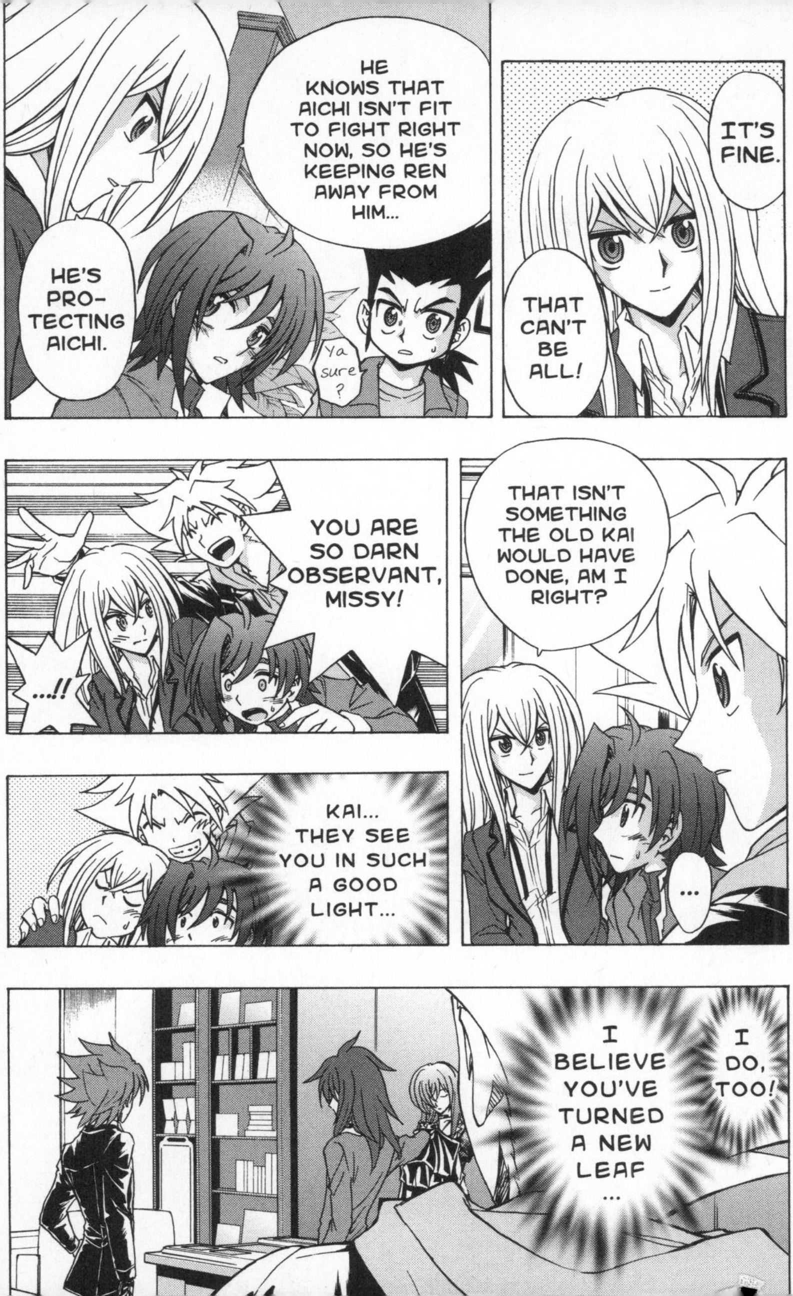
IT'S FINE.
THAT CAN'T BE ALL!
HE KNOWS THAT AICHI ISN'T FIT TO FIGHT RIGHT NOW, SO HE'S KEEPING REN AWAY FROM HIM...
Ya sure?
HE'S PRO-TECTING AICHI.
THAT ISN'T SOMETHING THE OLD KAI WOULD HAVE DONE, AM I RIGHT?
...
YOU ARE SO DARN OBSERVANT, MISSY!
...!!
KAI... THEY SEE YOU IN SUCH A GOOD LIGHT...
I DO, TOO!
I BELIEVE YOU'VE TURNED A NEW LEAF ...

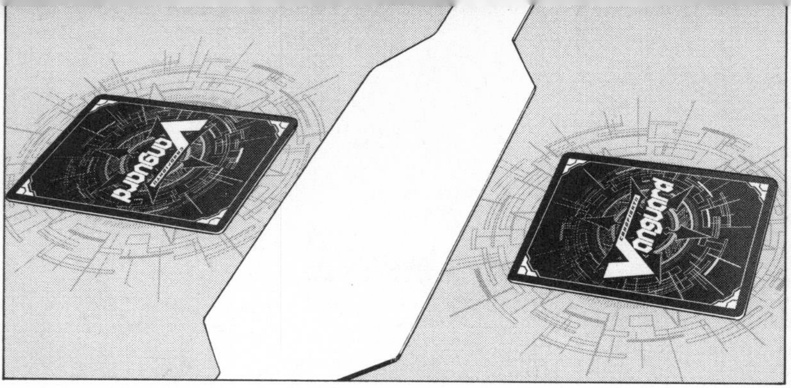
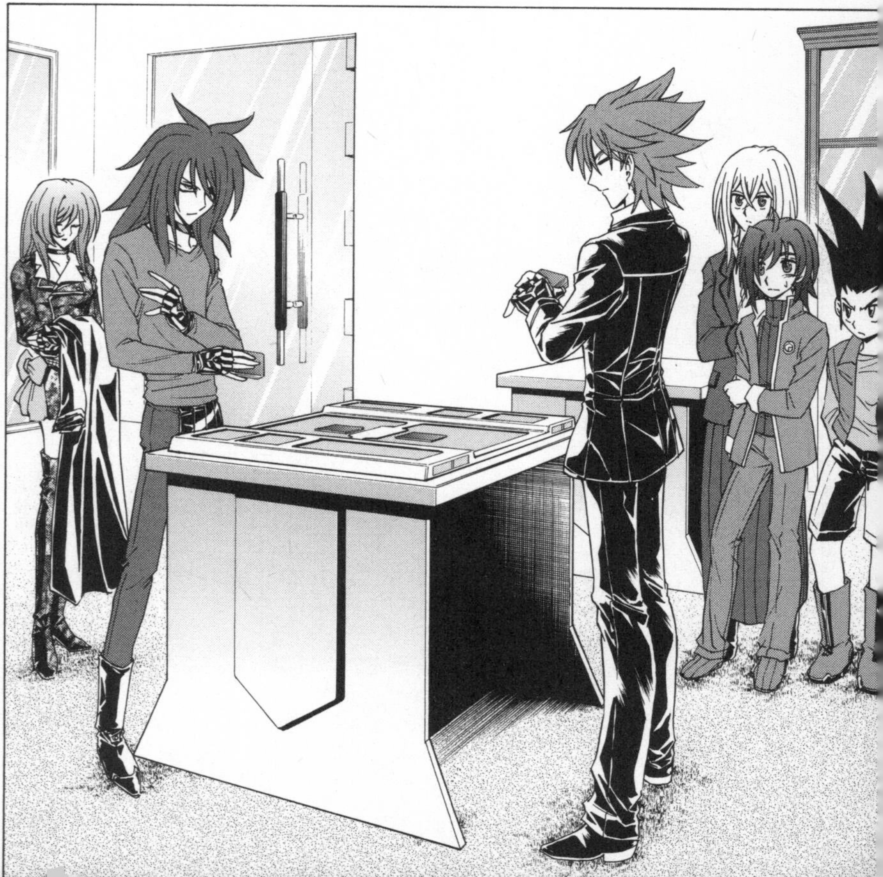

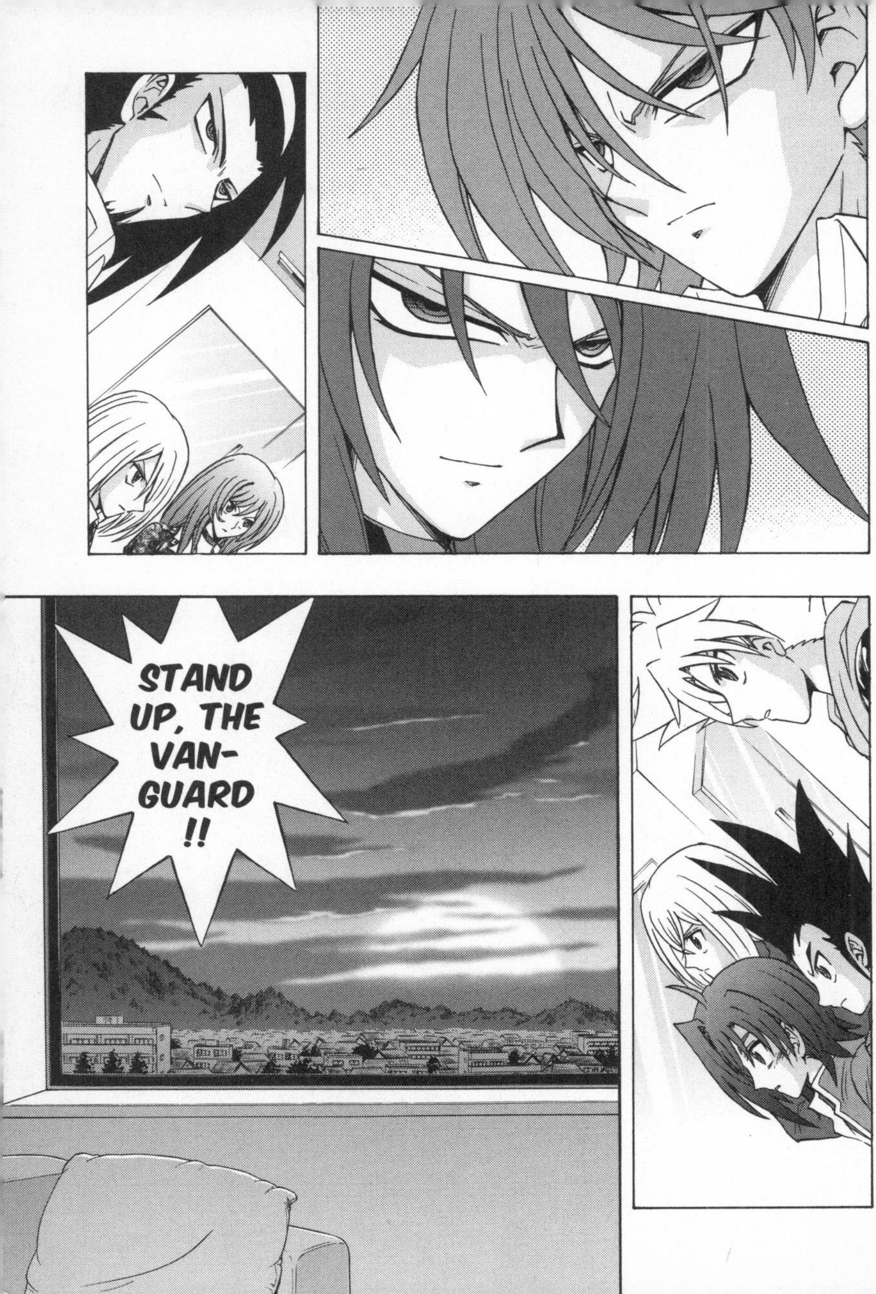
STAND UP, THE VAN-GUARD !!

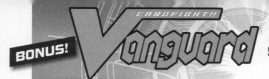

BONUS! CARDFIGHT!! Vanguard NEVER-BEFORE-SEEN IMAGE BOARDS

UNITS

We're continuing the hit series of Vanguard image boards! In this installment we'll show you brand-new units as well as casual clothes, summer clothes, and uniforms, mainly for Team Q4, in one fell swoop! As always, be sure to check out Mr. Akira Itou's handwritten notes on the sketches!

King of Knights, Alfred

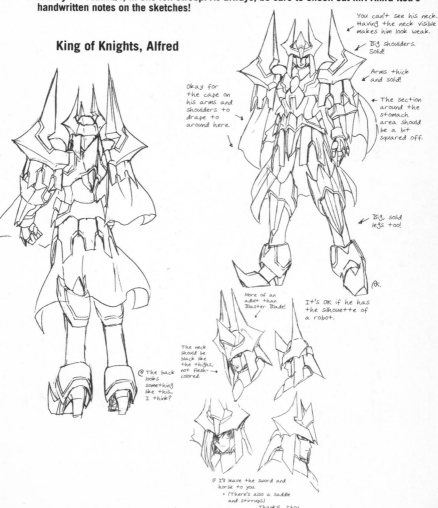

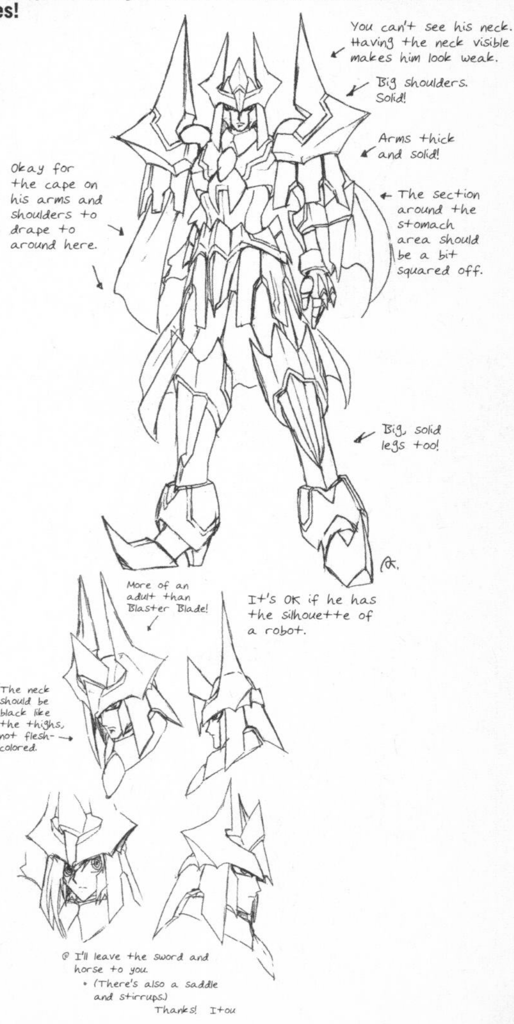
You can't see his neck. Having the neck visible makes him look weak.
Big shoulders. Solid!
Arms thick and solid!
Okay for the cape on his arms and shoulders to drape to around here.
The section around the stomach area should be a bit squared off.
Big, solid legs too!
More of an adult than Blaster Blade!
It's OK if he has the silhouette of a robot.
The neck should be black like the thighs, not flesh-colored.
@ I'll leave the sword and horse to you.
• (There's also a saddle and stirrups.)
Thanks! Itou

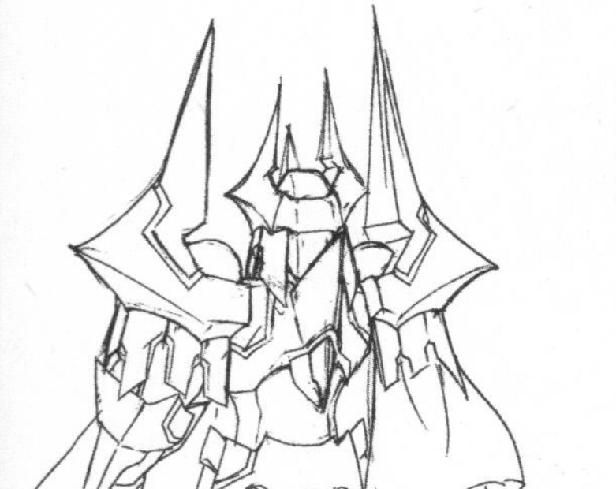
@ The back looks something like this... I think?

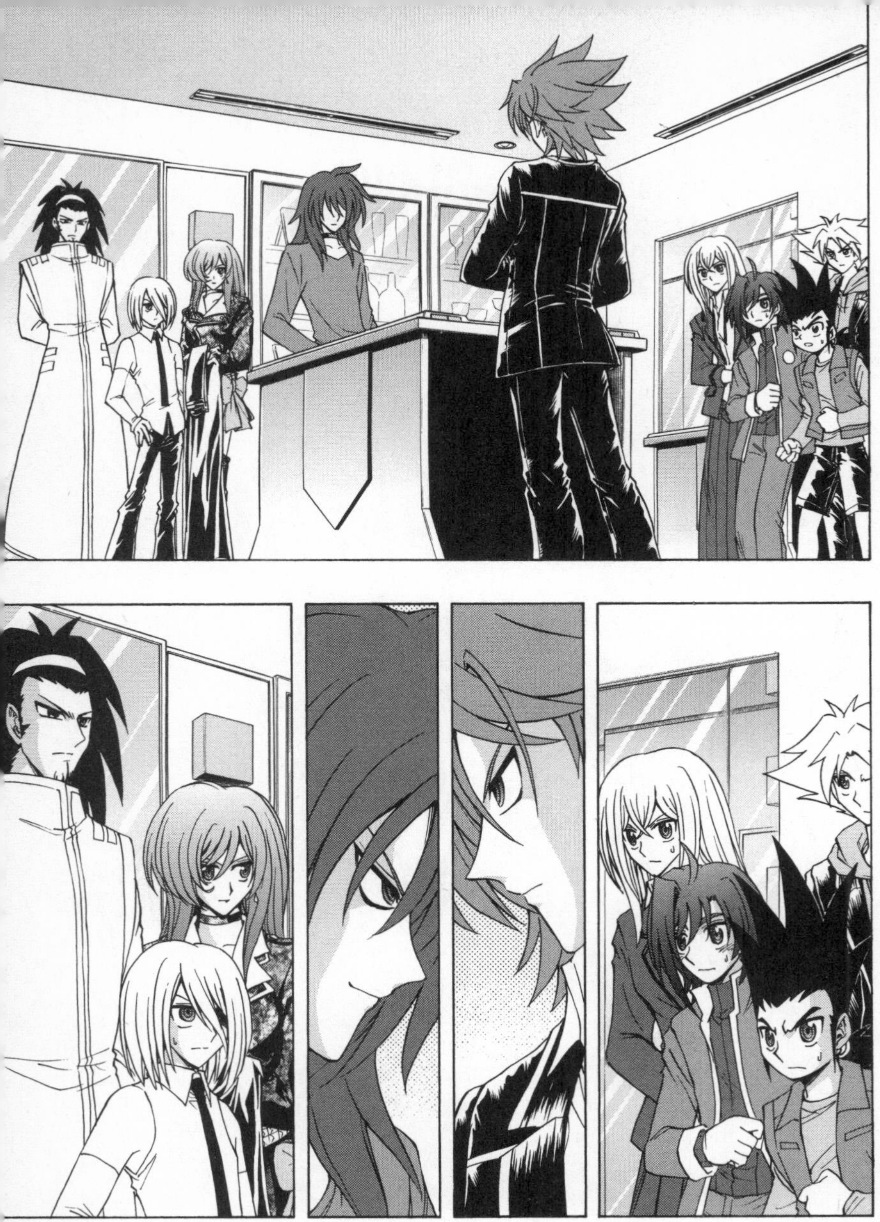

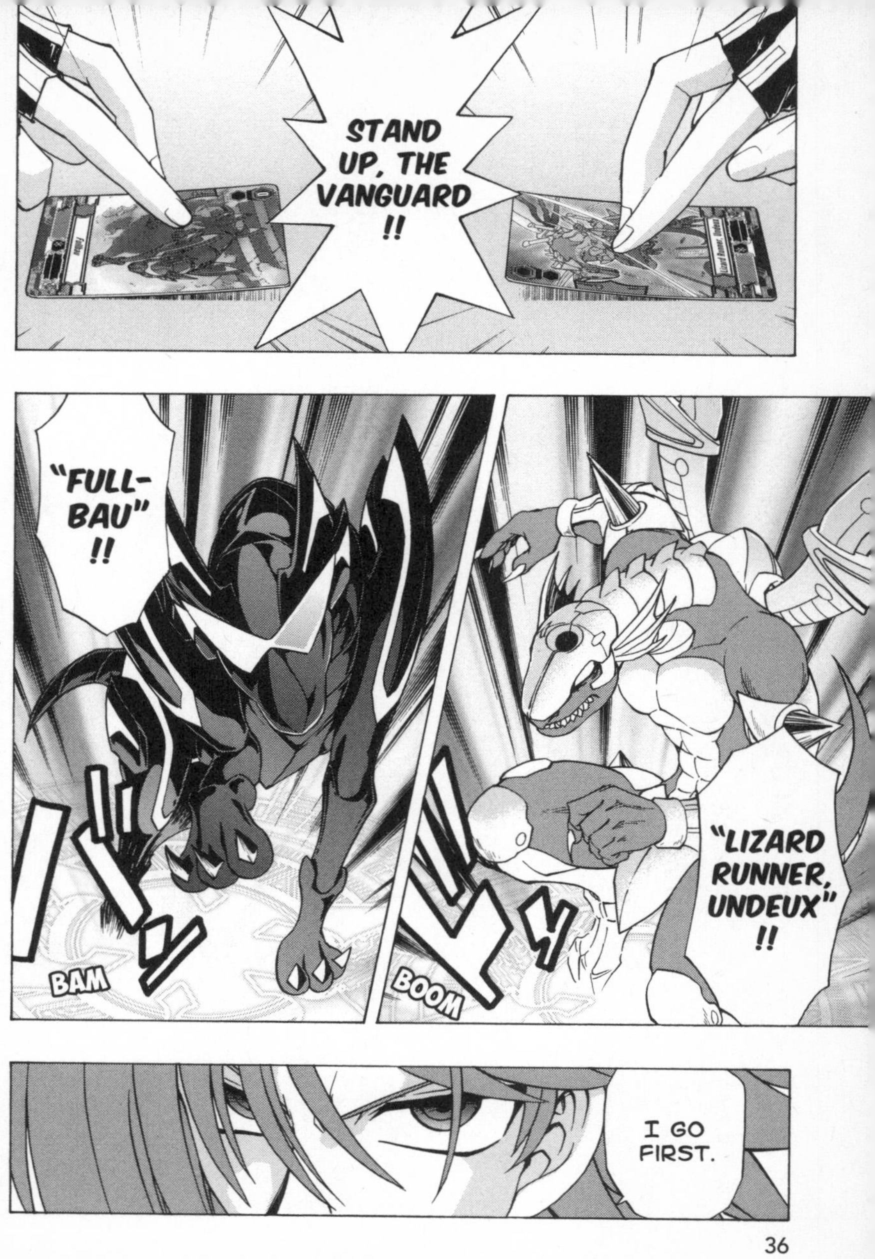
STAND UP, THE VANGUARD!!
"LIZARD RUNNER, UNDEUX"!!
BOOM
"FULL-BAU"!!
BAM
I GO FIRST.

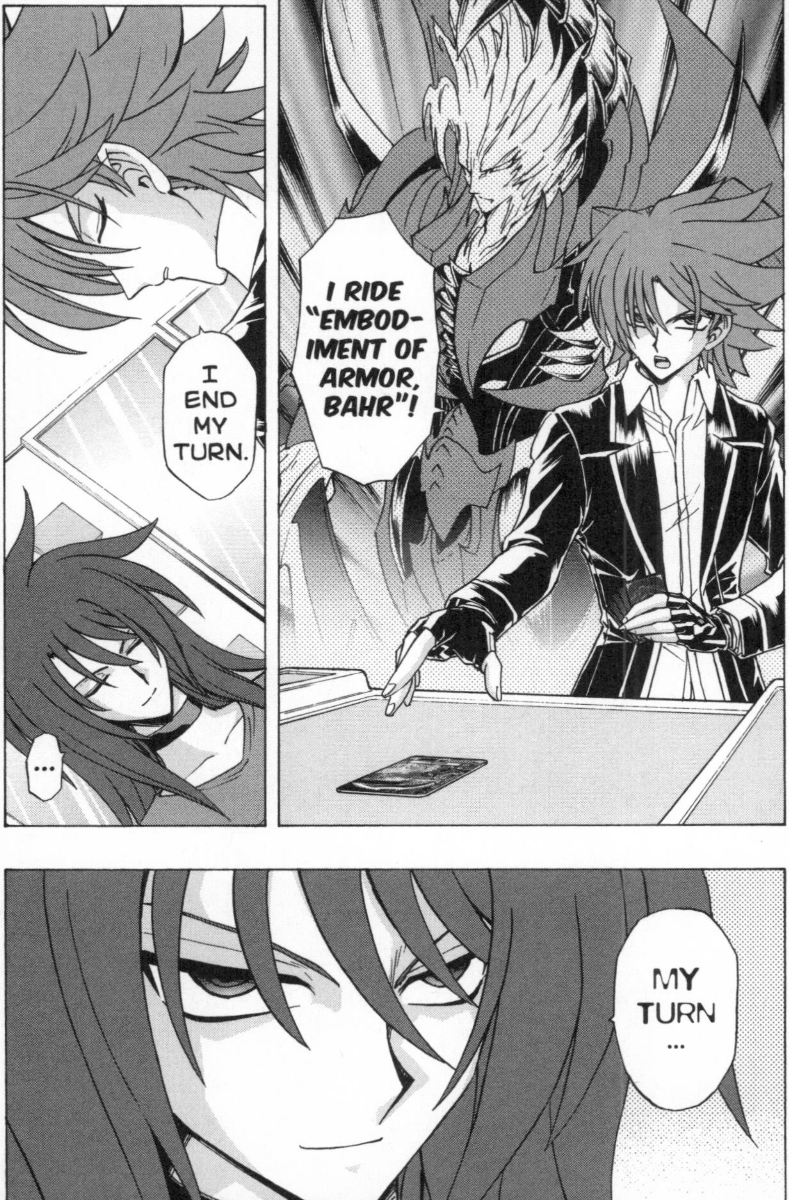
I RIDE "EMBODIMENT OF ARMOR, BAHR"!
I END MY TURN.
...
MY TURN ...

#016 DARK ABYSS

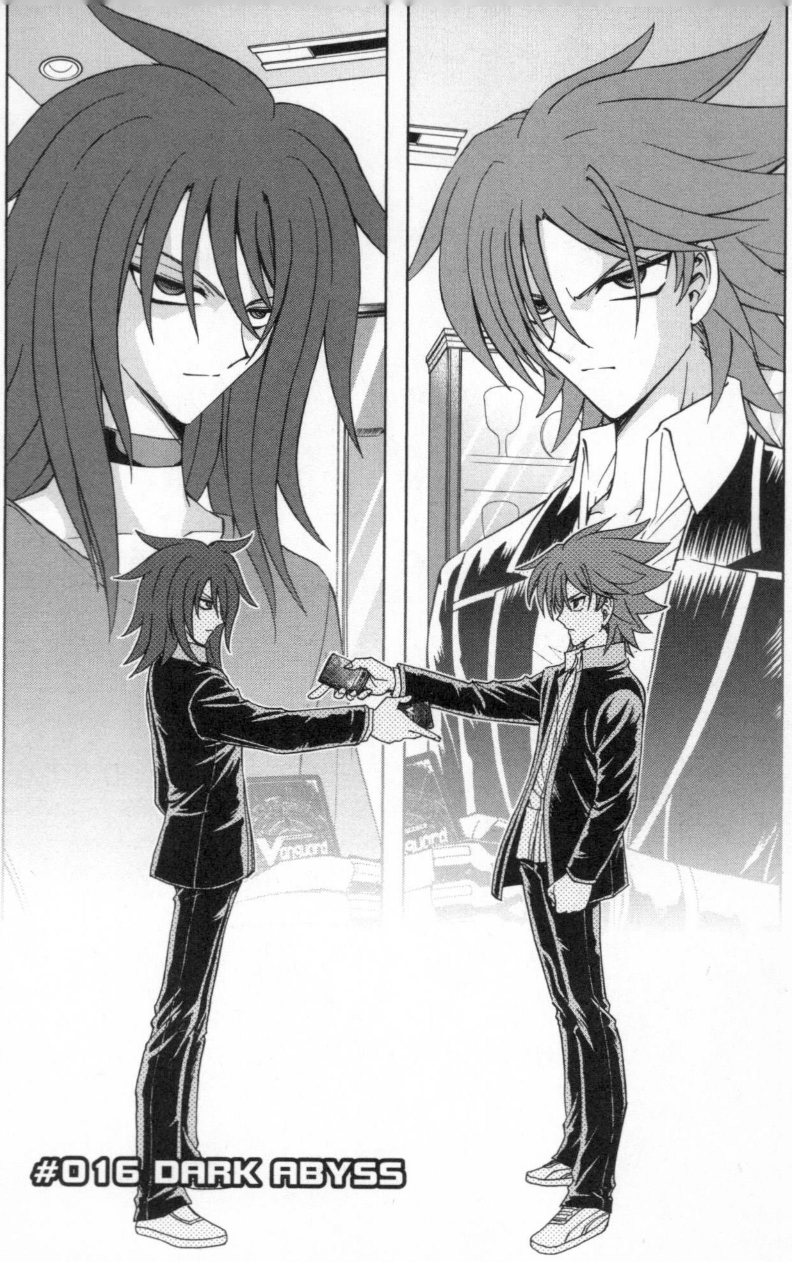

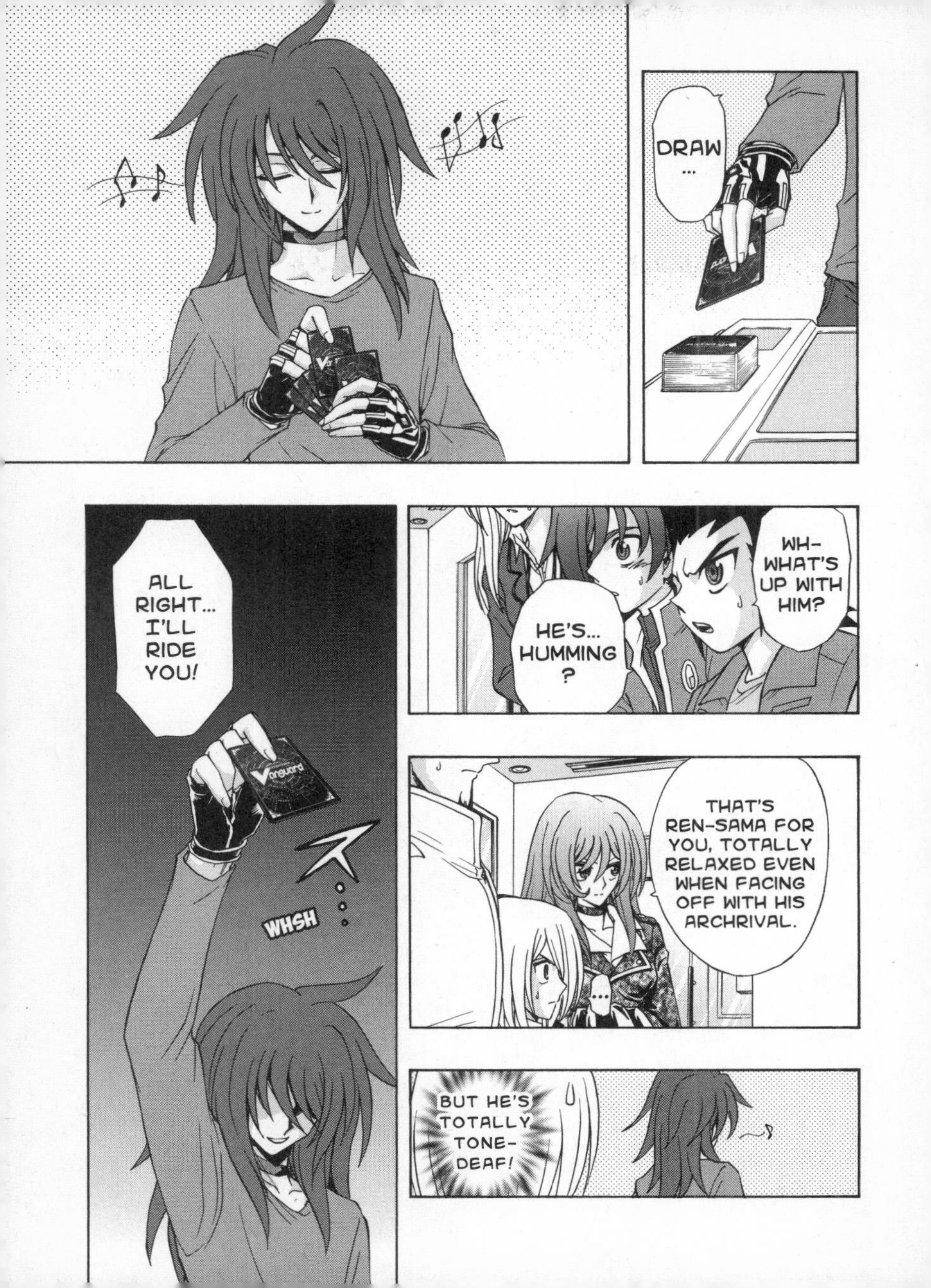
DRAW ...
WH- WHAT'S UP WITH HIM?
HE'S... HUMMING?
ALL RIGHT... I'LL RIDE YOU!
WHSH
THAT'S REN-SAMA FOR YOU, TOTALLY RELAXED EVEN WHEN FACING OFF WITH HIS ARCHRIVAL.
...
BUT HE'S TOTALLY TONE-DEAF!

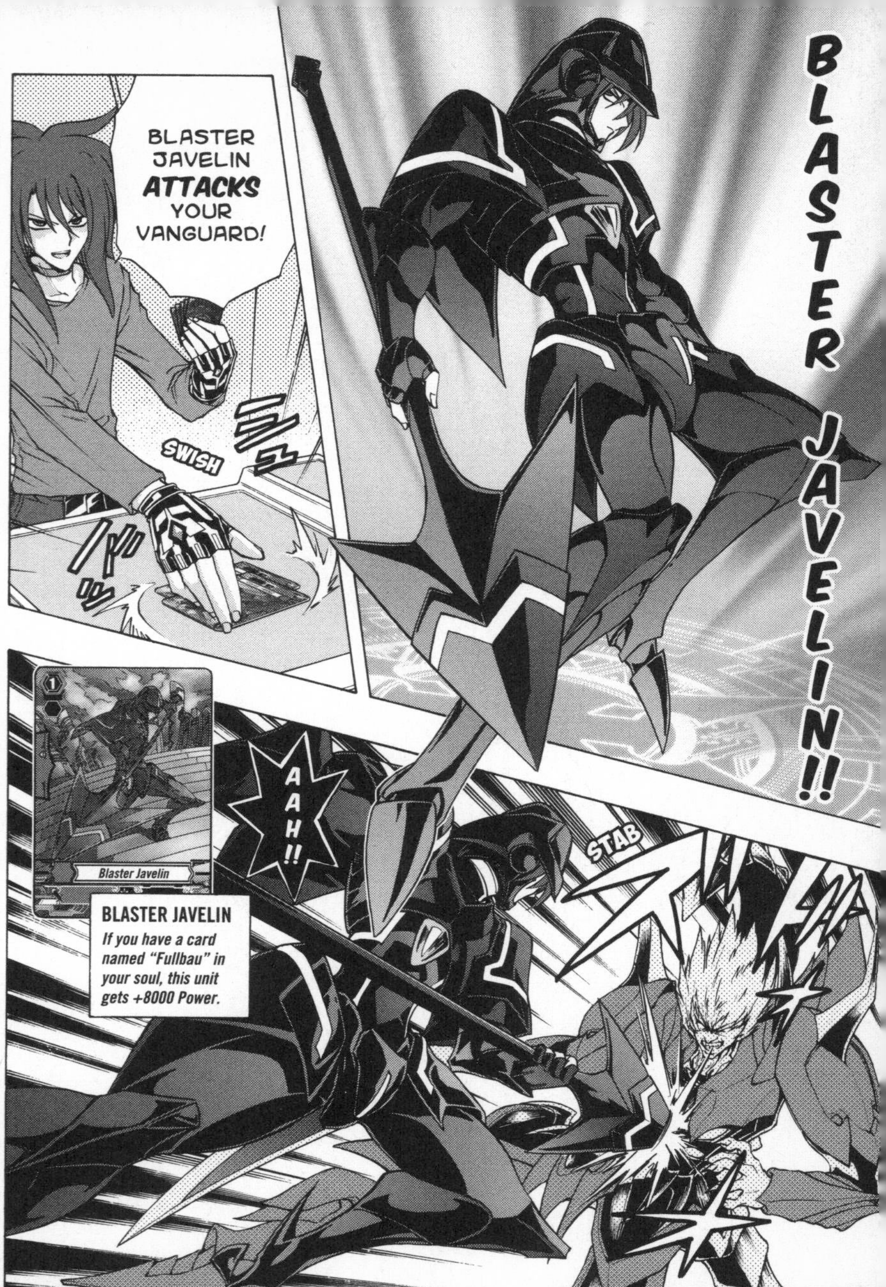
BLASTER JAVELIN!!
BLASTER JAVELIN ATTACKS YOUR VANGUARD!
SWISH
STAB
AAAH!!
Blaster Javelin
BLASTER JAVELIN
If you have a card named "Fullbau" in your soul, this unit gets +8000 Power.

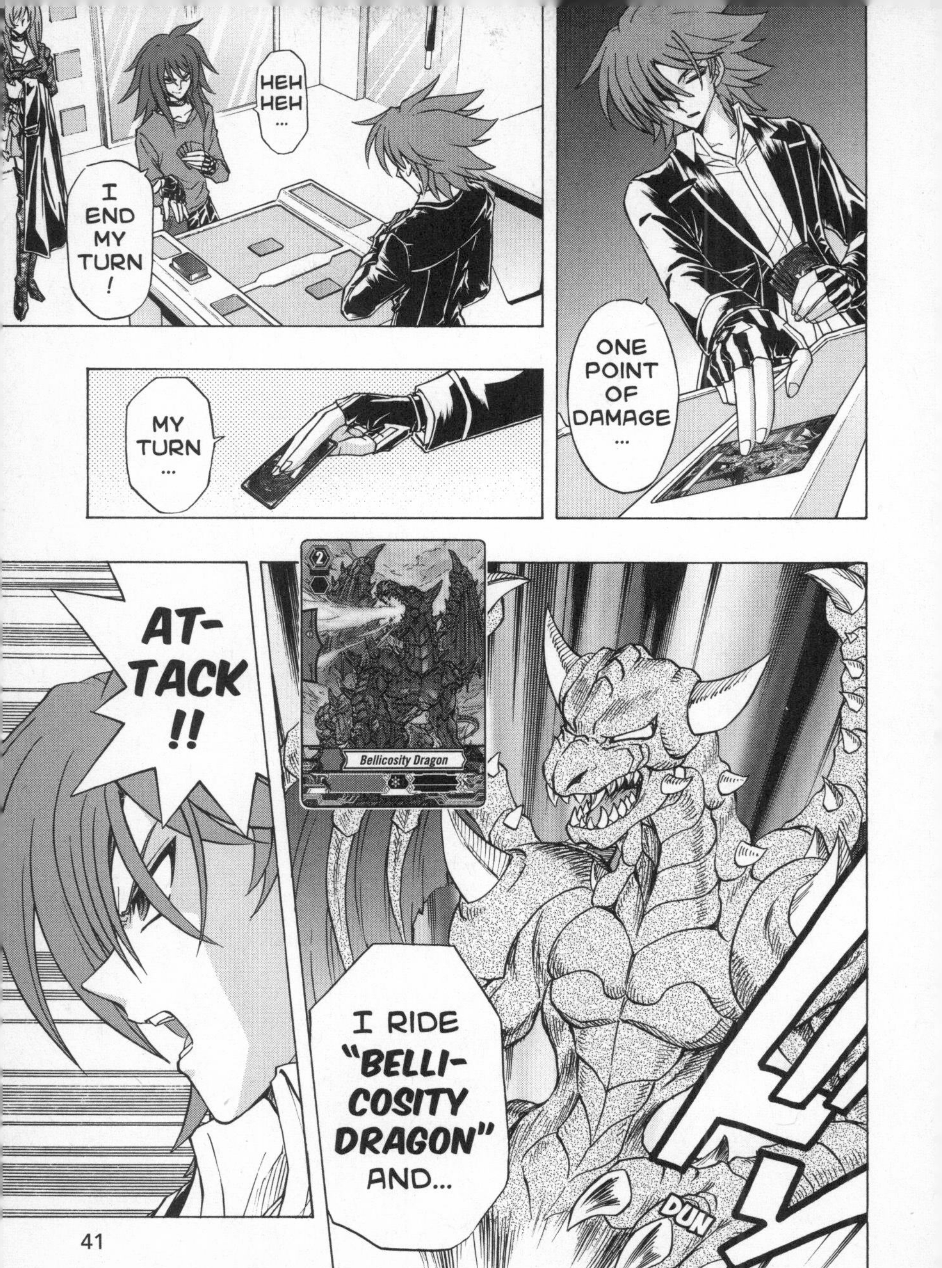
ONE POINT OF DAMAGE ...
HEH HEH ...
I END MY TURN !
MY TURN ...
Bellicosity Dragon
I RIDE "BELLICOSITY DRAGON" AND...
DUN
ATTACK !!

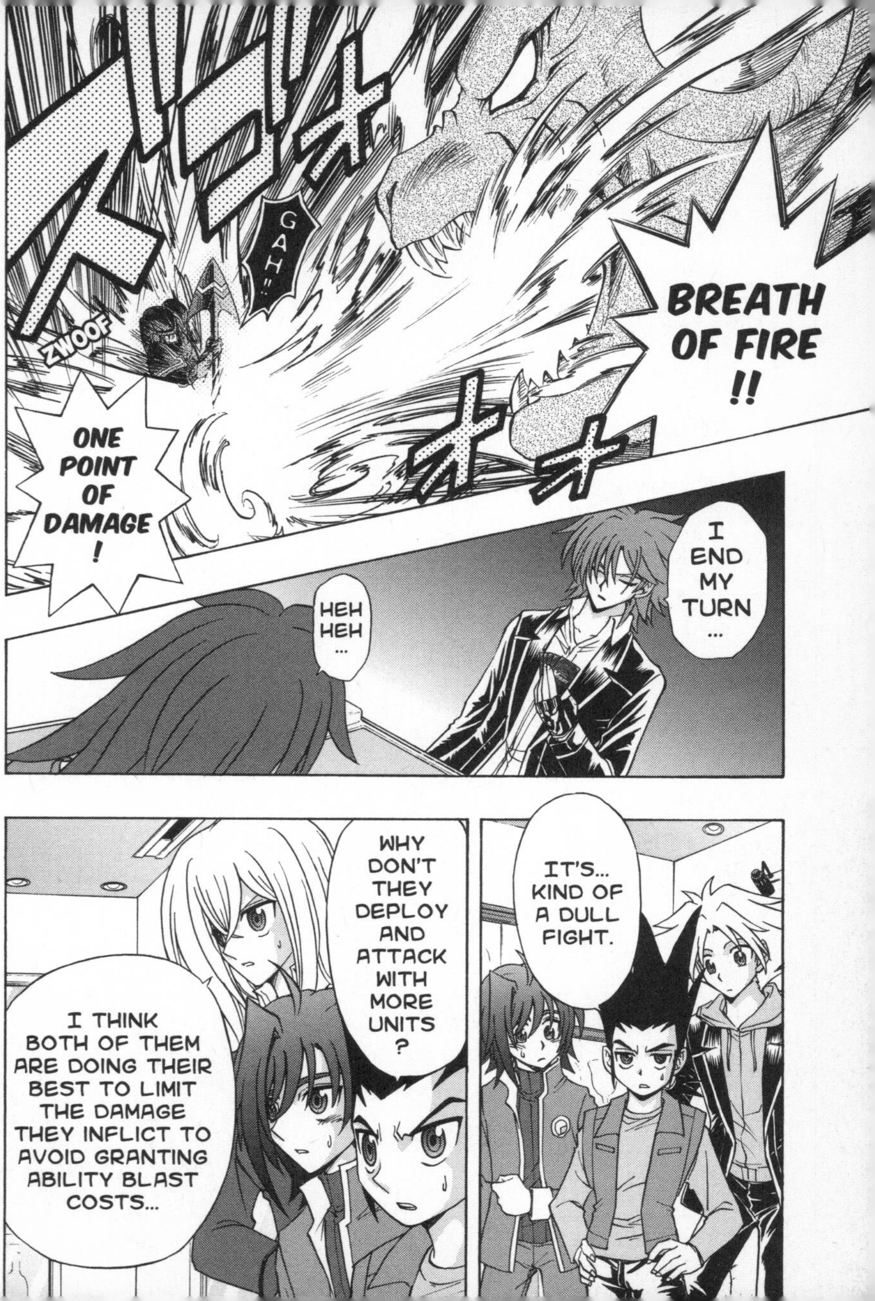
BREATH OF FIRE !!
GAH!!
ZWOOF
ONE POINT OF DAMAGE !
I END MY TURN ...
HEH HEH ...
IT'S... KIND OF A DULL FIGHT.
WHY DON'T THEY DEPLOY AND ATTACK WITH MORE UNITS ?
I THINK BOTH OF THEM ARE DOING THEIR BEST TO LIMIT THE DAMAGE THEY INFLICT TO AVOID GRANTING ABILITY BLAST COSTS...

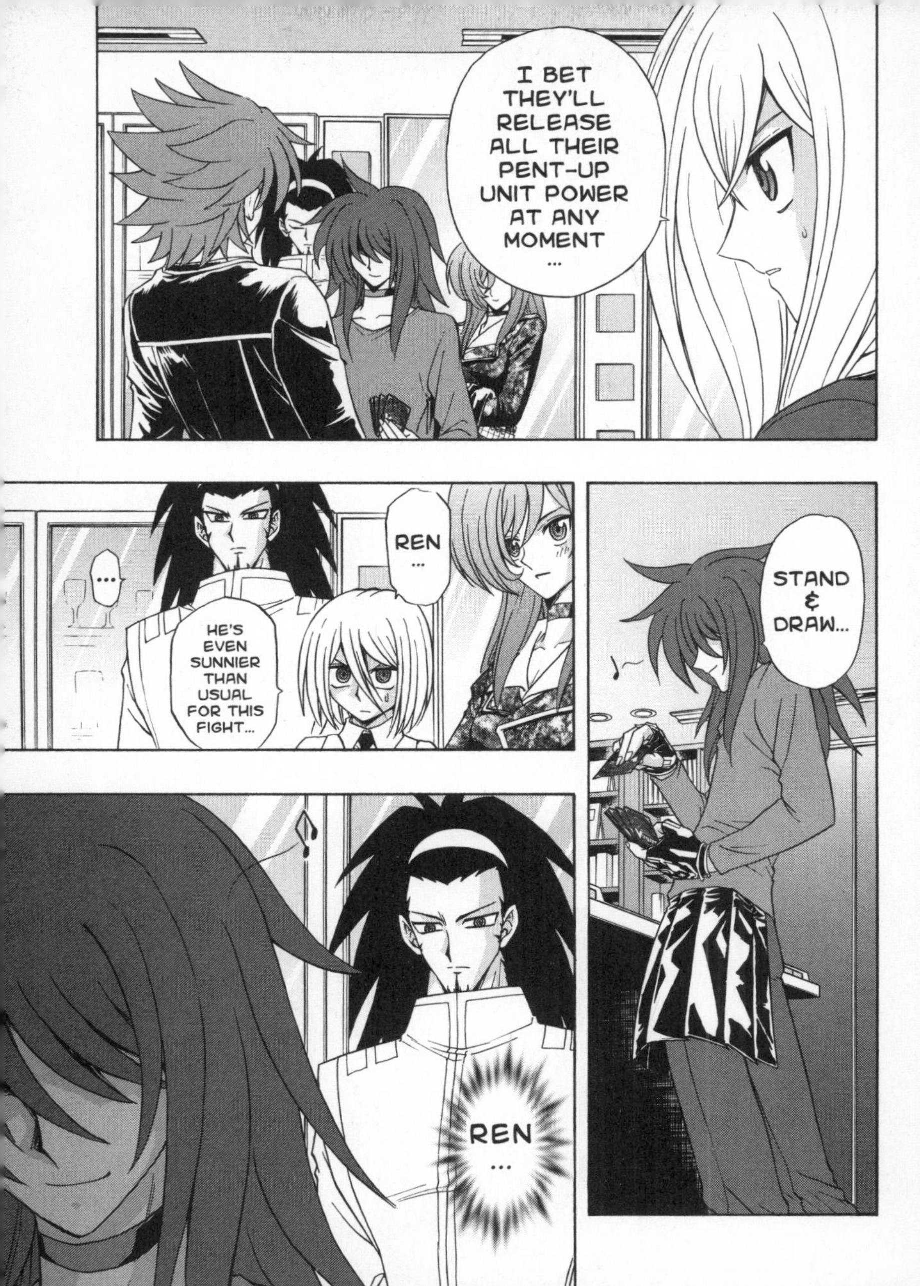
I BET THEY'LL RELEASE ALL THEIR PENT-UP UNIT POWER AT ANY MOMENT ...
STAND & DRAW...
REN ...
...
HE'S EVEN SUNNIER THAN USUAL FOR THIS FIGHT...
REN ...

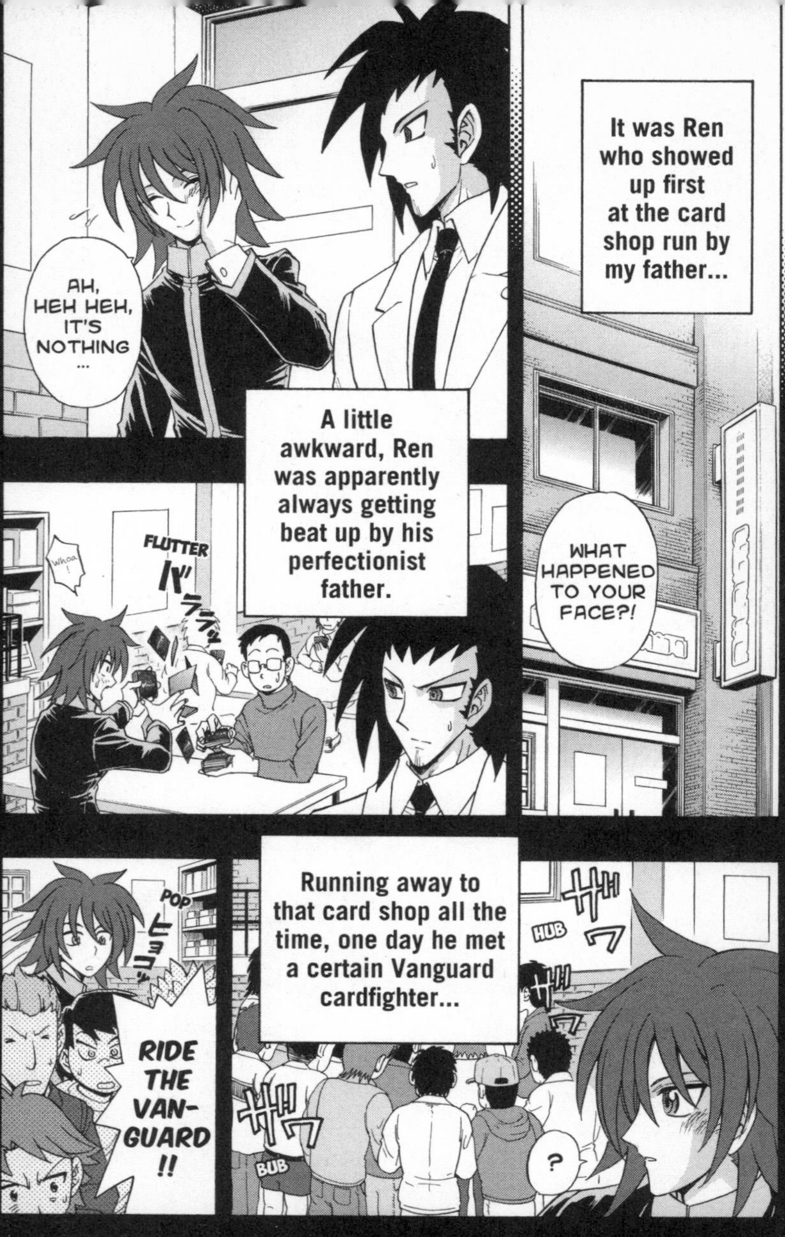

It was Ren who showed up first at the card shop run by my father...
WHAT HAPPENED TO YOUR FACE?!
AH, HEH HEH, IT'S NOTHING ...
A little awkward, Ren was apparently always getting beat up by his perfectionist father.
FLUTTER
Whoa!
Running away to that card shop all the time, one day he met a certain Vanguard cardfighter...
HUB
BUB
?
POP
RIDE THE VAN-GUARD !!

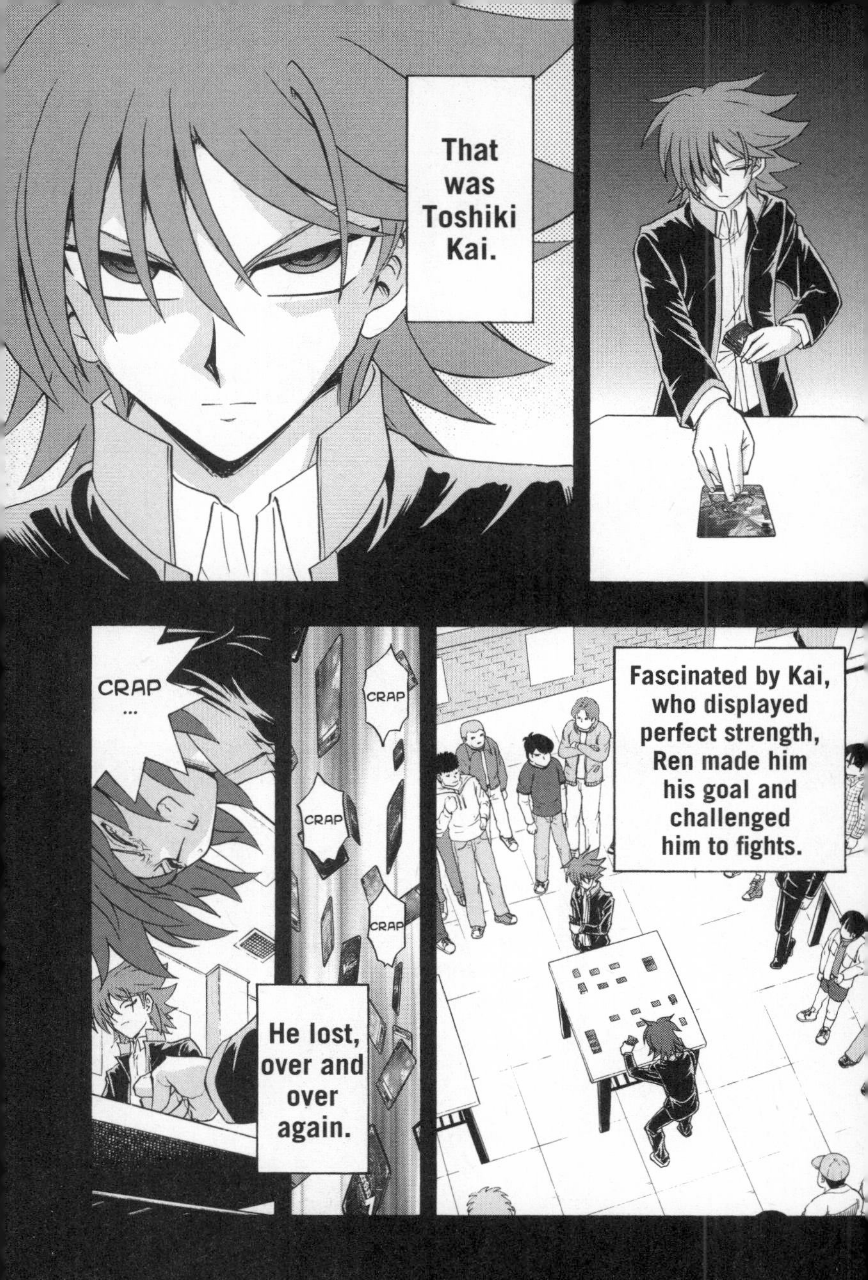
That was Toshiki Kai.
Fascinated by Kai, who displayed perfect strength, Ren made him his goal and challenged him to fights.
CRAP
CRAP
CRAP
CRAP ...
He lost, over and over again.

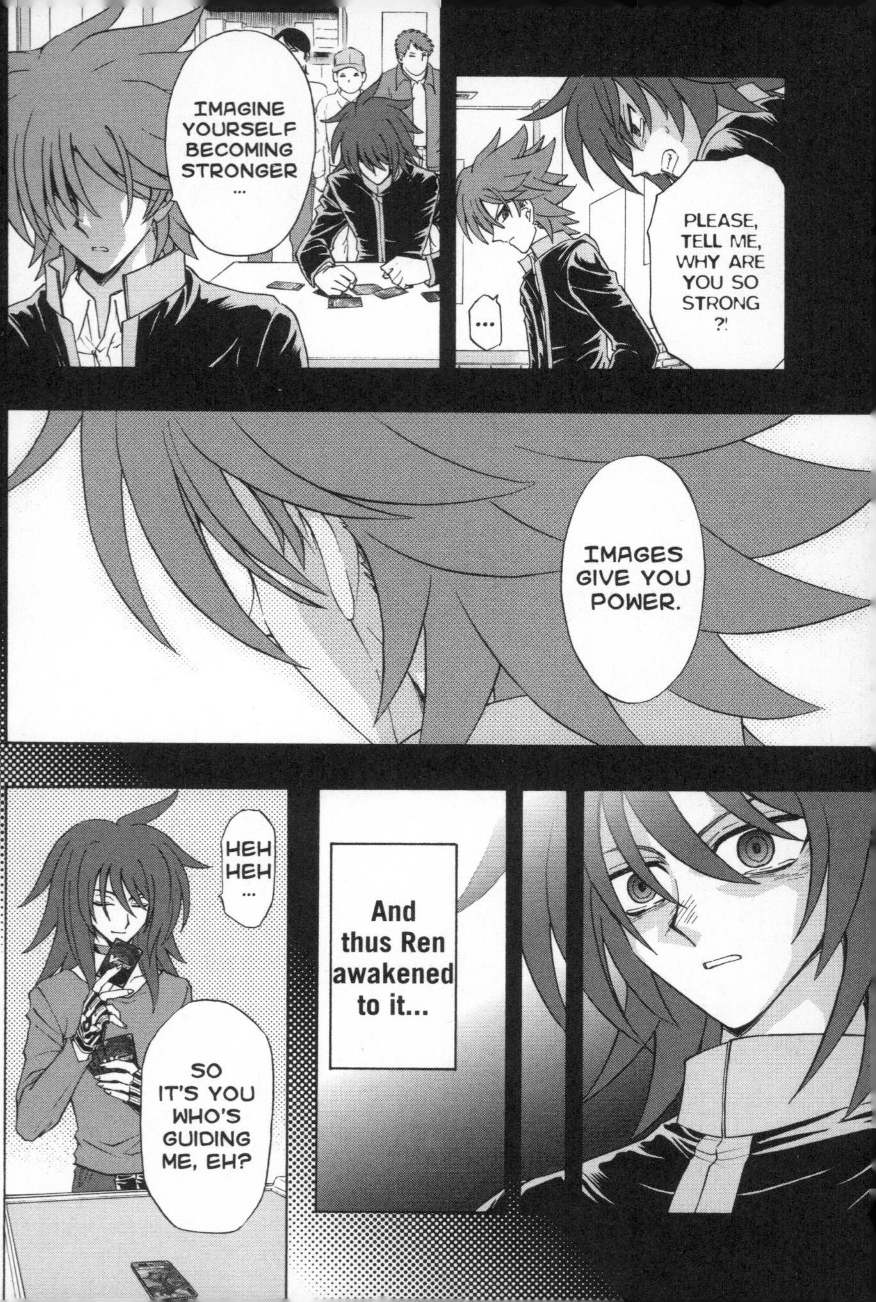
PLEASE, TELL ME, WHY ARE YOU SO STRONG ?!
...
IMAGINE YOURSELF BECOMING STRONGER ...
IMAGES GIVE YOU POWER.
And thus Ren awakened to it...
HEH HEH ...
SO IT'S YOU WHO'S GUIDING ME, EH?

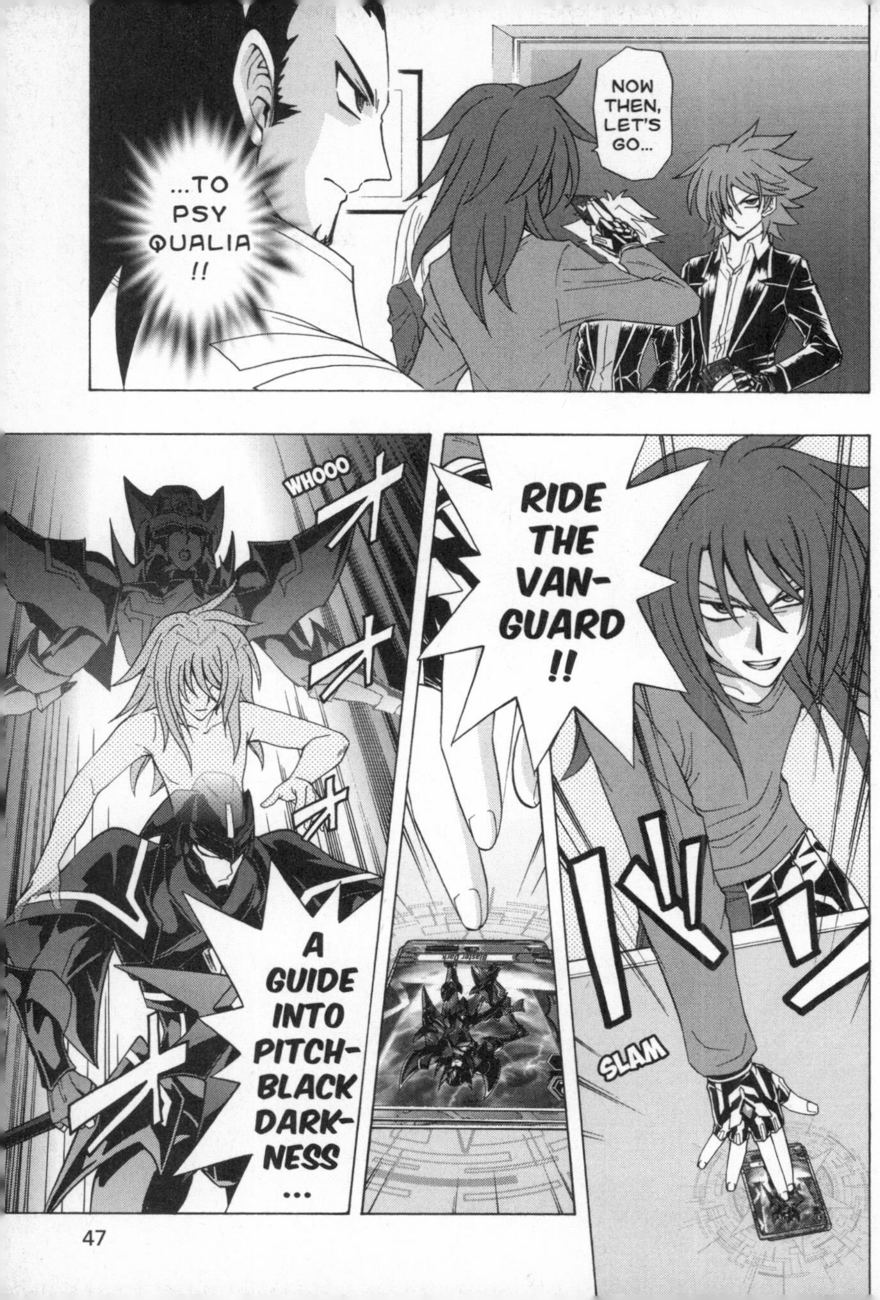
NOW THEN, LET'S GO...
...TO PSY QUALIA !!
RIDE THE VAN-GUARD !!
SLAM
WHOOO
A GUIDE INTO PITCH-BLACK DARKNESS ...

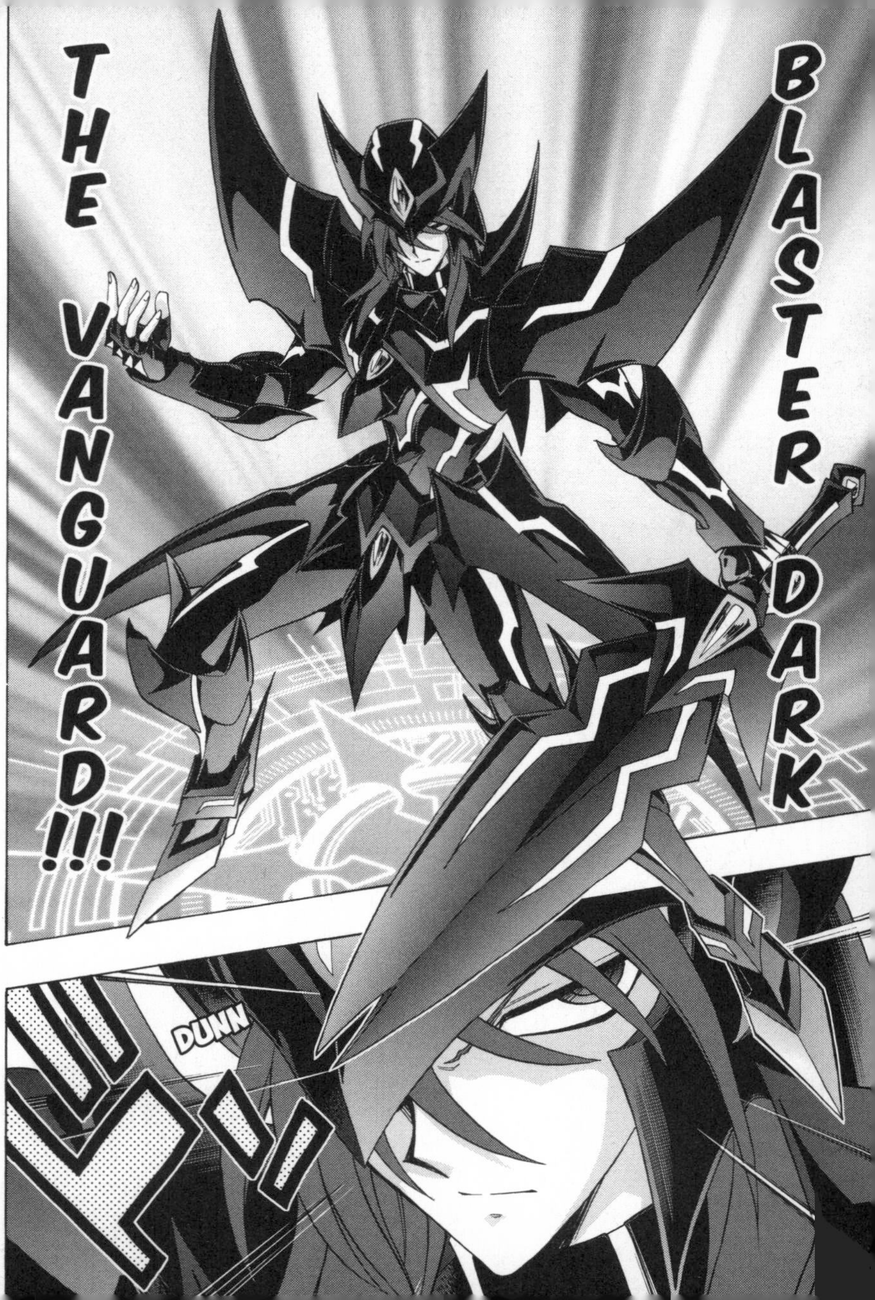
BLASTER DARK
THE VANGUARD!!!
DUNN

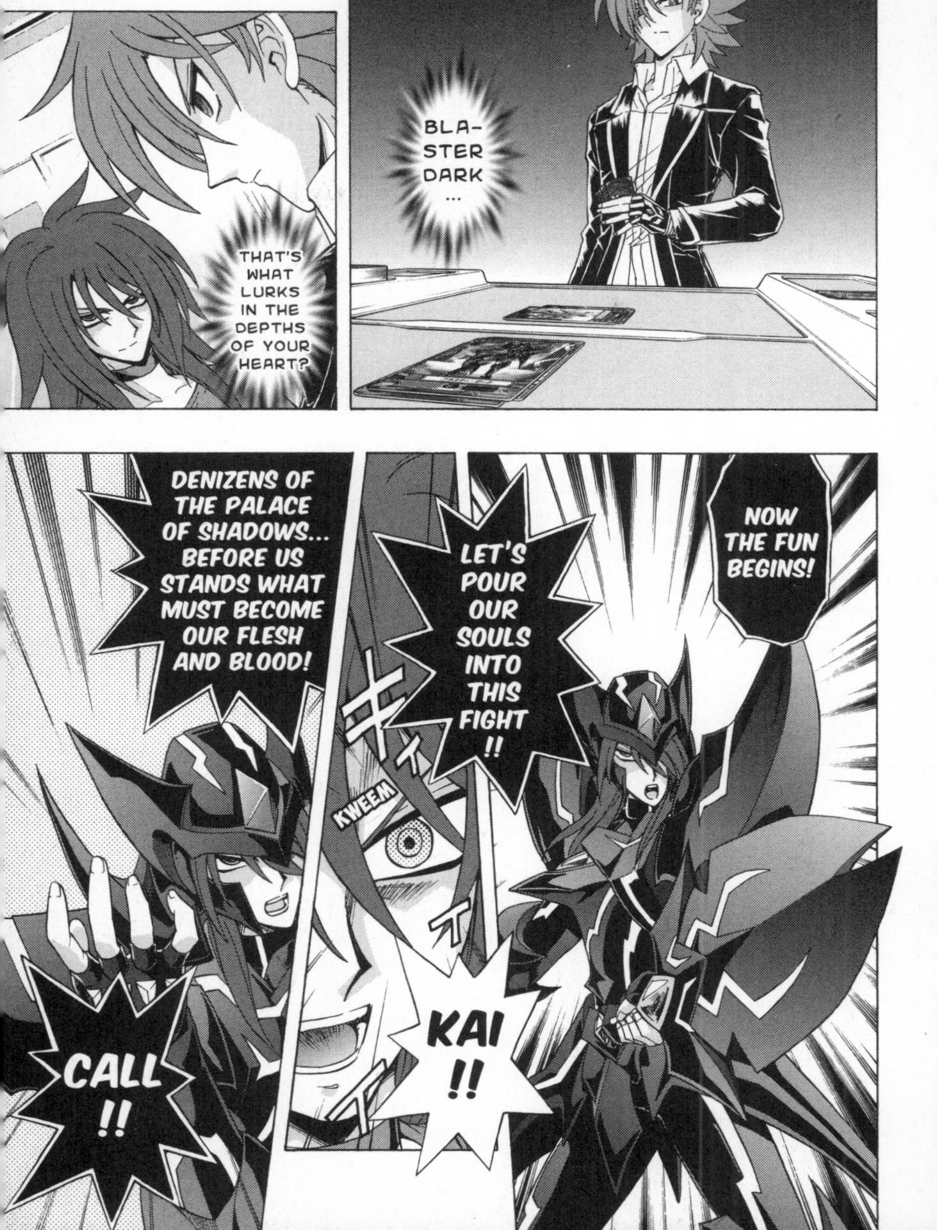
BLA-STER DARK ...
THAT'S WHAT LURKS IN THE DEPTHS OF YOUR HEART?
NOW THE FUN BEGINS!
LET'S POUR OUR SOULS INTO THIS FIGHT !!
キィ
KWEEM
KAI !!
DENIZENS OF THE PALACE OF SHADOWS... BEFORE US STANDS WHAT MUST BECOME OUR FLESH AND BLOOD!
CALL !!

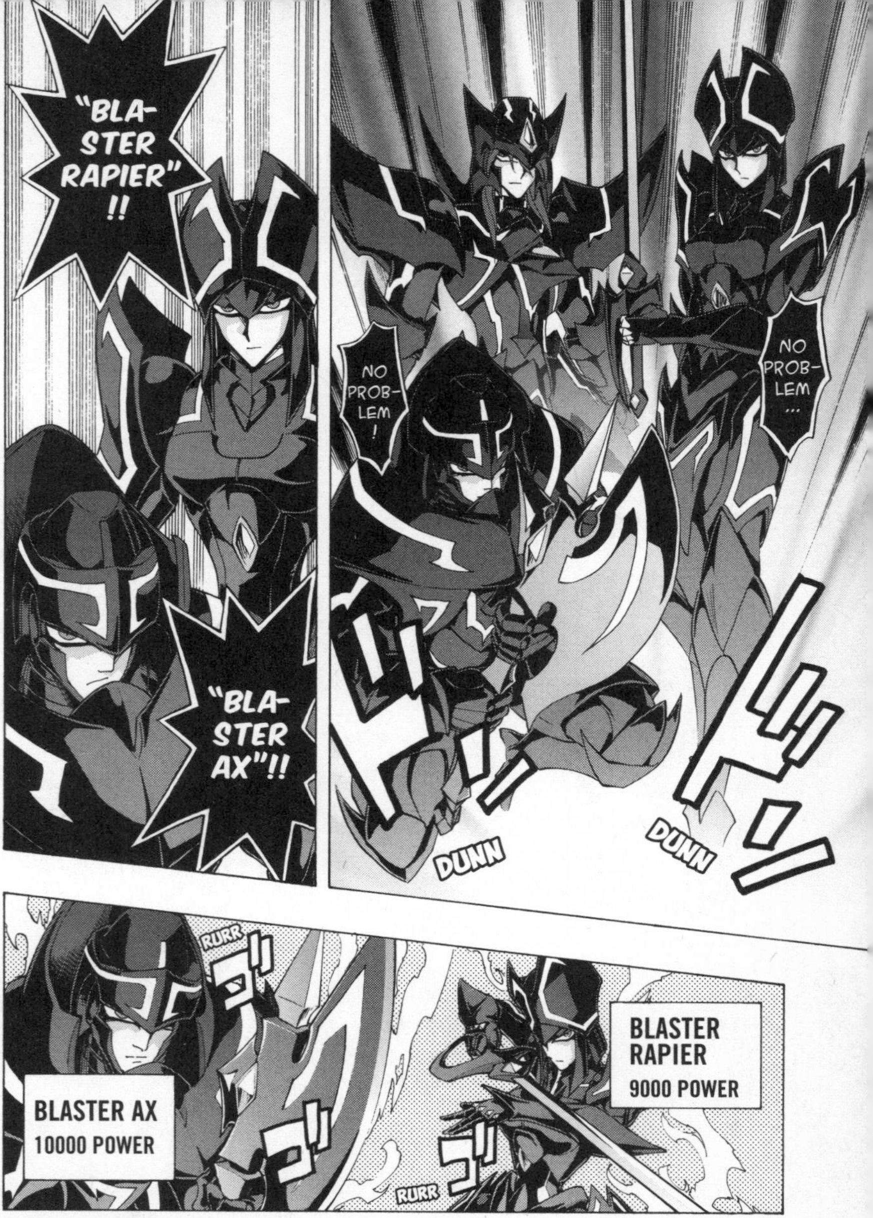
NO PROB-LEM...
NO PROB-LEM!
DUNN
DUNN
"BLA-STER RAPIER"!!
"BLA-STER AX"!!
BLASTER RAPIER 9000 POWER
RURR
RURR
BLASTER AX 10000 POWER

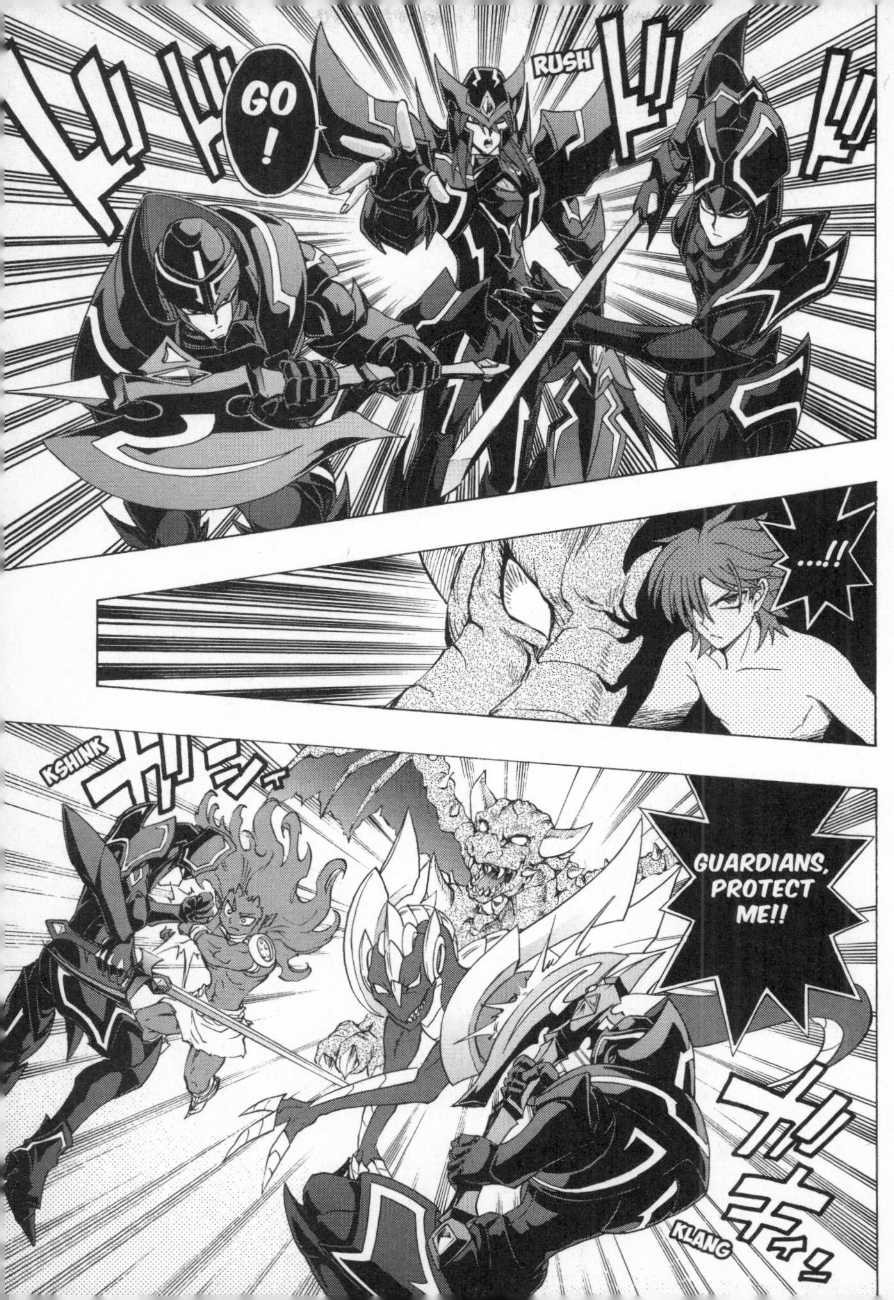
RUSH
GO!
...!!
GUARDIANS, PROTECT ME!!
KSHINK
KLANG

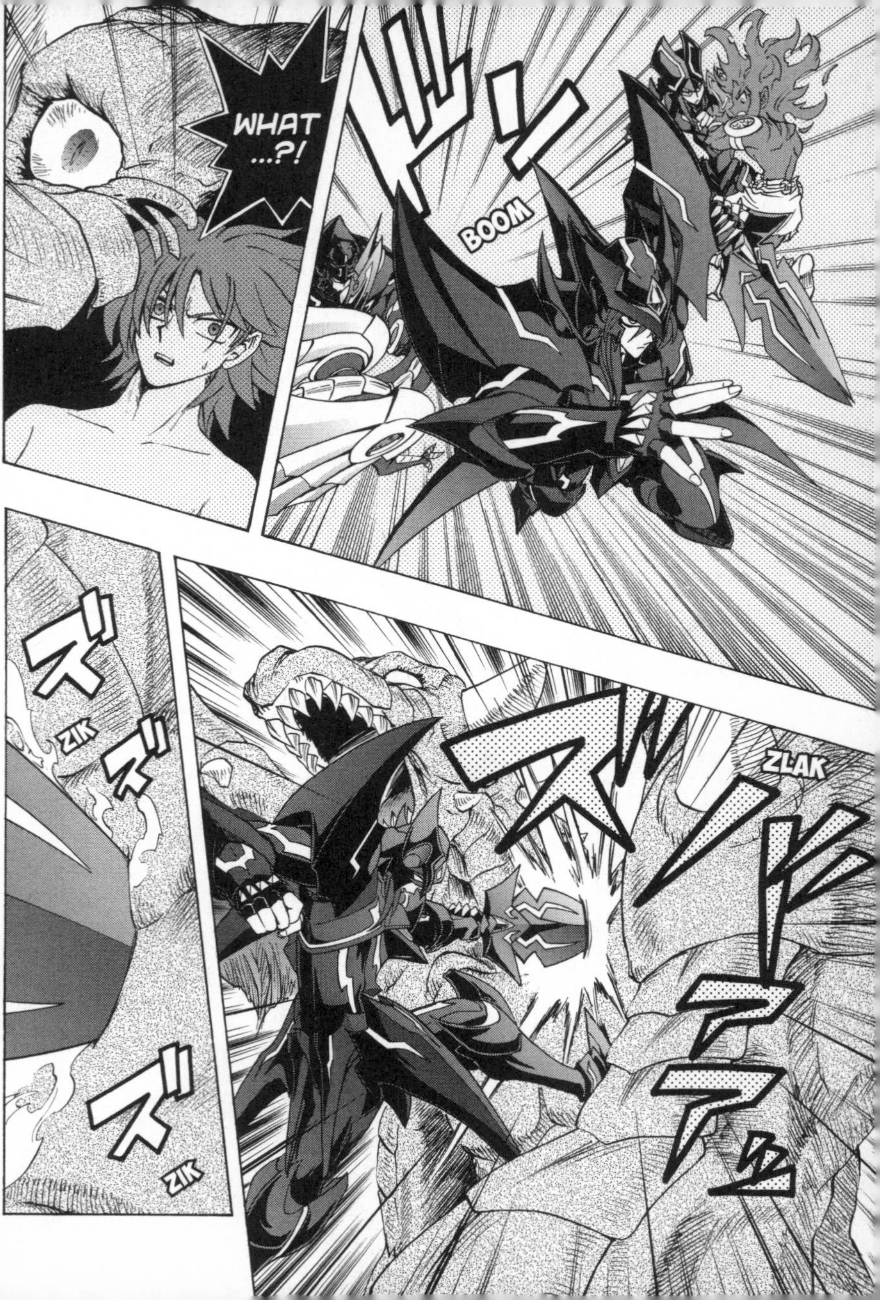
BOOM
WHAT ...?!
ZLAK
ZIK
ZIK

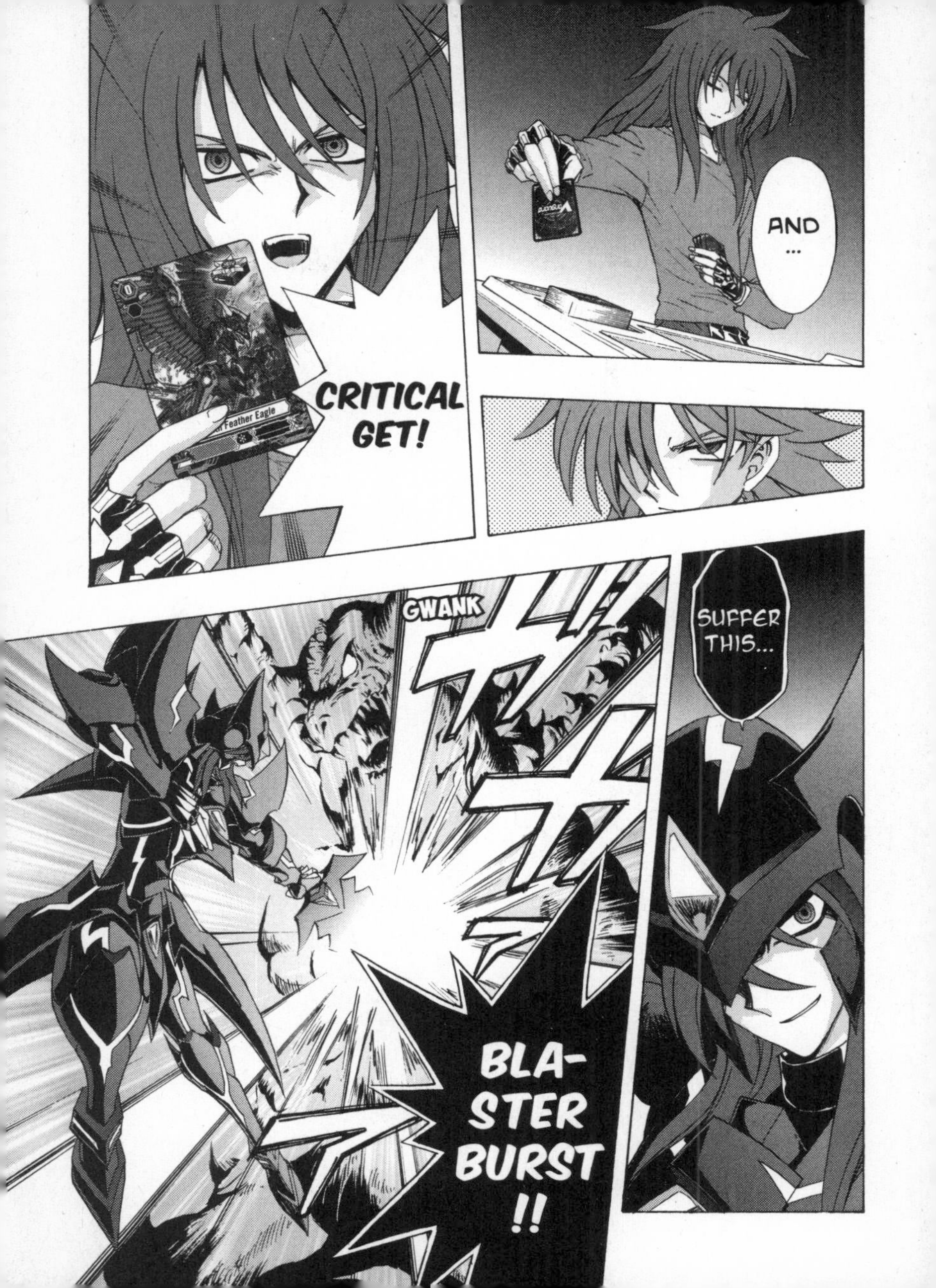
AND ...
CRITICAL GET!
SUFFER THIS...
GWANK
BLA-STER BURST !!

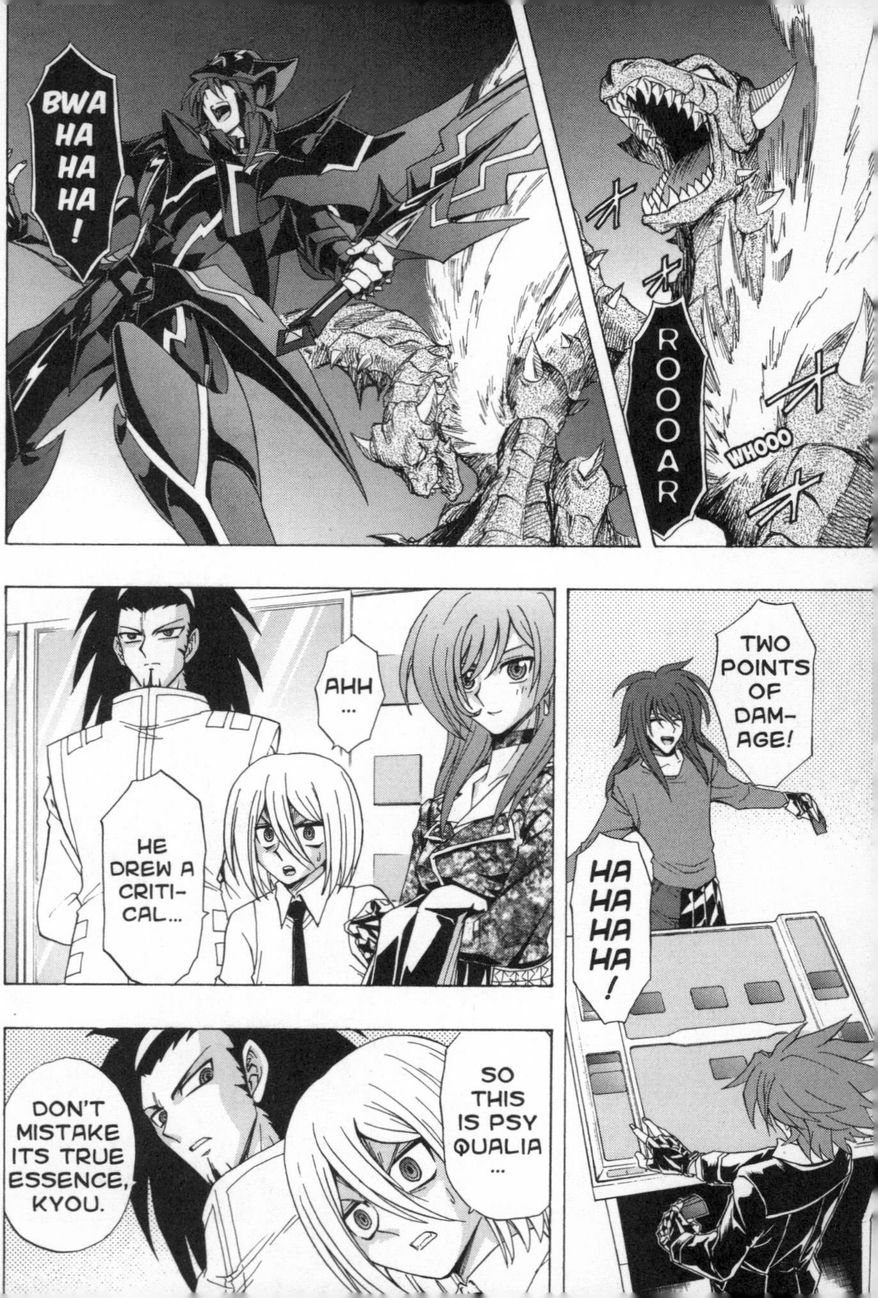

ROOOAR
WHOOO
BWA HA HA HA!
TWO POINTS OF DAM-AGE!
HA HA HA HA HA!
AHH...
HE DREW A CRITI-CAL...
SO THIS IS PSY QUALIA...
DON'T MISTAKE ITS TRUE ESSENCE, KYOU.

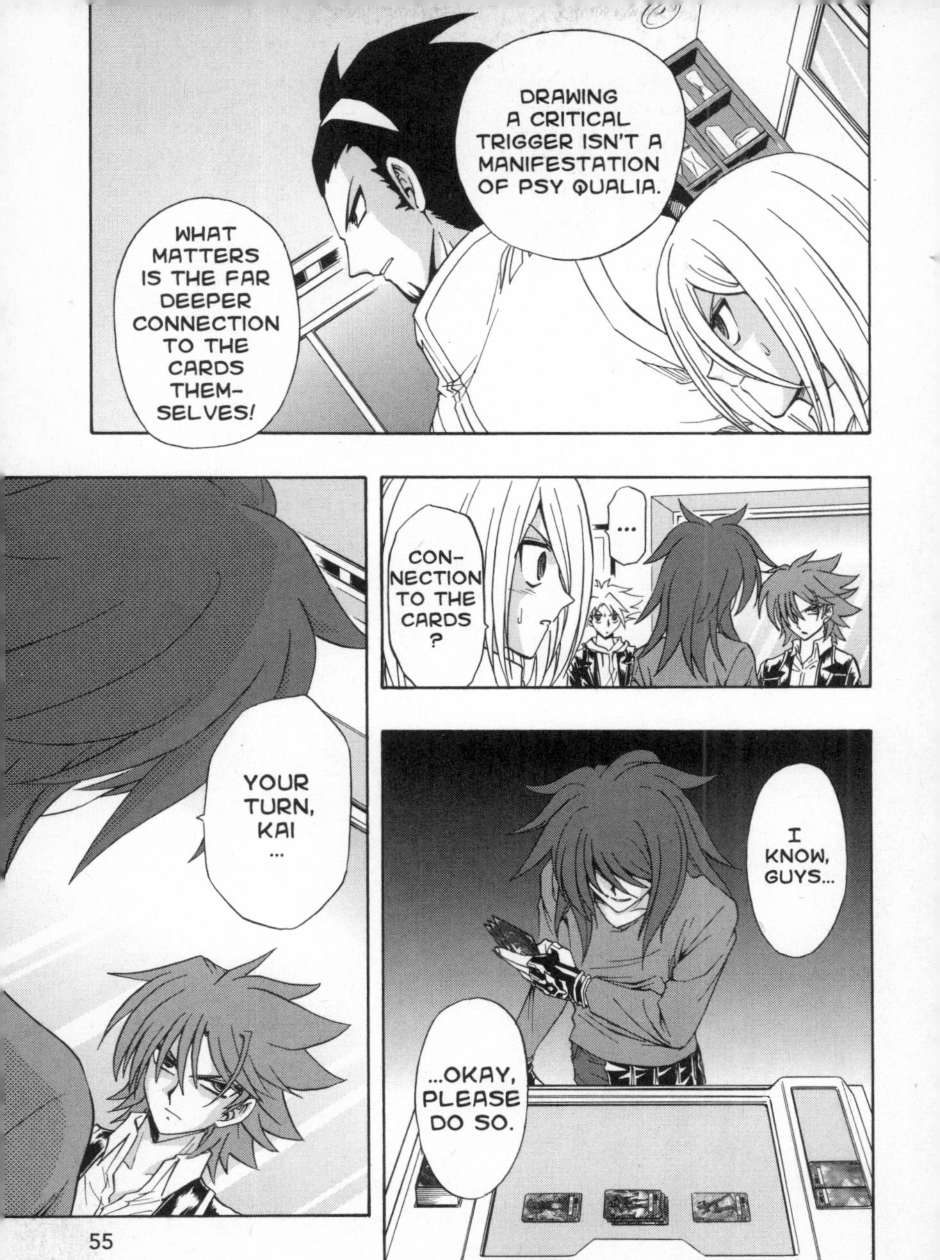
DRAWING A CRITICAL TRIGGER ISN'T A MANIFESTATION OF PSY QUALIA.
WHAT MATTERS IS THE FAR DEEPER CONNECTION TO THE CARDS THEM-SELVES!
...
CON-NECTION TO THE CARDS?
I KNOW, GUYS...
...OKAY, PLEASE DO SO.
YOUR TURN, KAI...

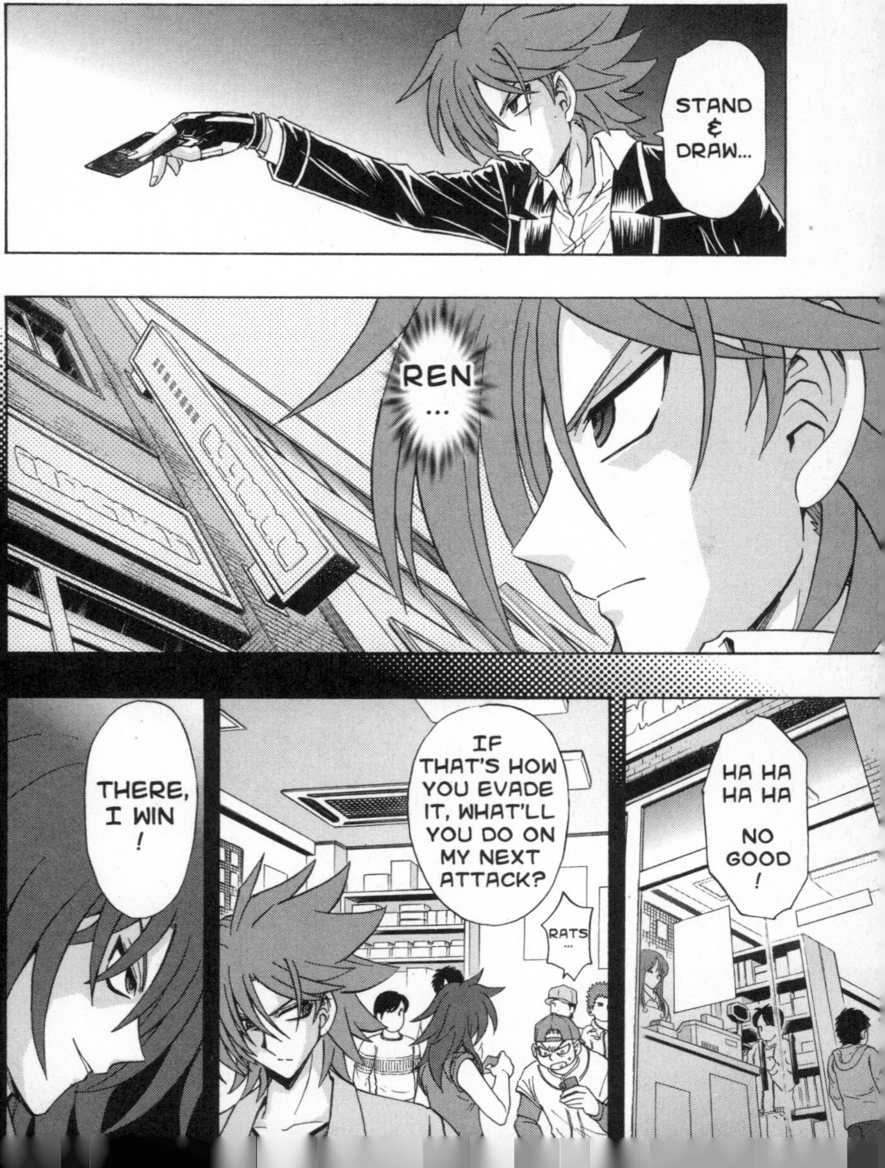
STAND & DRAW...
REN...
HA HA HA HA
NO GOOD!
IF THAT'S HOW YOU EVADE IT, WHAT'LL YOU DO ON MY NEXT ATTACK?
RATS...
THERE, I WIN!

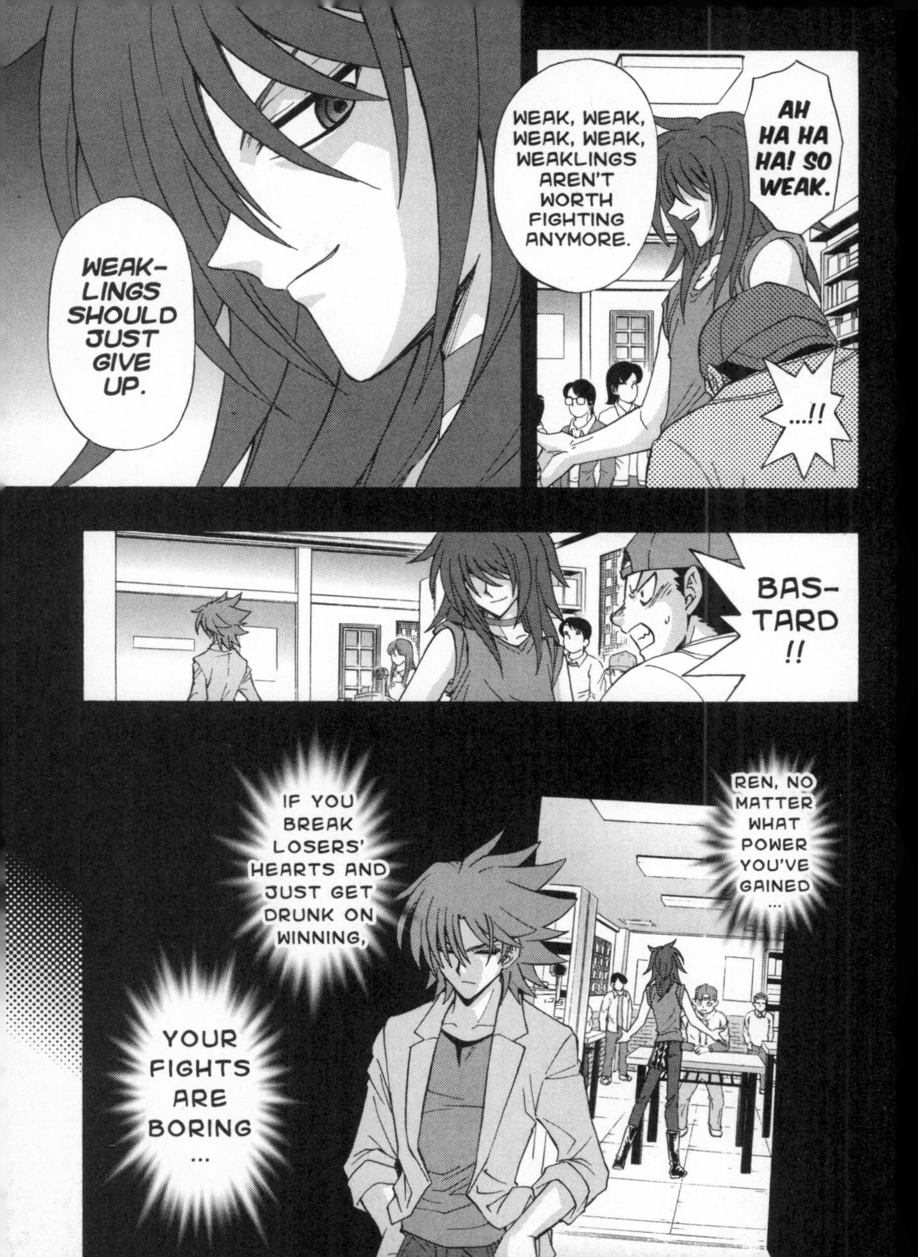
AH HA HA HA! SO WEAK.
WEAK, WEAK, WEAK, WEAK, WEAKLINGS AREN'T WORTH FIGHTING ANYMORE.
...!!
WEAK-LINGS SHOULD JUST GIVE UP.
BAS-TARD !!
REN, NO MATTER WHAT POWER YOU'VE GAINED ...
IF YOU BREAK LOSERS' HEARTS AND JUST GET DRUNK ON WINNING,
YOUR FIGHTS ARE BORING ...

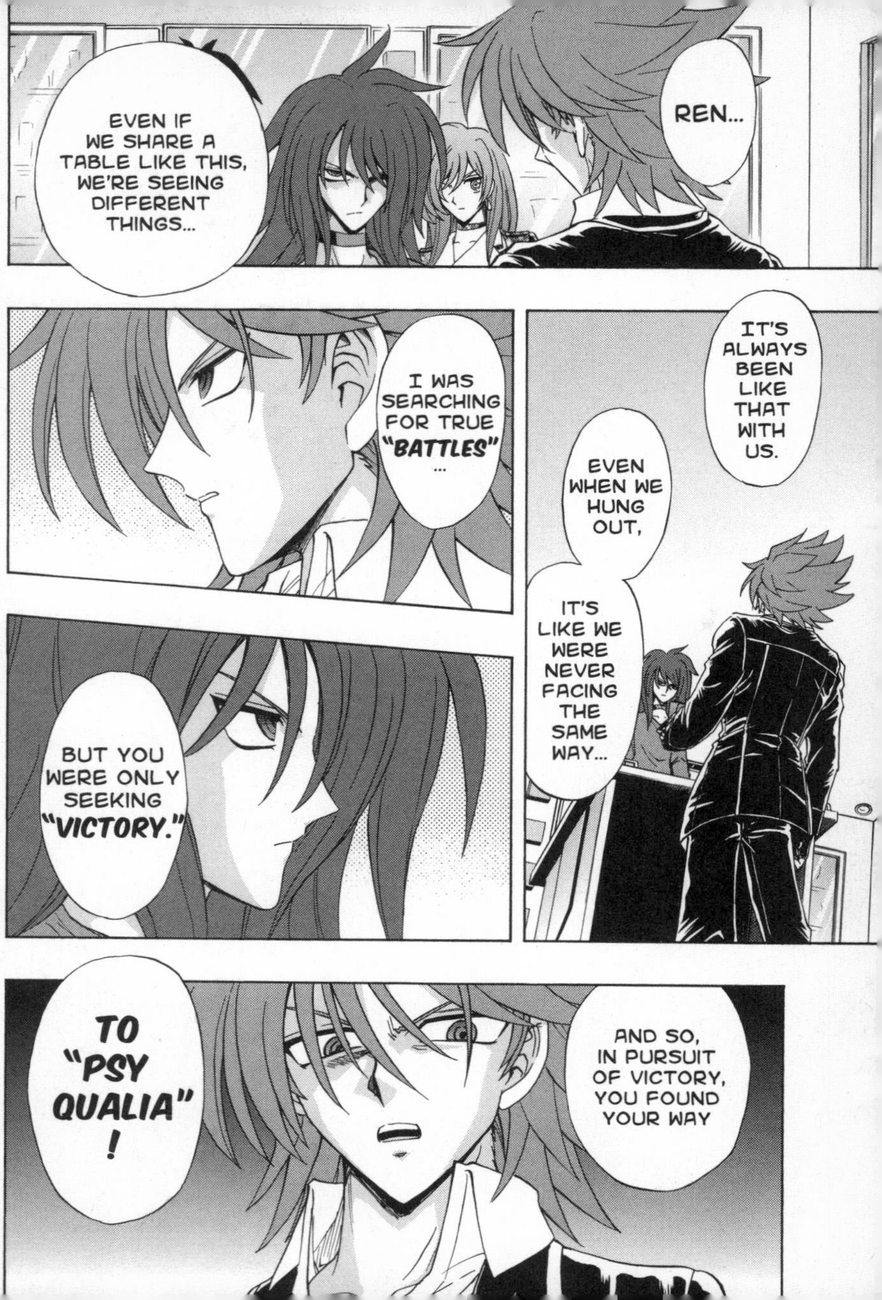
REN...
EVEN IF WE SHARE A TABLE LIKE THIS, WE'RE SEEING DIFFERENT THINGS...
IT'S ALWAYS BEEN LIKE THAT WITH US.
EVEN WHEN WE HUNG OUT,
IT'S LIKE WE WERE NEVER FACING THE SAME WAY...
I WAS SEARCHING FOR TRUE "BATTLES"...
BUT YOU WERE ONLY SEEKING "VICTORY."
AND SO, IN PURSUIT OF VICTORY, YOU FOUND YOUR WAY
TO "PSY QUALIA"!

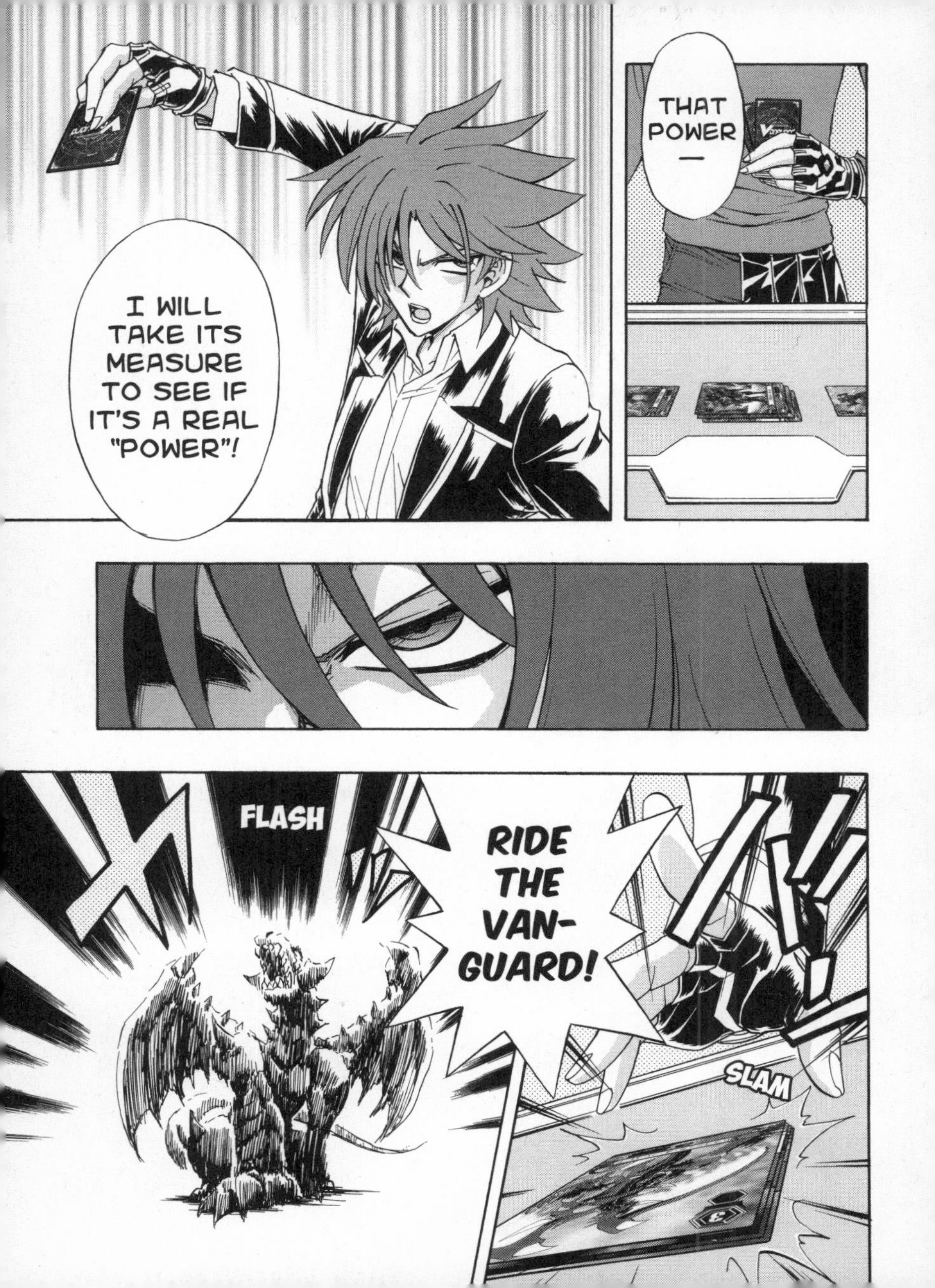
THAT POWER —
I WILL TAKE ITS MEASURE TO SEE IF IT'S A REAL "POWER"!
RIDE THE VAN-GUARD!
FLASH
SLAM

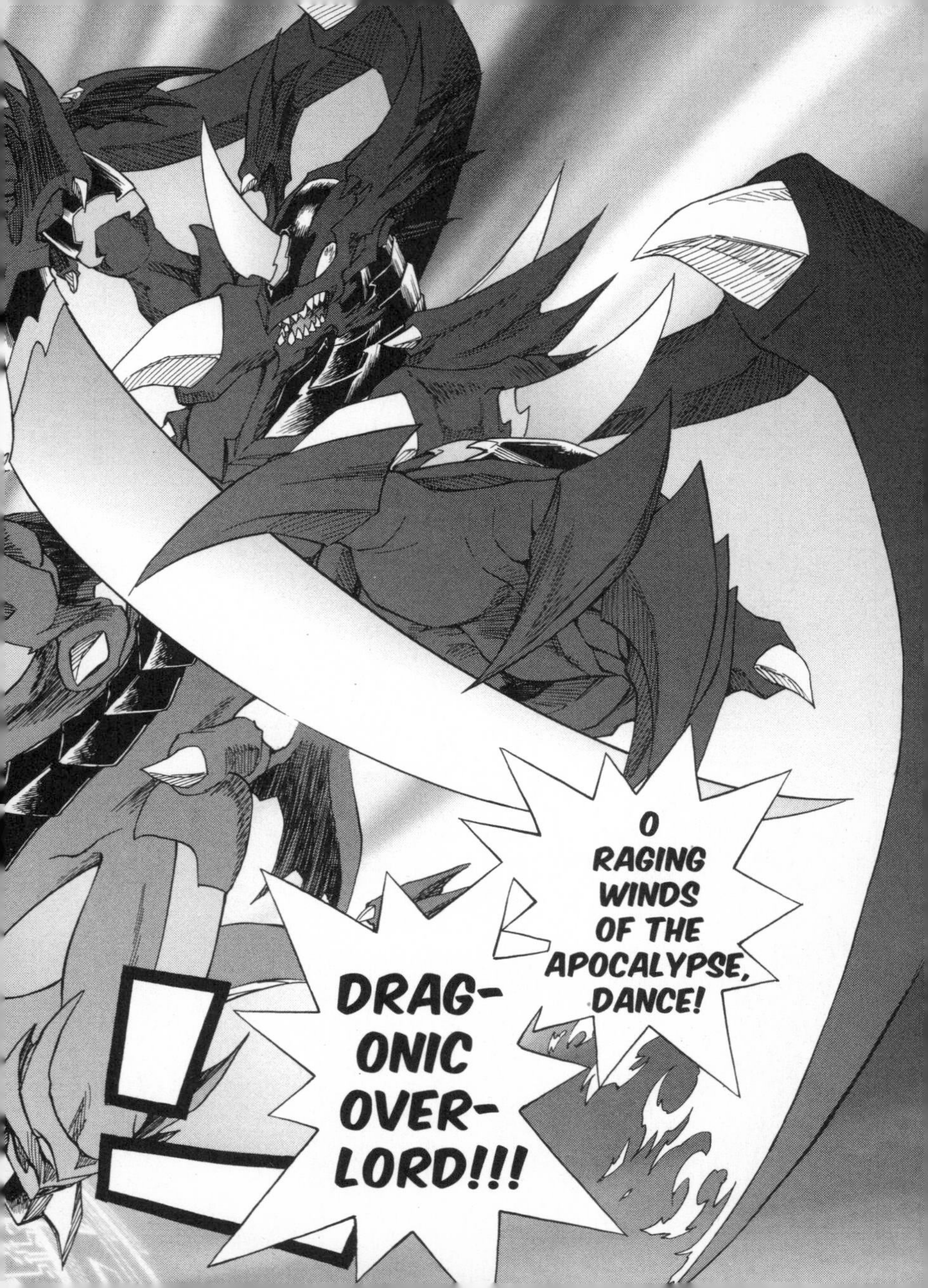
O RAGING WINDS OF THE APOCALYPSE, DANCE!
DRAG-ONIC OVER-LORD!!!

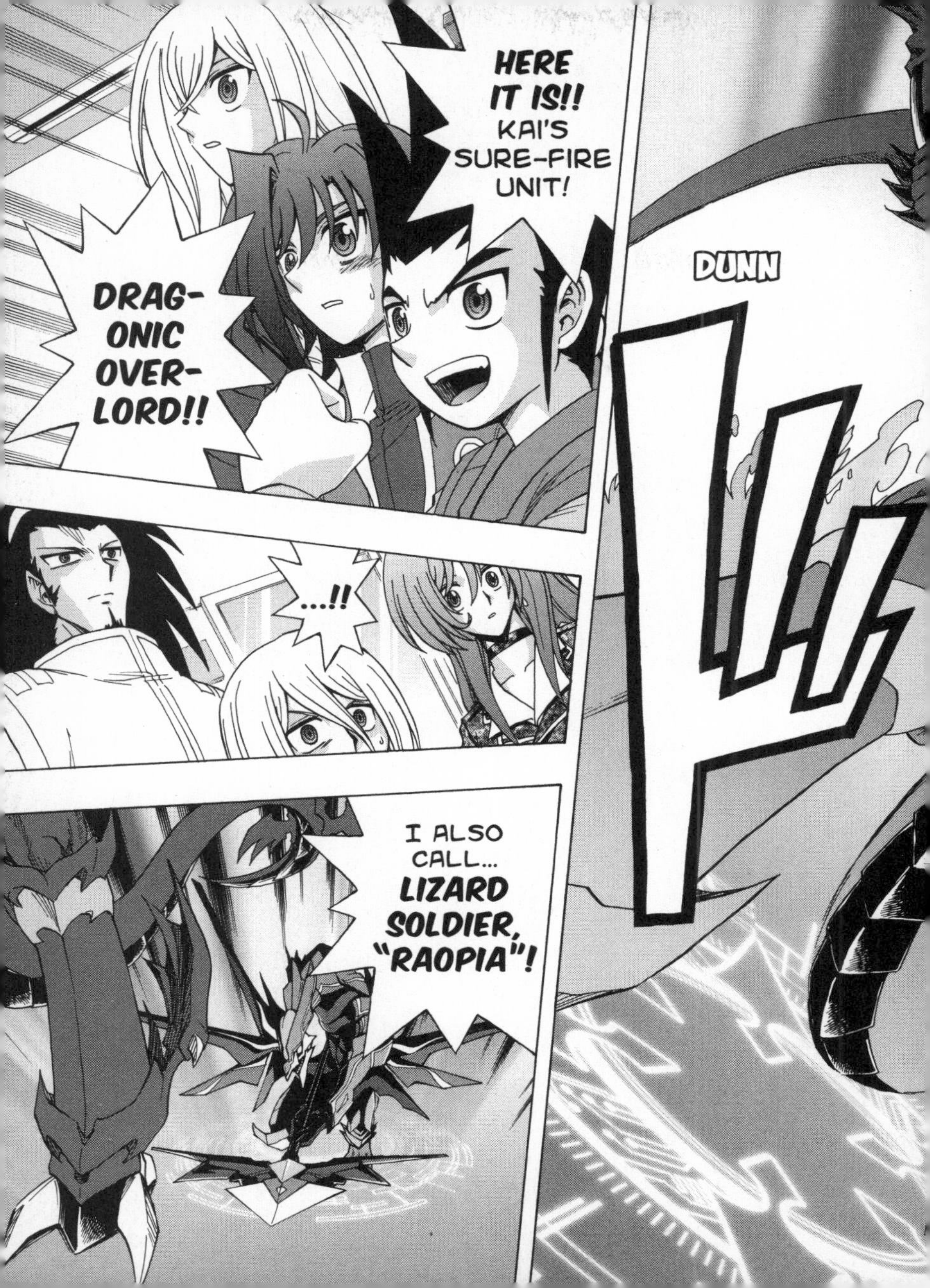
DUNN
HERE IT IS!! KAI'S SURE-FIRE UNIT!
DRAG-ONIC OVER-LORD!!
...!!
I ALSO CALL... LIZARD SOLDIER, "RAOPIA"!

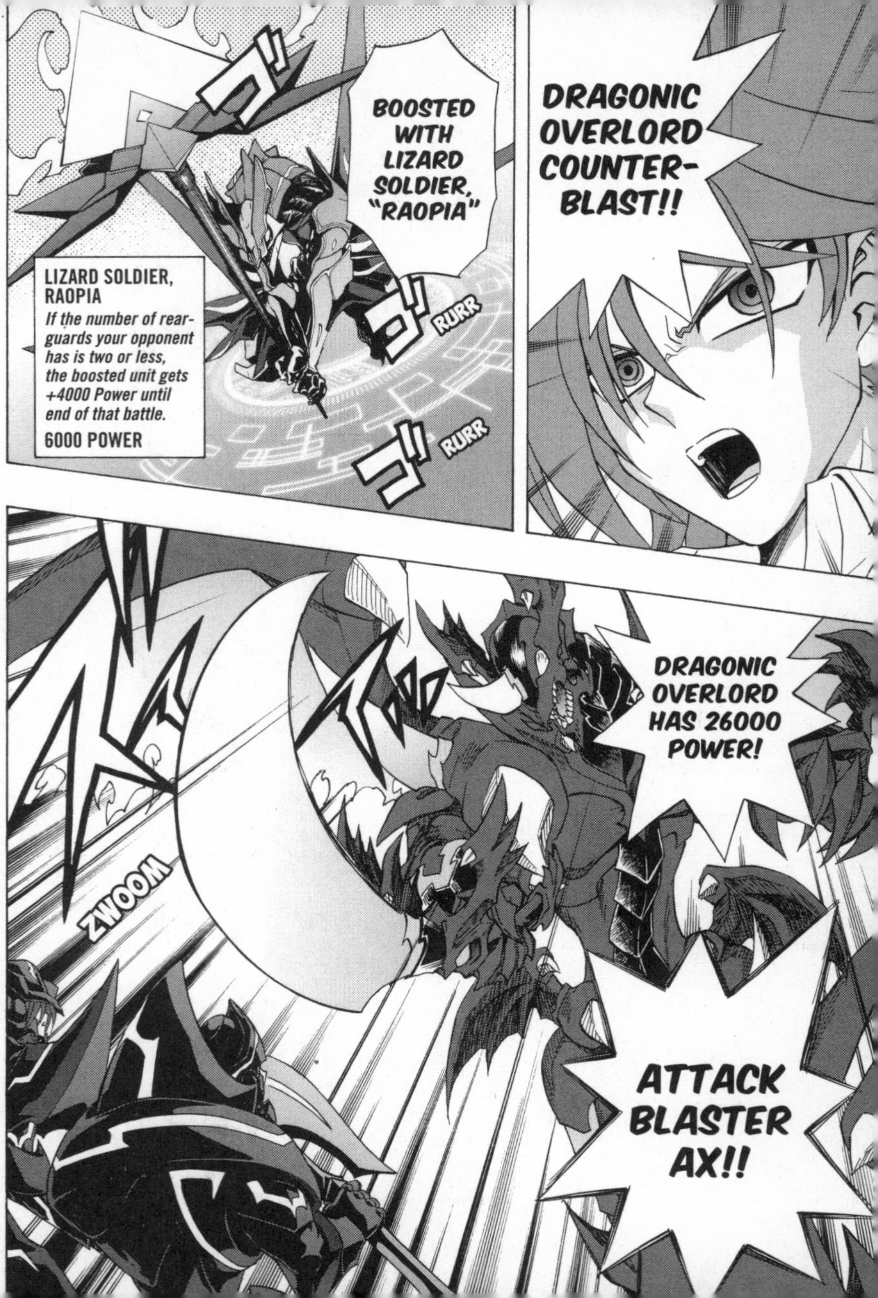
DRAGONIC OVERLORD COUNTER-BLAST!!
BOOSTED WITH LIZARD SOLDIER, "RAOPIA"
LIZARD SOLDIER, RAOPIA
If the number of rear-guards your opponent has is two or less, the boosted unit gets +4000 Power until end of that battle.
6000 POWER
RURR
RURR
DRAGONIC OVERLORD HAS 26000 POWER!
ATTACK BLASTER AX!!
ZWOOM

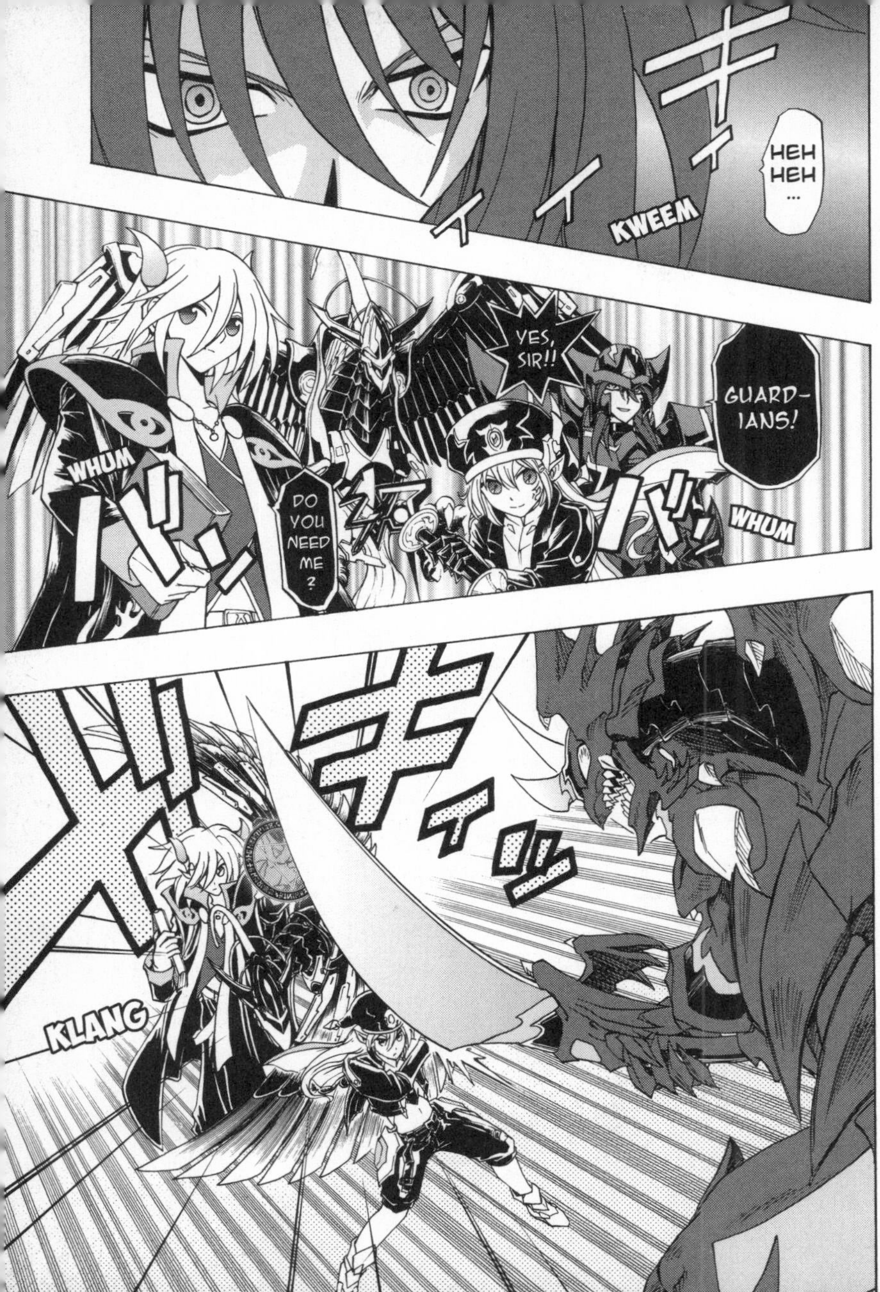
HEH HEH ...
KWEEM
GUARD-IANS!
WHUM
YES, SIR!!
DO YOU NEED ME?
WHUM
KLANG

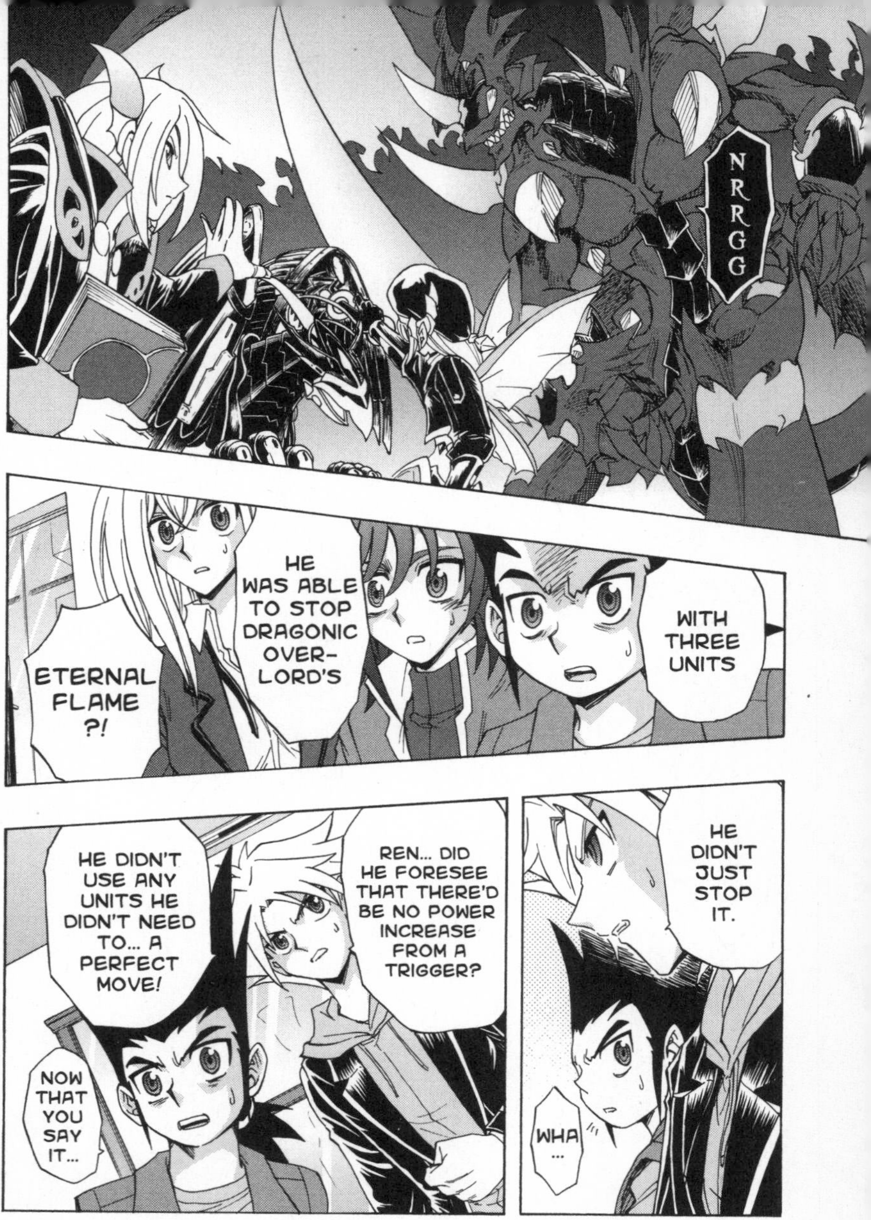
NRRGG
WITH THREE UNITS
HE WAS ABLE TO STOP DRAGONIC OVER-LORD'S
ETERNAL FLAME ?!
HE DIDN'T JUST STOP IT.
WHA ...
REN... DID HE FORESEE THAT THERE'D BE NO POWER INCREASE FROM A TRIGGER?
HE DIDN'T USE ANY UNITS HE DIDN'T NEED TO... A PERFECT MOVE!
NOW THAT YOU SAY IT...

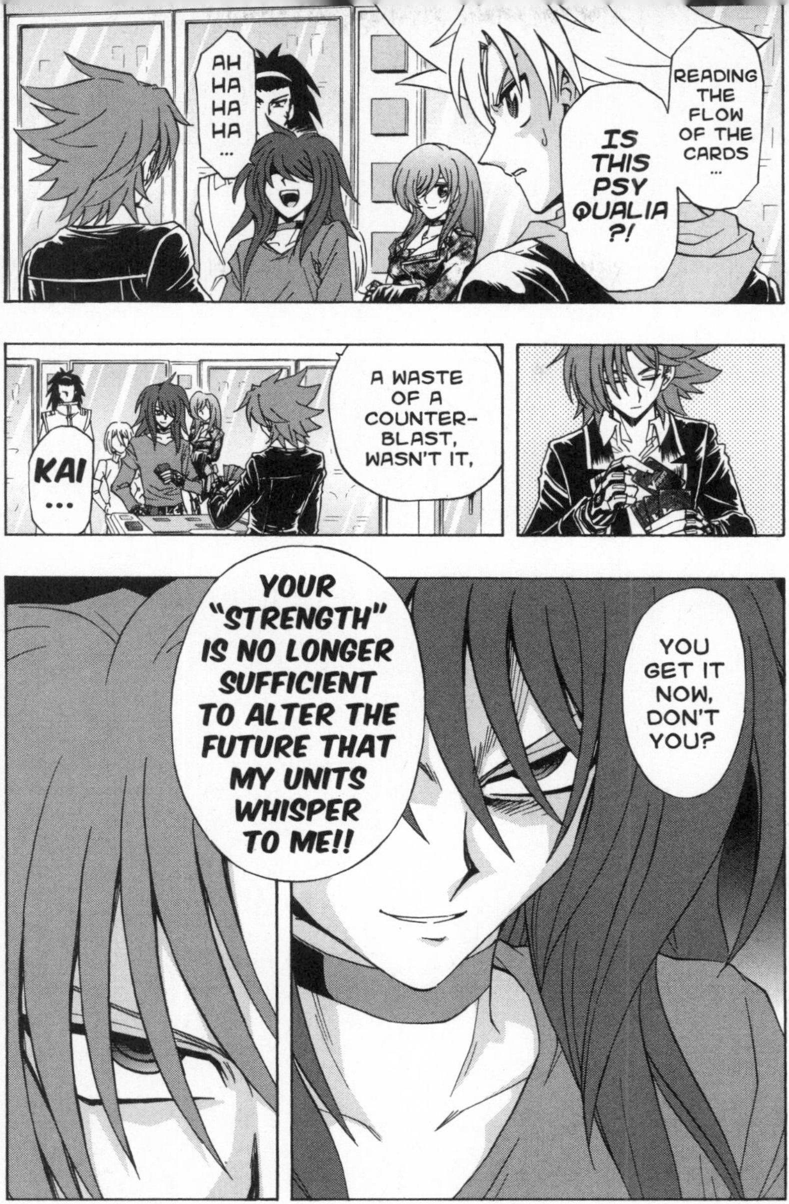
READING THE FLOW OF THE CARDS ...
IS THIS PSY QUALIA ?!
AH HA HA HA ...
A WASTE OF A COUNTER-BLAST, WASN'T IT,
KAI ...
YOU GET IT NOW, DON'T YOU?
YOUR "STRENGTH" IS NO LONGER SUFFICIENT TO ALTER THE FUTURE THAT MY UNITS WHISPER TO ME!!

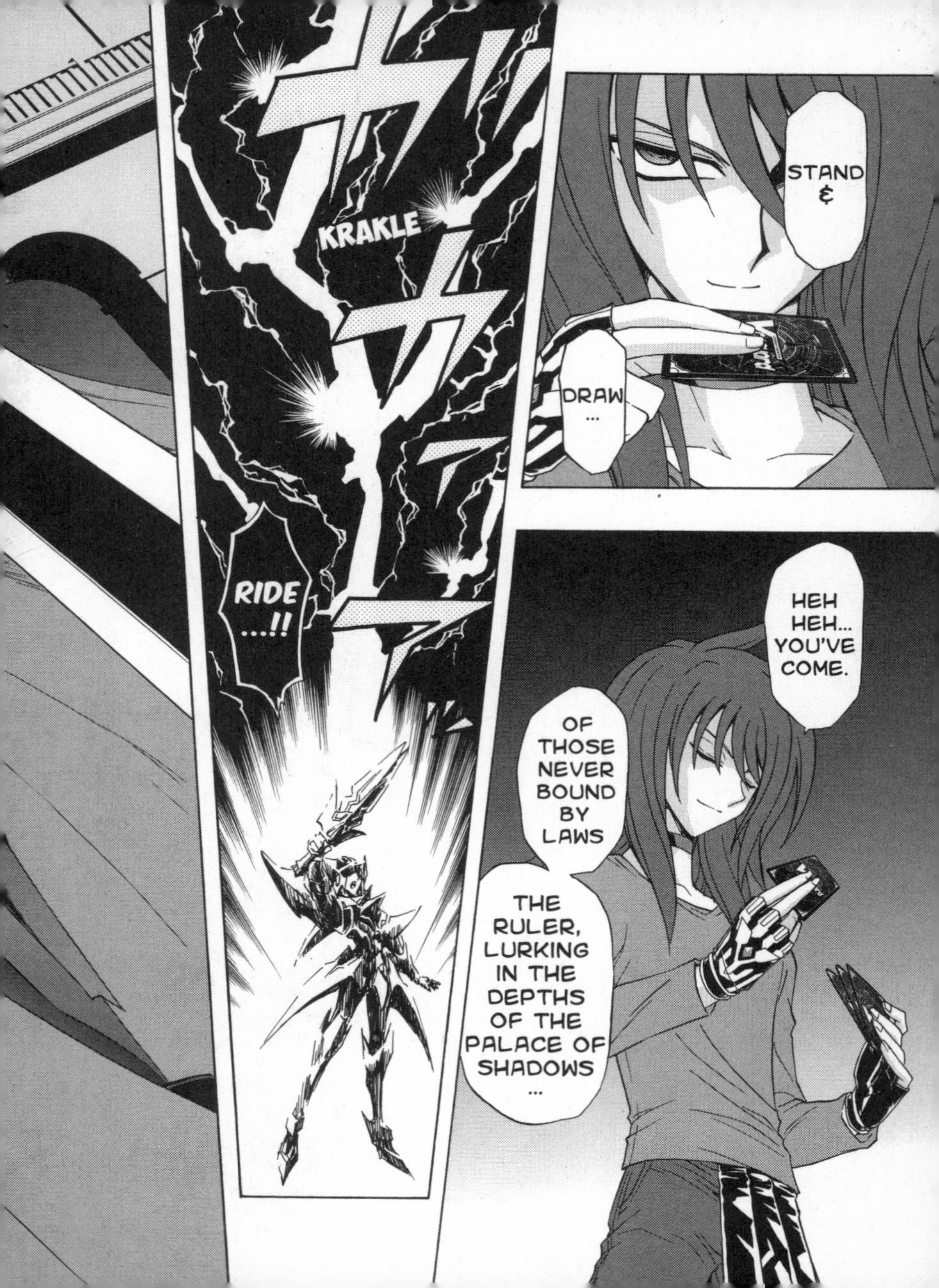
STAND &
DRAW ...
HEH HEH... YOU'VE COME.
OF THOSE NEVER BOUND BY LAWS
THE RULER, LURKING IN THE DEPTHS OF THE PALACE OF SHADOWS ...
KRAKLE
RIDE ....!!

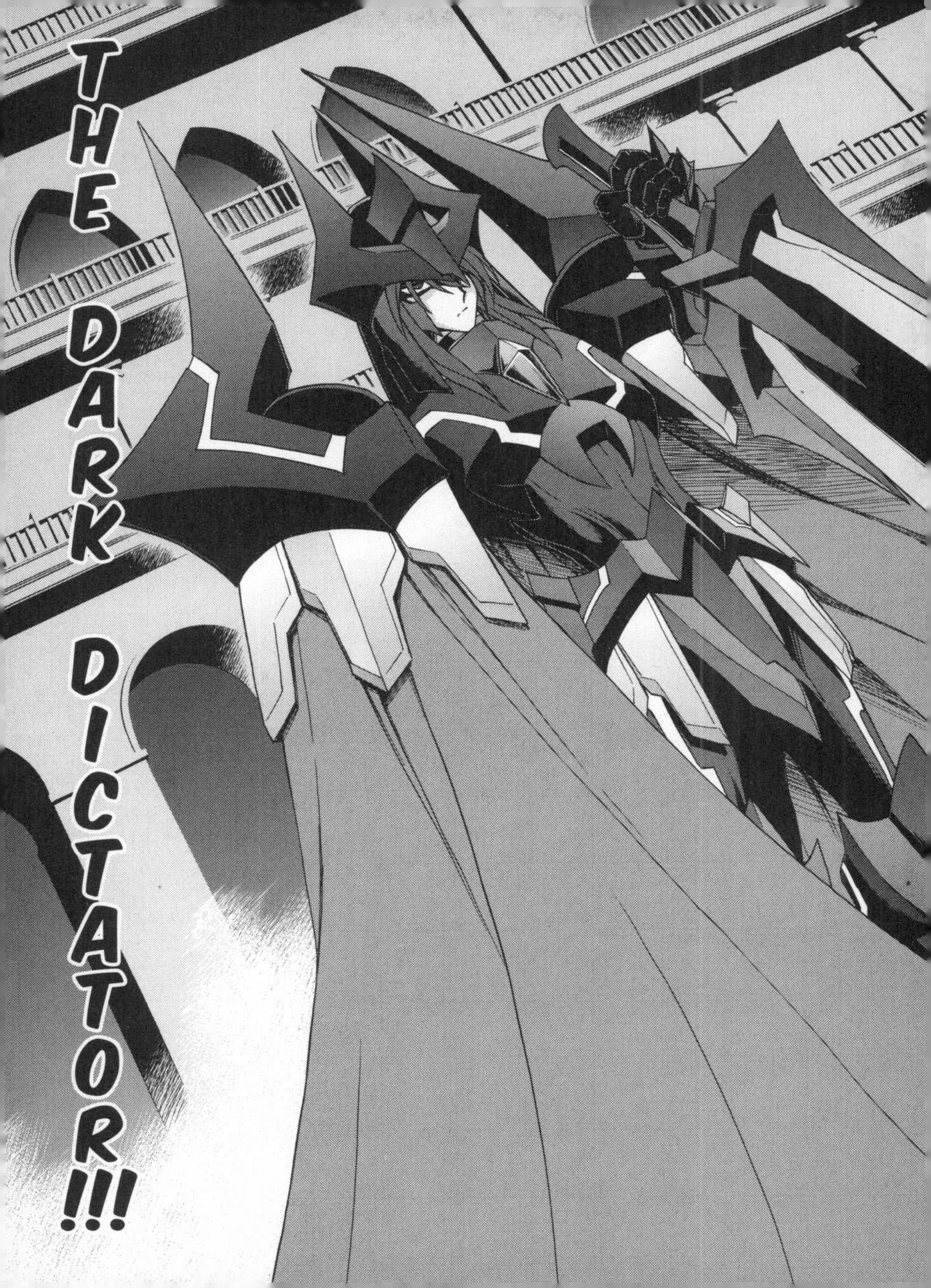
THE DARK DICTATOR!!

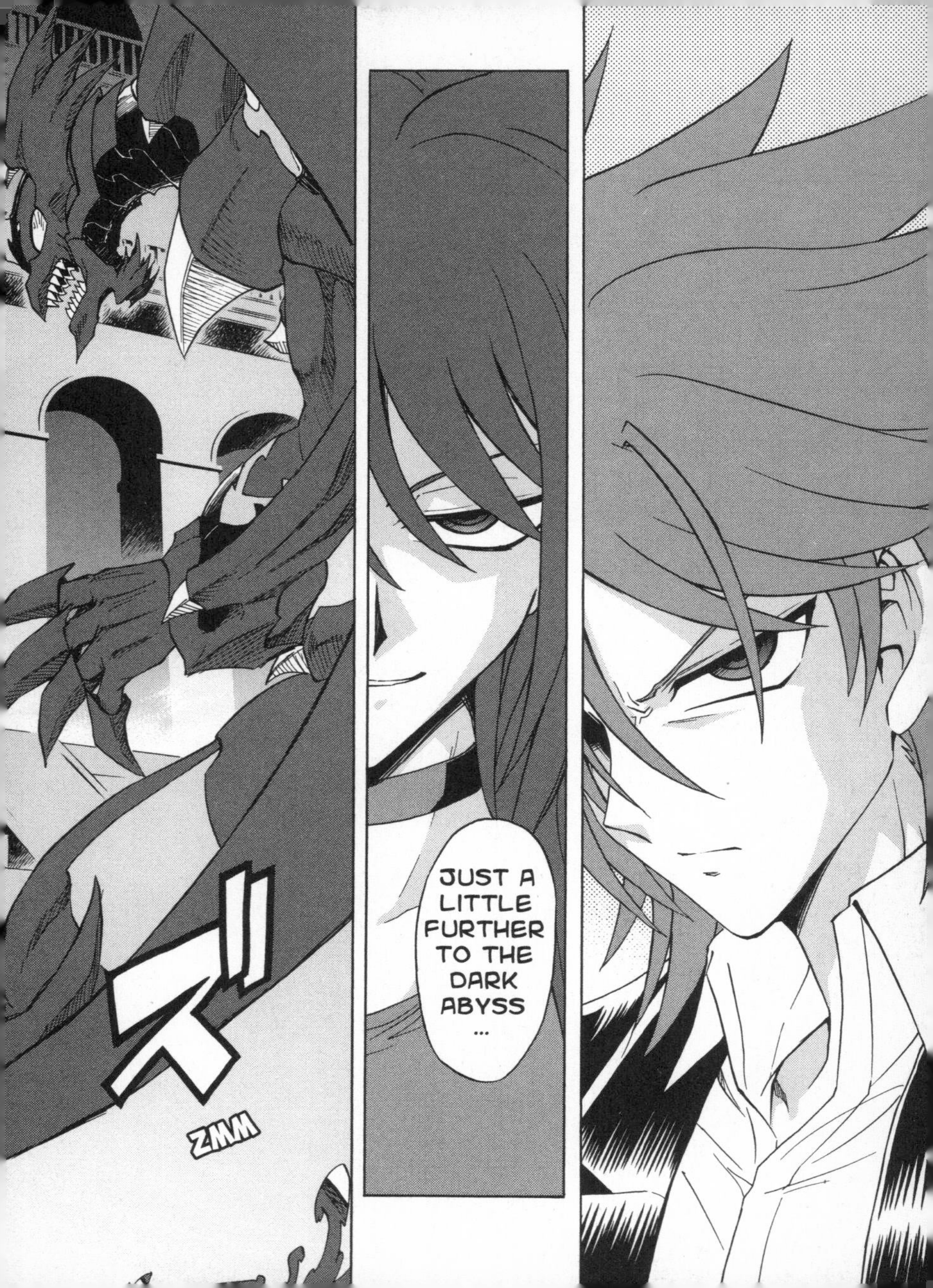
JUST A LITTLE FURTHER TO THE DARK ABYSS ...
ZMM

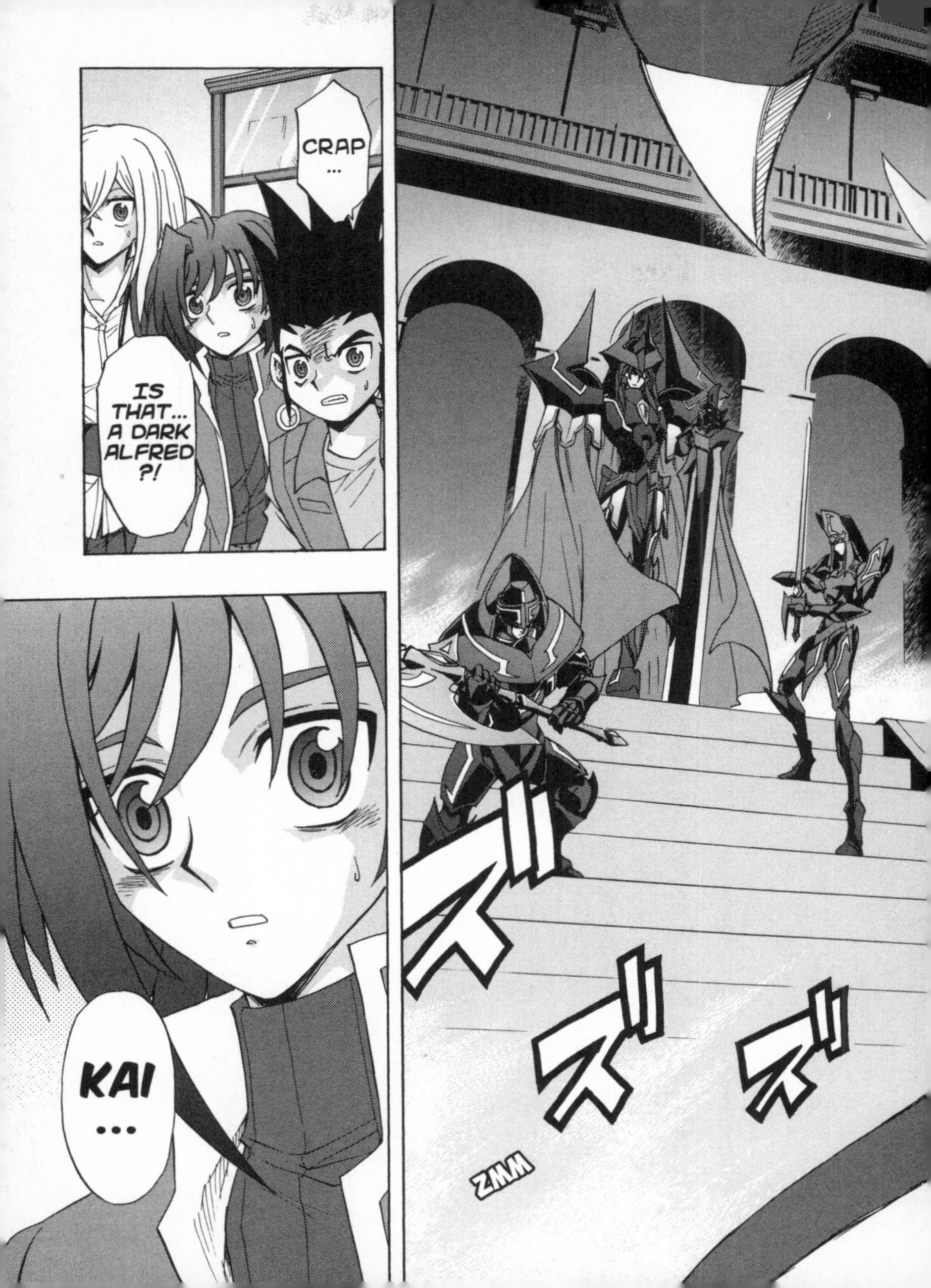
ズズズ
ZMM
CRAP ...
IS THAT... A DARK ALFRED ?!
KAI ...

BONUS! CARDFIGHT!! Vanguard NEVER-BEFORE-SEEN IMAGE BOARDS

UNITS

Majestic Lord Blaster

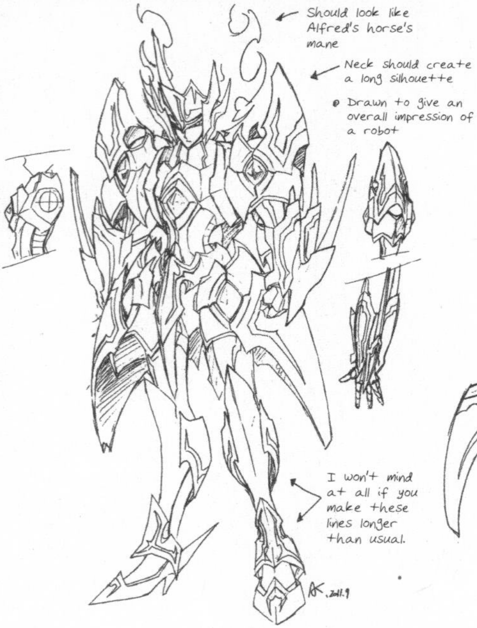
Should look like Alfred's horse's mane
Neck should create a long silhouette
@ Drawn to give an overall impression of a robot
I won't mind at all if you make these lines longer than usual.
AK. 2011.9

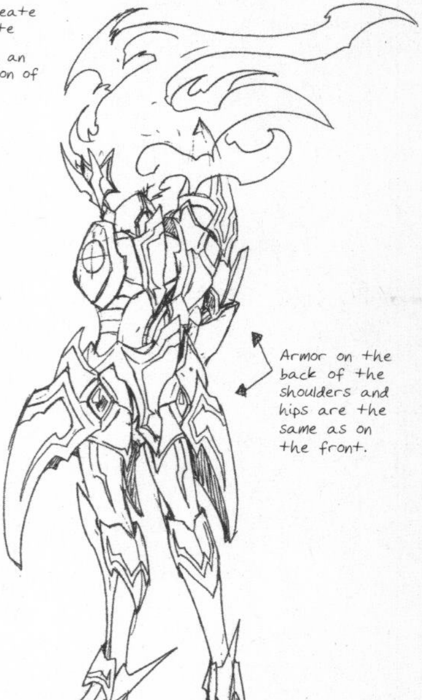
Armor on the back of the shoulders and hips are the same as on the front.

@ His Majesty's weapon

Blaster Photon Blade

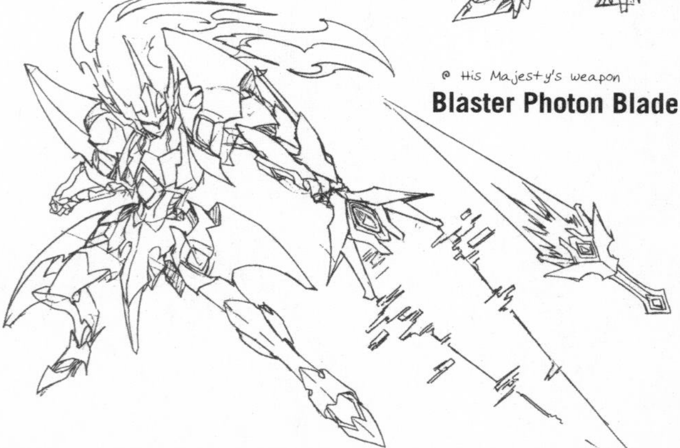

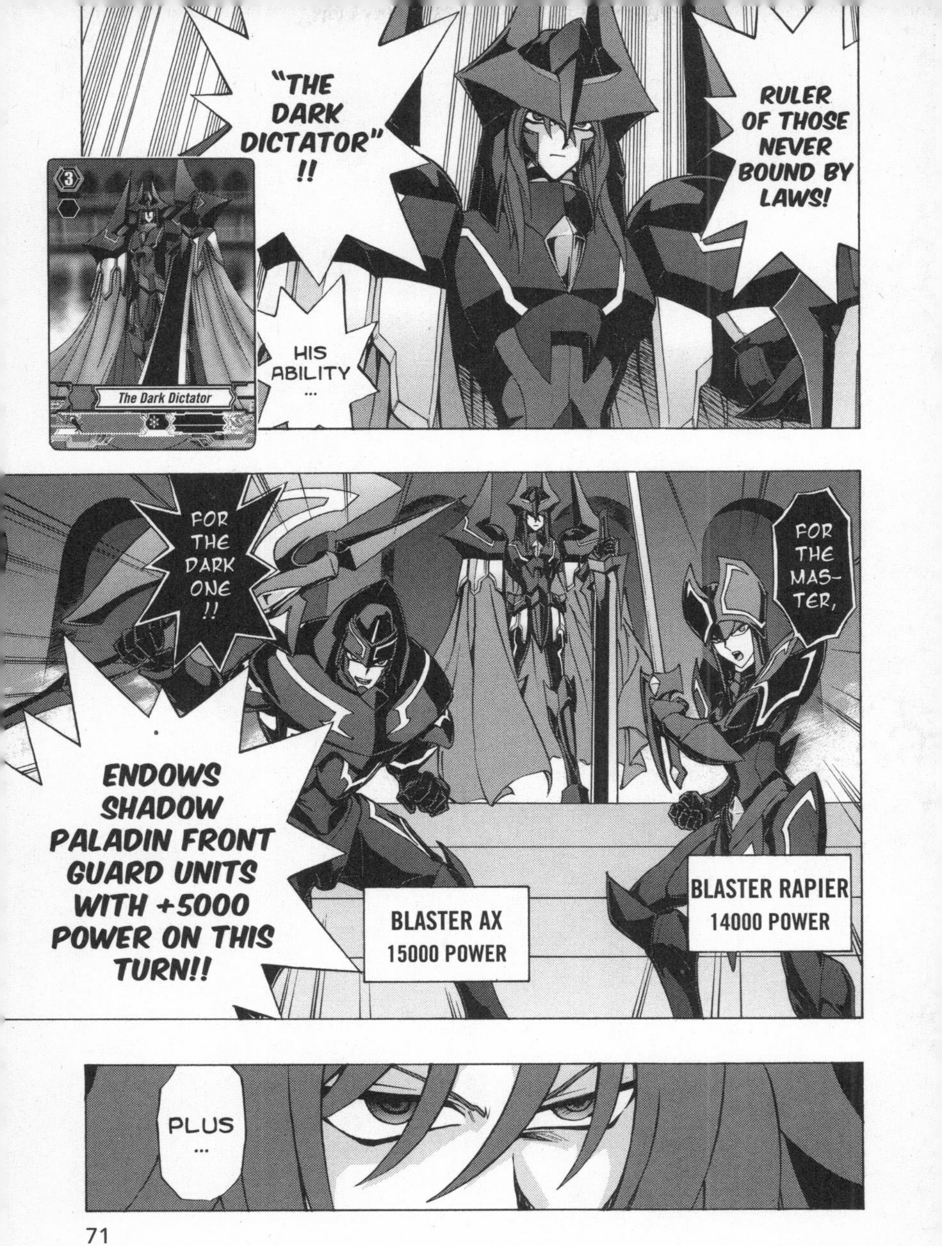
RULER OF THOSE NEVER BOUND BY LAWS!
"THE DARK DICTATOR" !!
3
The Dark Dictator
HIS ABILITY ...
FOR THE MAS- TER,
FOR THE DARK ONE !!
ENDOWS SHADOW PALADIN FRONT GUARD UNITS WITH +5000 POWER ON THIS TURN!!
BLASTER RAPIER 14000 POWER
BLASTER AX 15000 POWER
PLUS ...

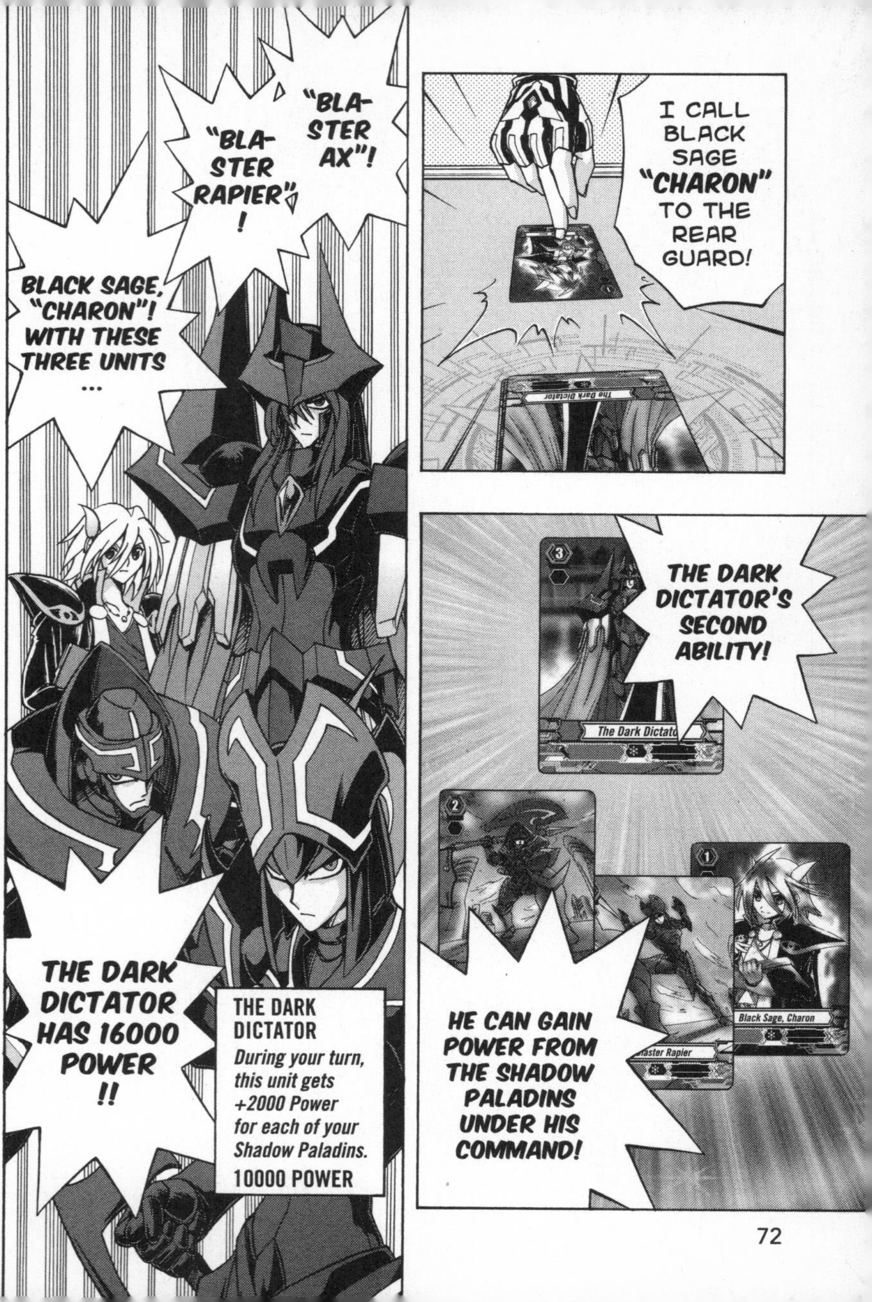
I CALL BLACK SAGE "CHARON" TO THE REAR GUARD!
THE DARK DICTATOR'S SECOND ABILITY!
Black Sage, Charon
HE CAN GAIN POWER FROM THE SHADOW PALADINS UNDER HIS COMMAND!
"BLA-STER AX"!
"BLA-STER RAPIER"!
BLACK SAGE, "CHARON"! WITH THESE THREE UNITS ...
THE DARK DICTATOR HAS 16000 POWER !!
THE DARK DICTATOR
During your turn, this unit gets +2000 Power for each of your Shadow Paladins.
10000 POWER

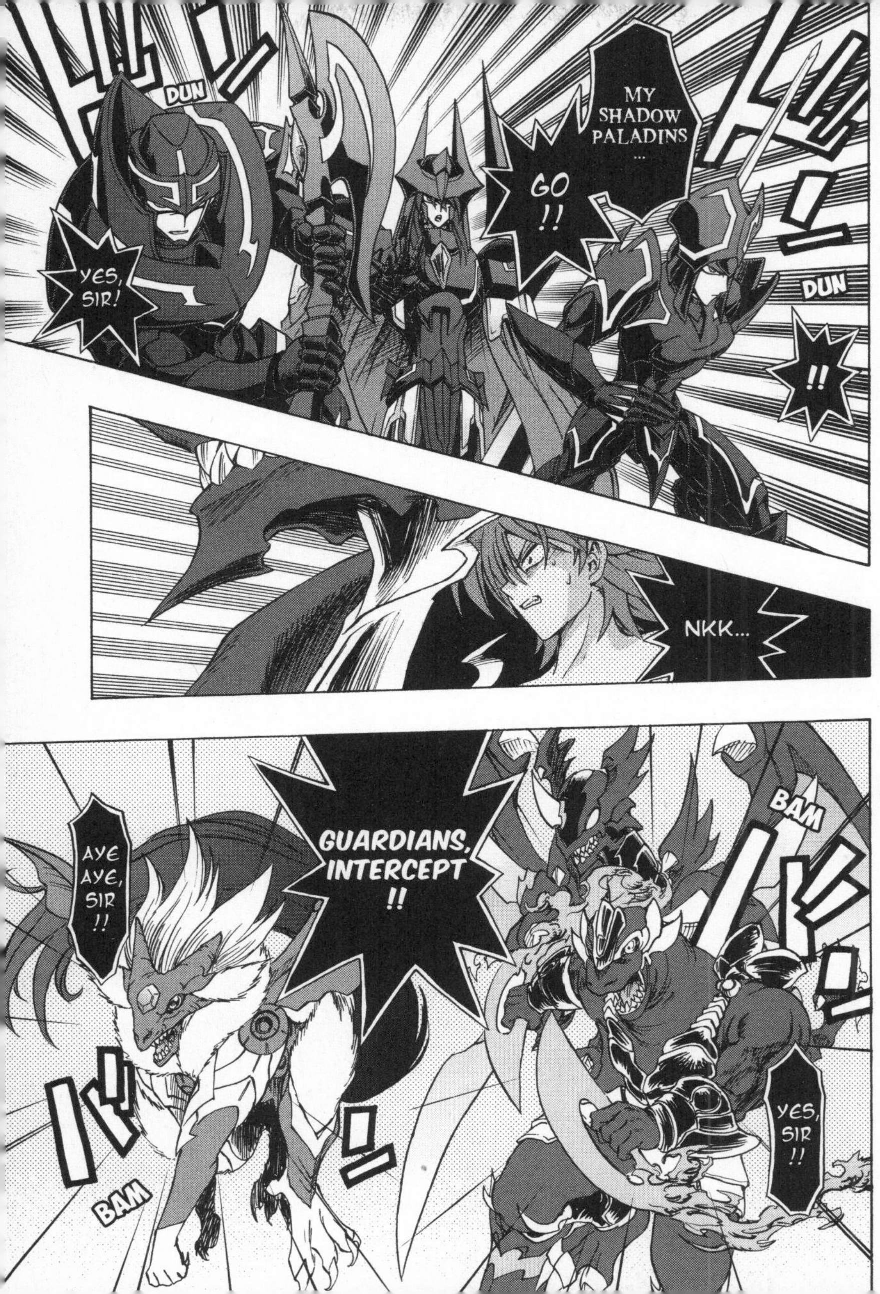
MY SHADOW PALADINS ...
GO !!
DUN
!!
DUN
YES, SIR!
NKK...
BAM
GUARDIANS, INTERCEPT !!
YES, SIR !!
AYE AYE, SIR !!
BAM

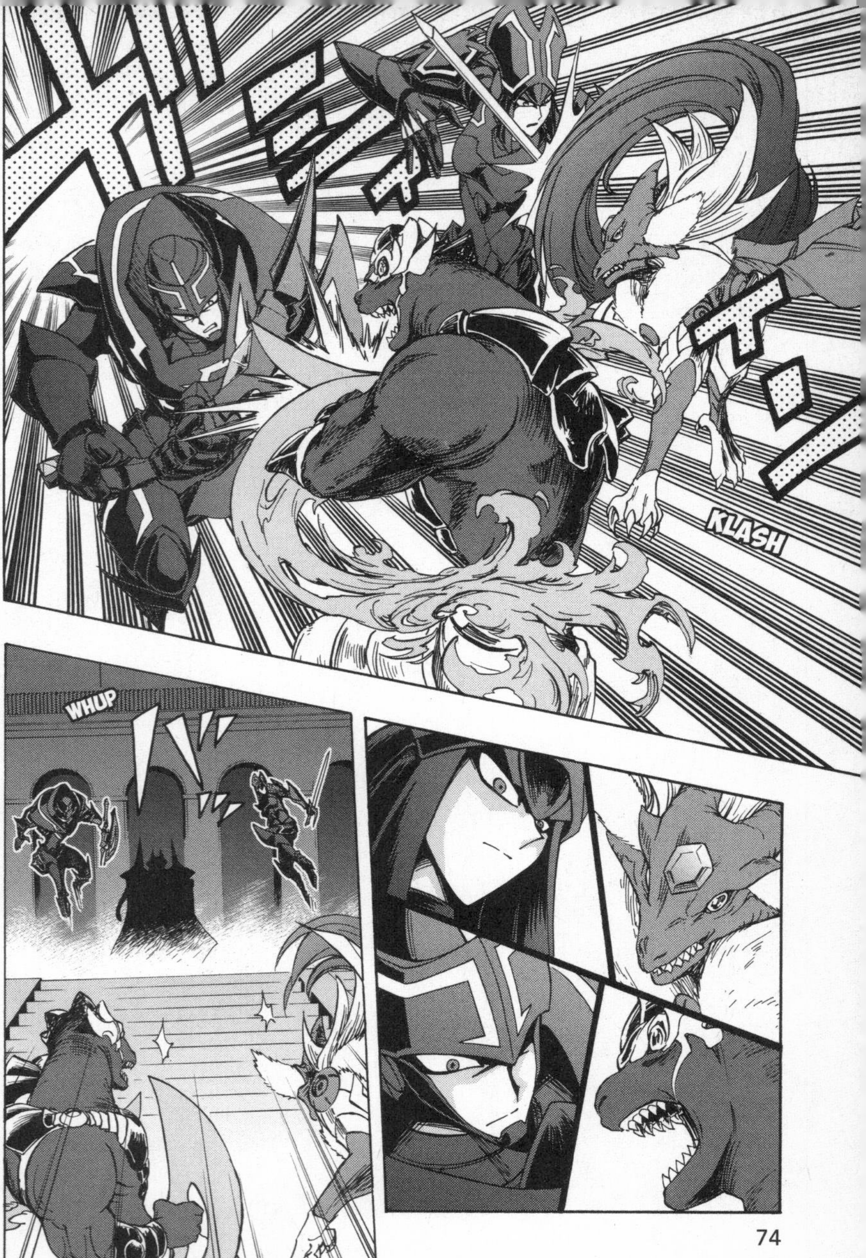
KLASH
WHUP

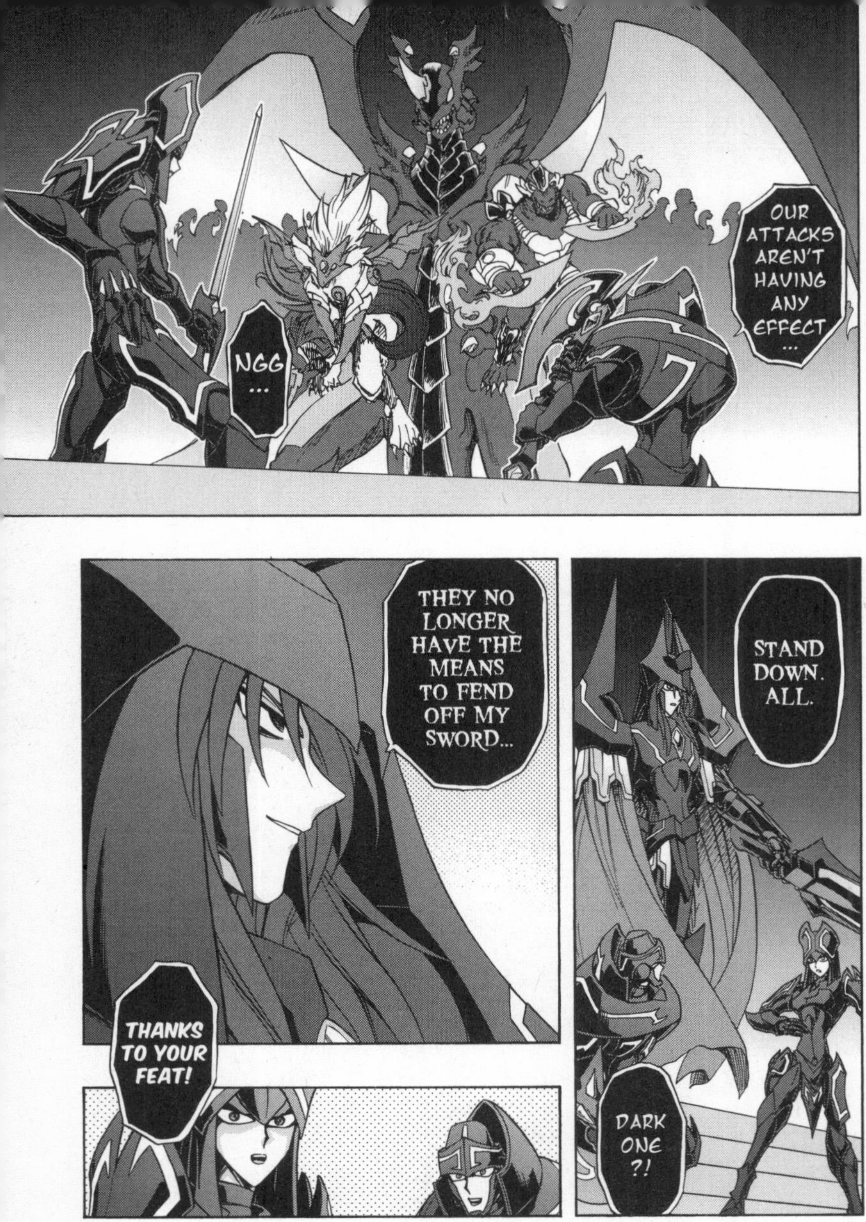
OUR ATTACKS AREN'T HAVING ANY EFFECT...
NGG...
STAND DOWN. ALL.
DARK ONE?!
THEY NO LONGER HAVE THE MEANS TO FEND OFF MY SWORD...
THANKS TO YOUR FEAT!

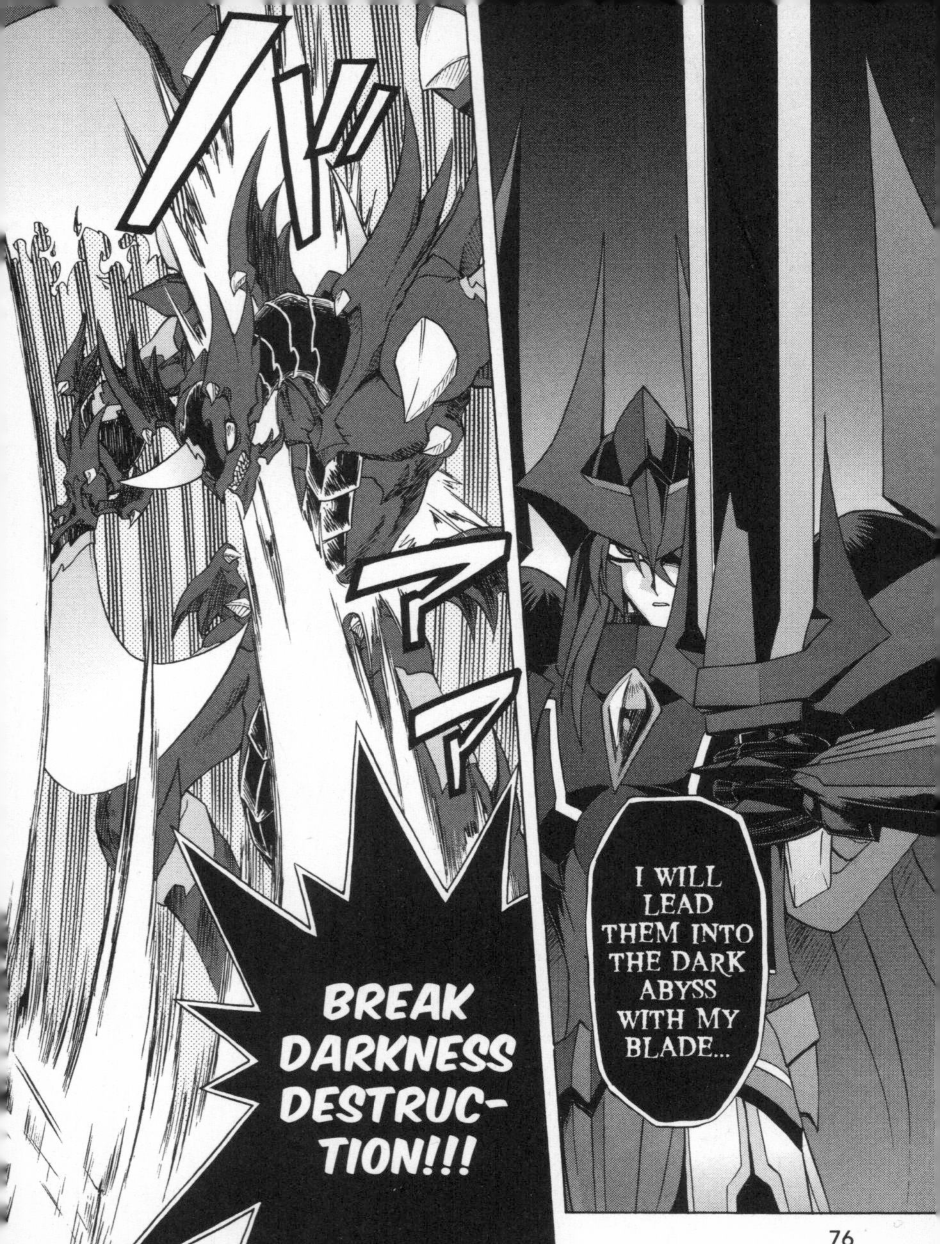
I WILL LEAD THEM INTO THE DARK ABYSS WITH MY BLADE...
BREAK DARKNESS DESTRUC-TION!!!

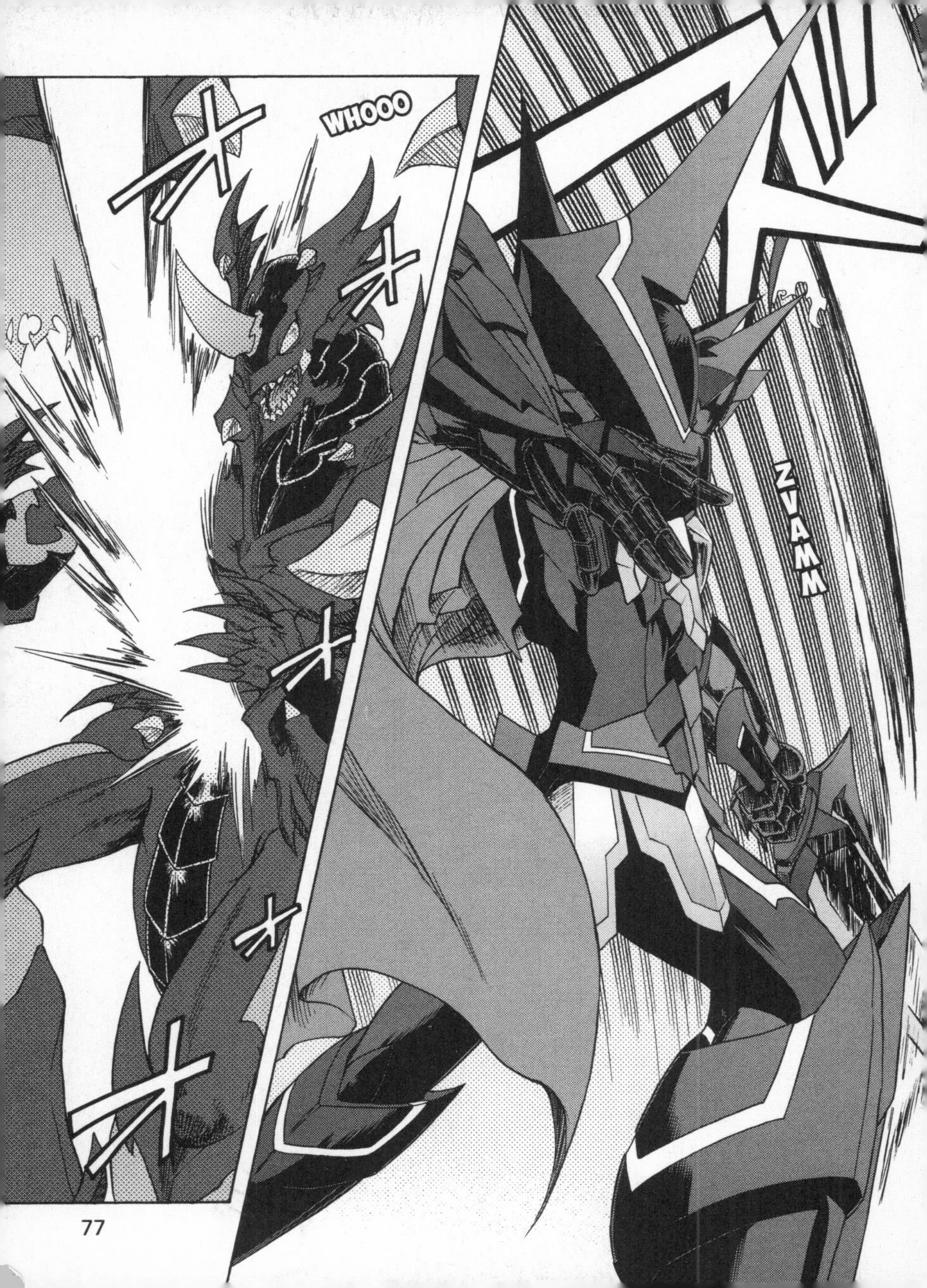
ZVAMM
WHOOO

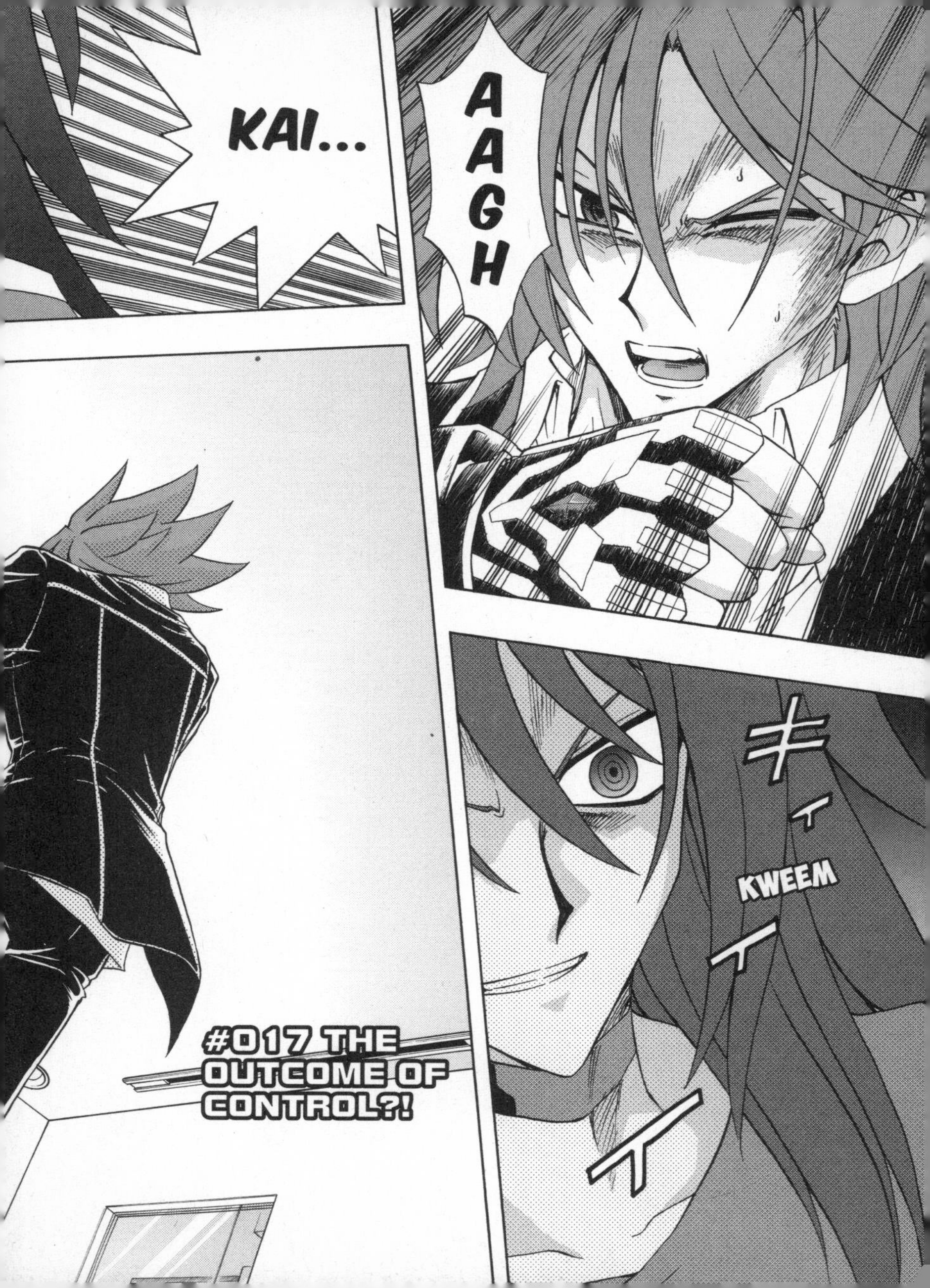
AAGH
KAI...
キィイイ
KWEEM
#017 THE OUTCOME OF CONTROL?!

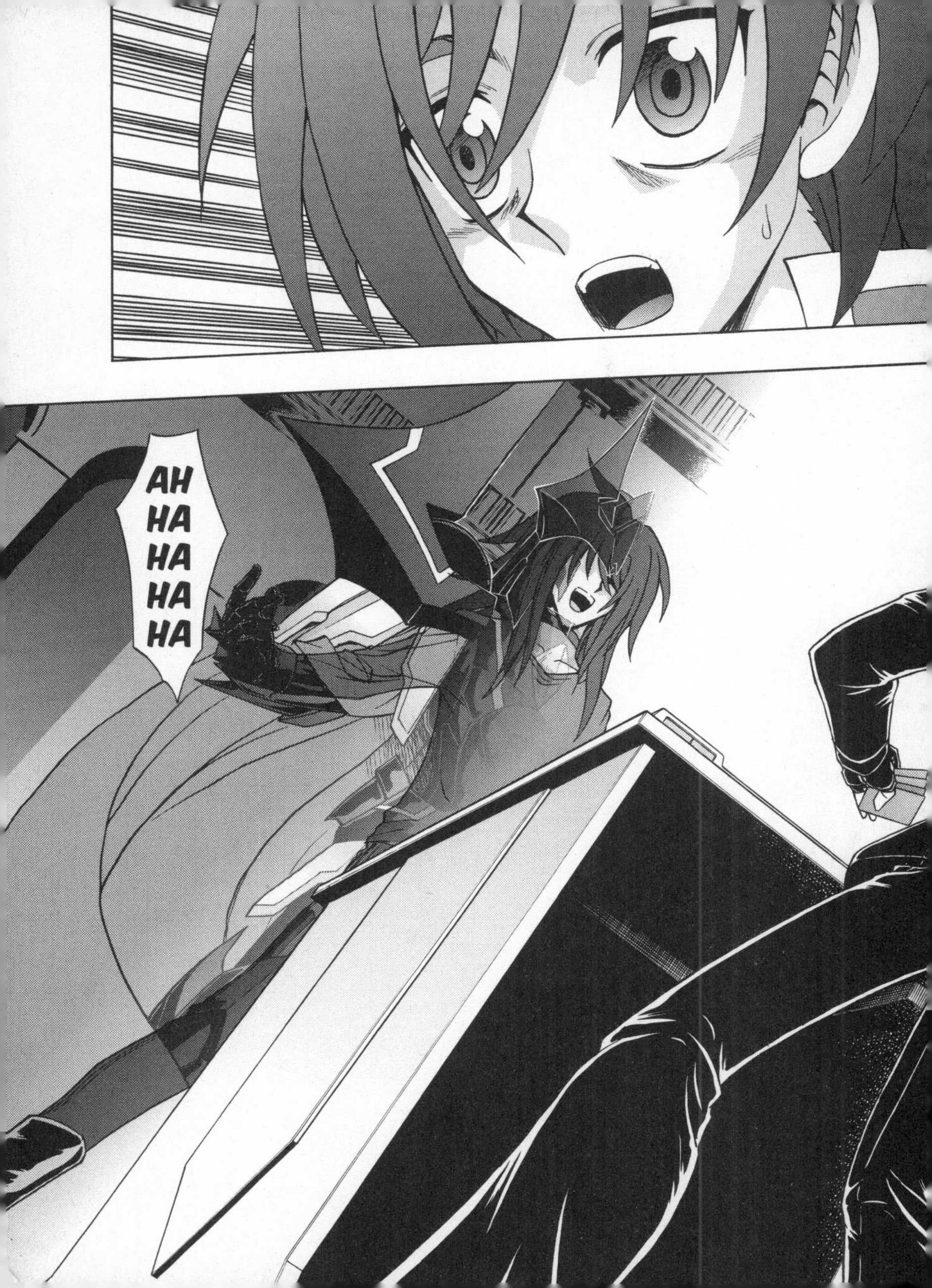
AH HA HA HA HA HA

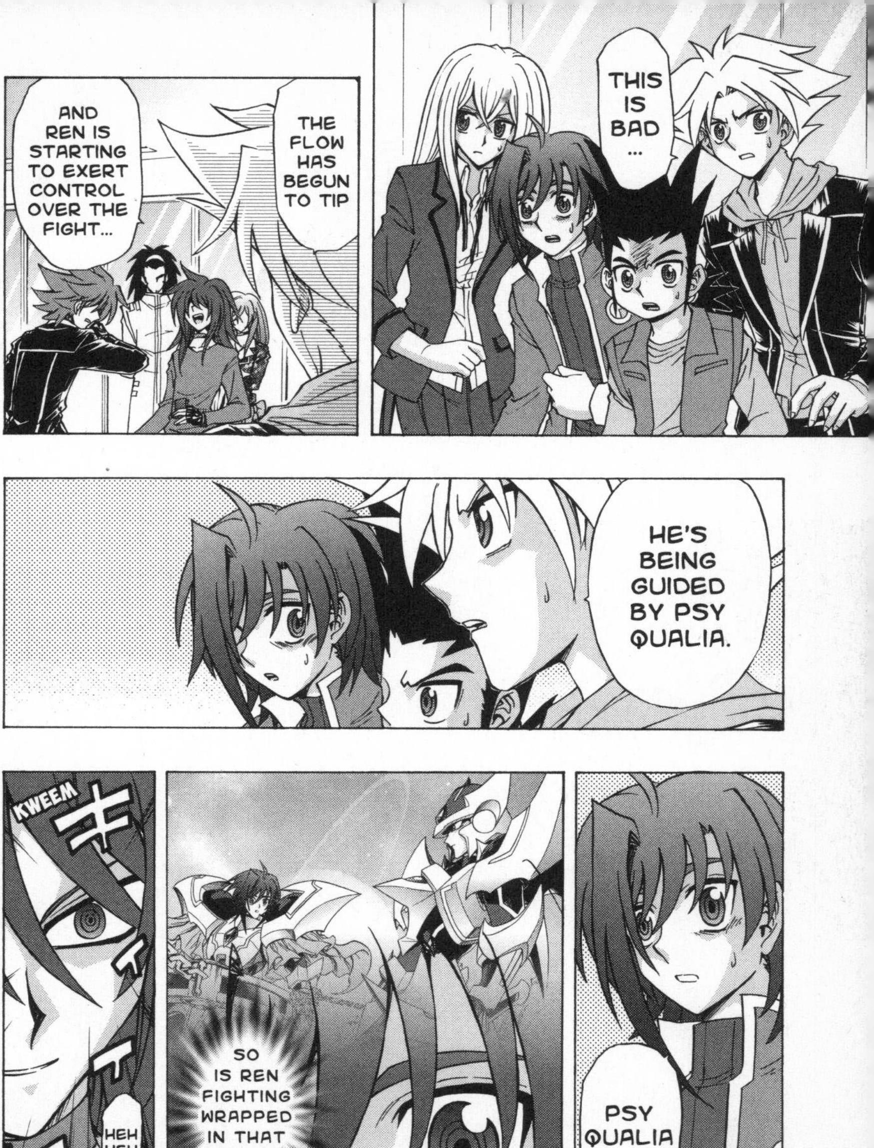
THIS IS BAD...
THE FLOW HAS BEGUN TO TIP
AND REN IS STARTING TO EXERT CONTROL OVER THE FIGHT...
HE'S BEING GUIDED BY PSY QUALIA.
PSY QUALIA...
SO IS REN FIGHTING WRAPPED IN THAT FEELING?
KWEEM
HEH HEH...

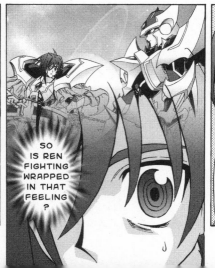

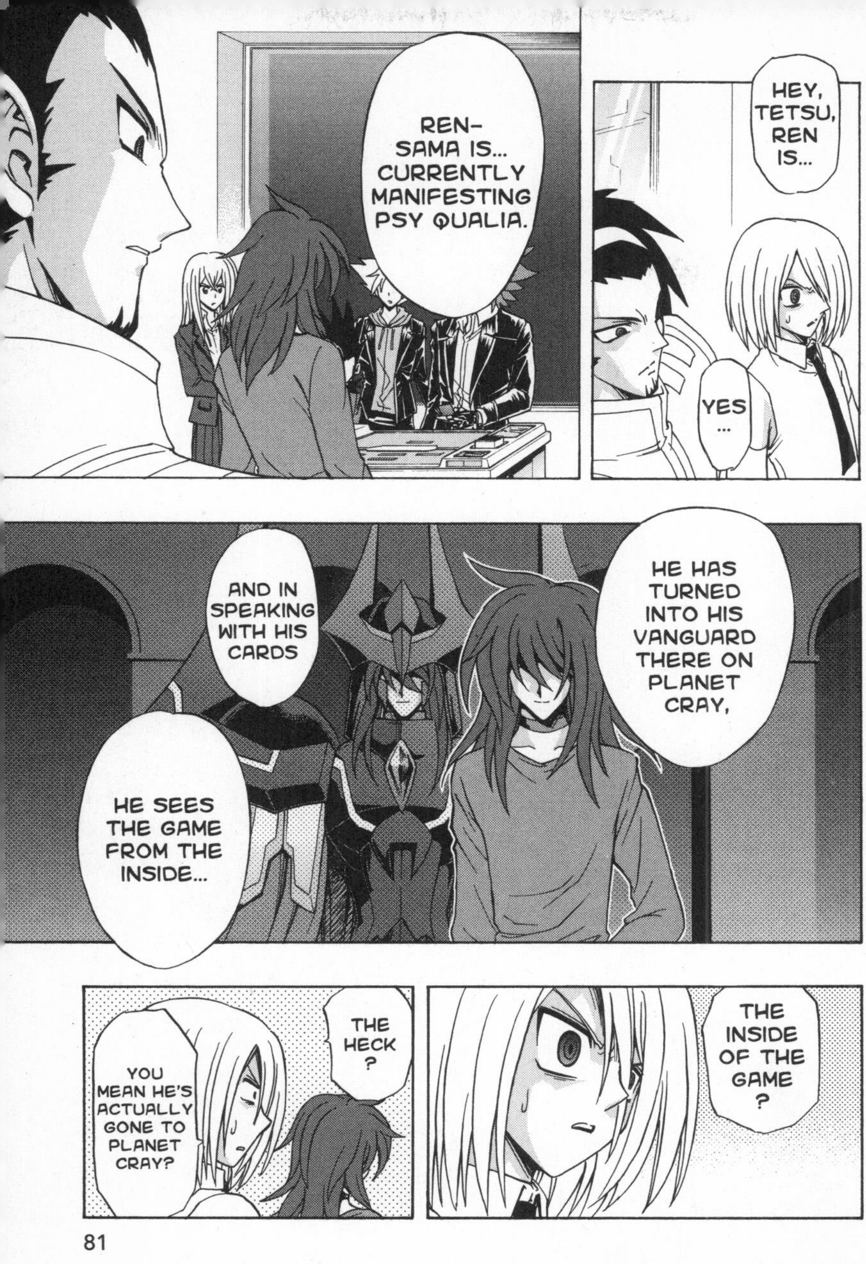
HEY, TETSU, REN IS...
YES...
REN-SAMA IS... CURRENTLY MANIFESTING PSY QUALIA.
HE HAS TURNED INTO HIS VANGUARD THERE ON PLANET CRAY,
AND IN SPEAKING WITH HIS CARDS
HE SEES THE GAME FROM THE INSIDE...
THE INSIDE OF THE GAME?
THE HECK?
YOU MEAN HE'S ACTUALLY GONE TO PLANET CRAY?

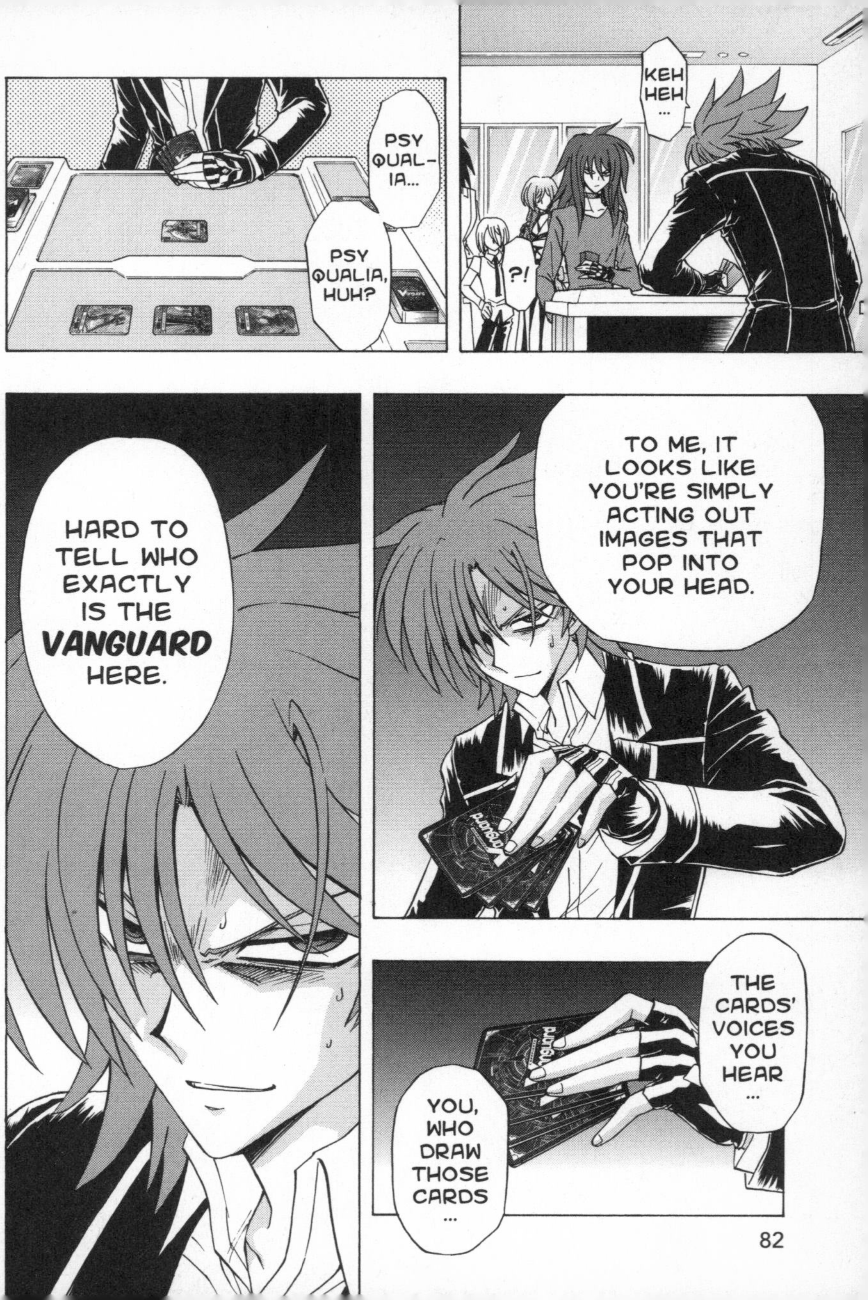
KEH HEH ...
?!
PSY QUALIA...
PSY QUALIA, HUH?
TO ME, IT LOOKS LIKE YOU'RE SIMPLY ACTING OUT IMAGES THAT POP INTO YOUR HEAD.
THE CARDS' VOICES YOU HEAR ...
YOU, WHO DRAW THOSE CARDS ...
HARD TO TELL WHO EXACTLY IS THE VANGUARD HERE.

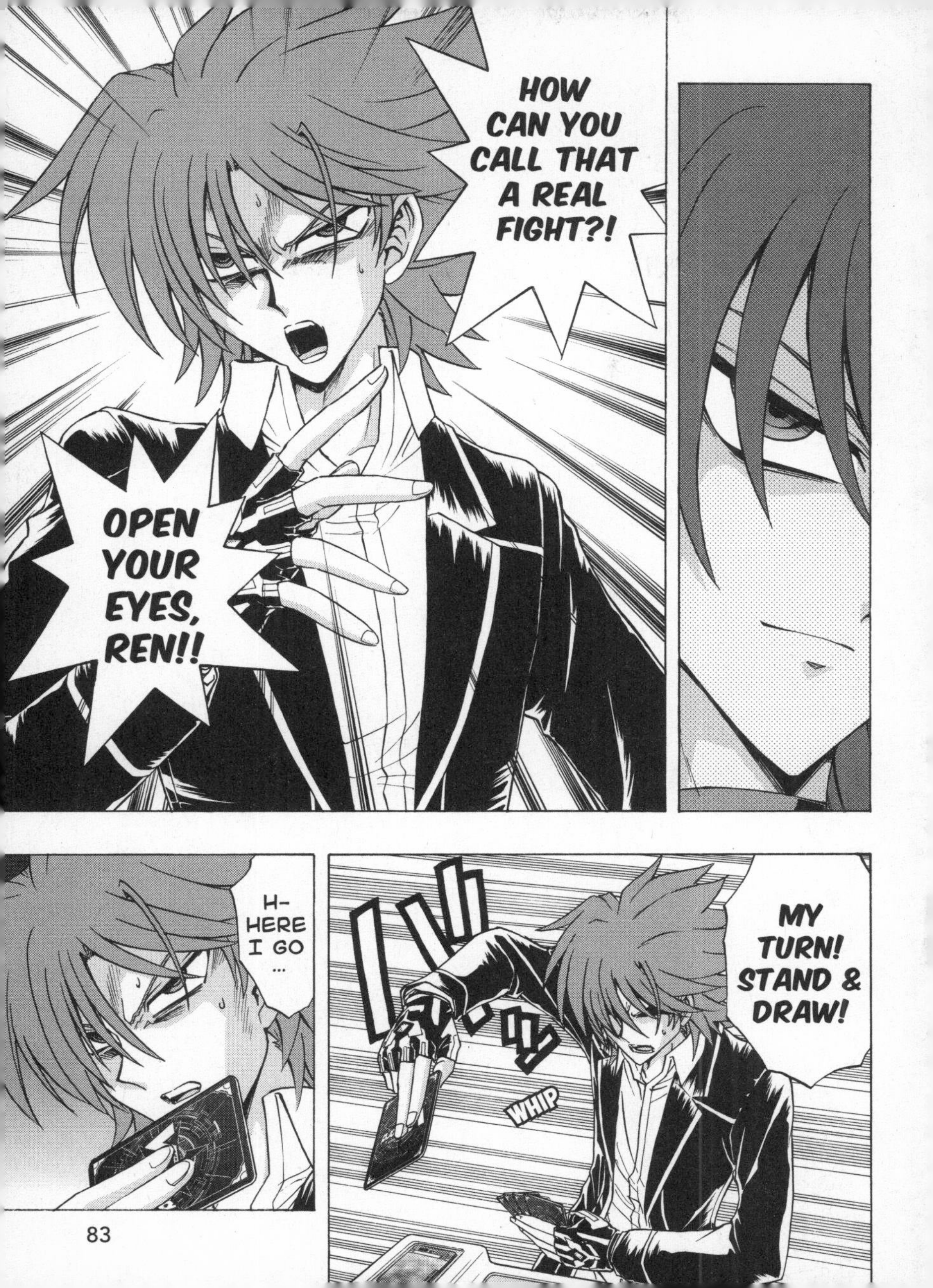
HOW CAN YOU CALL THAT A REAL FIGHT?!
OPEN YOUR EYES, REN!!
MY TURN! STAND & DRAW!
WHIP
H- HERE I GO ...

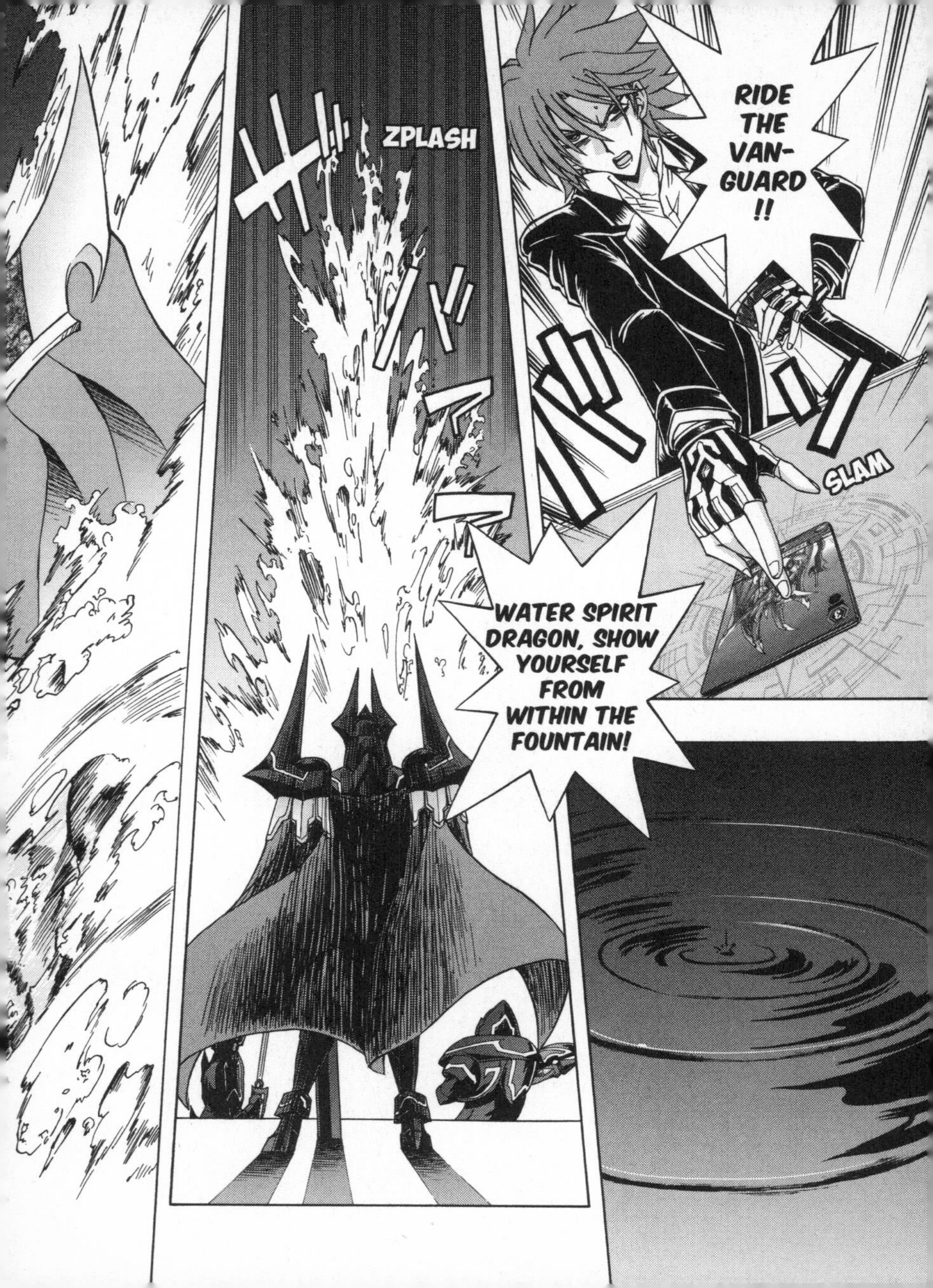
RIDE THE VAN-GUARD !!
SLAM
WATER SPIRIT DRAGON, SHOW YOURSELF FROM WITHIN THE FOUNTAIN!
ZPLASH

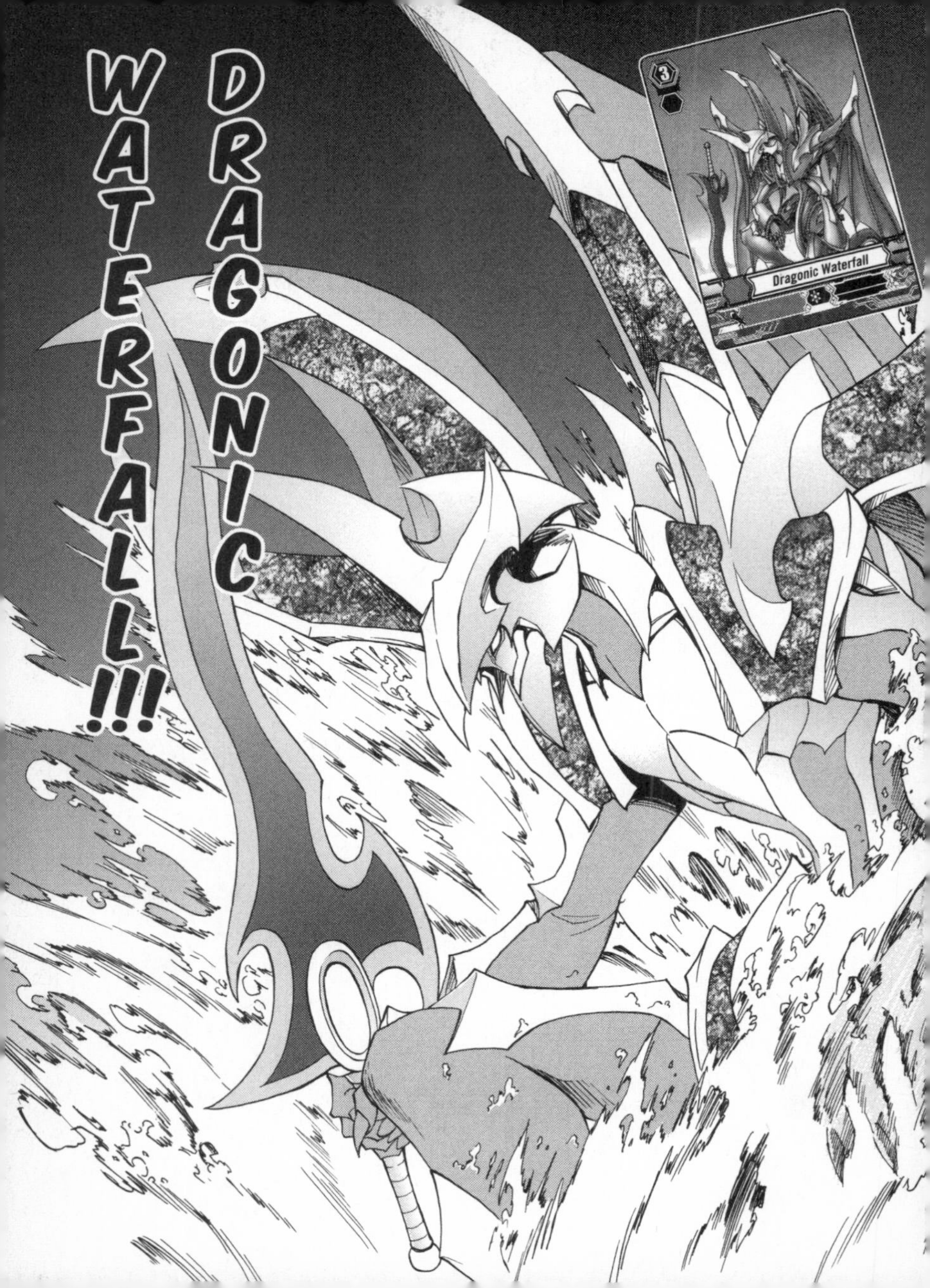
3
Dragonic Waterfall
DRAGONIC
WATERFALL!!!

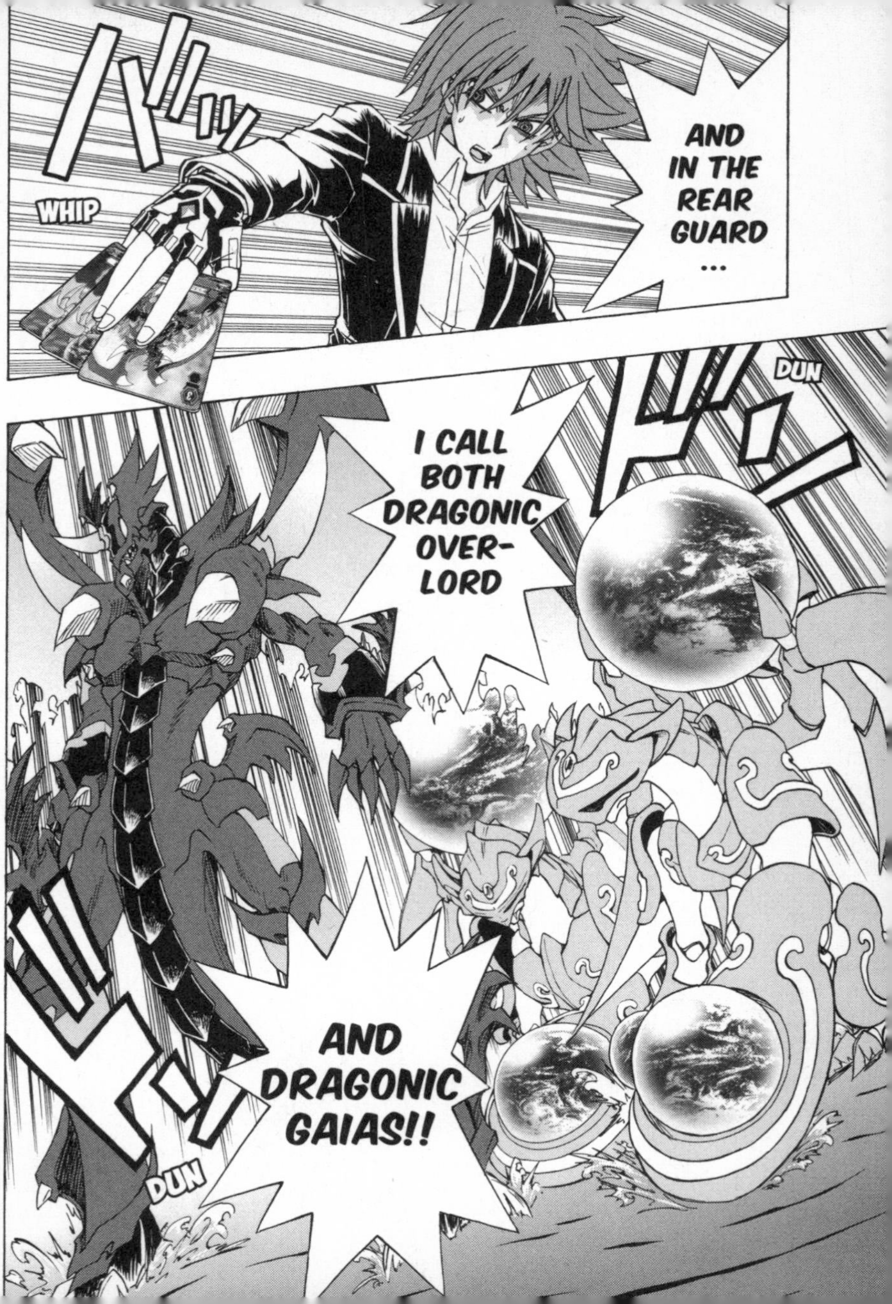
AND IN THE REAR GUARD ...
WHIP
DUN
I CALL BOTH DRAGONIC OVER-LORD
AND DRAGONIC GAIAS!!
DUN

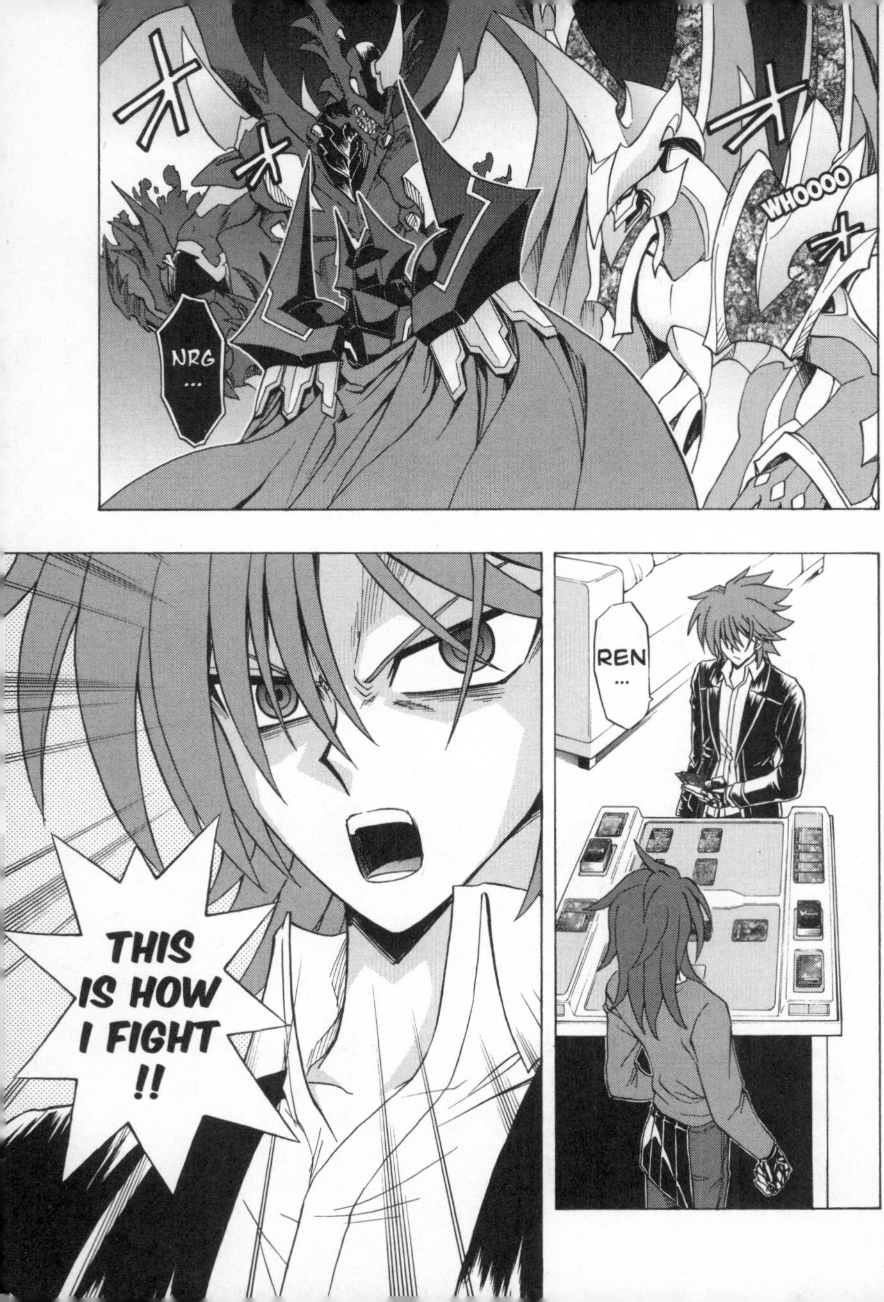
WHOOOO
NRG ...
REN ...
THIS IS HOW I FIGHT !!

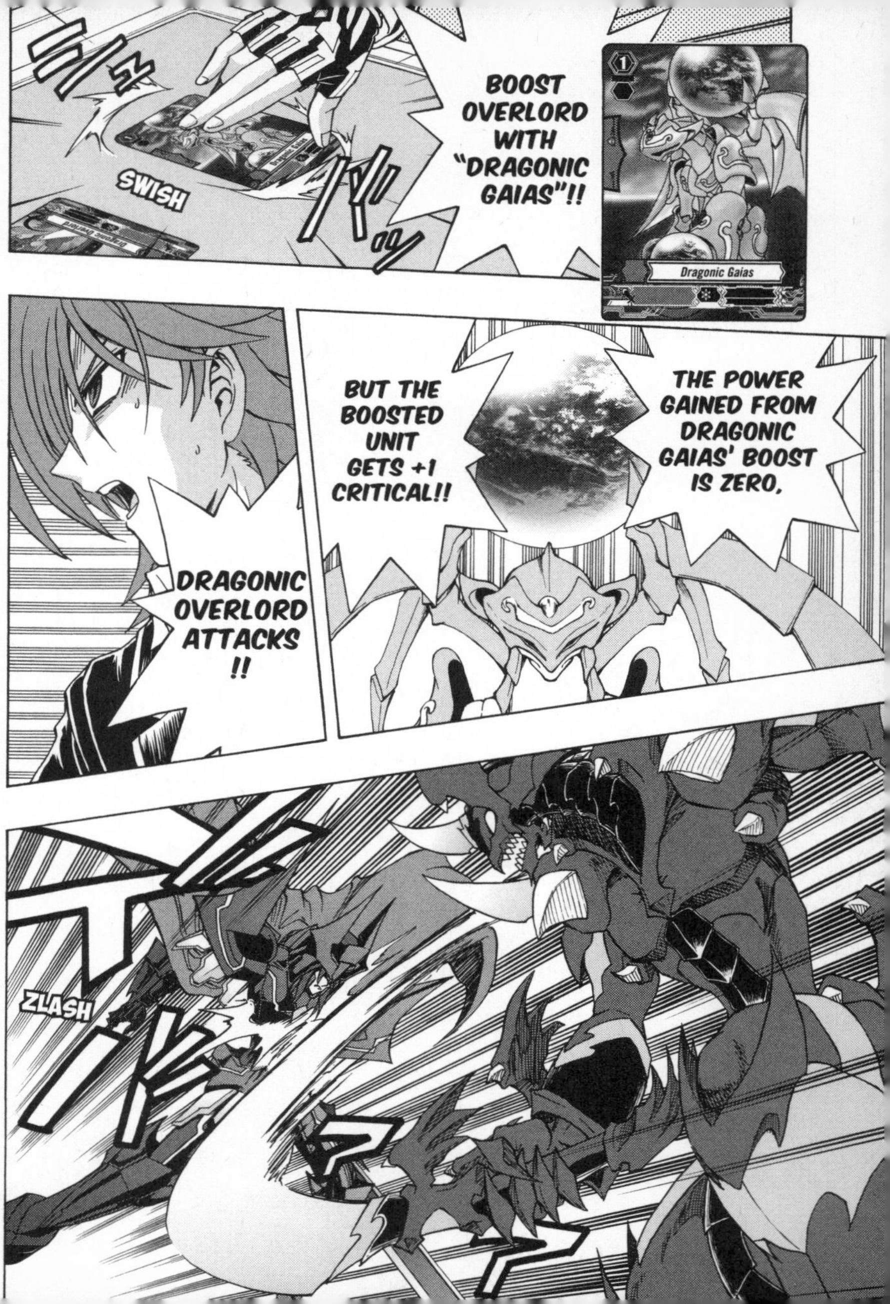
Dragonic Gaias
BOOST OVERLORD WITH "DRAGONIC GAIAS"!!
SWISH
THE POWER GAINED FROM DRAGONIC GAIAS' BOOST IS ZERO,
BUT THE BOOSTED UNIT GETS +1 CRITICAL!!
DRAGONIC OVERLORD ATTACKS !!
ZLASH

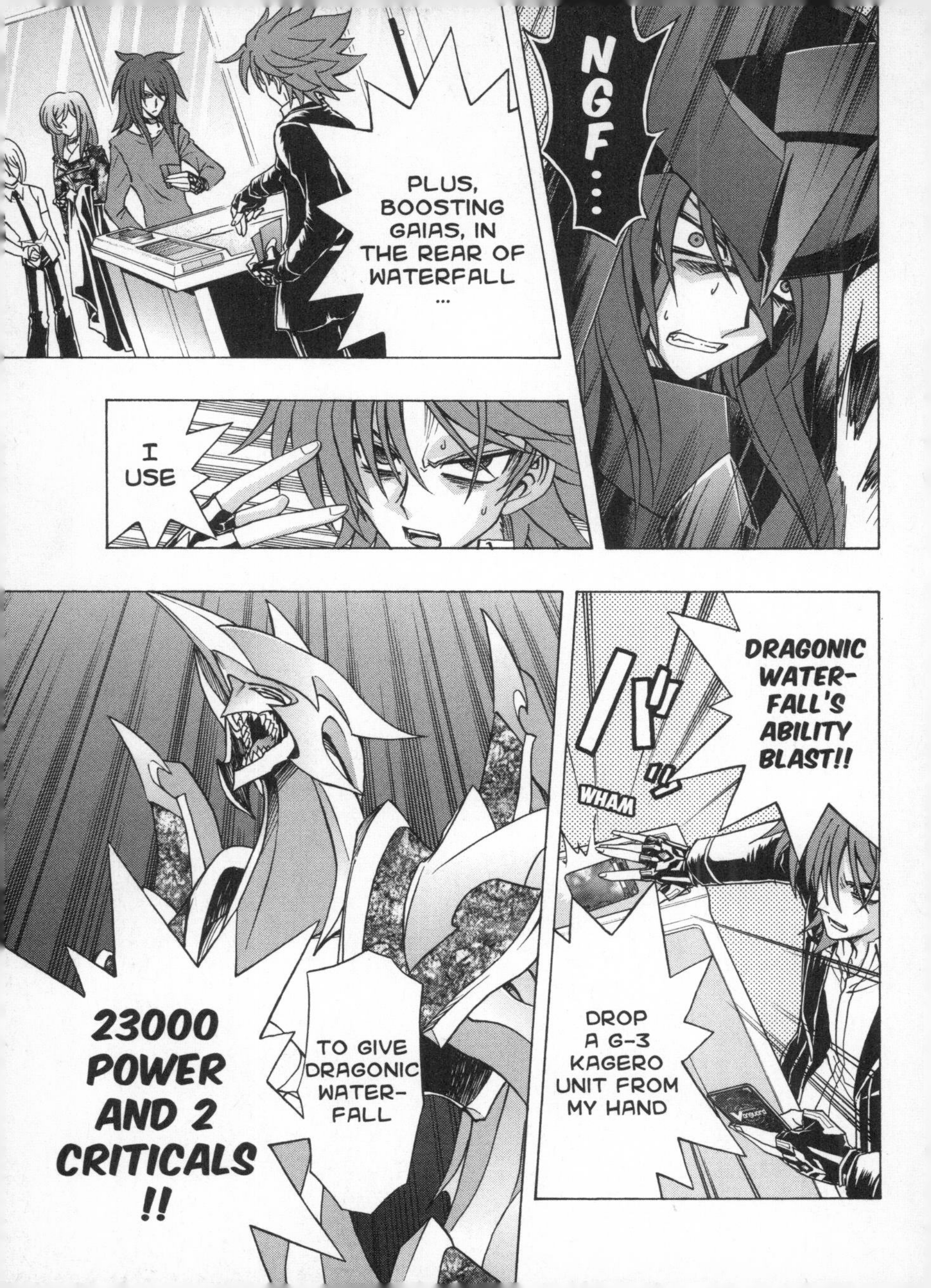
NGF...
PLUS, BOOSTING GAIAS, IN THE REAR OF WATERFALL ...
I USE
DRAGONIC WATER-FALL'S ABILITY BLAST!!
WHAM
DROP A G-3 KAGERO UNIT FROM MY HAND
TO GIVE DRAGONIC WATER-FALL
23000 POWER AND 2 CRITICALS !!

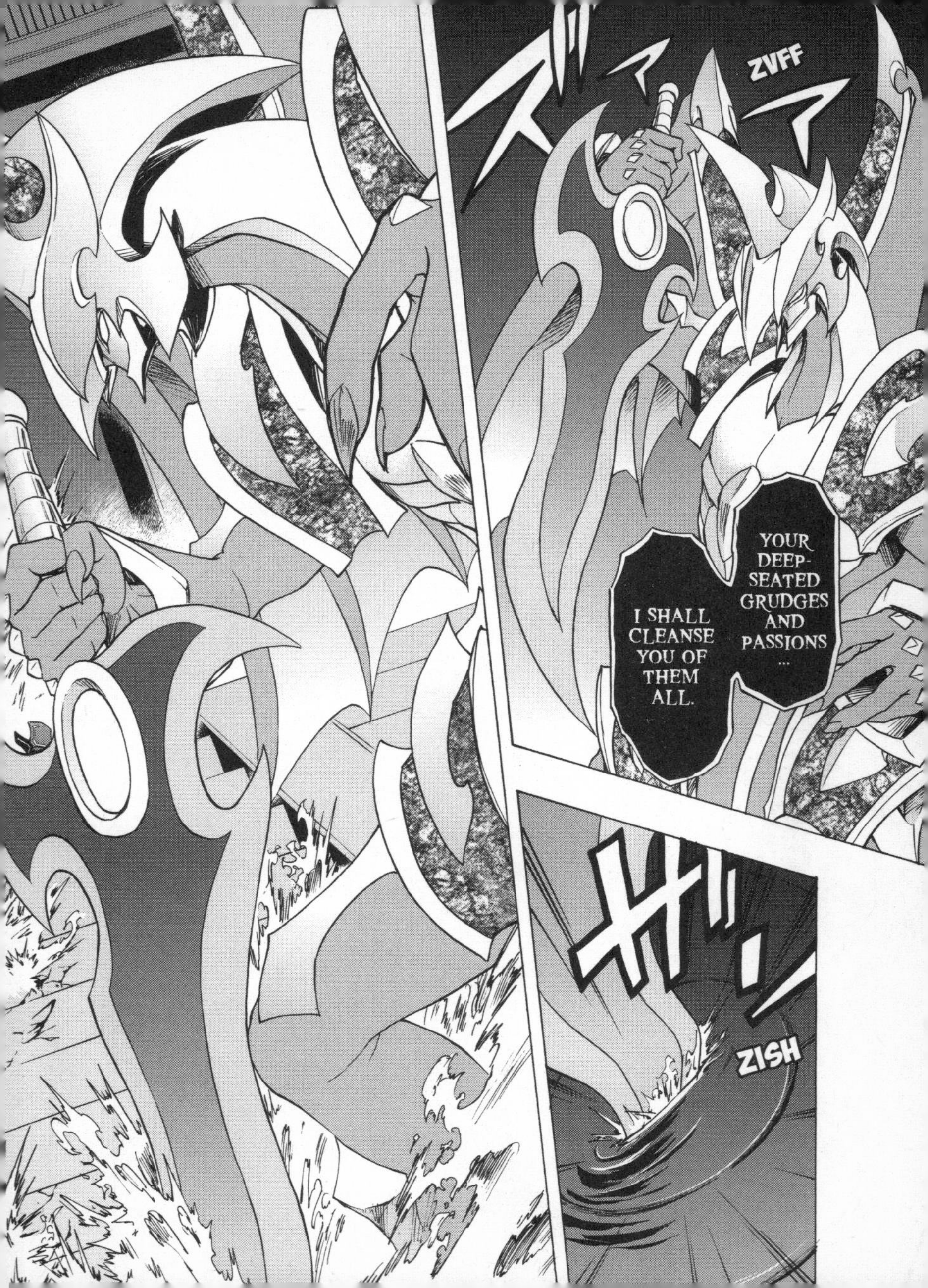
ZVFF
YOUR DEEP-SEATED GRUDGES AND PASSIONS ...
I SHALL CLEANSE YOU OF THEM ALL.
ZISH

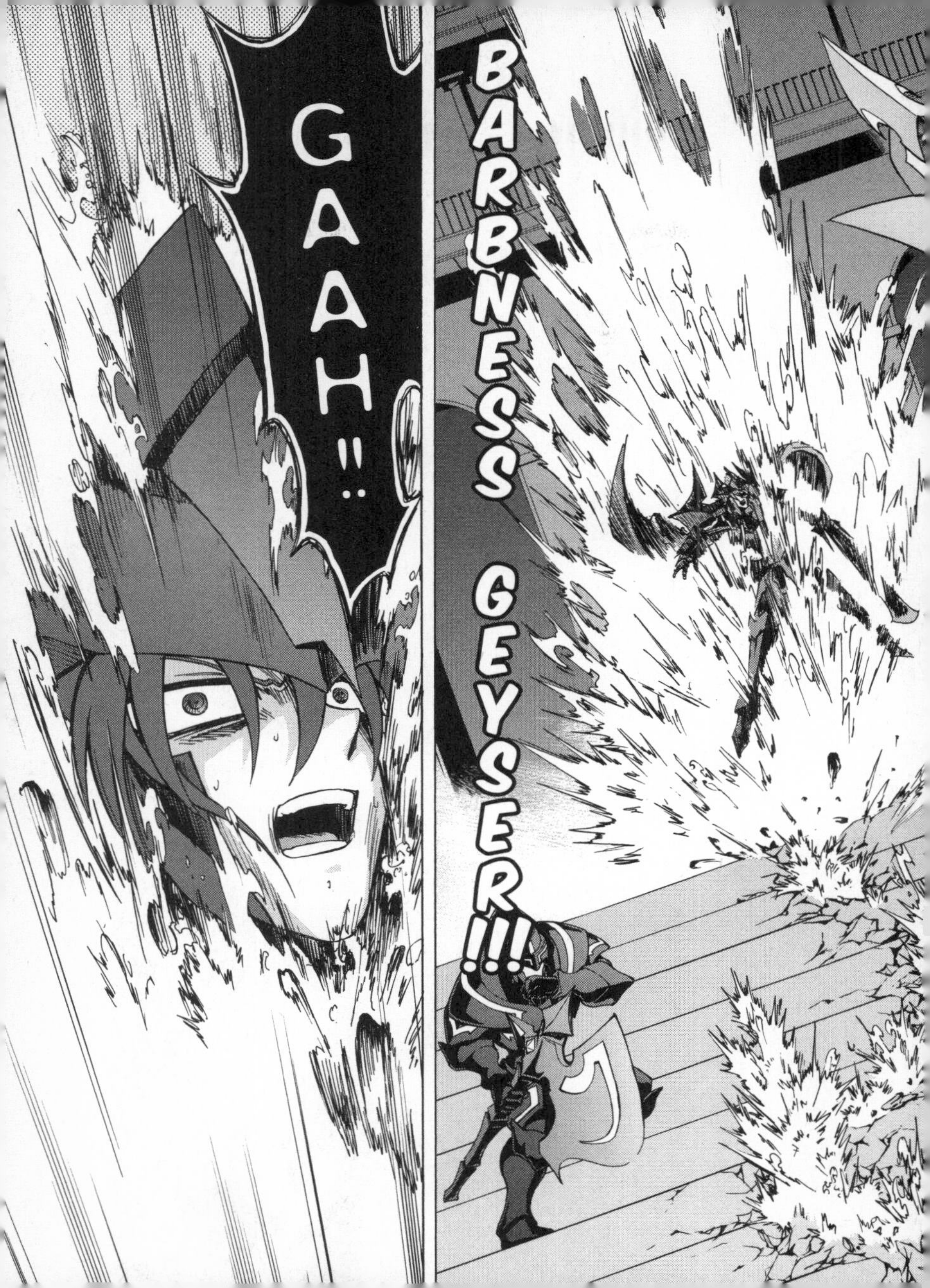
BARBNESS GEYSER!!!
GAH!!

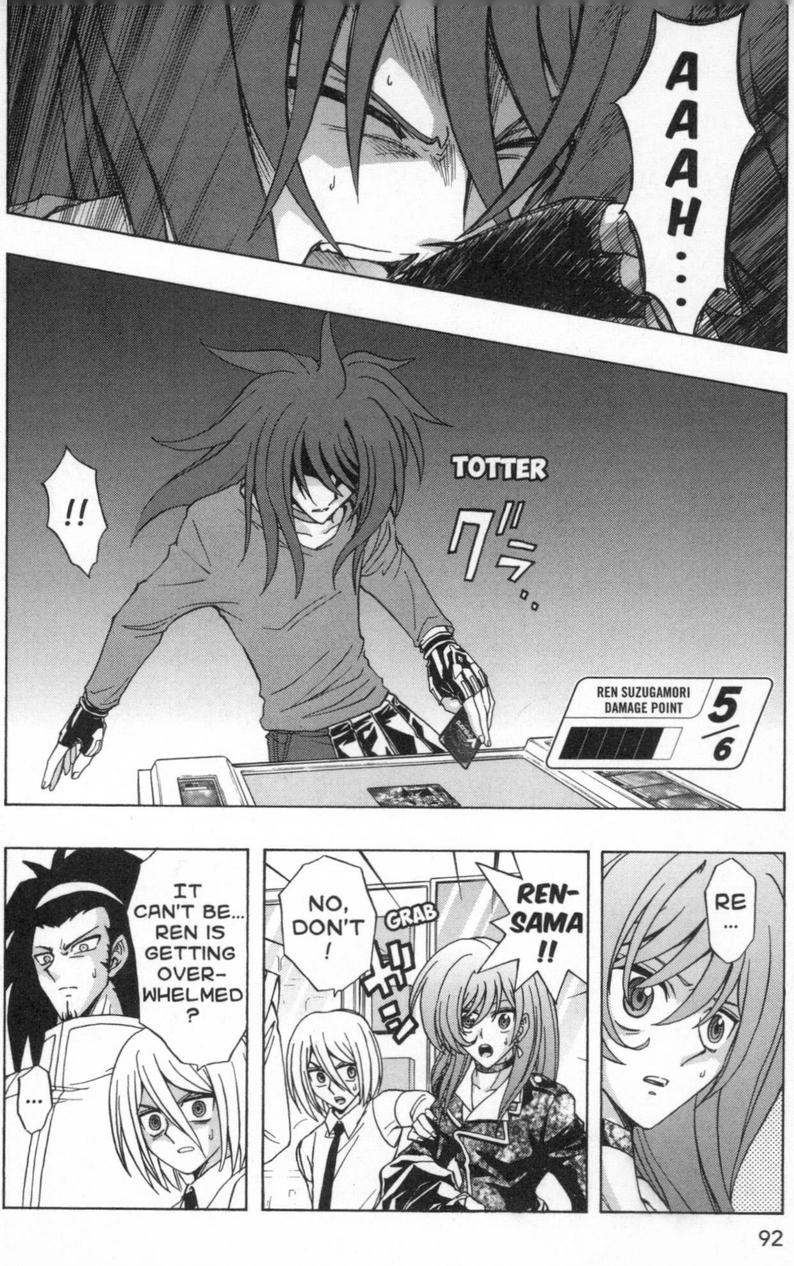
AAAH...
TOTTER
グラ..
!!
REN SUZUGAMORI DAMAGE POINT
5/6
RE ...
REN-SAMA!!
GRAB
NO, DON'T!
IT CAN'T BE... REN IS GETTING OVER-WHELMED?
...

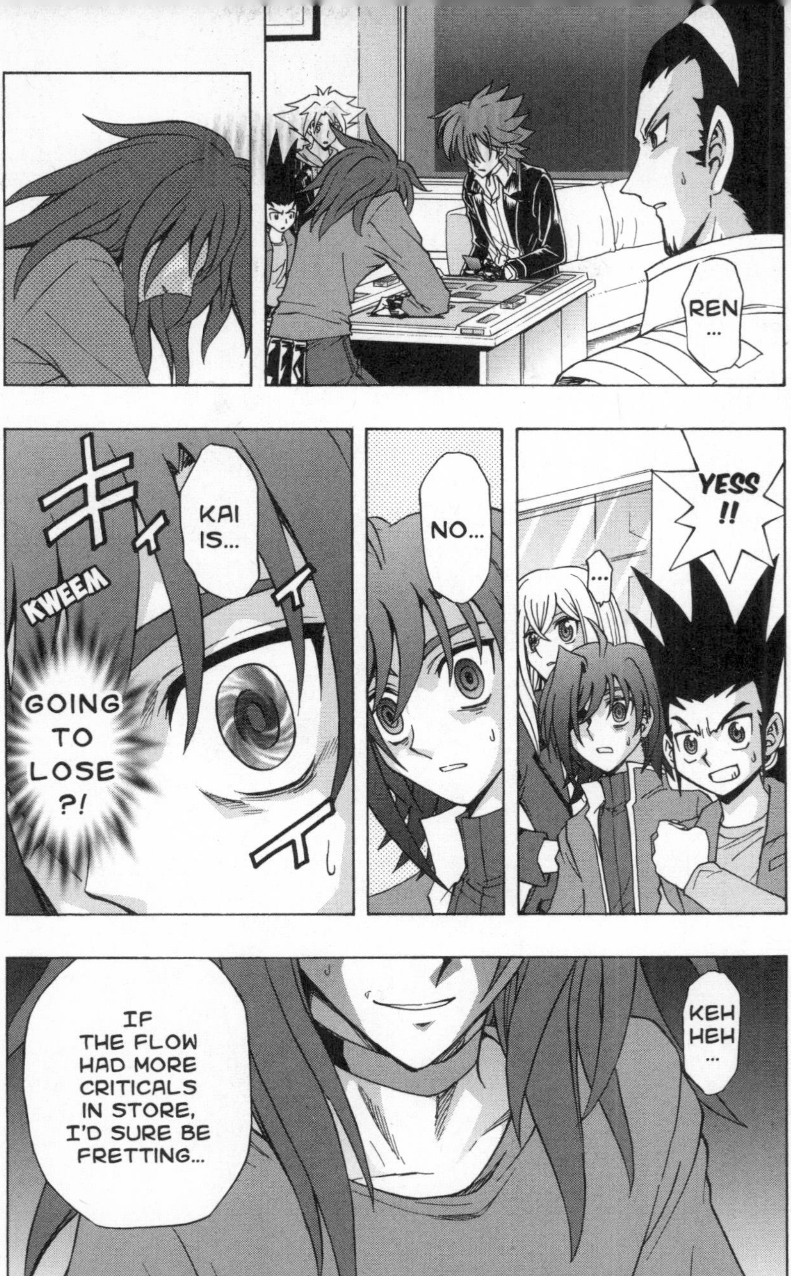
REN...
YESS!!
...
NO...
KAI IS...
KWEEM
GOING TO LOSE?!
KEH HEH...
IF THE FLOW HAD MORE CRITICALS IN STORE, I'D SURE BE FRETTING...

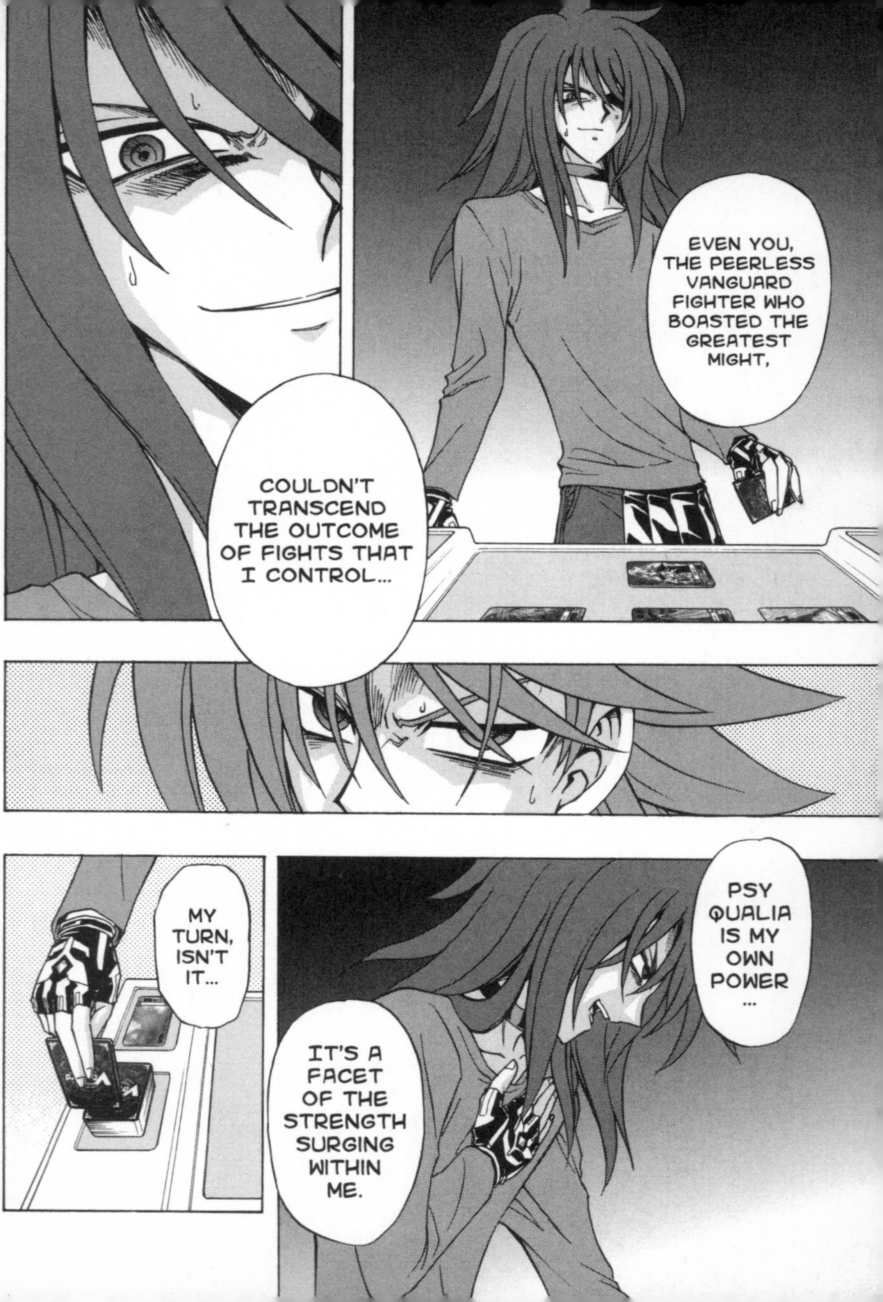
EVEN YOU, THE PEERLESS VANGUARD FIGHTER WHO BOASTED THE GREATEST MIGHT,
COULDN'T TRANSCEND THE OUTCOME OF FIGHTS THAT I CONTROL...
PSY QUALIA IS MY OWN POWER ...
IT'S A FACET OF THE STRENGTH SURGING WITHIN ME.
MY TURN, ISN'T IT...

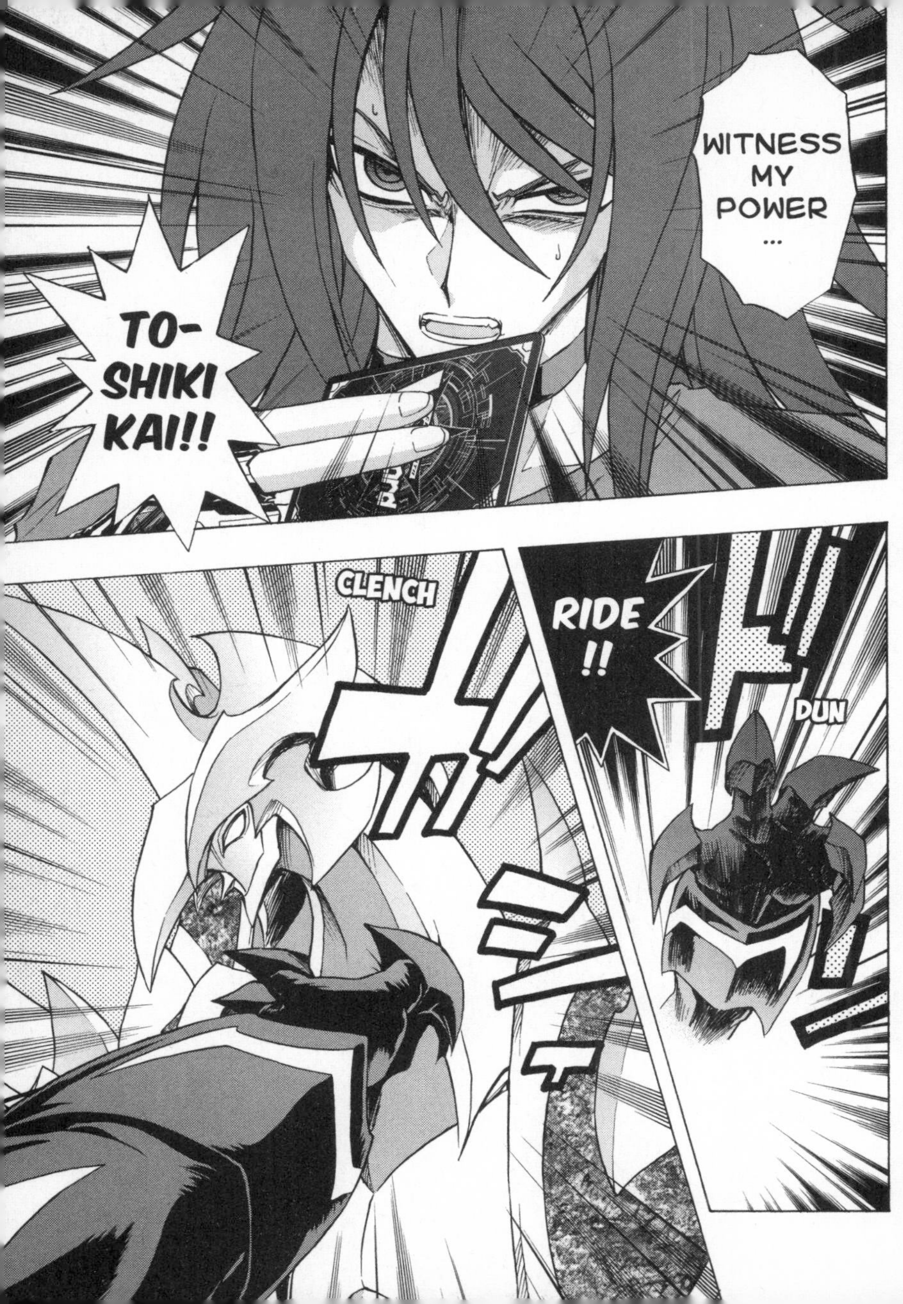
WITNESS MY POWER ...
TO-SHIKI KAI!!
RIDE !!
DUN
CLENCH

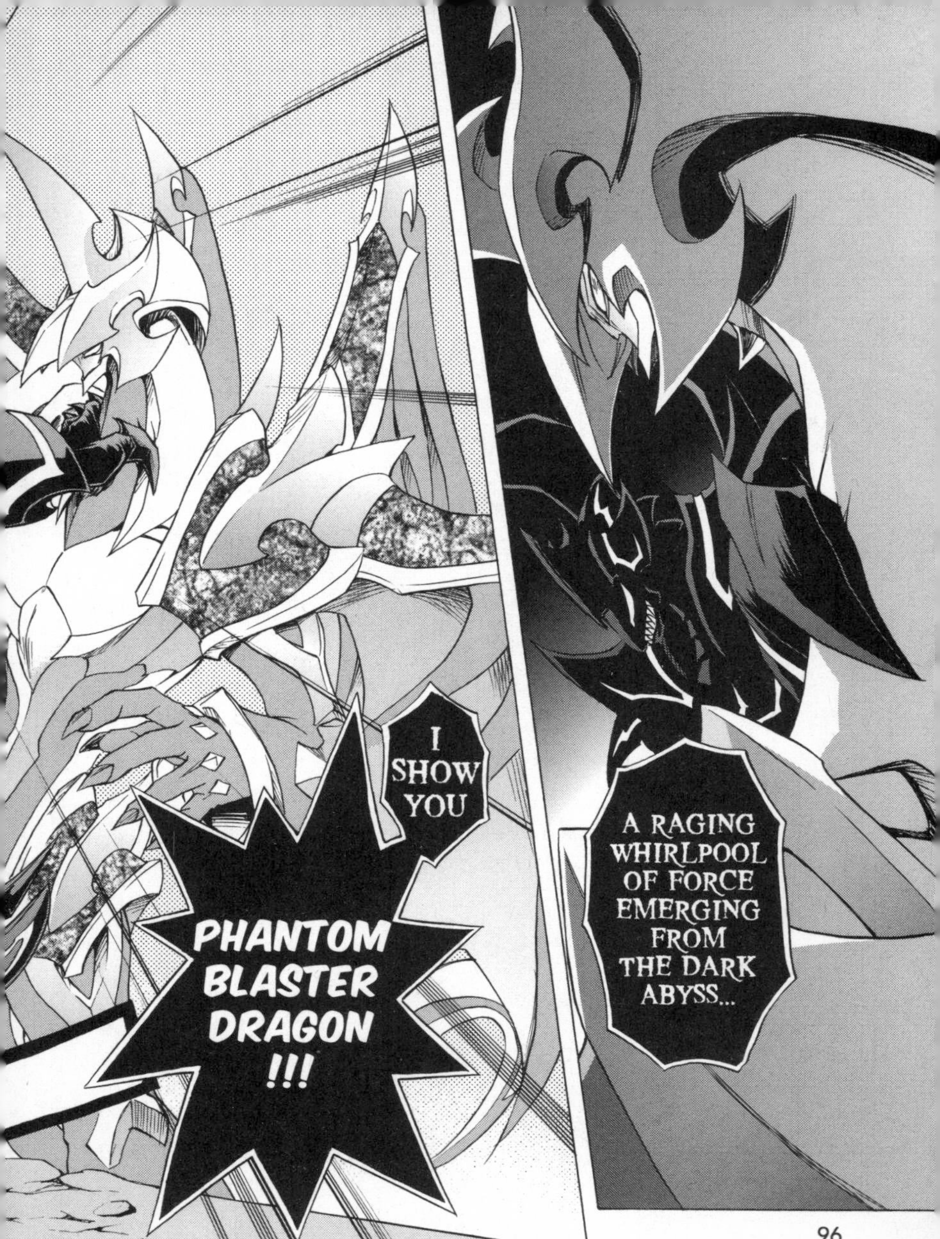
A RAGING WHIRLPOOL OF FORCE EMERGING FROM THE DARK ABYSS...
I SHOW YOU
PHANTOM BLASTER DRAGON !!!

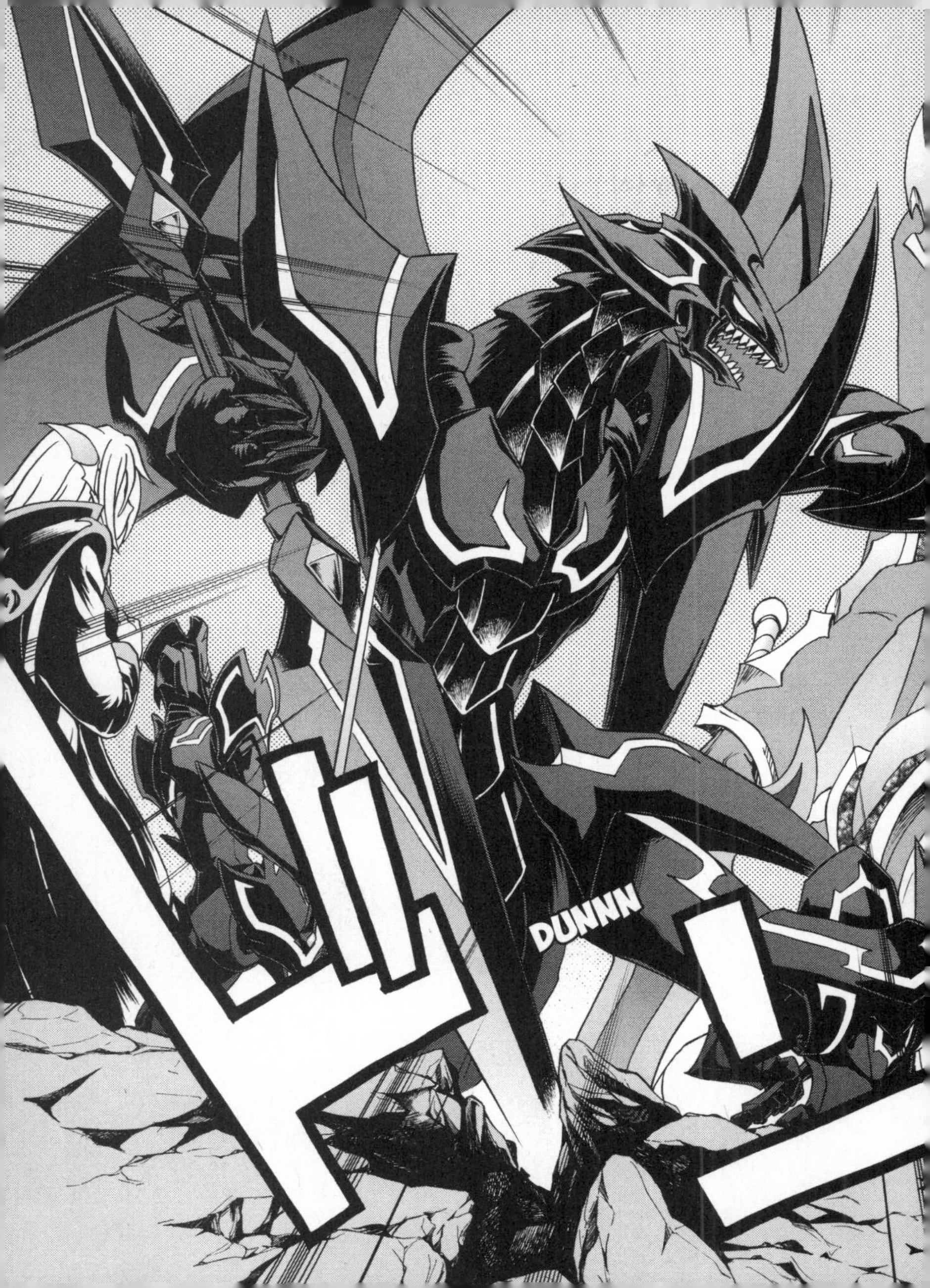
DUNNN

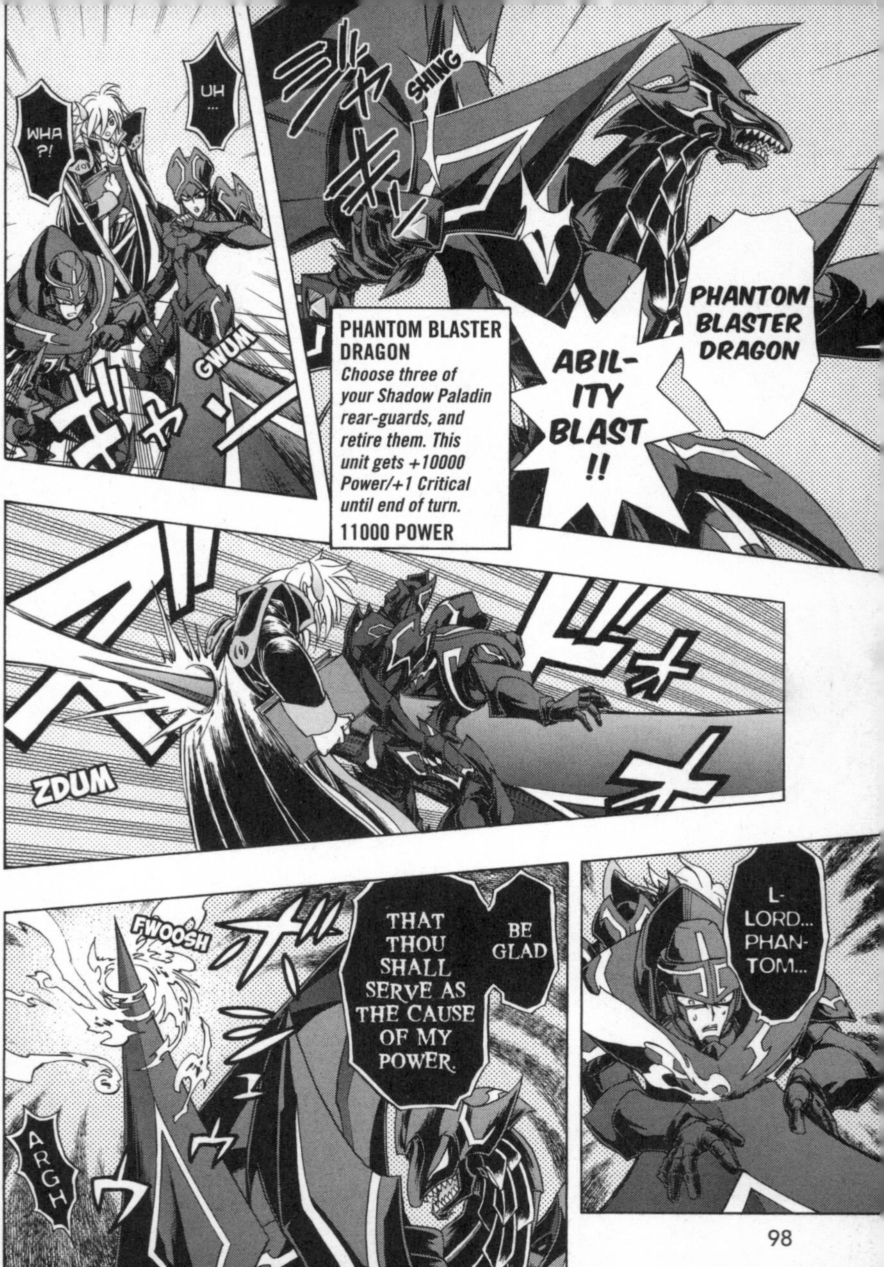
SHING
PHANTOM BLASTER DRAGON
ABIL-ITY BLAST!!
PHANTOM BLASTER DRAGON
Choose three of your Shadow Paladin rear-guards, and retire them. This unit gets +10000 Power/+1 Critical until end of turn.
11000 POWER
UH...
WHA?!
GWUM
ZDUM
L-LORD... PHAN-TOM...
BE GLAD
THAT THOU SHALL SERVE AS THE CAUSE OF MY POWER.
FWOOSH
ARGH

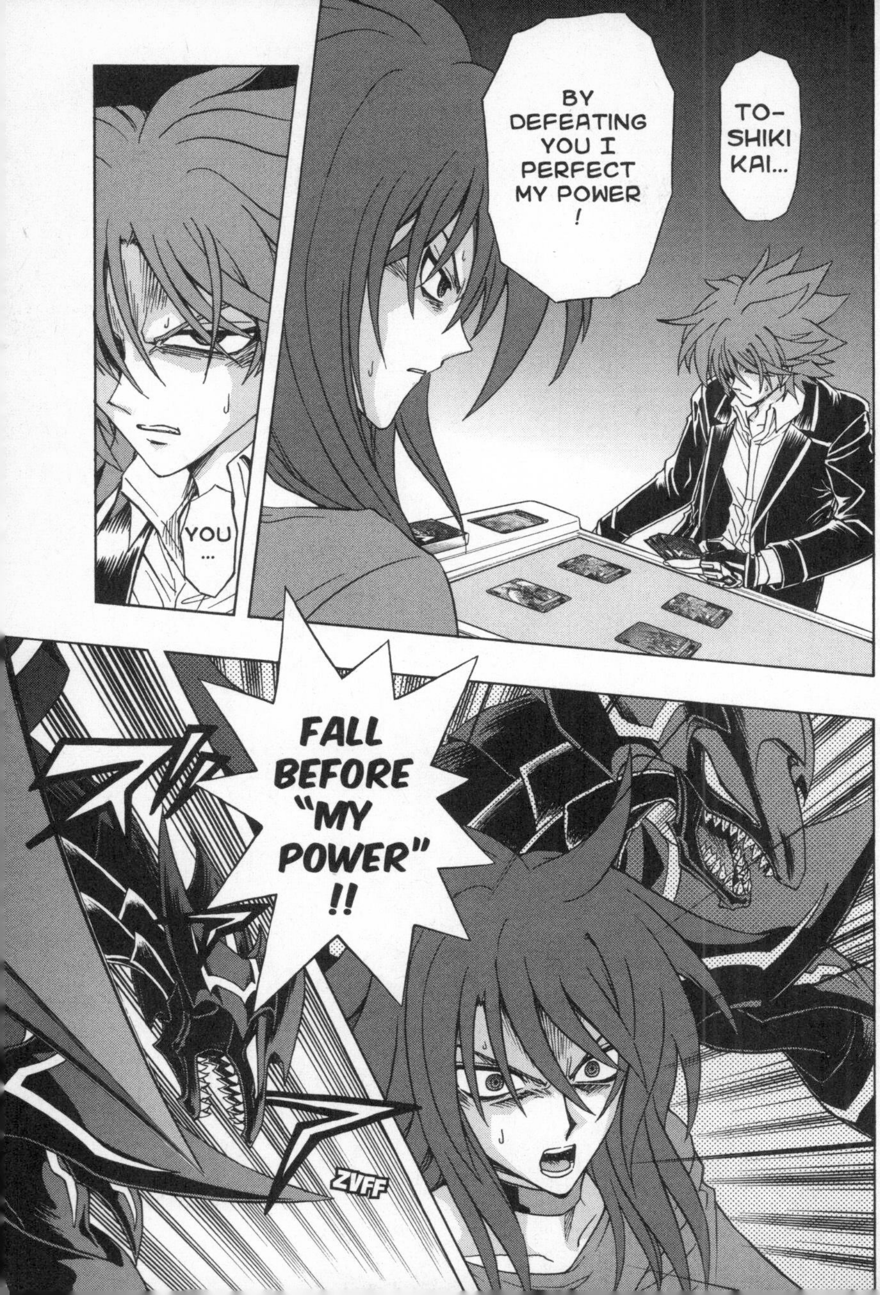
TO-SHIKI KAI...
BY DEFEATING YOU I PERFECT MY POWER!
YOU...
FALL BEFORE "MY POWER"!!
ZVFF

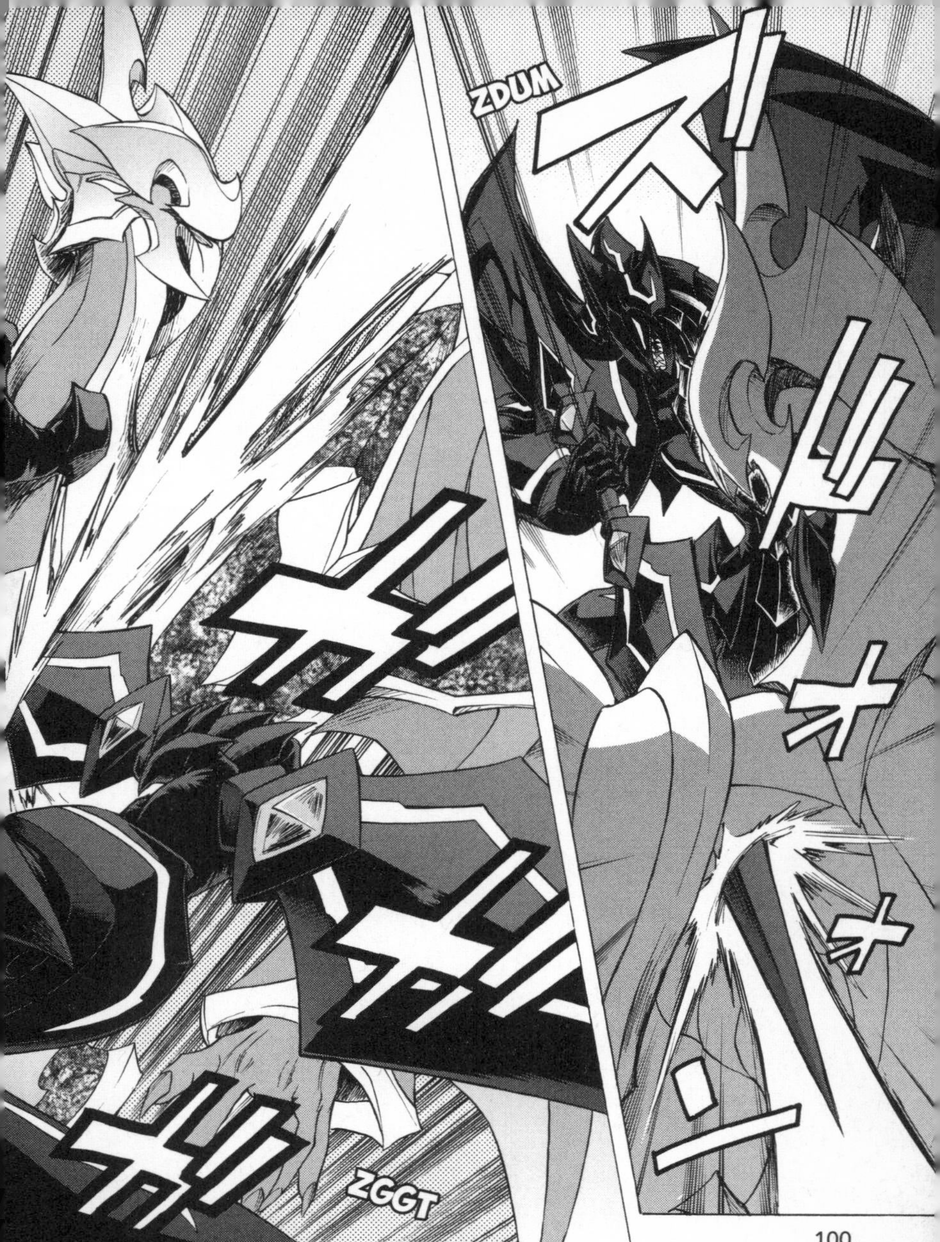
ZDUM
ZGGT

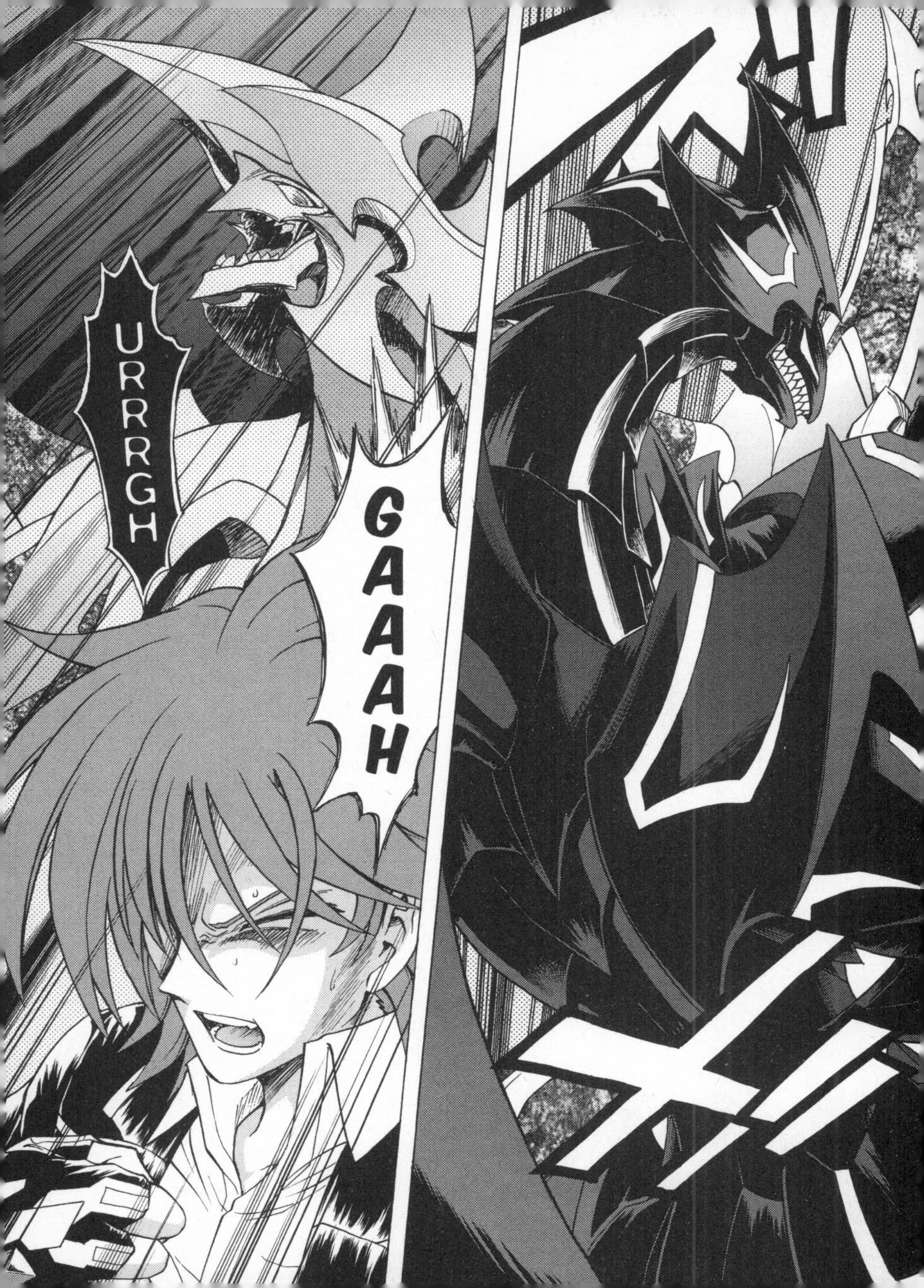
URRRGH
GAAAH

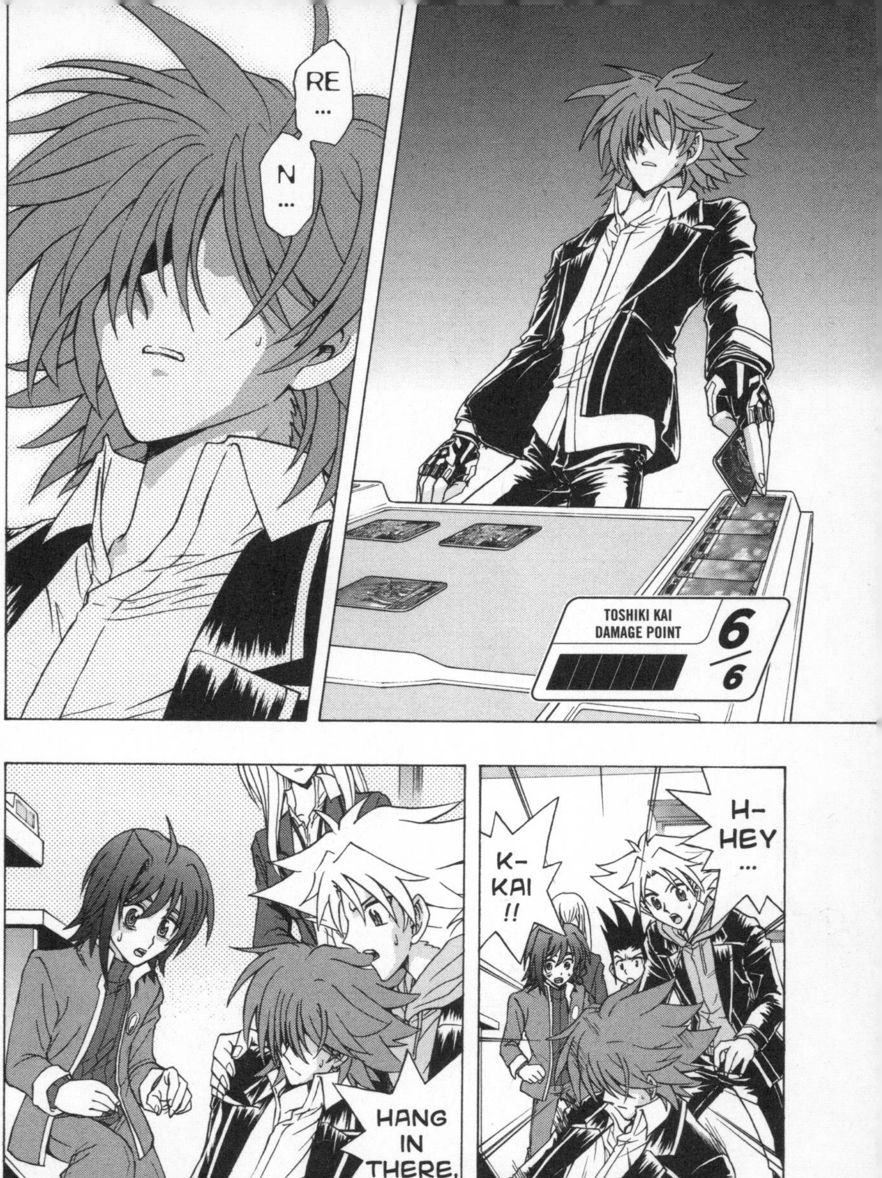
TOSHIKI KAI
DAMAGE POINT
6/6
RE... N...
H-HEY...
K-KAI!!
HANG IN THERE, KAI!!

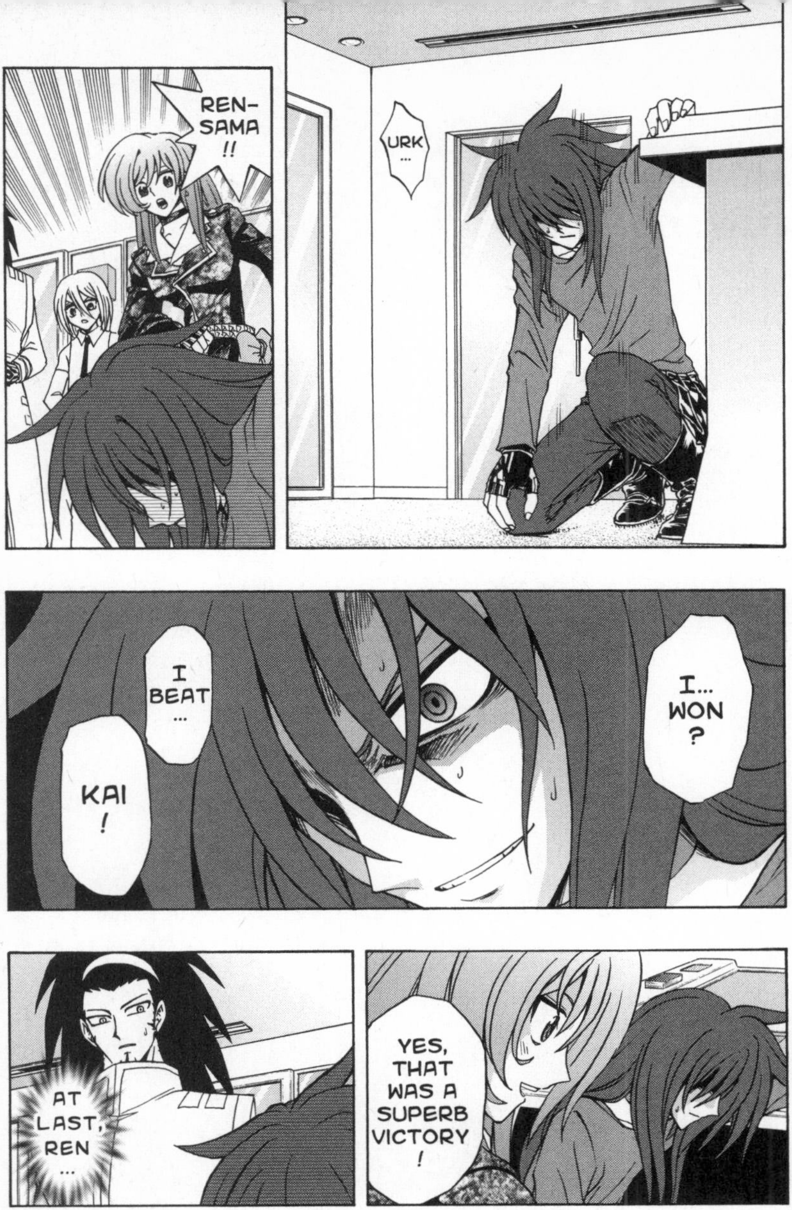
URK...
REN-SAMA!!
I... WON?
I BEAT... KAI!
YES, THAT WAS A SUPERB VICTORY!
AT LAST, REN...

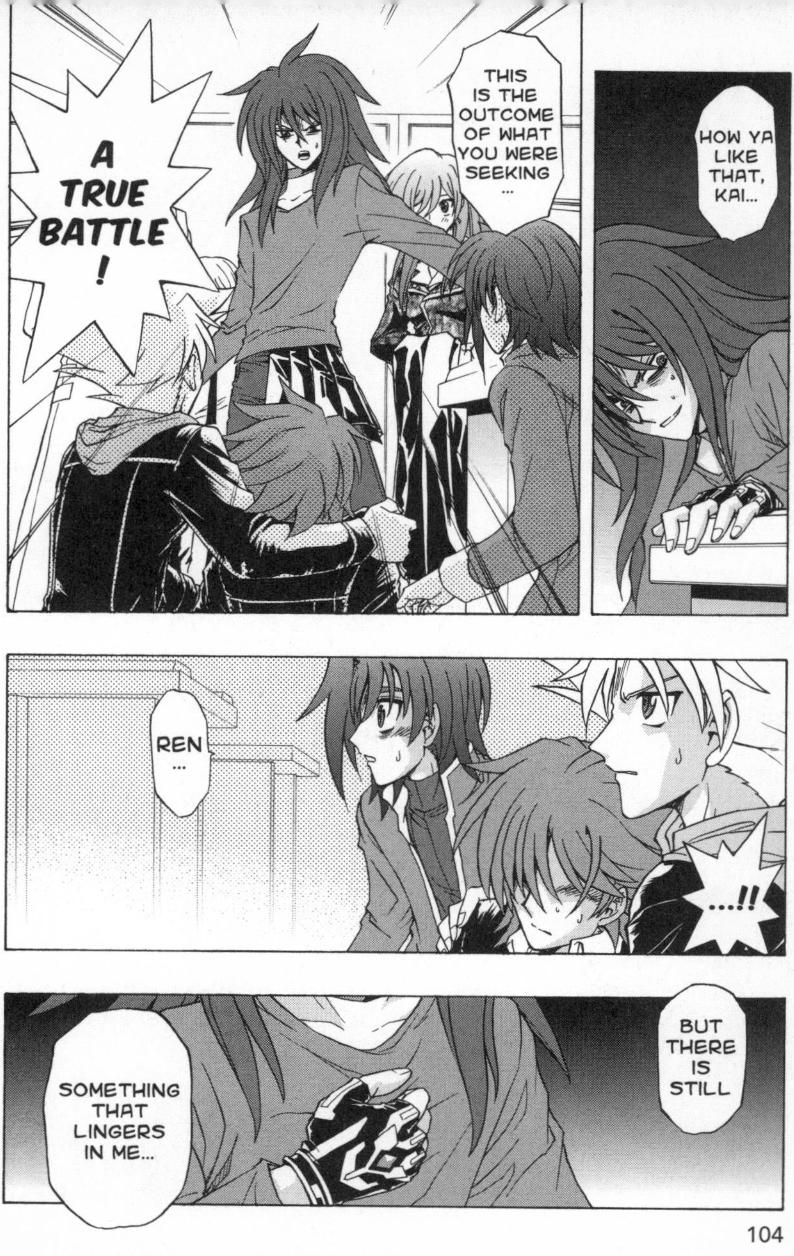
HOW YA LIKE THAT, KAI...
THIS IS THE OUTCOME OF WHAT YOU WERE SEEKING ...
A TRUE BATTLE !
REN ...
...!!
BUT THERE IS STILL
SOMETHING THAT LINGERS IN ME...

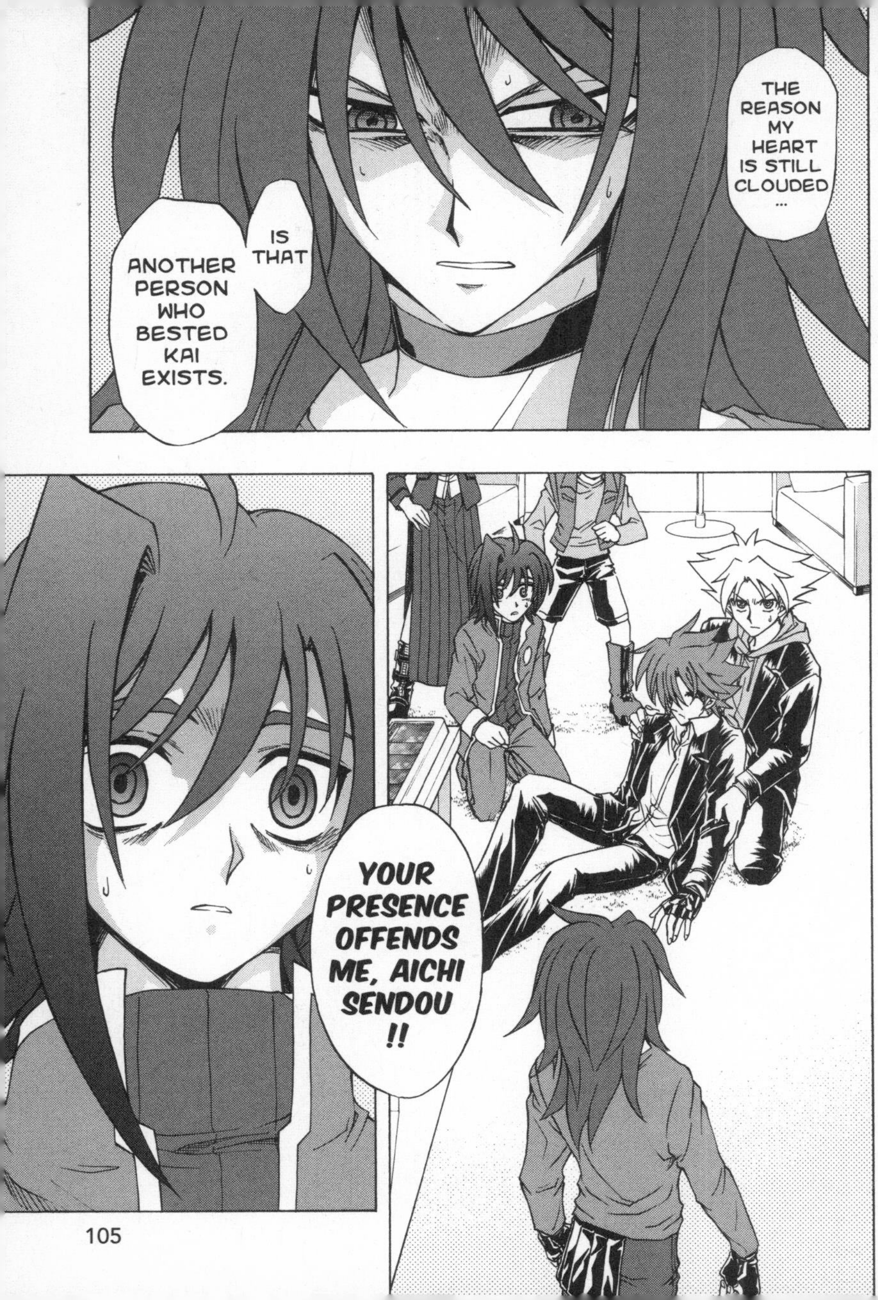
THE REASON MY HEART IS STILL CLOUDED ...
IS THAT
ANOTHER PERSON WHO BESTED KAI EXISTS.
YOUR PRESENCE OFFENDS ME, AICHI SENDOU !!

BONUS! CARDFIGHT!! Vanguard NEVER-BEFORE-SEEN IMAGE BOARDS

UNITS

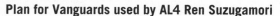

Plan for Vanguards used by AL4 Ren Suzugamori

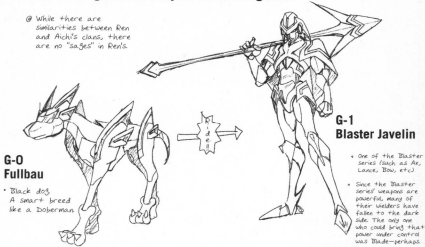

@ While there are similarities between Ren and Aichi's clans, there are no "sages" in Ren's.

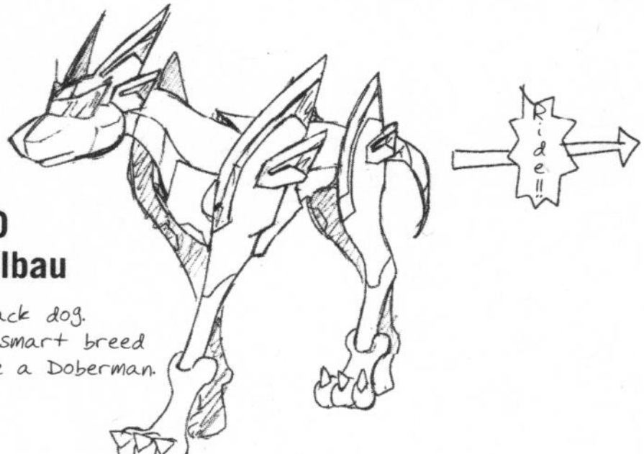

Ride!!

G-0
Fullbau

• Black dog. A smart breed like a Doberman.

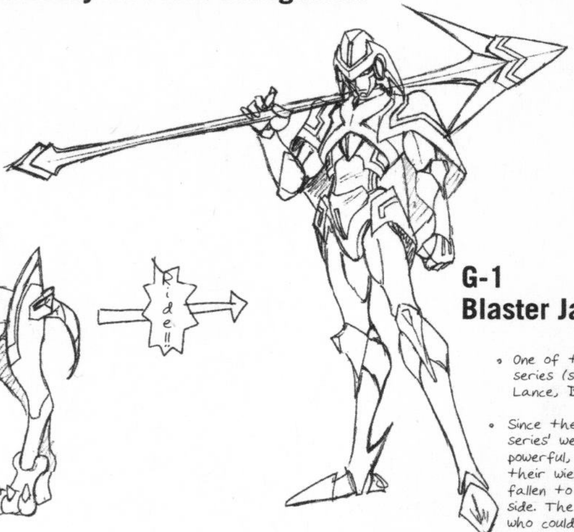

G-1
Blaster Javelin

• One of the Blaster series (such as Ax, Lance, Bow, etc.)

• Since the Blaster series' weapons are powerful, many of their wielders have fallen to the dark side. The only one who could bring that power under control was Blade—perhaps.

G-2
Blaster Dark

• To make it clear that he's the clan's command tower, he's simply called "Dark."

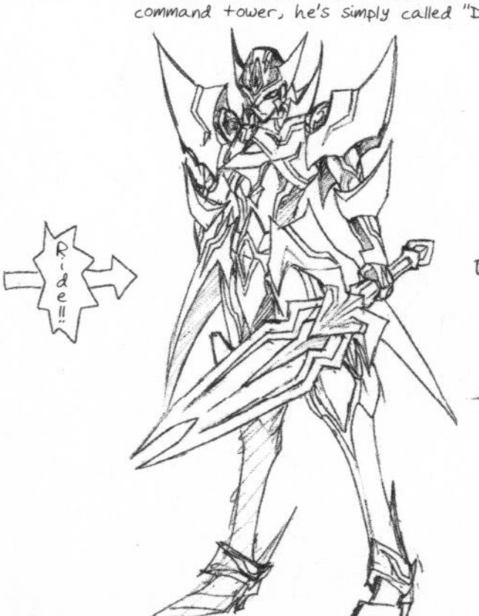

Ride!!

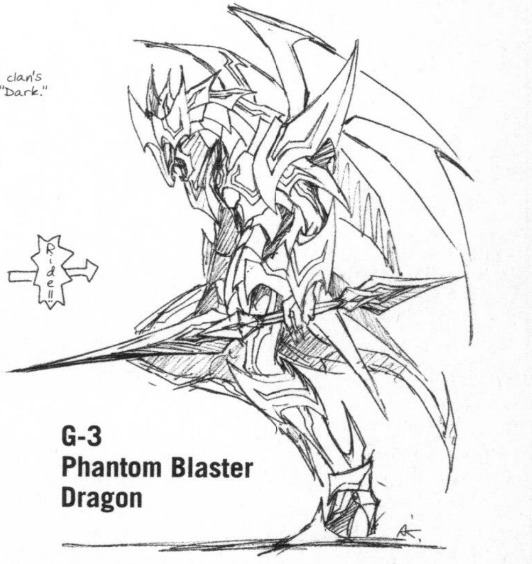

Ride!!

G-3
Phantom Blaster Dragon

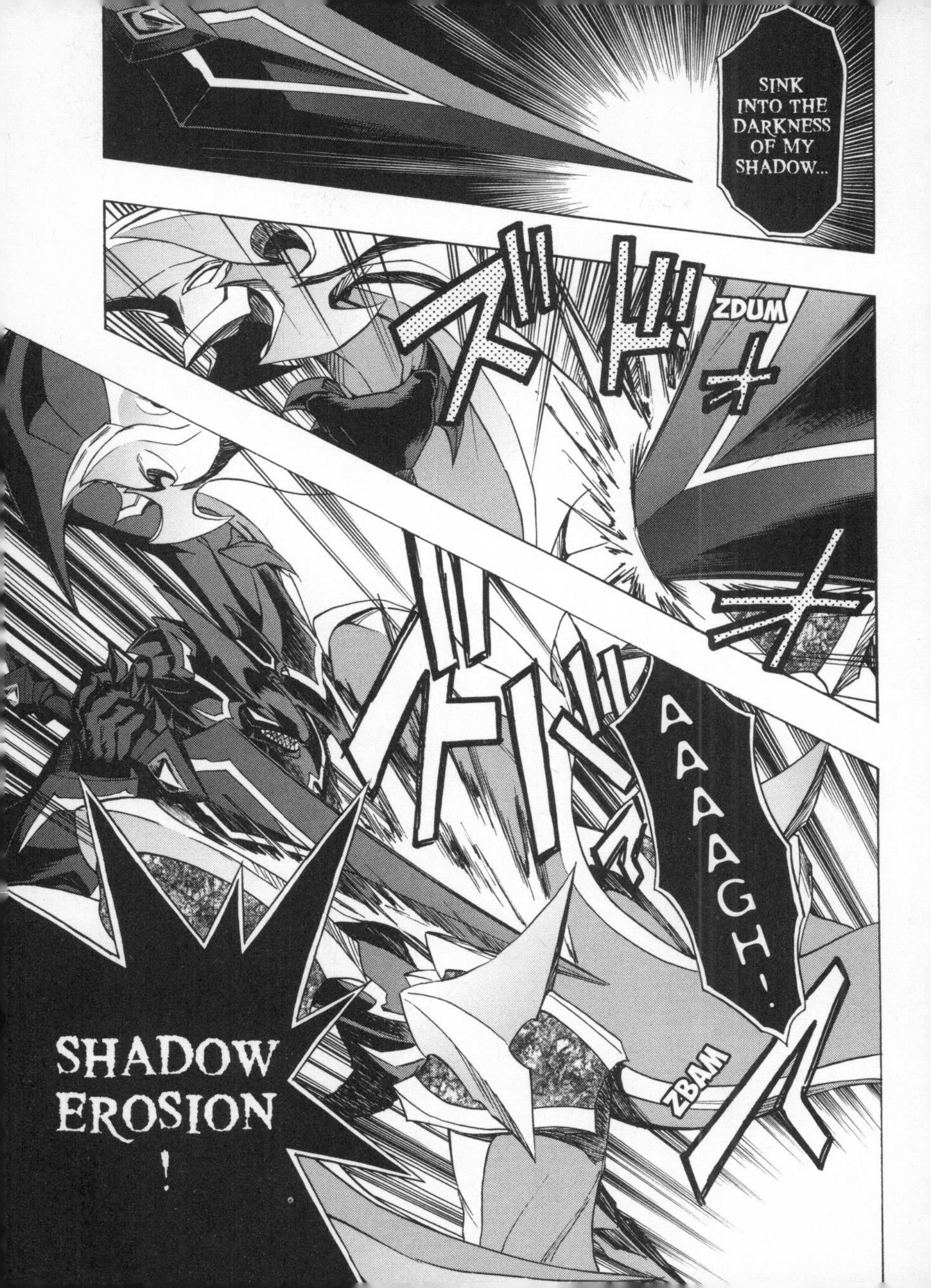
SINK INTO THE DARKNESS OF MY SHADOW...
ZDUM
AAAAGH-!
ZBAM
SHADOW EROSION !

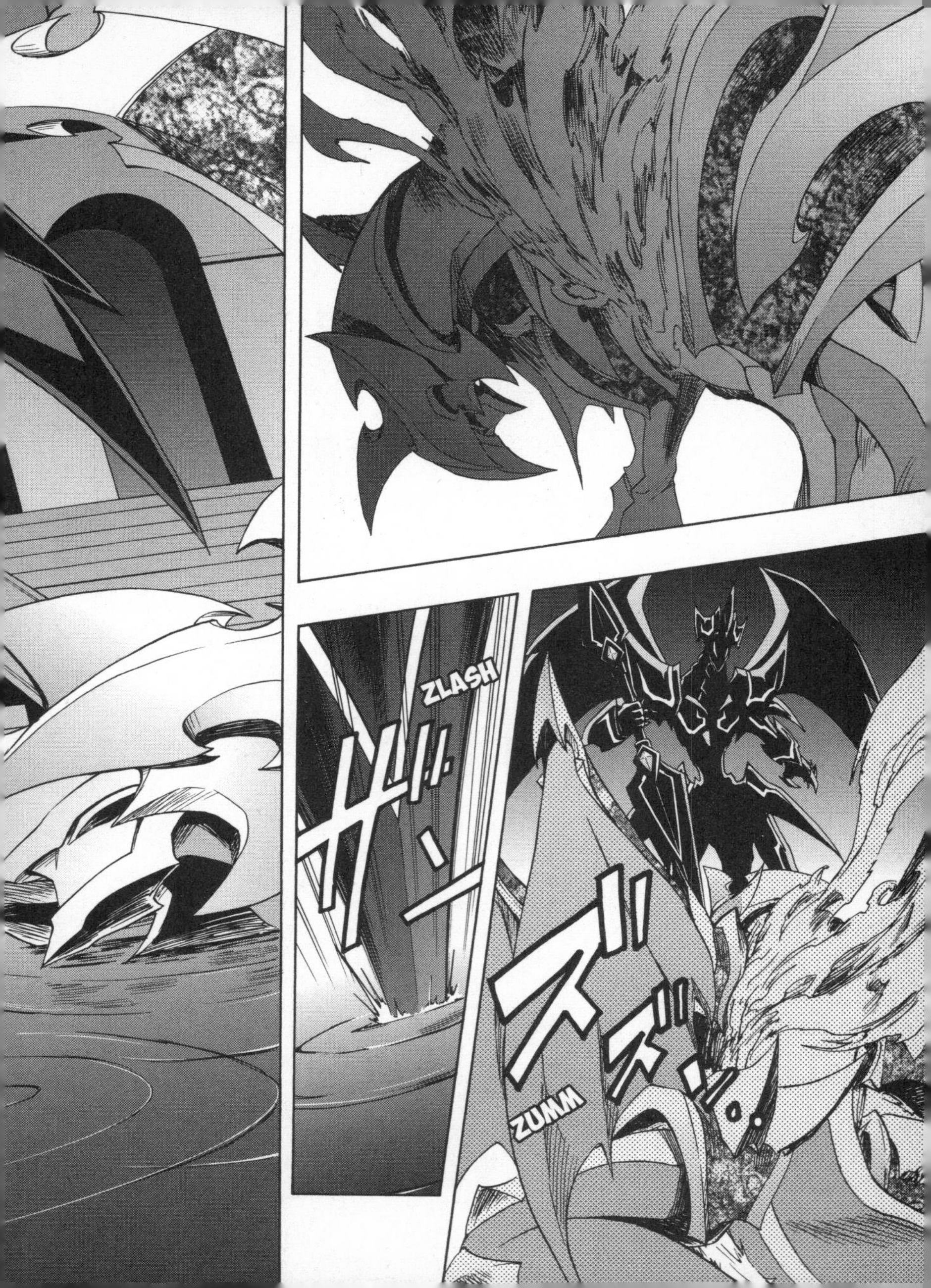
ZLASH
ZUMM

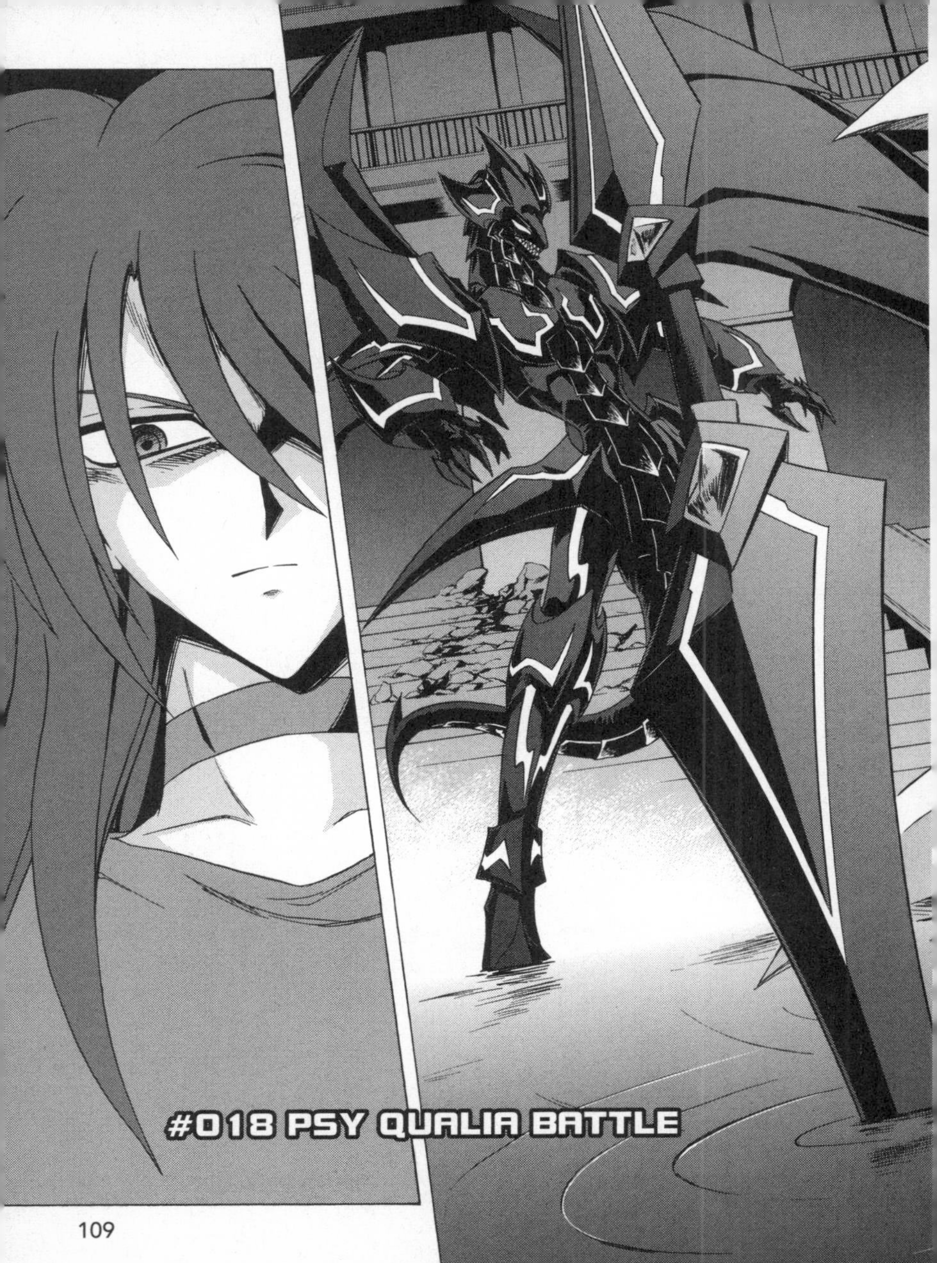
#018 PSY QUALIA BATTLE

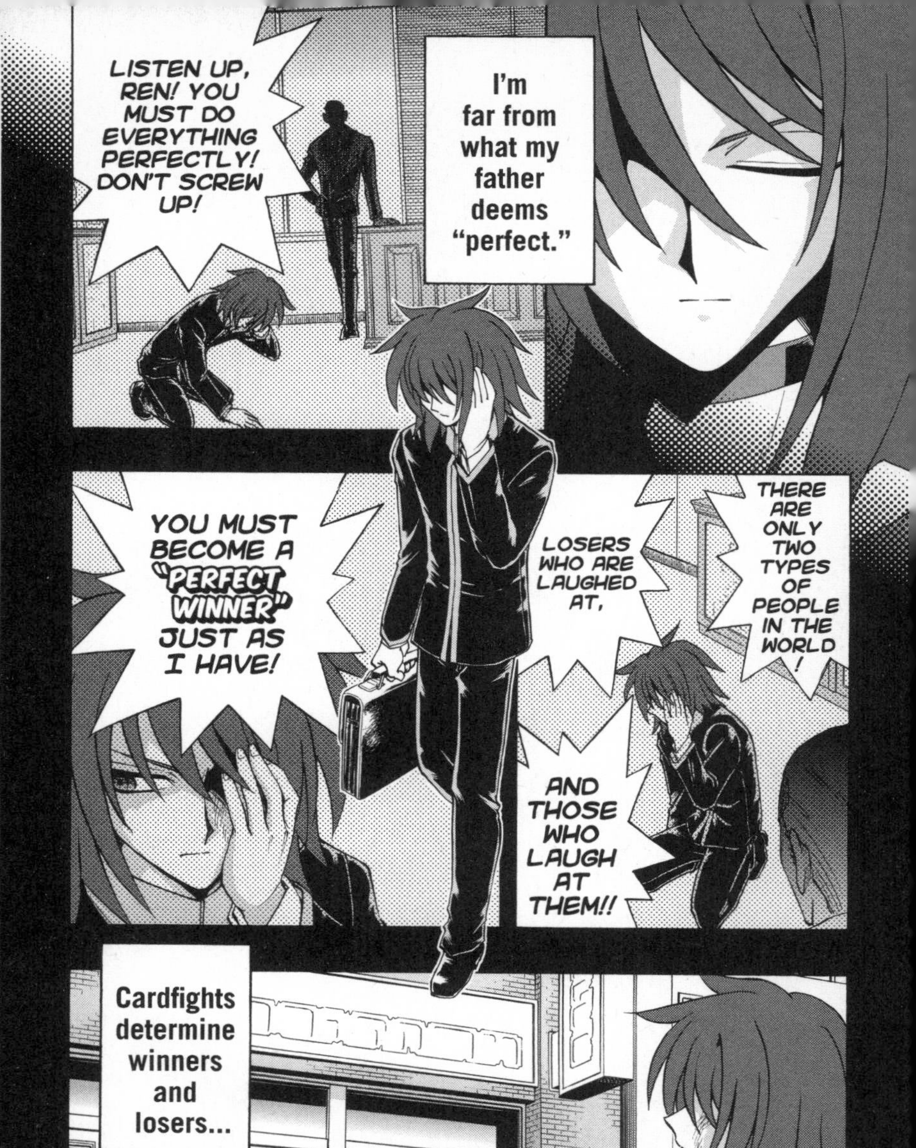
I'm far from what my father deems "perfect."
LISTEN UP, REN! YOU MUST DO EVERYTHING PERFECTLY! DON'T SCREW UP!
THERE ARE ONLY TWO TYPES OF PEOPLE IN THE WORLD!
LOSERS WHO ARE LAUGHED AT,
AND THOSE WHO LAUGH AT THEM!!
YOU MUST BECOME A "PERFECT WINNER" JUST AS I HAVE!
Cardfights determine winners and losers...

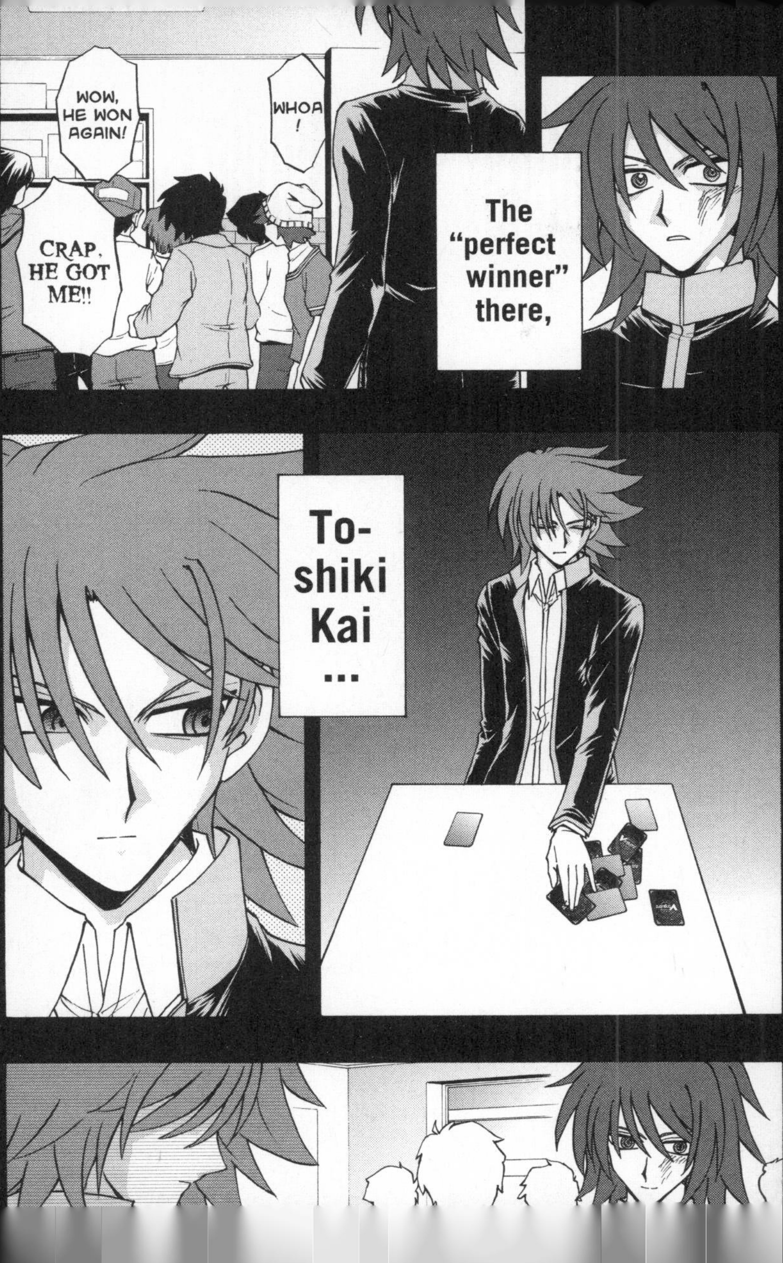

WHOA!
WOW, HE WON AGAIN!
CRAP, HE GOT ME!!
The "perfect winner" there,
To-shiki Kai...

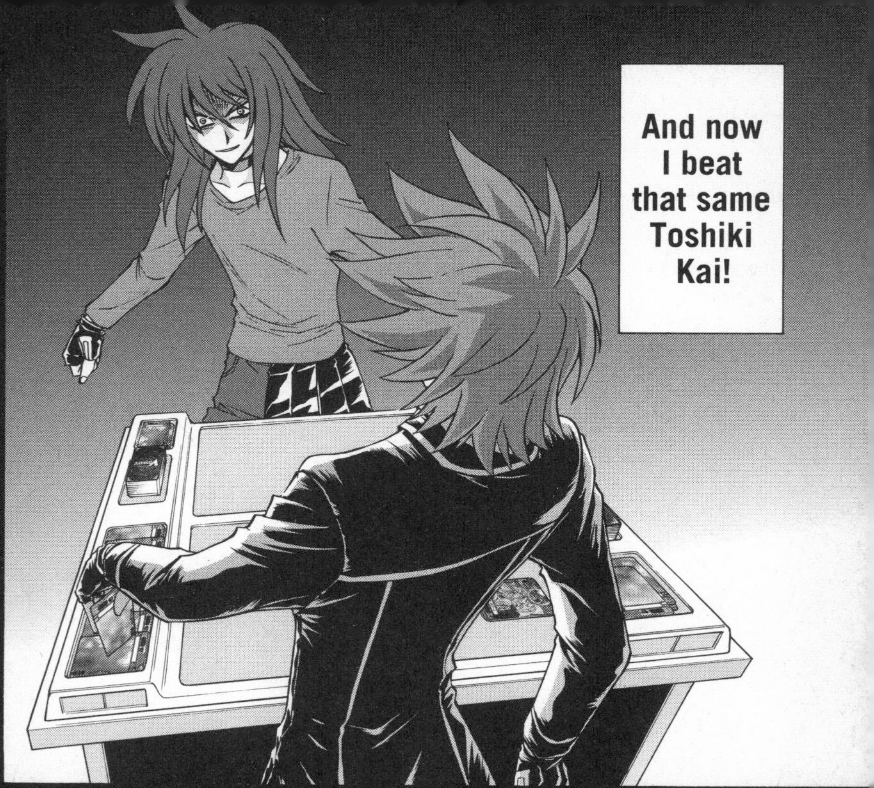
And now I beat that same Toshiki Kai!

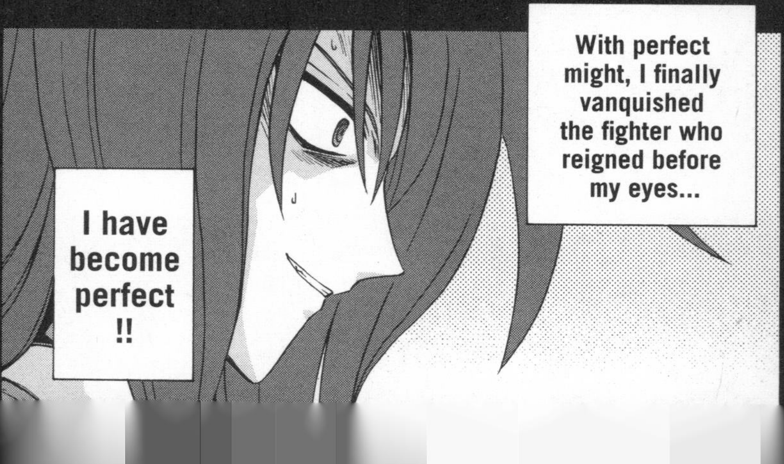
With perfect might, I finally vanquished the fighter who reigned before my eyes...
I have become perfect !!

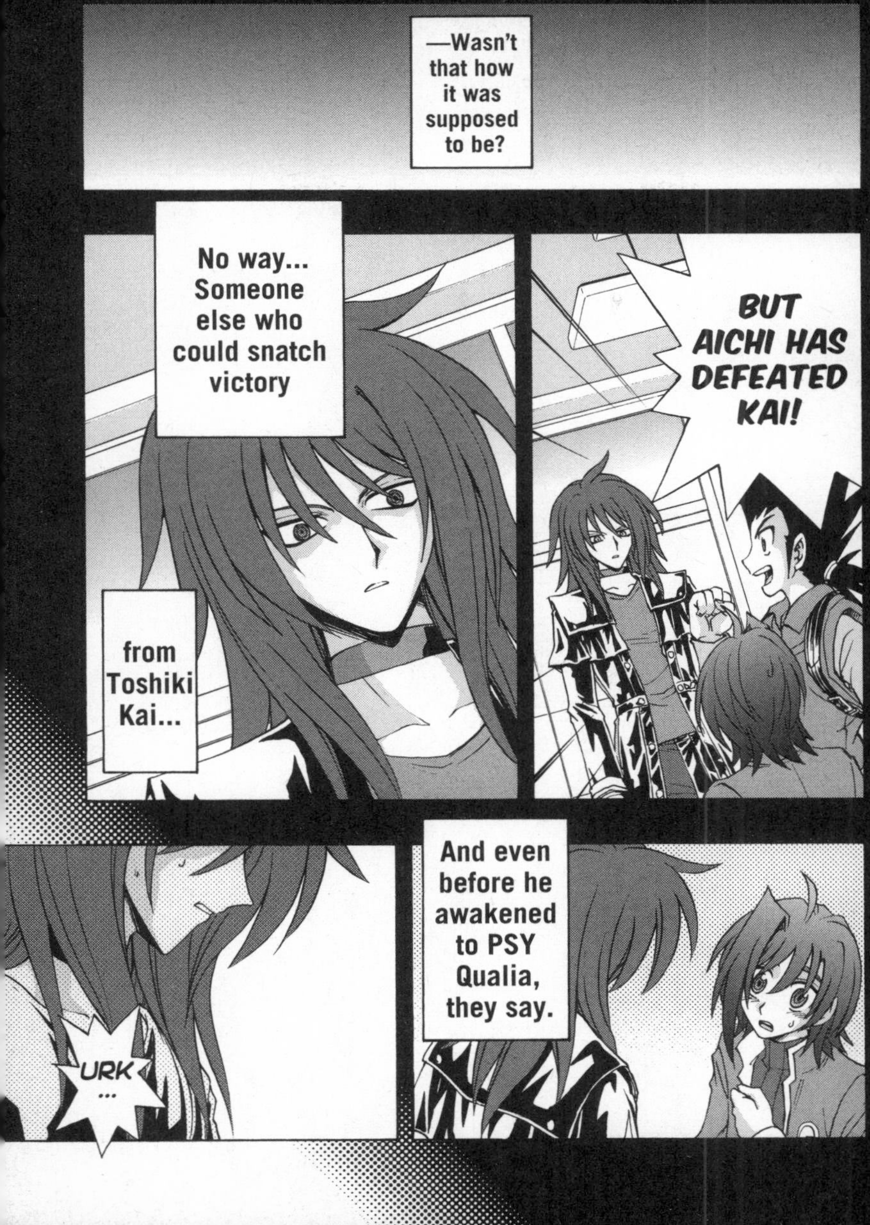
—Wasn't that how it was supposed to be?
BUT AICHI HAS DEFEATED KAI!
No way... Someone else who could snatch victory
from Toshiki Kai...
And even before he awakened to PSY Qualia, they say.
URK ...

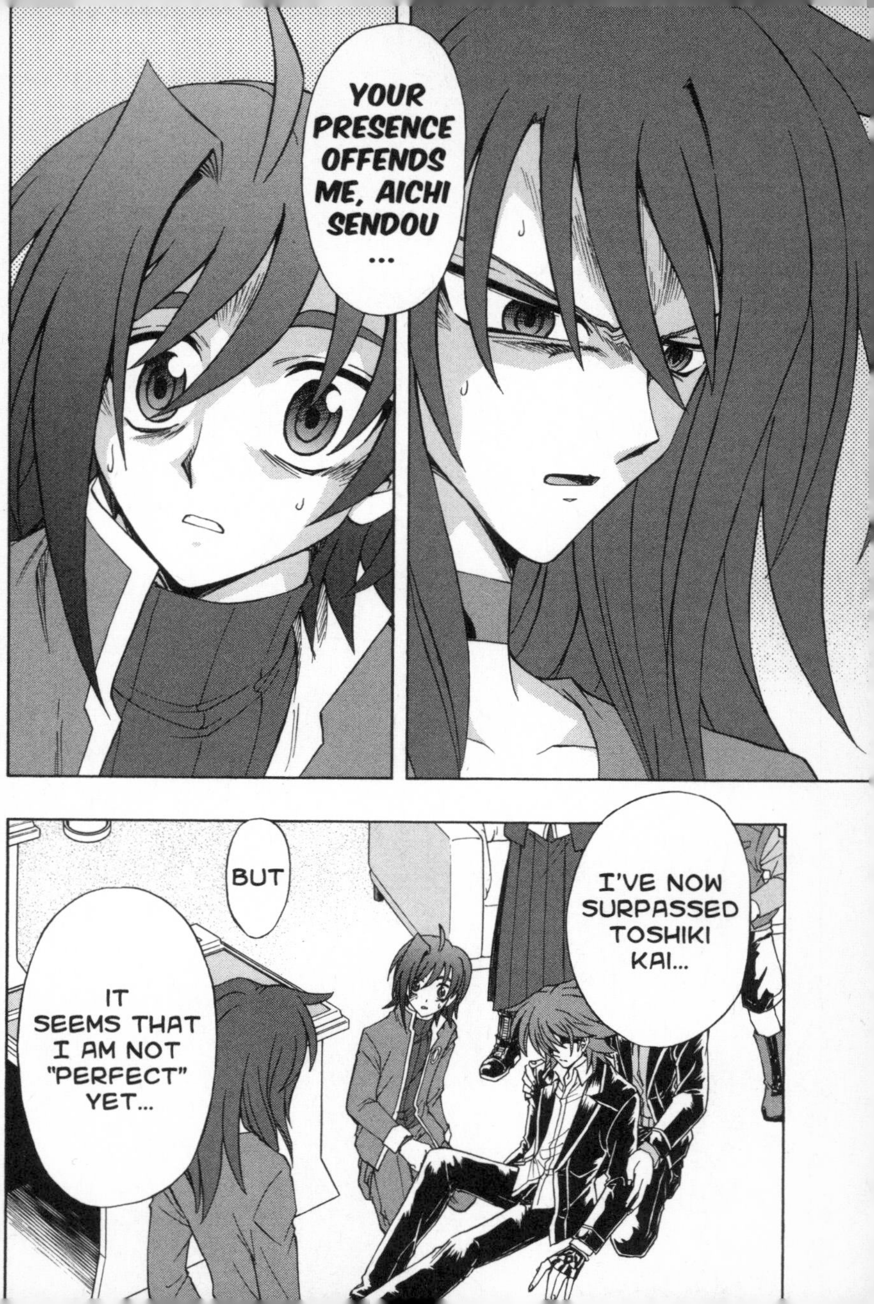
YOUR PRESENCE OFFENDS ME, AICHI SENDOU ...
I'VE NOW SURPASSED TOSHIKI KAI...
BUT
IT SEEMS THAT I AM NOT "PERFECT" YET...

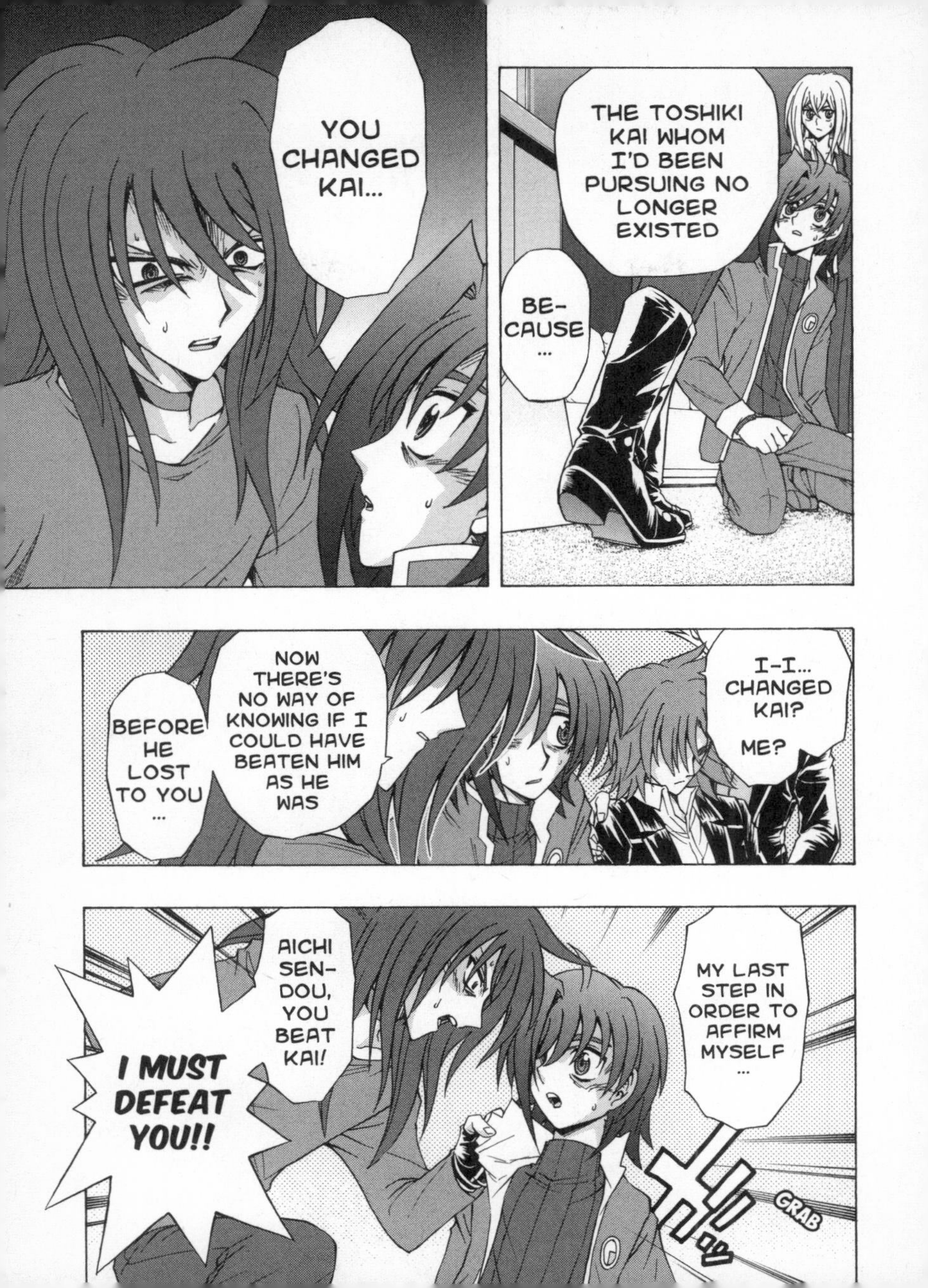
THE TOSHIKI KAI WHOM I'D BEEN PURSUING NO LONGER EXISTED
BE-CAUSE ...
YOU CHANGED KAI...
I-I... CHANGED KAI?
ME?
NOW THERE'S NO WAY OF KNOWING IF I COULD HAVE BEATEN HIM AS HE WAS
BEFORE HE LOST TO YOU ...
MY LAST STEP IN ORDER TO AFFIRM MYSELF ...
AICHI SEN-DOU, YOU BEAT KAI!
I MUST DEFEAT YOU!!
GRAB

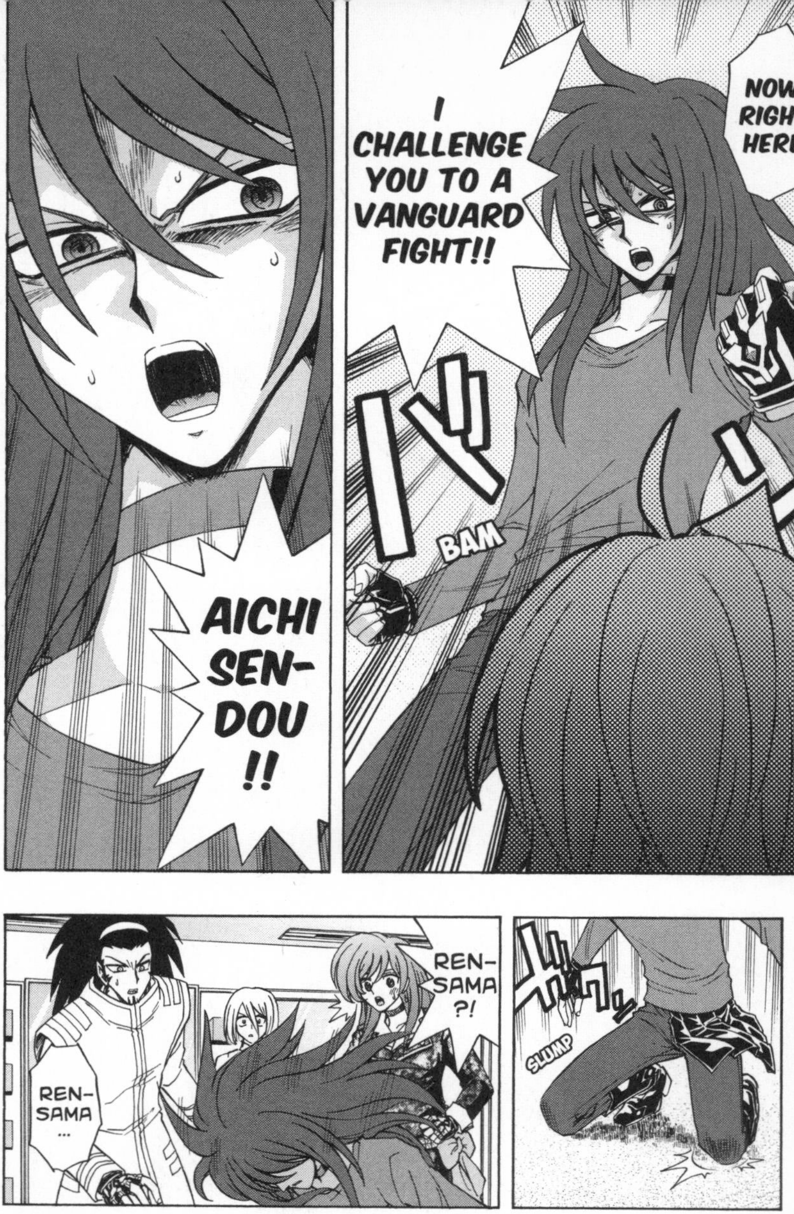
NOW, RIGHT HERE,
I CHALLENGE YOU TO A VANGUARD FIGHT!!
BAM
AICHI SEN-DOU !!
SLUMP
REN-SAMA ?!
REN-SAMA ...

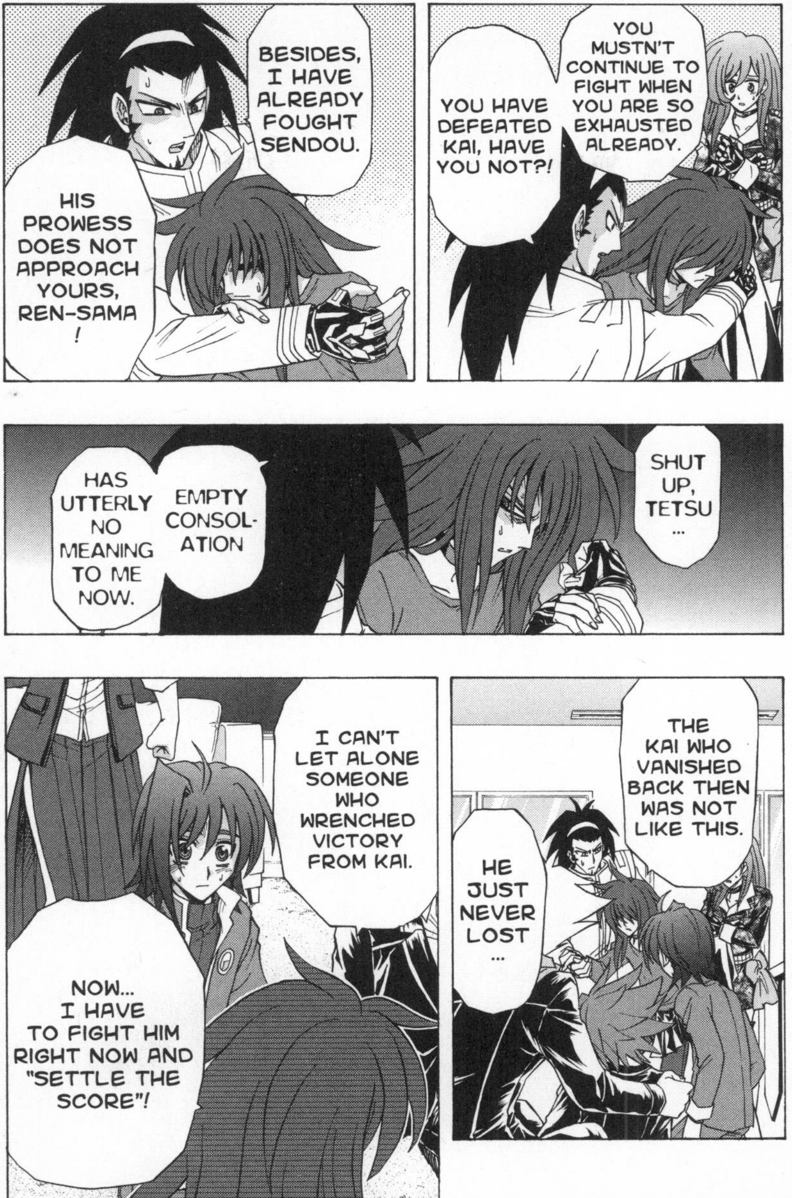
YOU MUSTN'T CONTINUE TO FIGHT WHEN YOU ARE SO EXHAUSTED ALREADY.
YOU HAVE DEFEATED KAI, HAVE YOU NOT?!
BESIDES, I HAVE ALREADY FOUGHT SENDOU.
HIS PROWESS DOES NOT APPROACH YOURS, REN-SAMA!
SHUT UP, TETSU...
EMPTY CONSOLATION
HAS UTTERLY NO MEANING TO ME NOW.
THE KAI WHO VANISHED BACK THEN WAS NOT LIKE THIS.
HE JUST NEVER LOST...
I CAN'T LET ALONE SOMEONE WHO WRENCHED VICTORY FROM KAI.
NOW... I HAVE TO FIGHT HIM RIGHT NOW AND "SETTLE THE SCORE"!

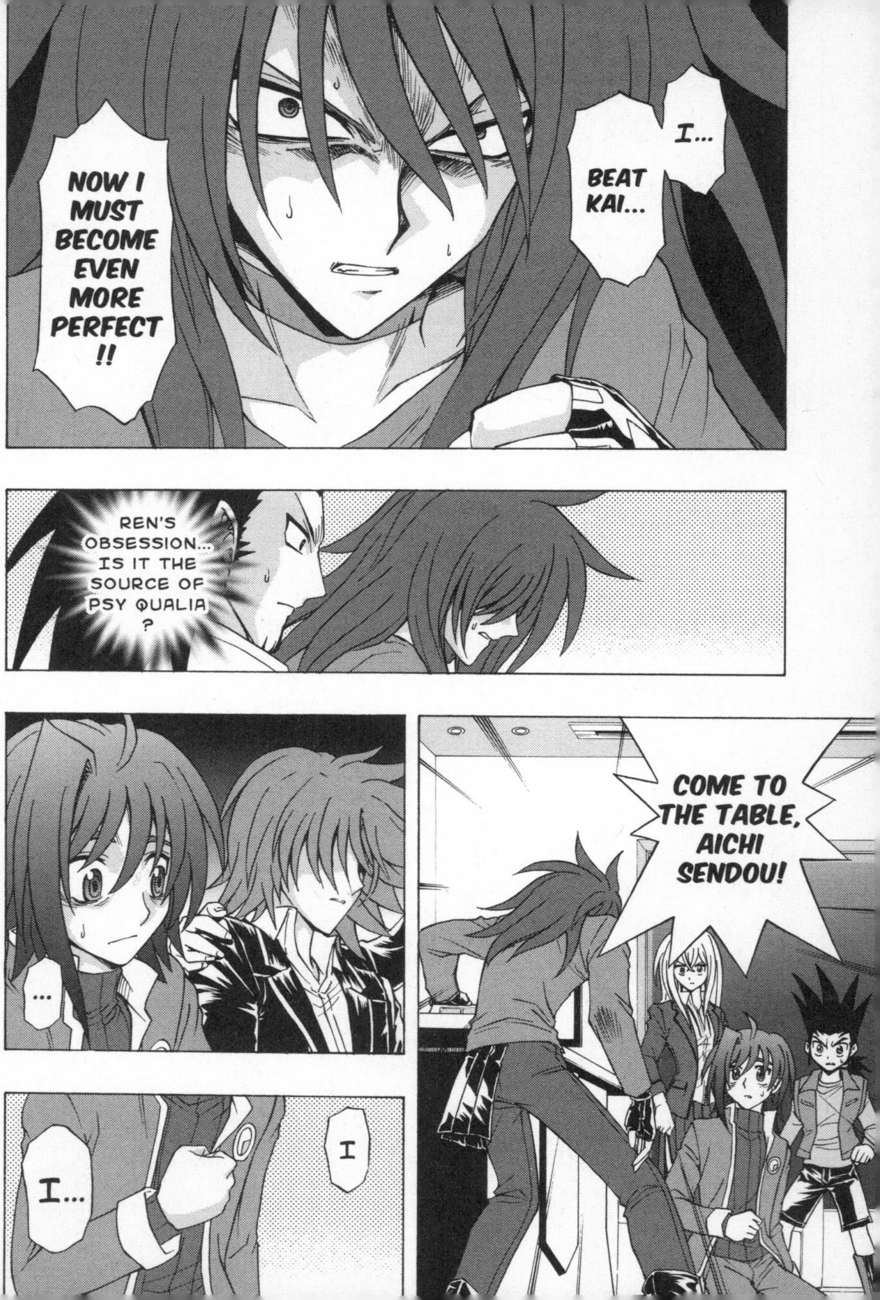
I...
BEAT KAI...
NOW I MUST BECOME EVEN MORE PERFECT !!
REN'S OBSESSION... IS IT THE SOURCE OF PSY QUALIA ?
COME TO THE TABLE, AICHI SENDOU!
...
I
I...

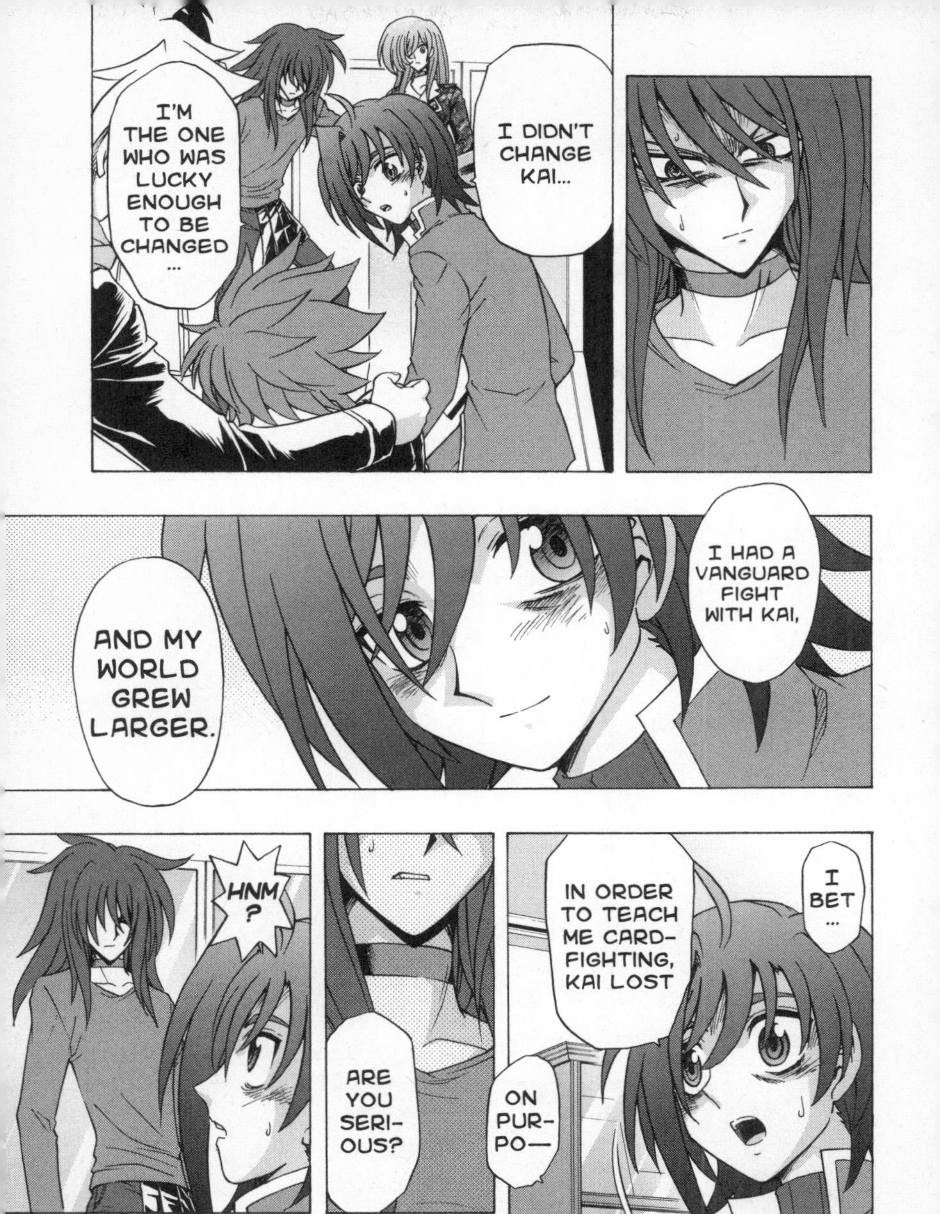
I DIDN'T CHANGE KAI...
I'M THE ONE WHO WAS LUCKY ENOUGH TO BE CHANGED ...
I HAD A VANGUARD FIGHT WITH KAI,
AND MY WORLD GREW LARGER.
I BET ...
IN ORDER TO TEACH ME CARD-FIGHTING, KAI LOST
ON PUR-PO—
ARE YOU SERI-OUS?
HNM ?

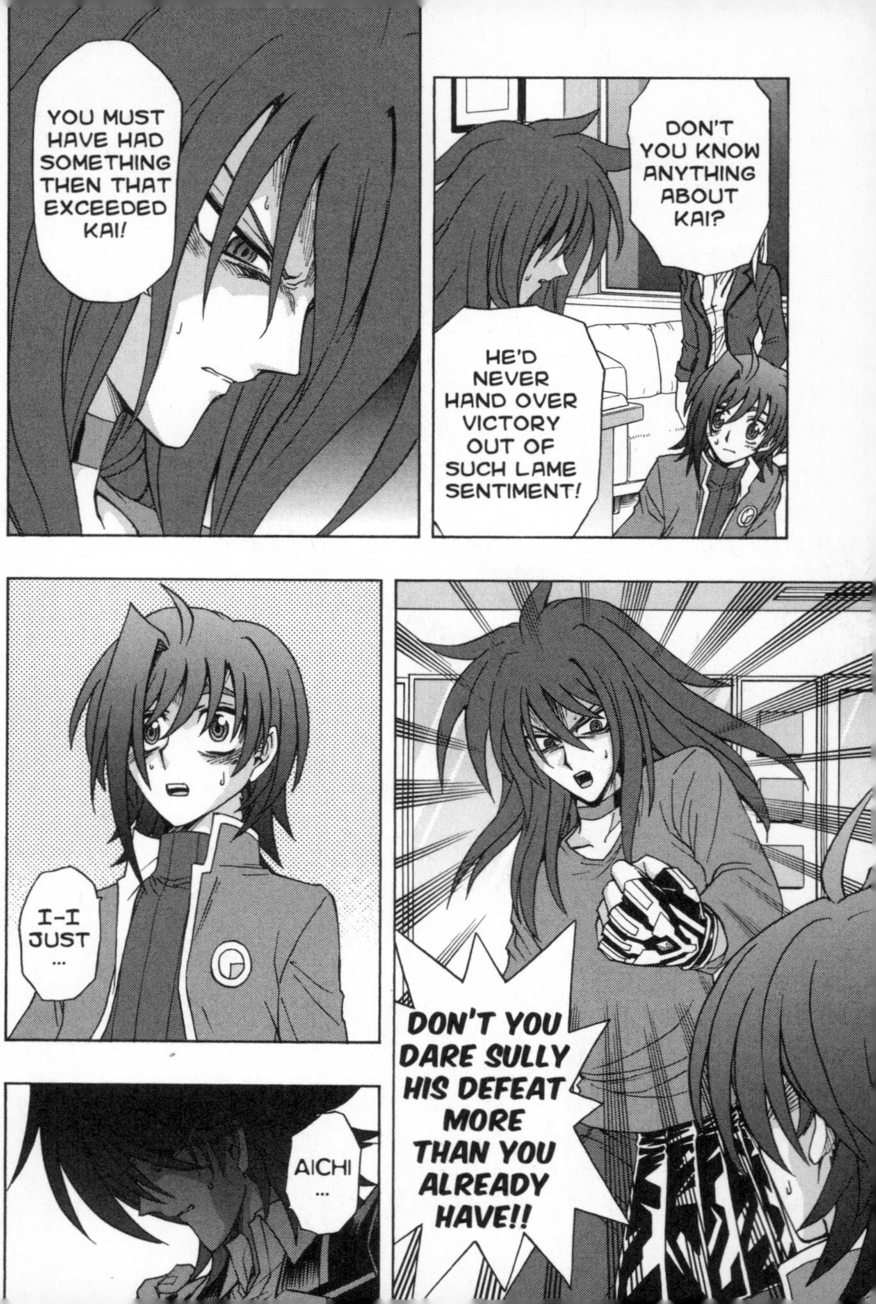
DON'T YOU KNOW ANYTHING ABOUT KAI?
HE'D NEVER HAND OVER VICTORY OUT OF SUCH LAME SENTIMENT!
YOU MUST HAVE HAD SOMETHING THEN THAT EXCEEDED KAI!
DON'T YOU DARE SULLY HIS DEFEAT MORE THAN YOU ALREADY HAVE!!
I-I JUST ...
AICHI ...

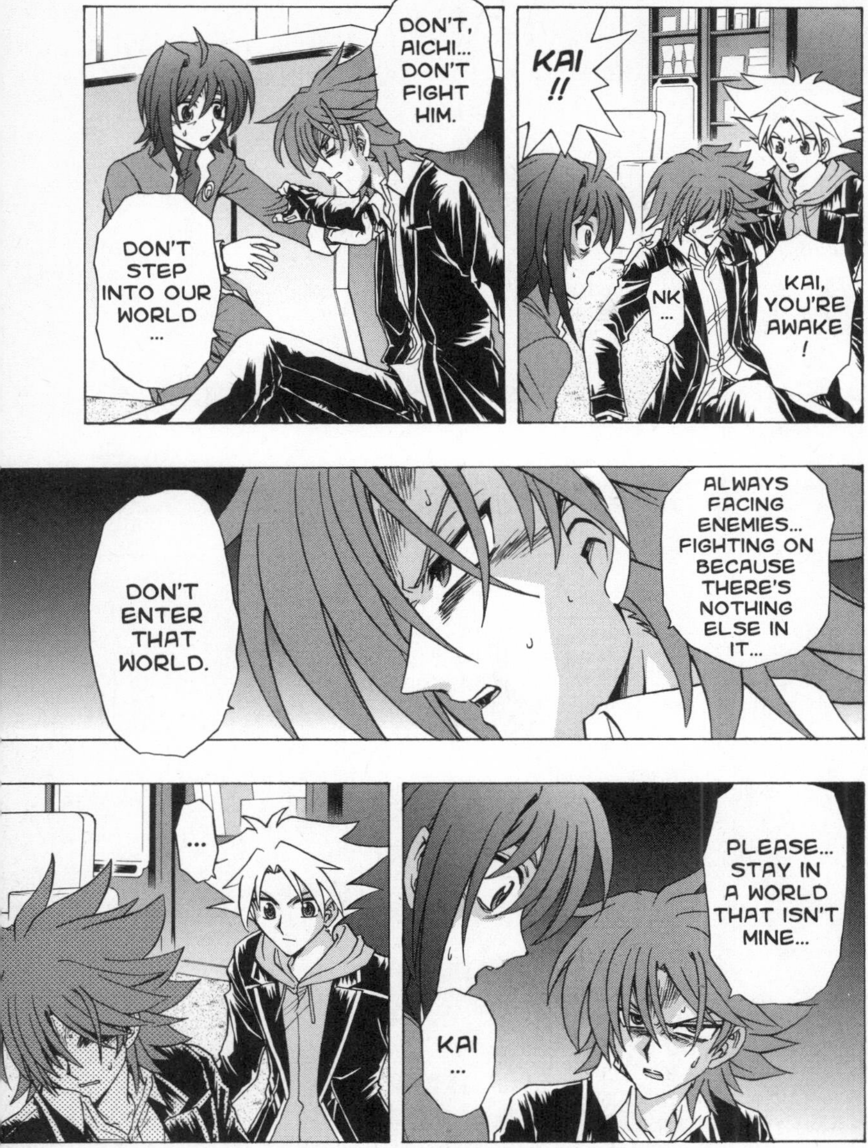
KAI !!
KAI, YOU'RE AWAKE !
NK ...
DON'T, AICHI... DON'T FIGHT HIM.
DON'T STEP INTO OUR WORLD ...
ALWAYS FACING ENEMIES... FIGHTING ON BECAUSE THERE'S NOTHING ELSE IN IT...
DON'T ENTER THAT WORLD.
PLEASE... STAY IN A WORLD THAT ISN'T MINE...
KAI ...
...

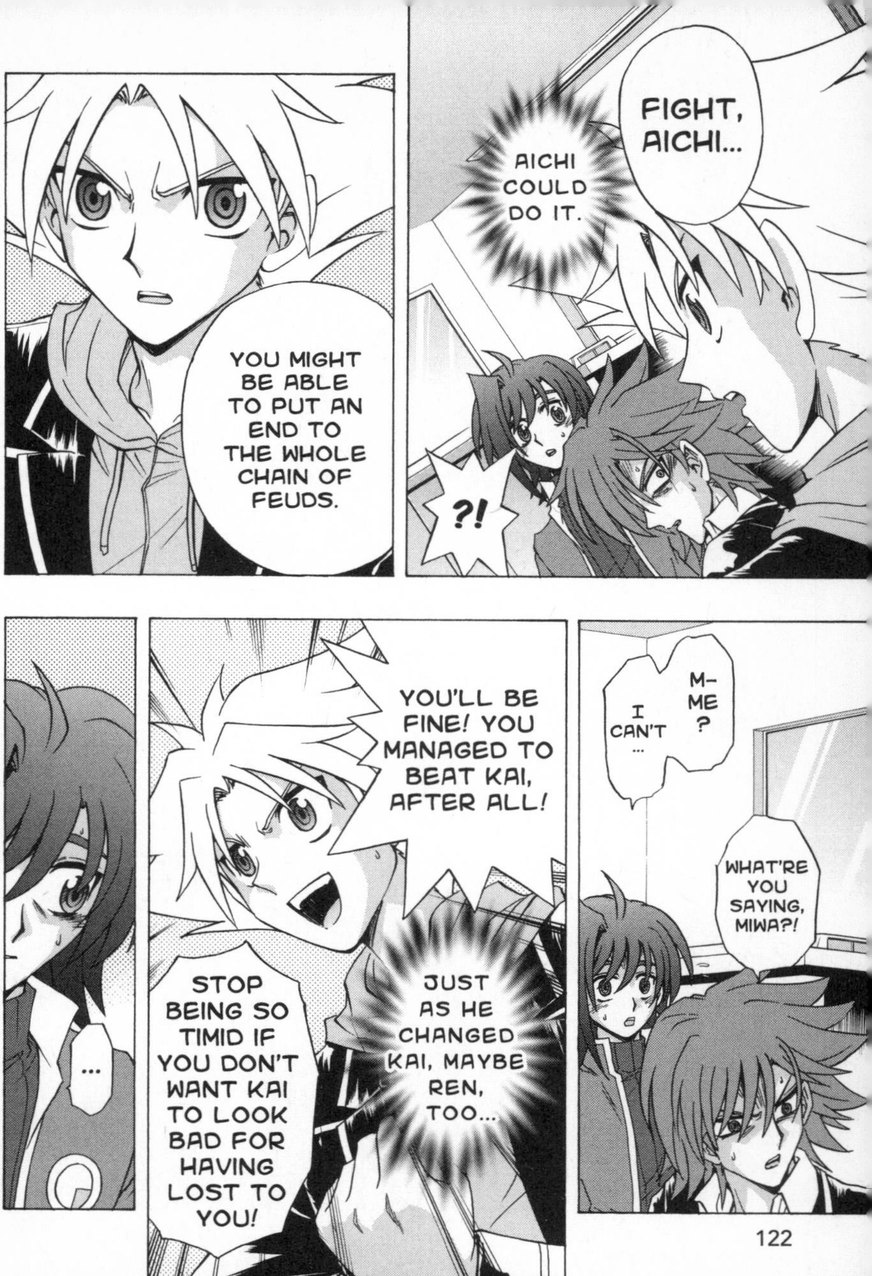
FIGHT, AICHI...
AICHI COULD DO IT.
?!
YOU MIGHT BE ABLE TO PUT AN END TO THE WHOLE CHAIN OF FEUDS.
M-ME?
I CAN'T...
WHAT'RE YOU SAYING, MIWA?!
YOU'LL BE FINE! YOU MANAGED TO BEAT KAI, AFTER ALL!
JUST AS HE CHANGED KAI, MAYBE REN, TOO...
STOP BEING SO TIMID IF YOU DON'T WANT KAI TO LOOK BAD FOR HAVING LOST TO YOU!
...

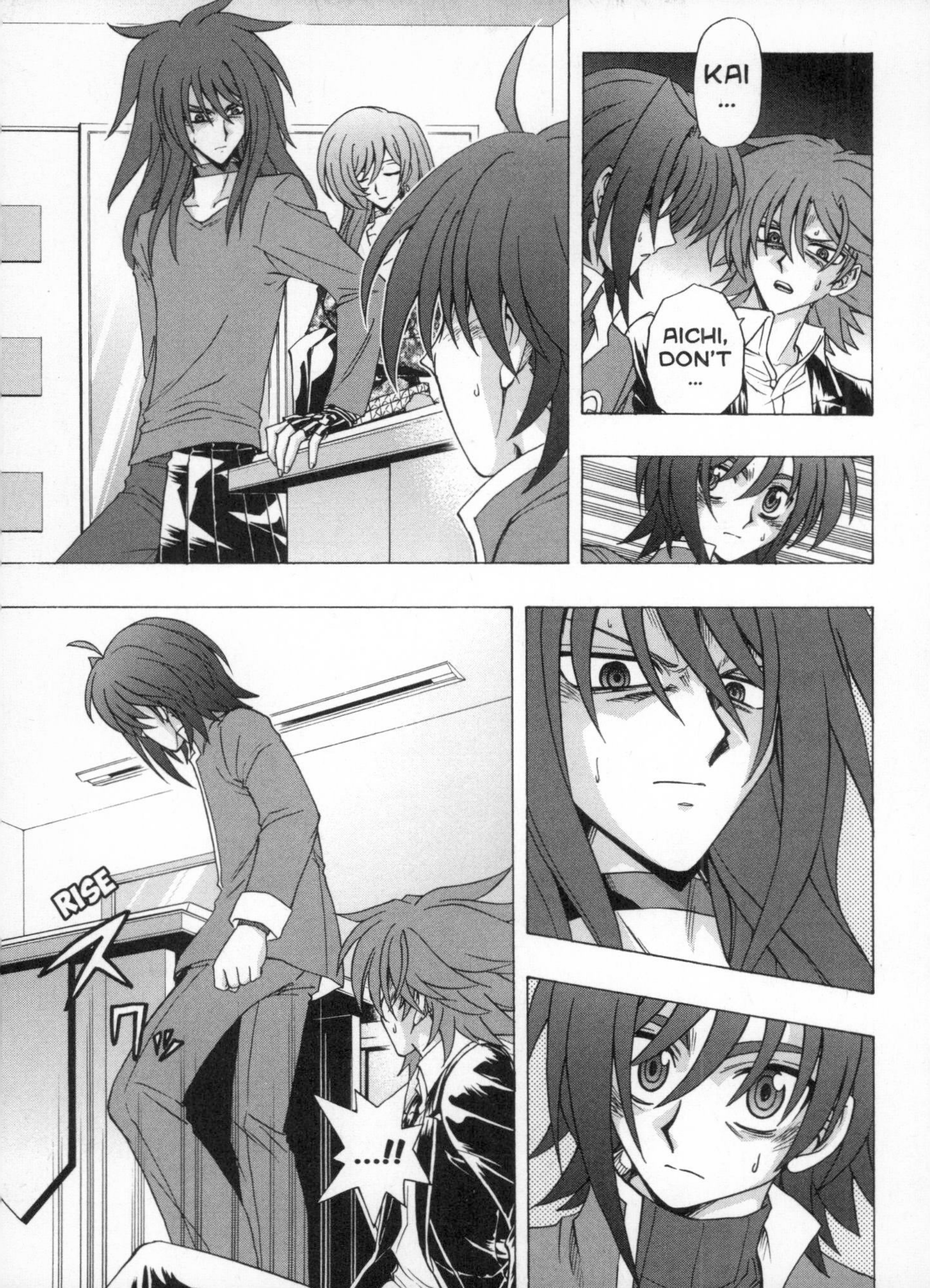
KAI ...
AICHI, DON'T ...
RISE
...!!

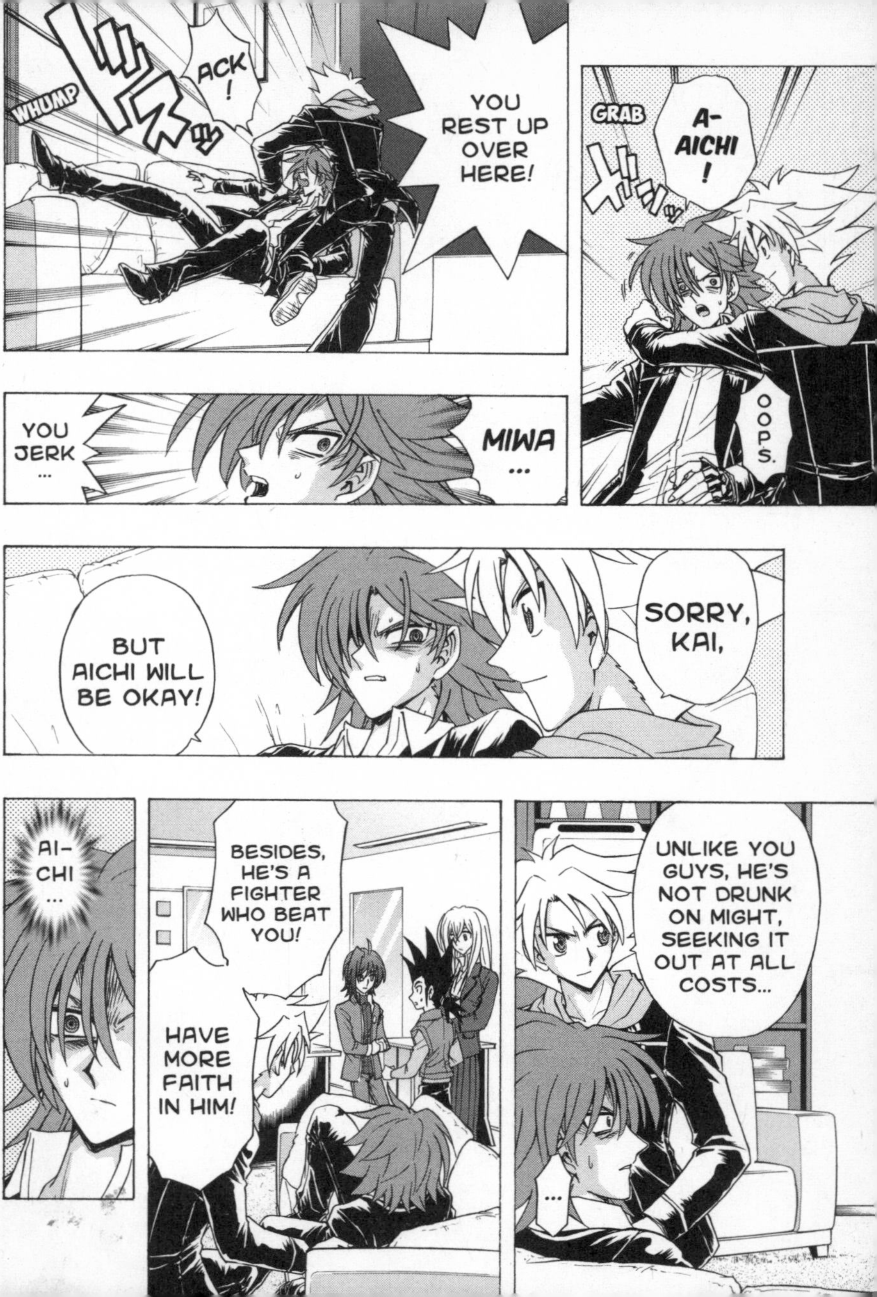
GRAB
A-AICHI!
OOPS.
YOU REST UP OVER HERE!
ACK!
WHUMP
MIWA...
YOU JERK...
SORRY, KAI,
BUT AICHI WILL BE OKAY!
UNLIKE YOU GUYS, HE'S NOT DRUNK ON MIGHT, SEEKING IT OUT AT ALL COSTS...
...
BESIDES, HE'S A FIGHTER WHO BEAT YOU!
HAVE MORE FAITH IN HIM!
AI-CHI...

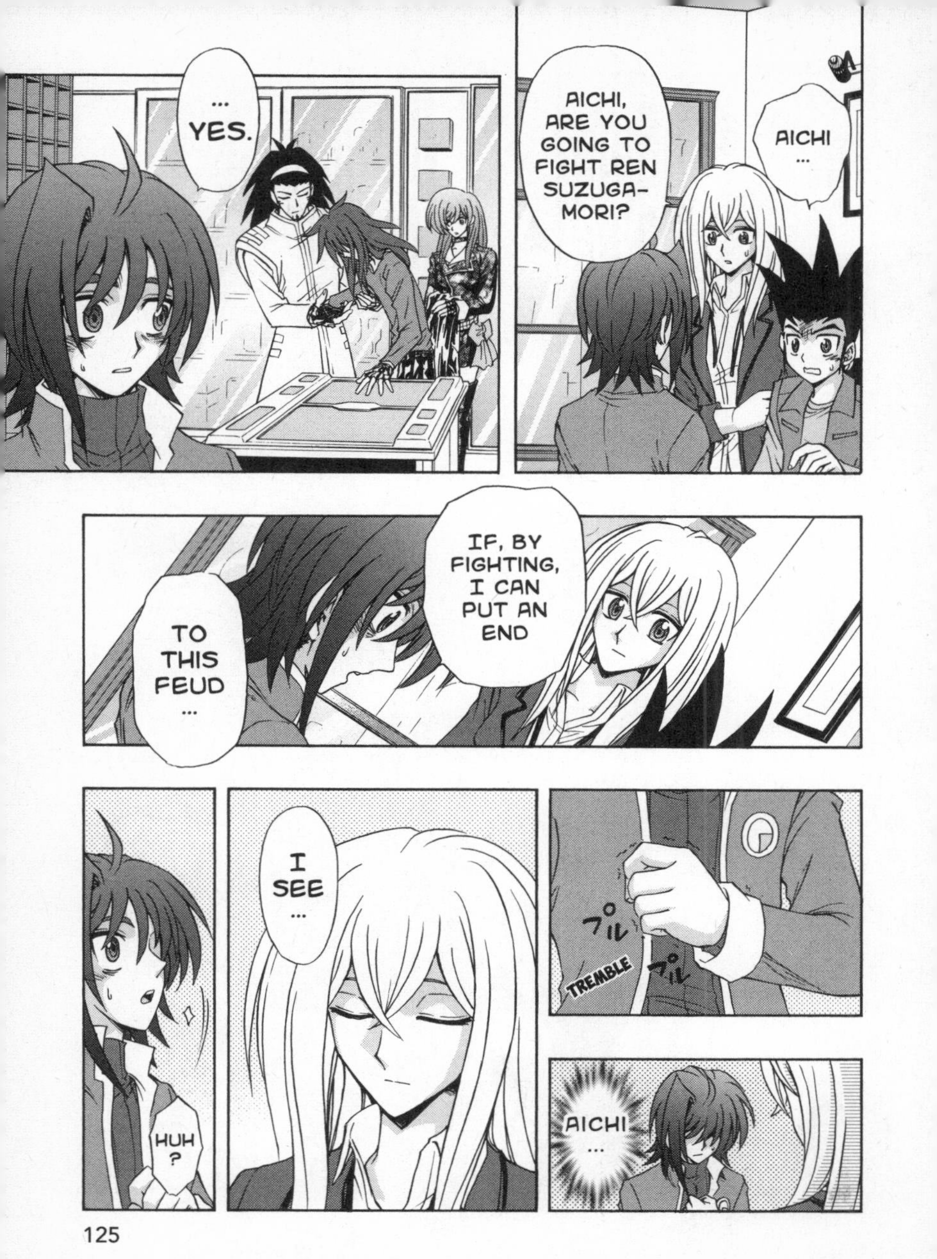
AICHI ...
AICHI, ARE YOU GOING TO FIGHT REN SUZUGA-MORI?
... YES.
IF, BY FIGHTING, I CAN PUT AN END
TO THIS FEUD ...
プル
プル
TREMBLE
AICHI ...
I SEE ...
HUH ?

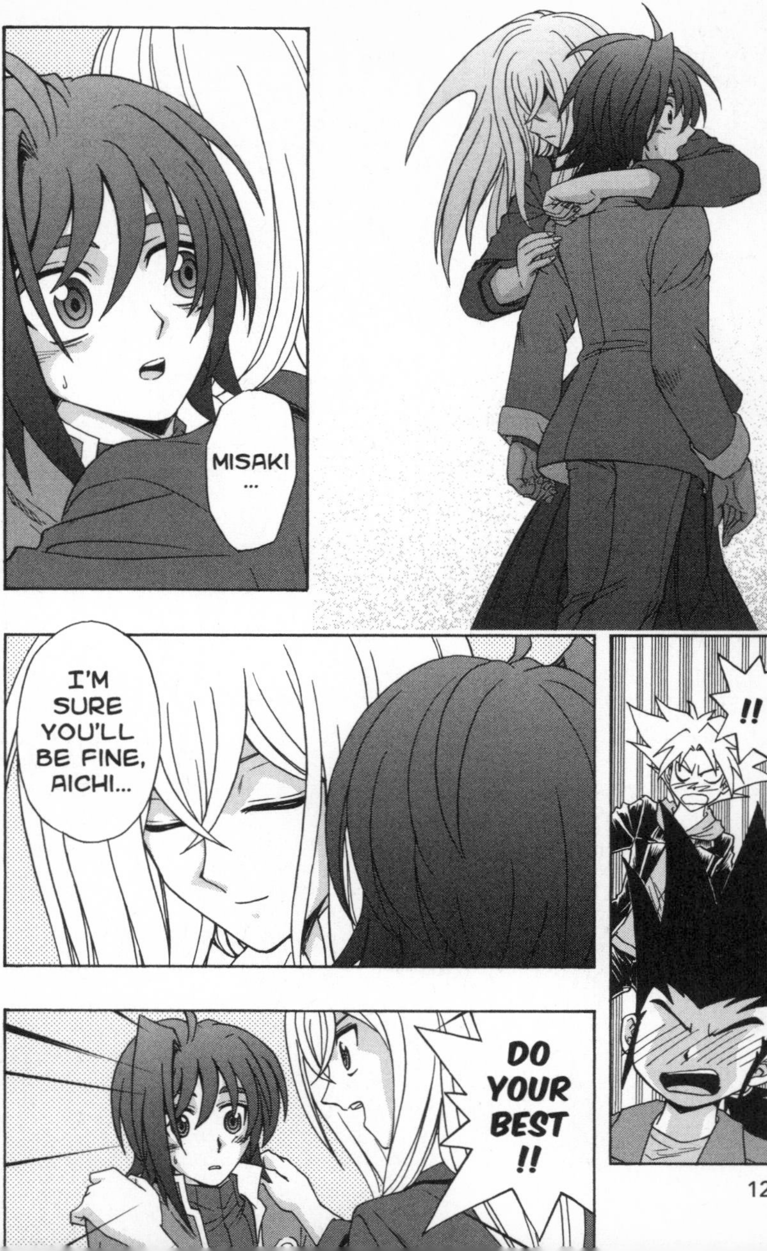
MISAKI ...
!!
I'M SURE YOU'LL BE FINE, AICHI...
DO YOUR BEST !!

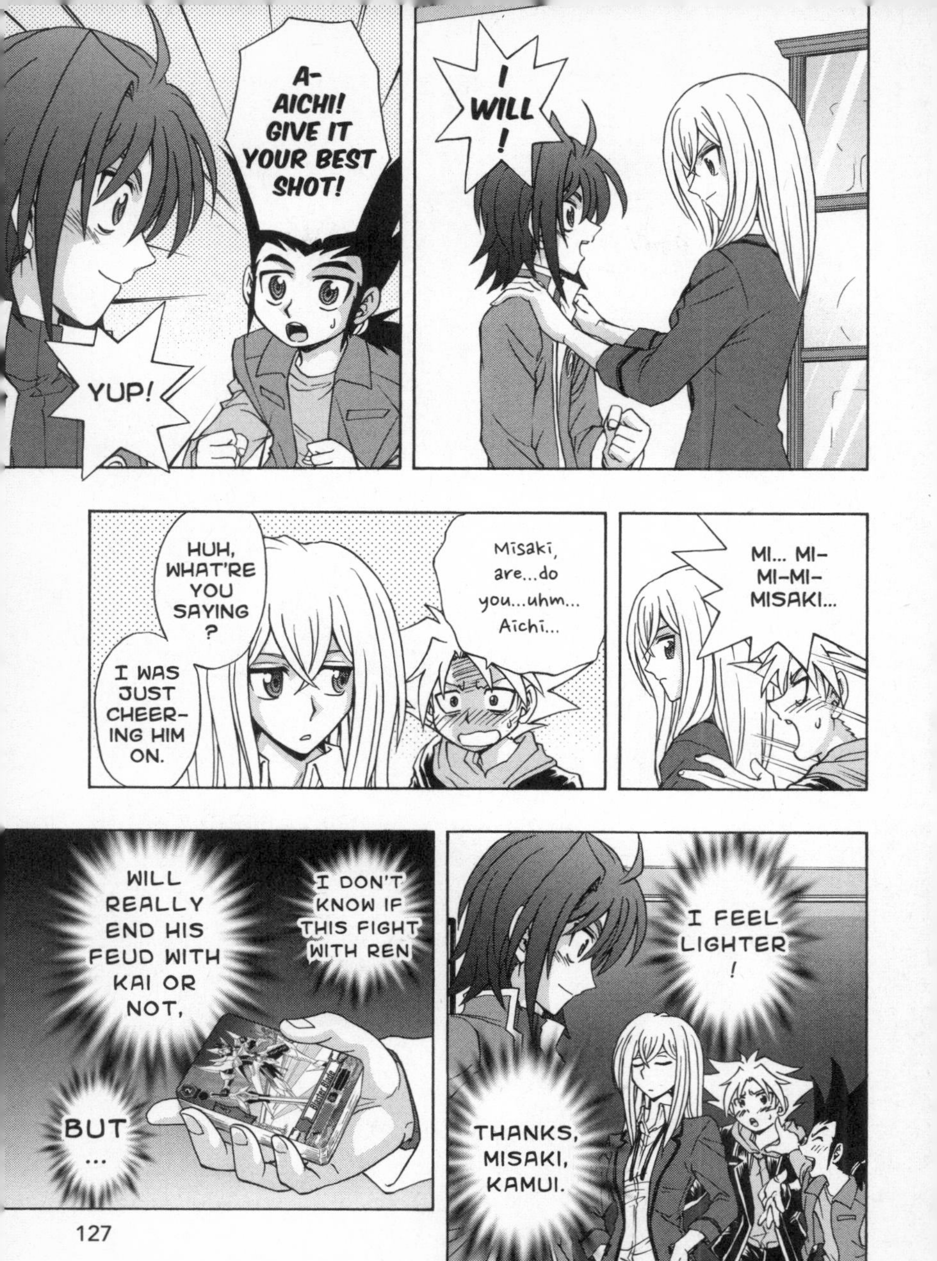
I WILL!
A-AICHI! GIVE IT YOUR BEST SHOT!
YUP!
MI... MI-MI-MI-MISAKI...
Misaki, are...do you...uhm... Aichi...
HUH, WHAT'RE YOU SAYING?
I WAS JUST CHEERING HIM ON.
I FEEL LIGHTER!
THANKS, MISAKI, KAMUI.
I DON'T KNOW IF THIS FIGHT WITH REN
WILL REALLY END HIS FEUD WITH KAI OR NOT,
BUT...

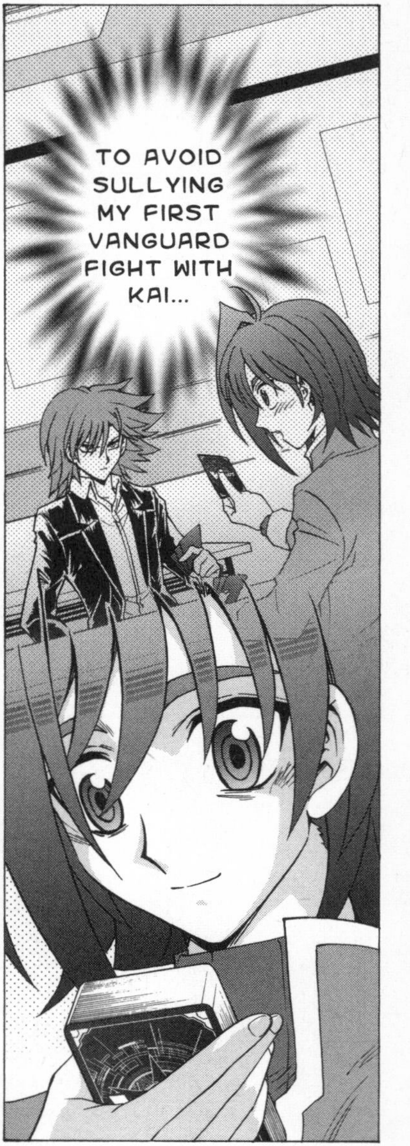
TO AVOID SULLYING MY FIRST VANGUARD FIGHT WITH KAI...

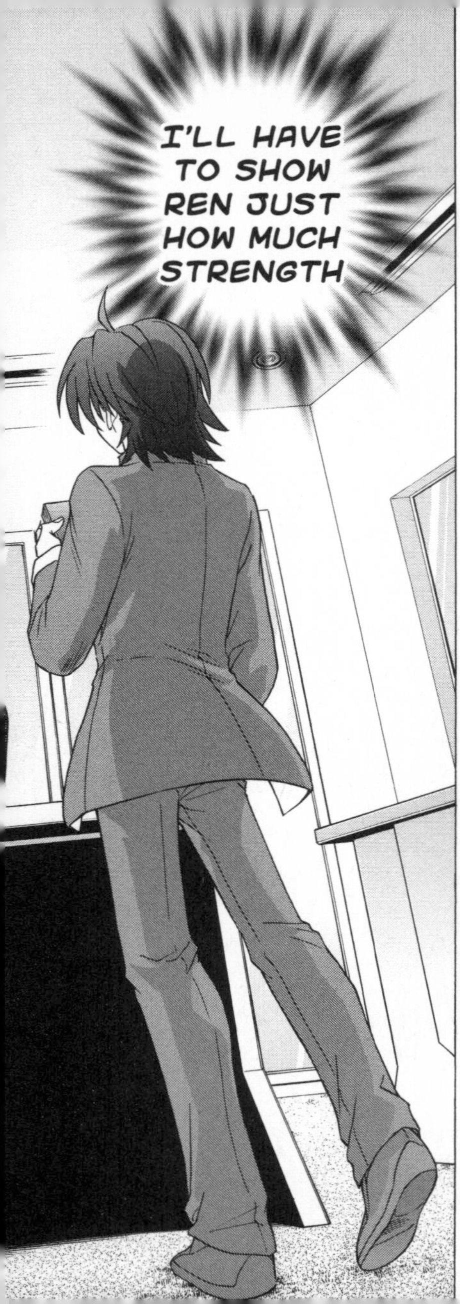
I'LL HAVE TO SHOW REN JUST HOW MUCH STRENGTH

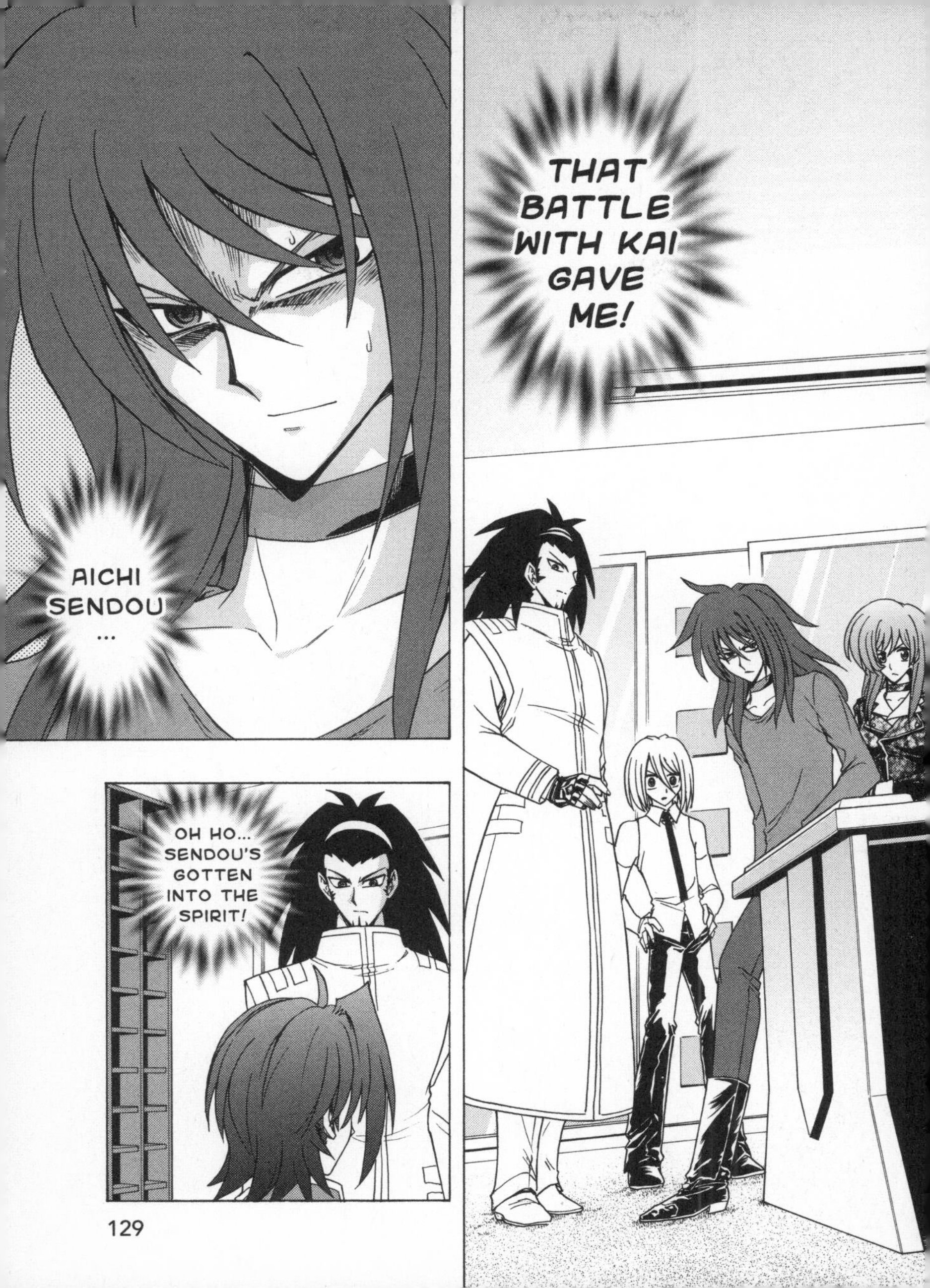
THAT BATTLE WITH KAI GAVE ME!
AICHI SENDOU ...
OH HO... SENDOU'S GOTTEN INTO THE SPIRIT!

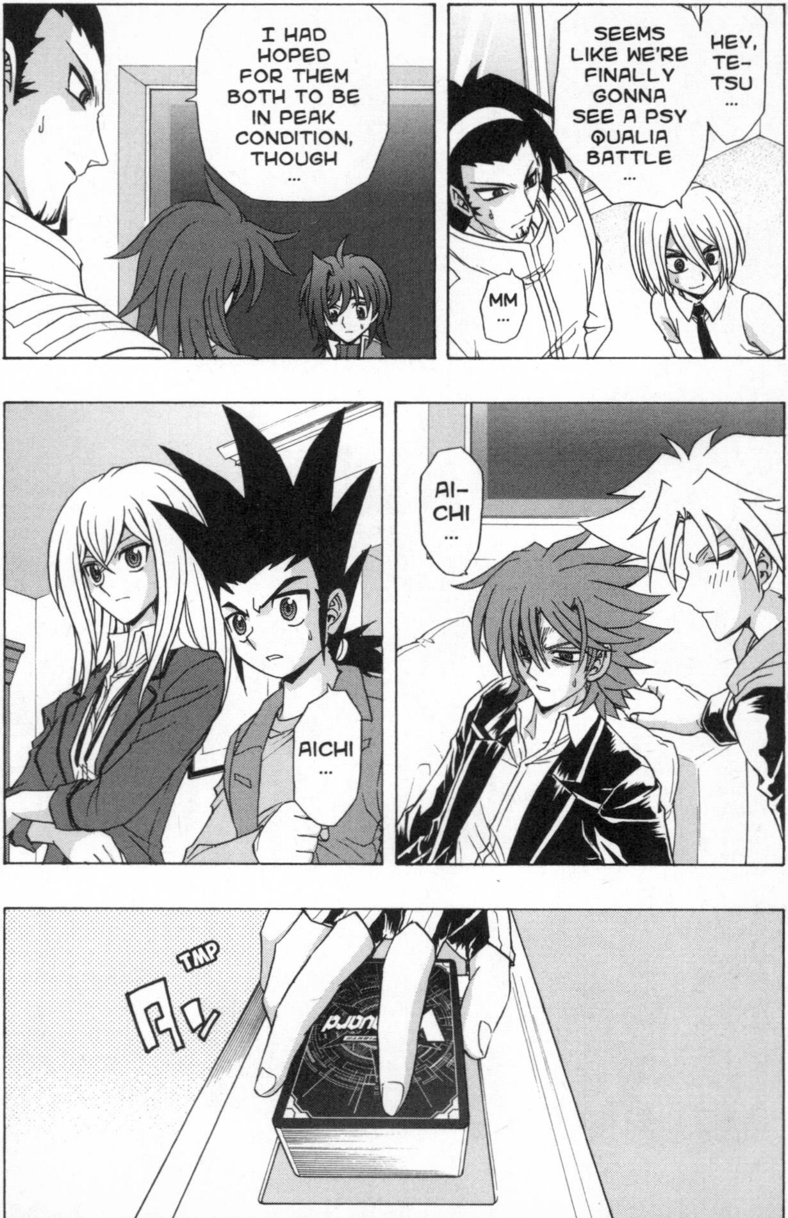
HEY, TE-TSU ...
SEEMS LIKE WE'RE FINALLY GONNA SEE A PSY QUALIA BATTLE ...
MM ...
I HAD HOPED FOR THEM BOTH TO BE IN PEAK CONDITION, THOUGH ...
AI-CHI ...
AICHI ...
TMP

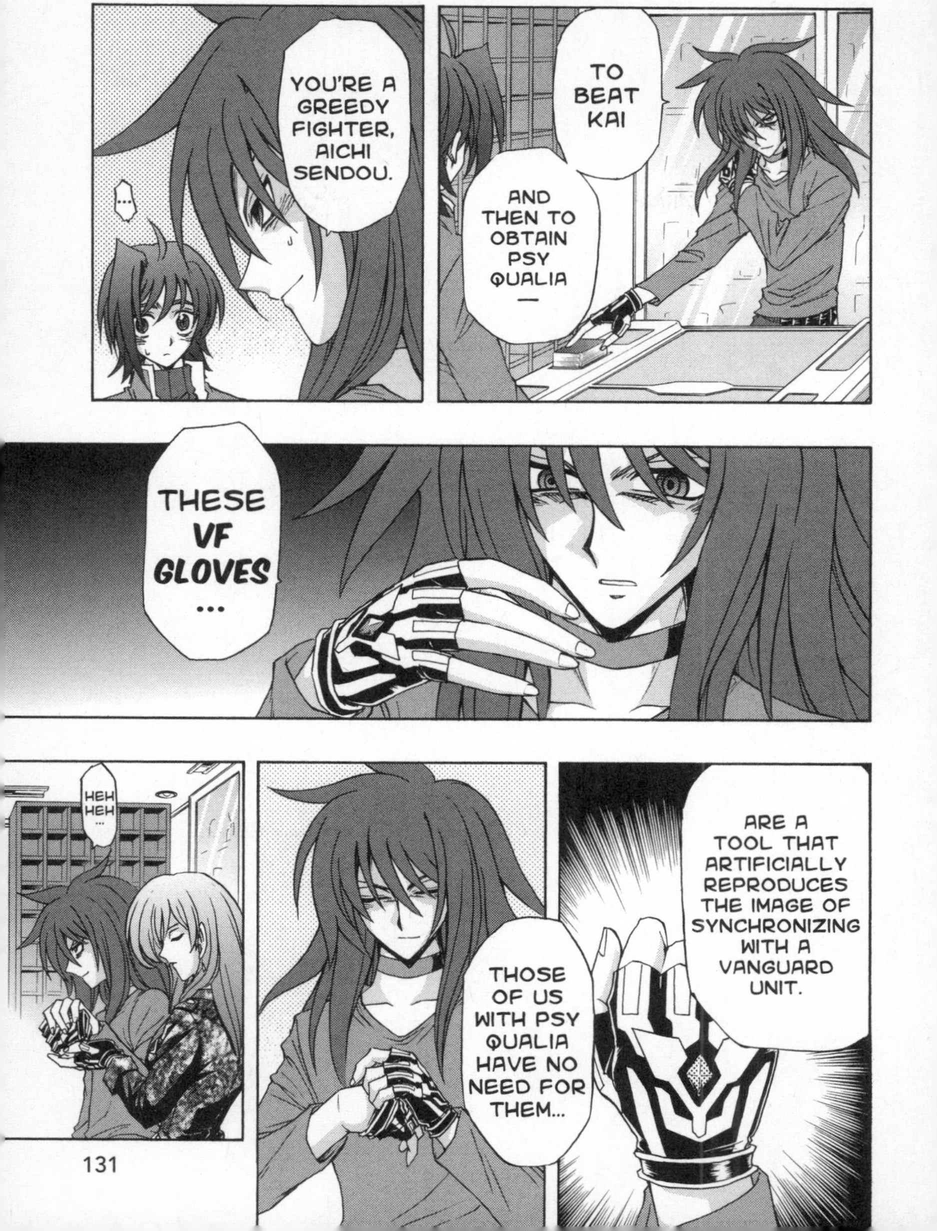
TO BEAT KAI
AND THEN TO OBTAIN PSY QUALIA —
YOU'RE A GREEDY FIGHTER, AICHI SENDOU.
...
THESE **VF GLOVES** ...
ARE A TOOL THAT ARTIFICIALLY REPRODUCES THE IMAGE OF SYNCHRONIZING WITH A VANGUARD UNIT.
THOSE OF US WITH PSY QUALIA HAVE NO NEED FOR THEM...
HEH HEH ...

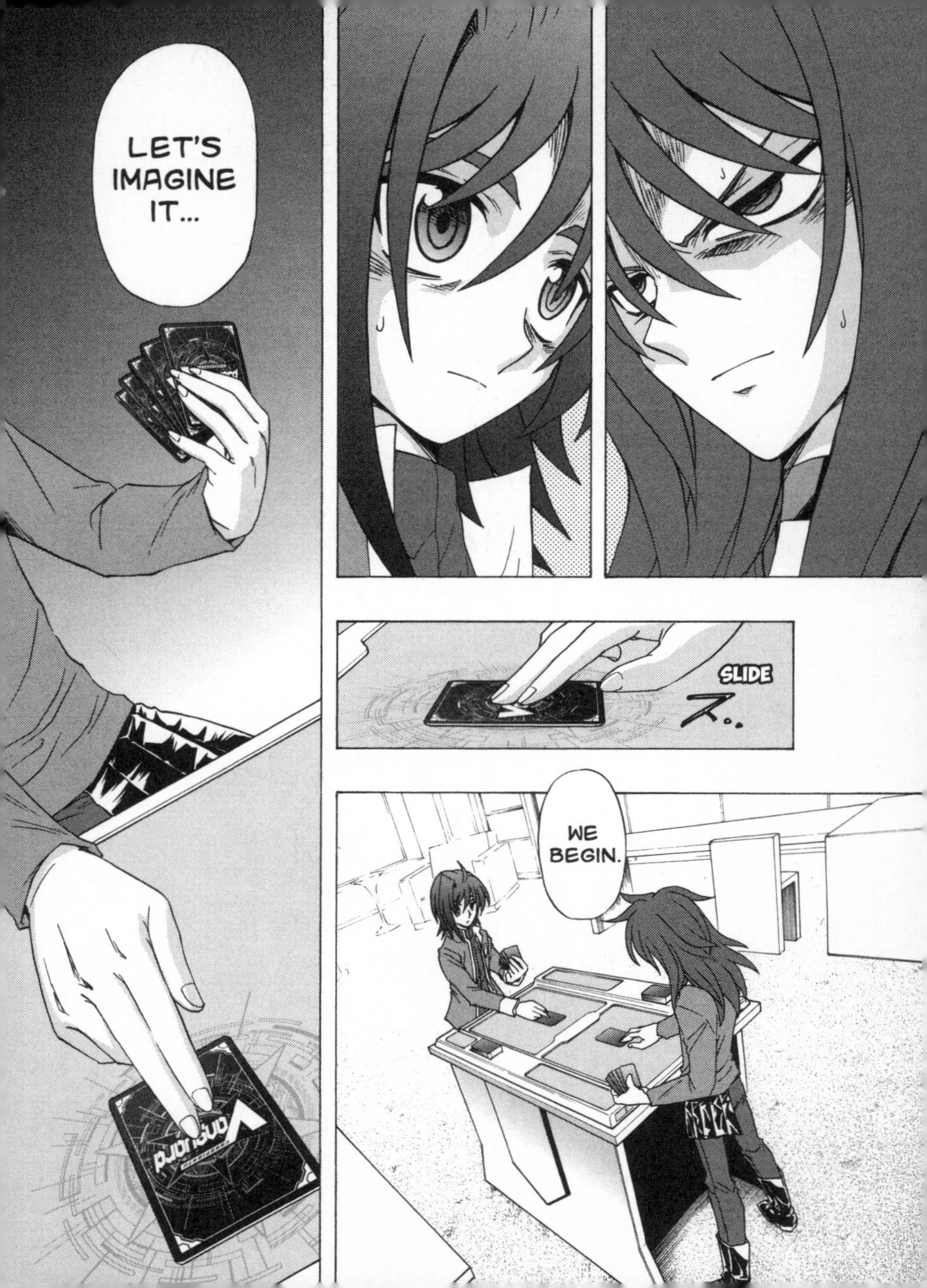
SLIDE
ス..
WE BEGIN.
LET'S IMAGINE IT...

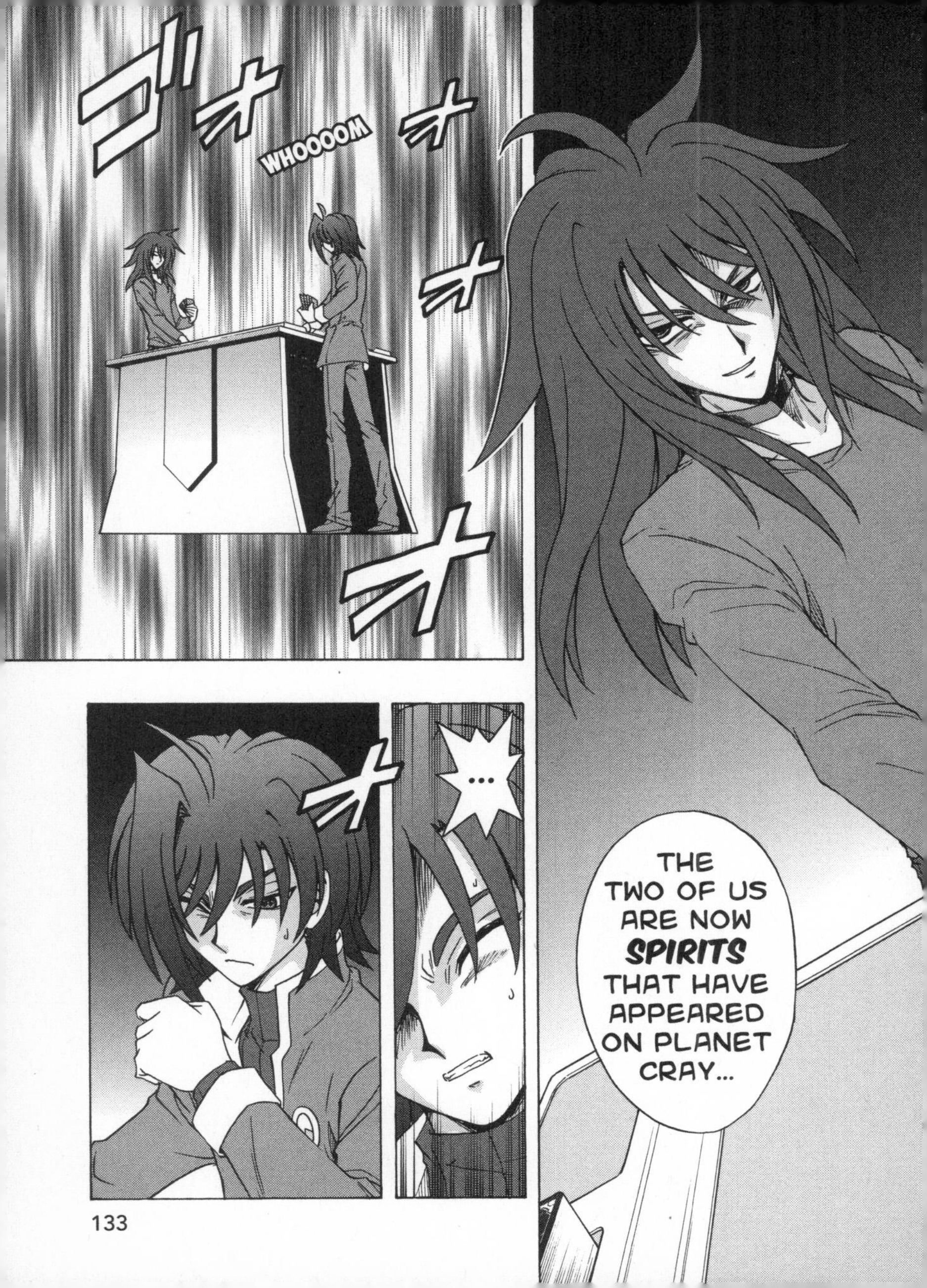
THE TWO OF US ARE NOW **SPIRITS** THAT HAVE APPEARED ON PLANET CRAY...
WHOOOOM
...

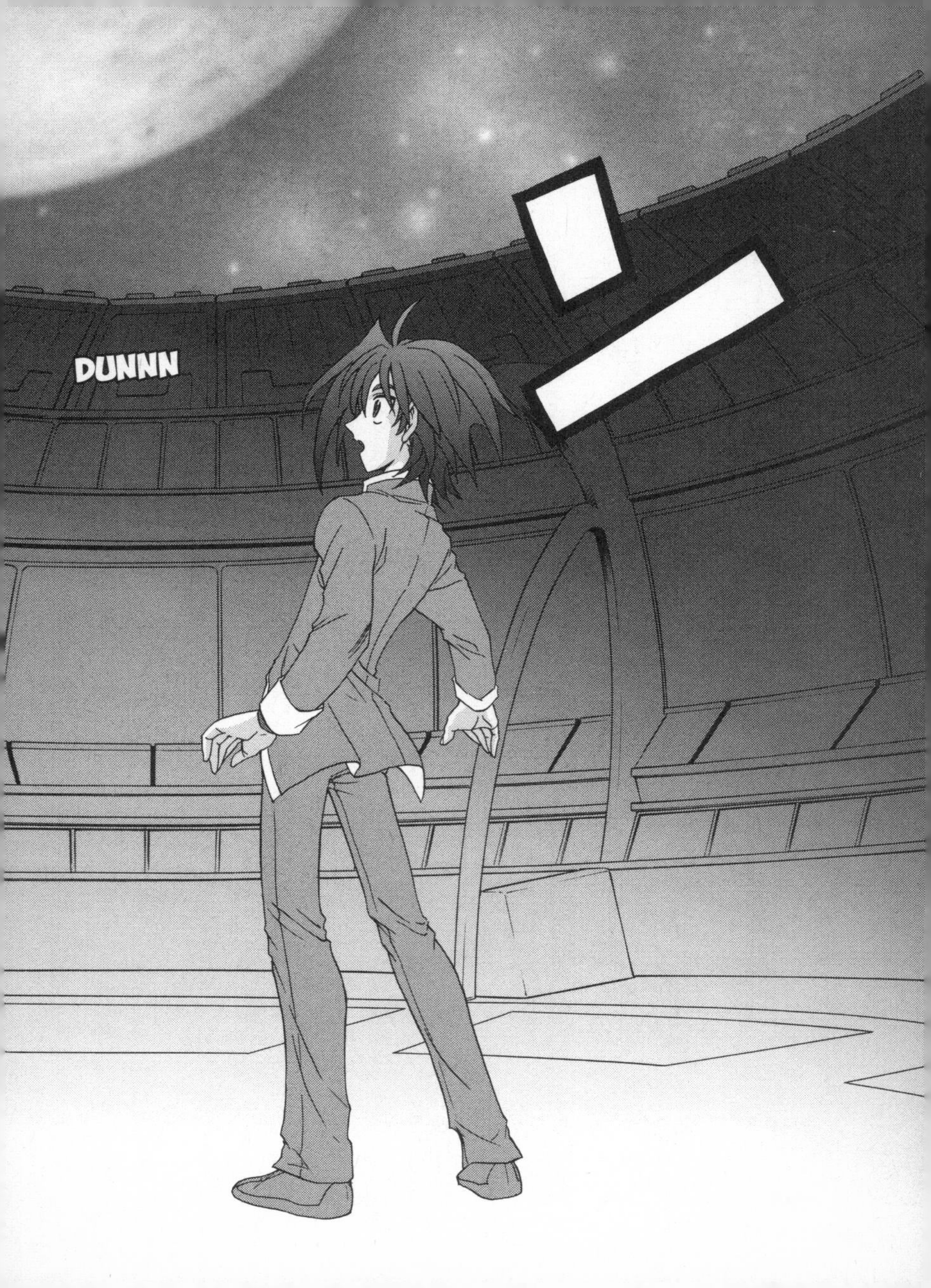
DUNNN

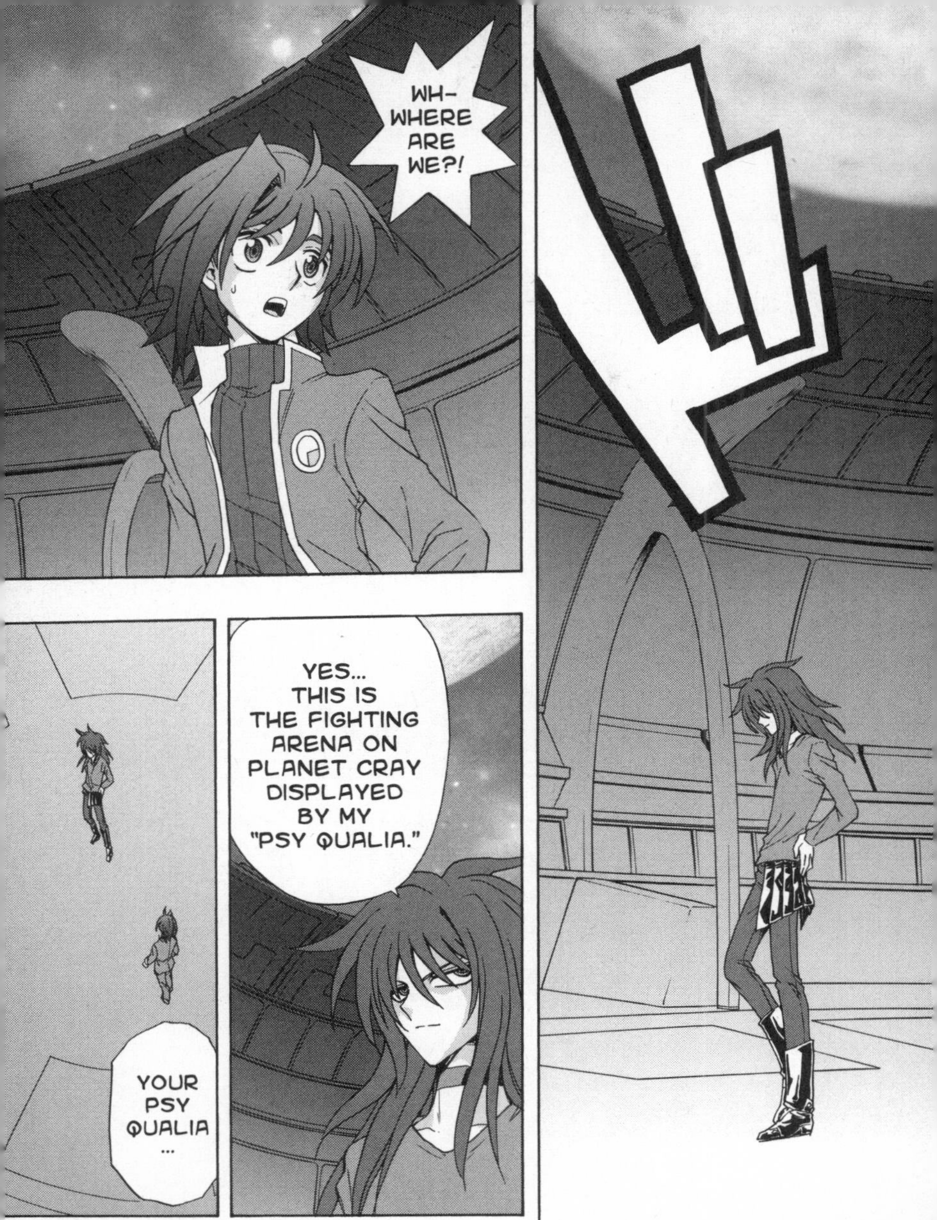
WH- WHERE ARE WE?!
YES... THIS IS THE FIGHTING ARENA ON PLANET CRAY DISPLAYED BY MY "PSY QUALIA."
YOUR PSY QUALIA ...

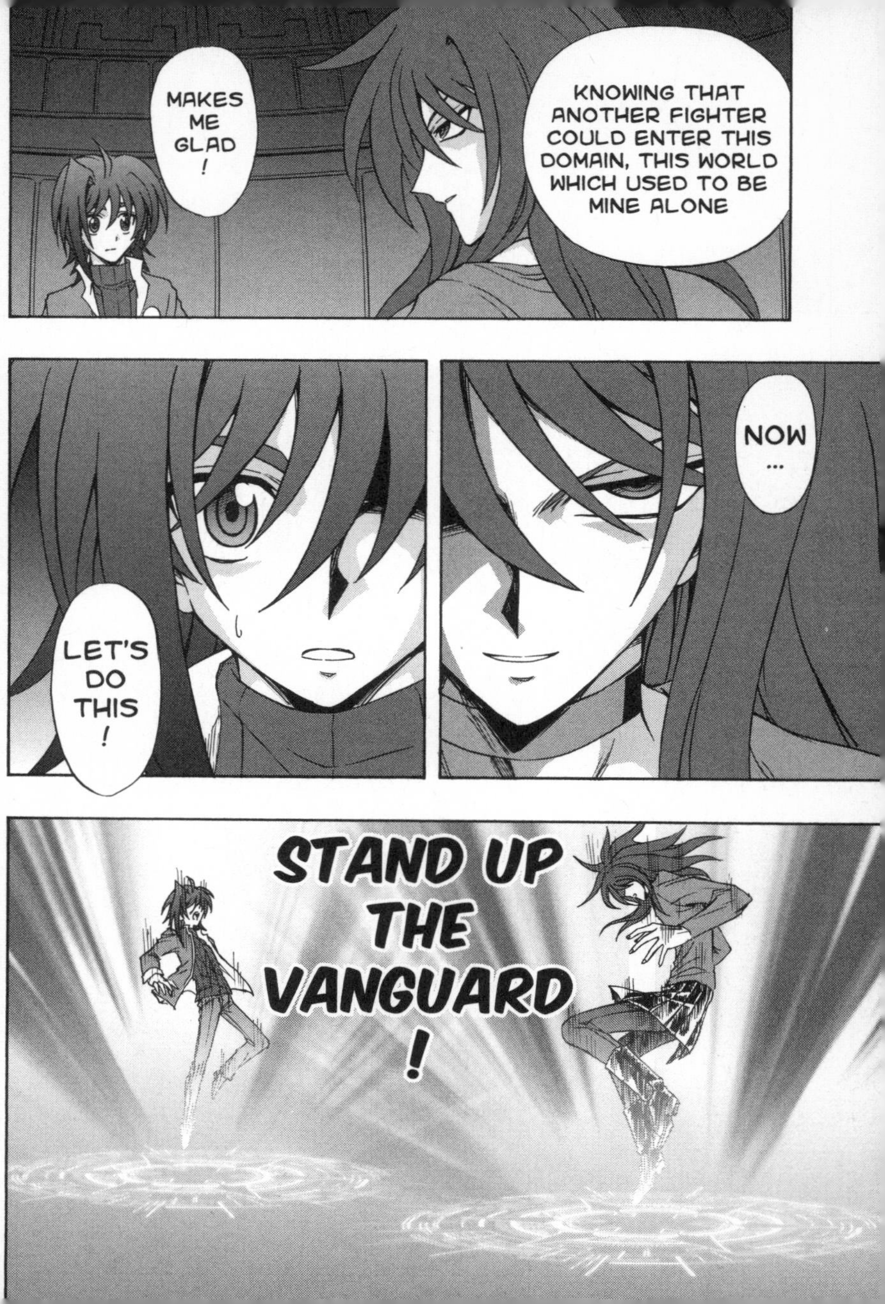
KNOWING THAT ANOTHER FIGHTER COULD ENTER THIS DOMAIN, THIS WORLD WHICH USED TO BE MINE ALONE
MAKES ME GLAD!
NOW...
LET'S DO THIS!
STAND UP THE VANGUARD!

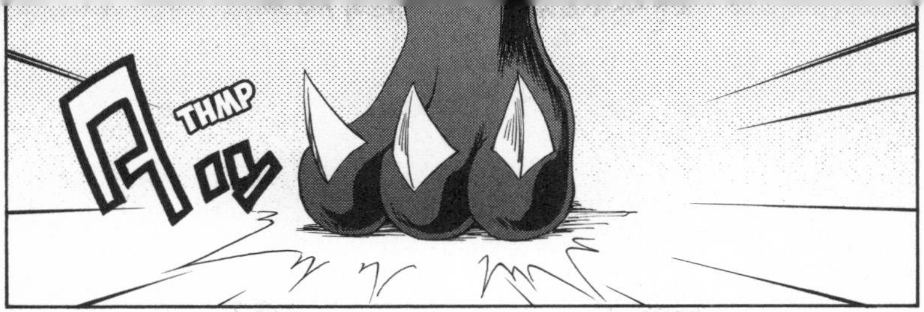
THMP
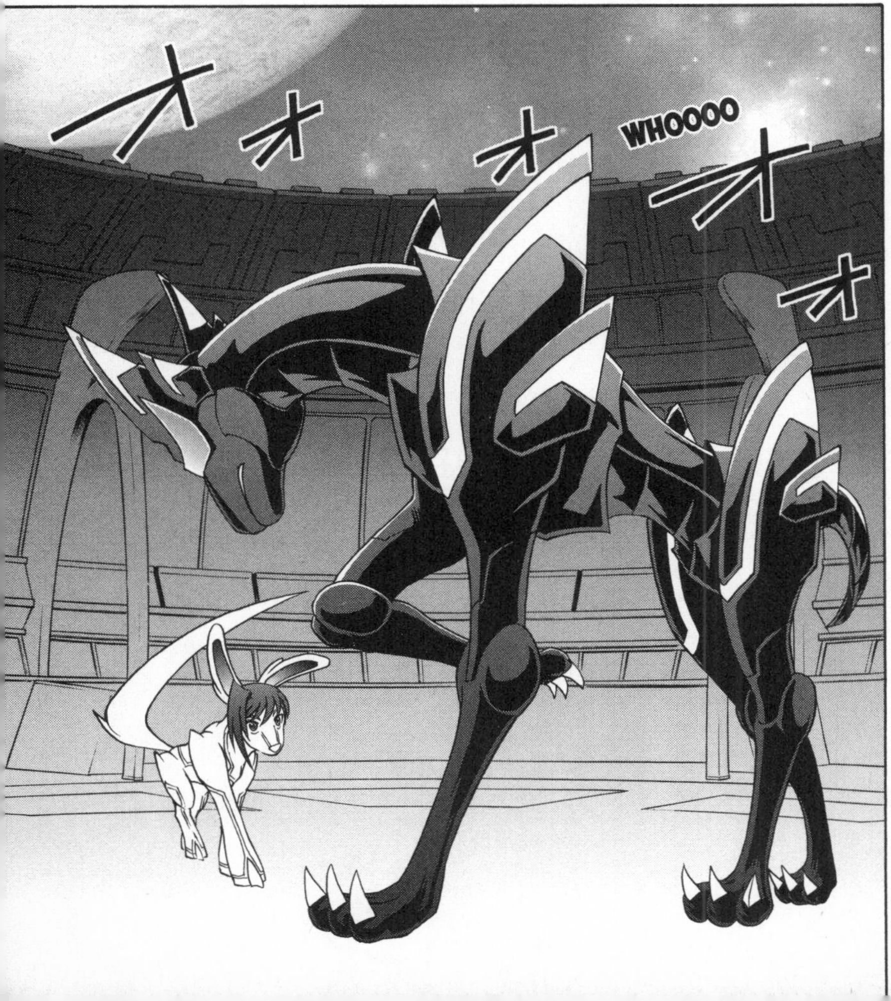
WHOOOO

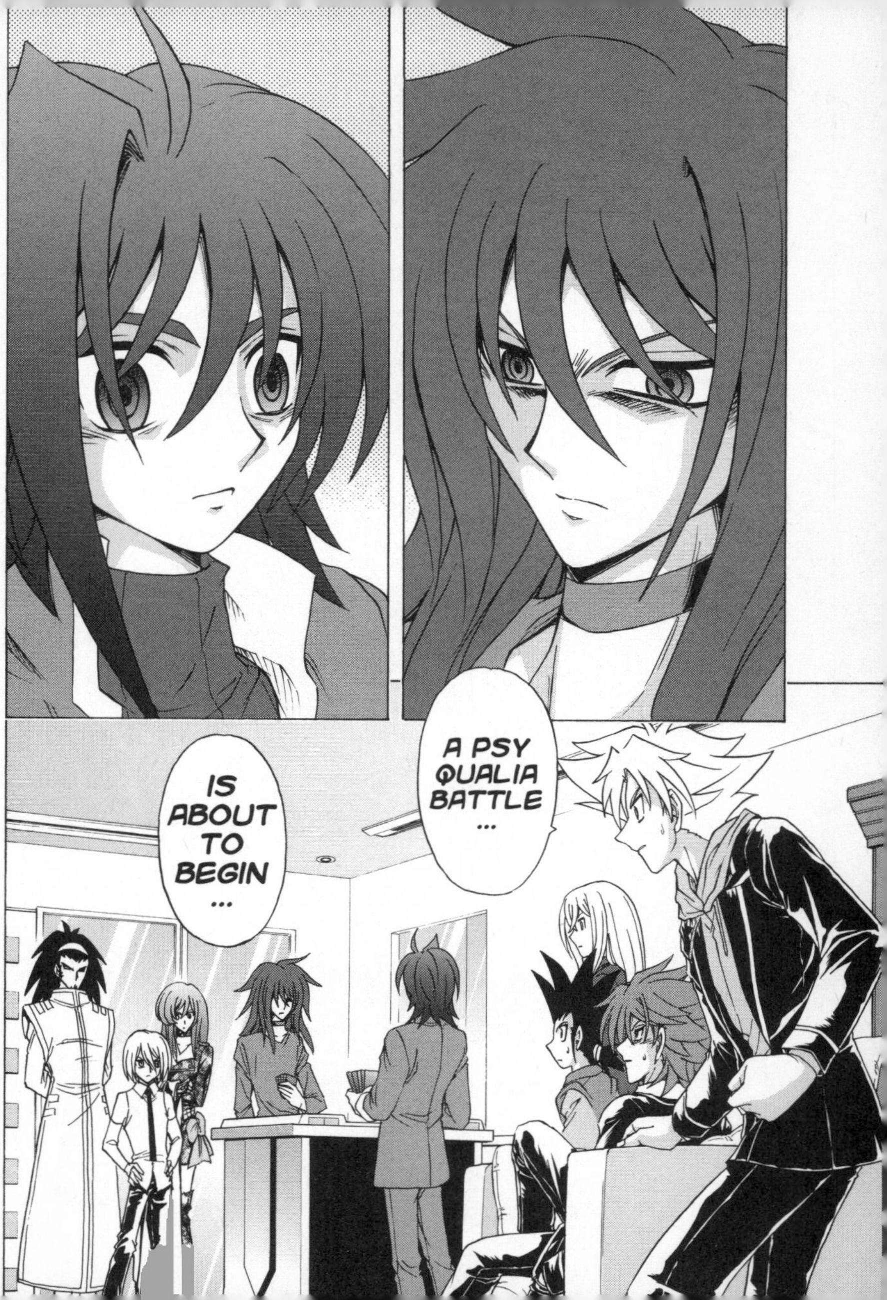
A PSY QUALIA BATTLE ...
IS ABOUT TO BEGIN ...

BONUS! CARDFIGHT!! Vanguard NEVER-BEFORE-SEEN IMAGE BOARDS — CHARACTERS

◎ Always in regular clothes other than when they're clearly going to and from school. No sending them to camp wearing school uniforms.

Summer Clothes (Fall Semester)

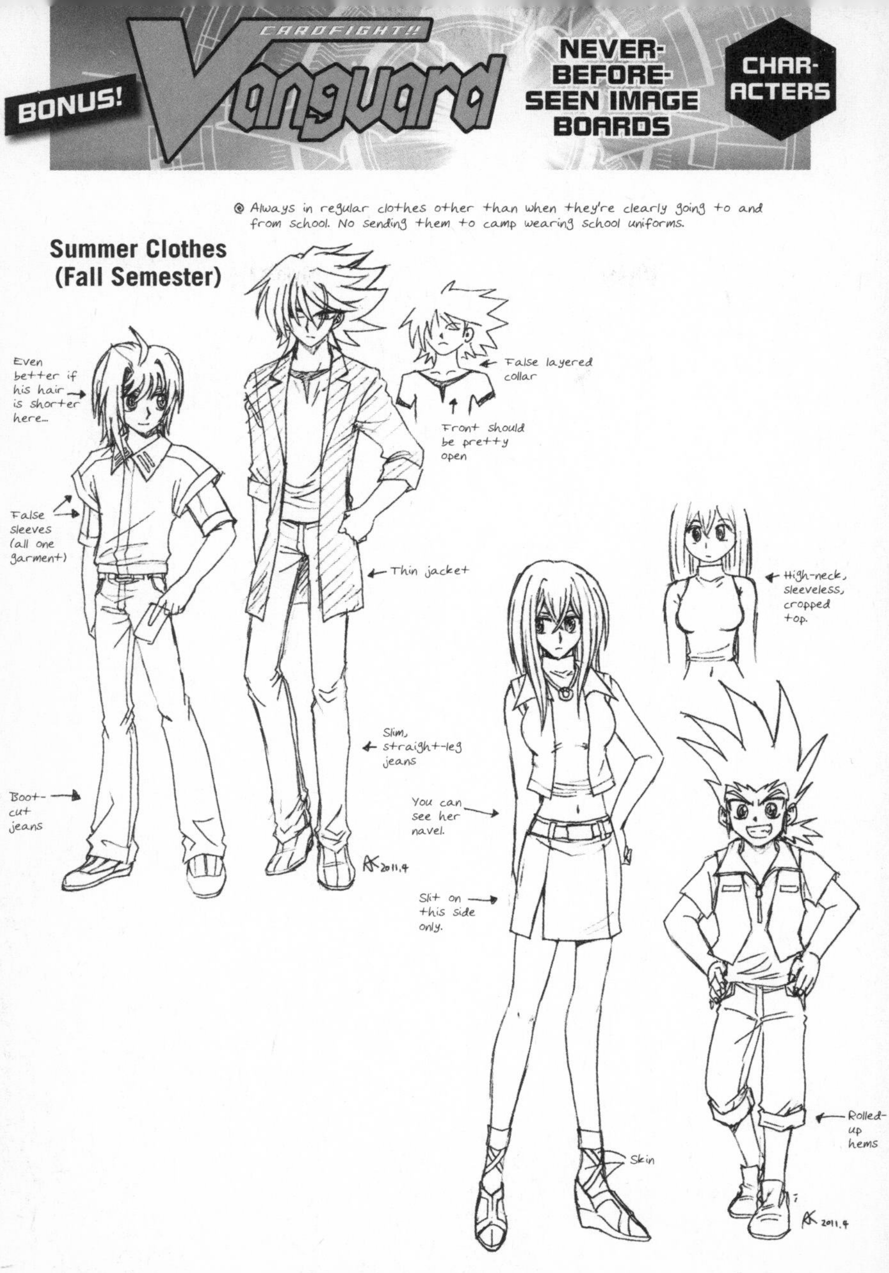

Even better if his hair is shorter here...
False sleeves (all one garment)
Boot-cut jeans
Thin jacket
Slim, straight-leg jeans
AK 2011.4
False layered collar
Front should be pretty open
High-neck, sleeveless, cropped top.
You can see her navel.
Slit on this side only.
Skin
Rolled-up hems
AK 2011.4

BONUS! CARDFIGHT!! Vanguard

NEVER-BEFORE-SEEN IMAGE BOARDS

CHAR-ACTERS

Hitsue Middle School Summer Uniforms

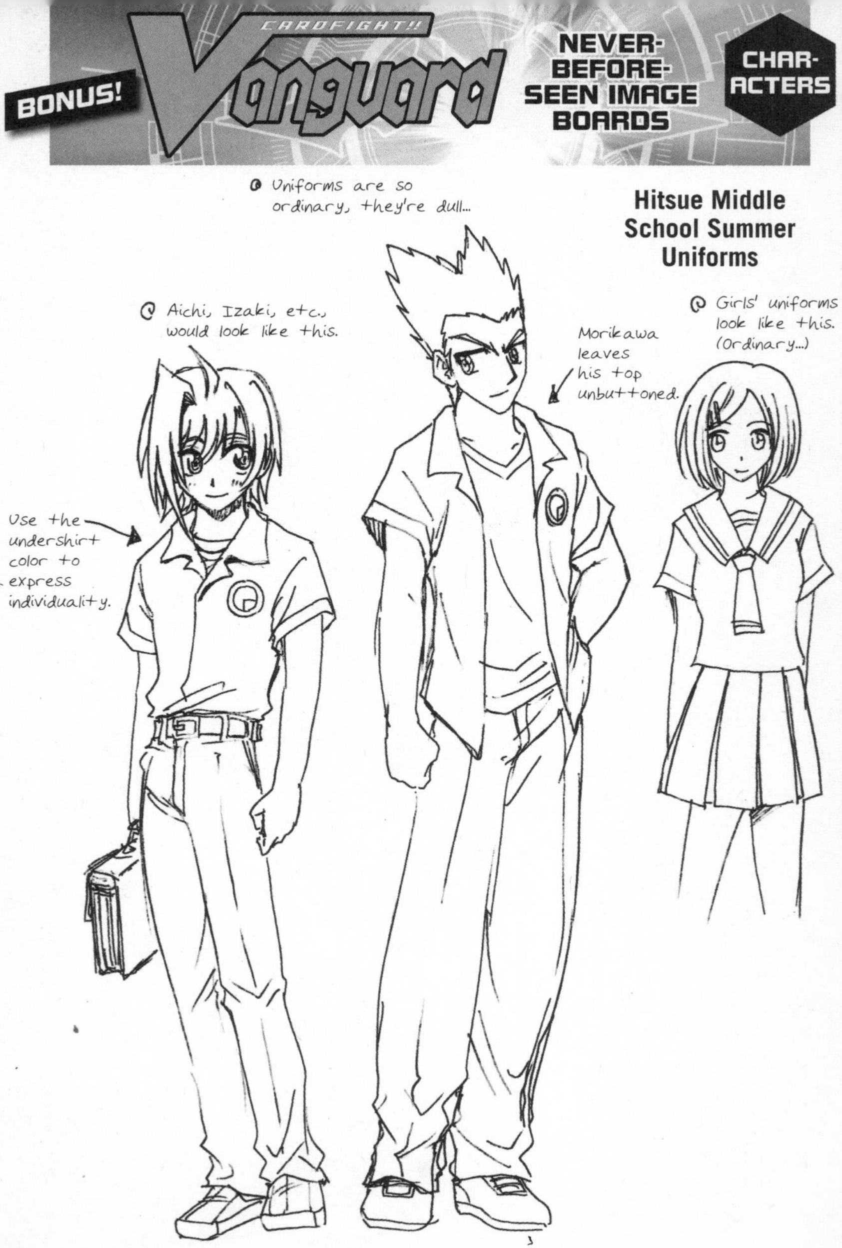

Uniforms are so ordinary, they're dull...
Aichi, Izaki, etc., would look like this.
Morikawa leaves his top unbuttoned.
Girls' uniforms look like this. (Ordinary...)
Use the undershirt color to express individuality.

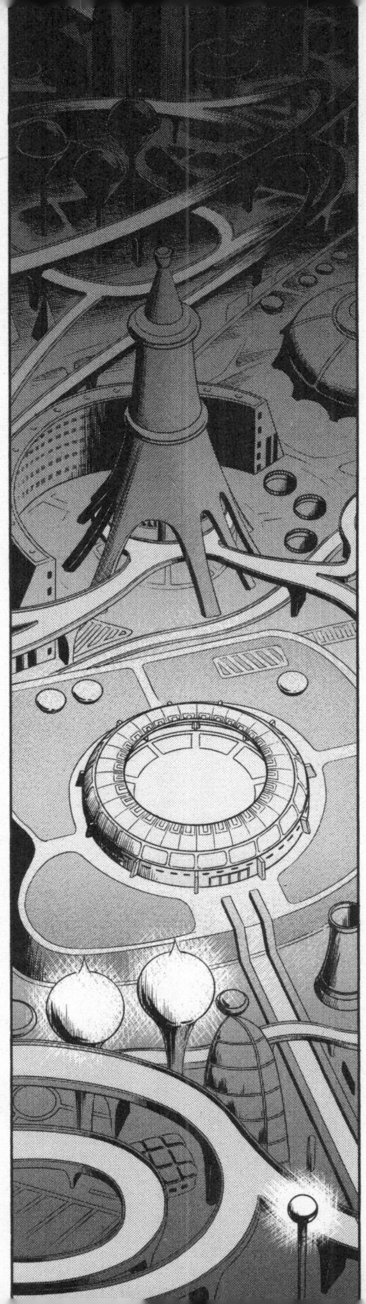

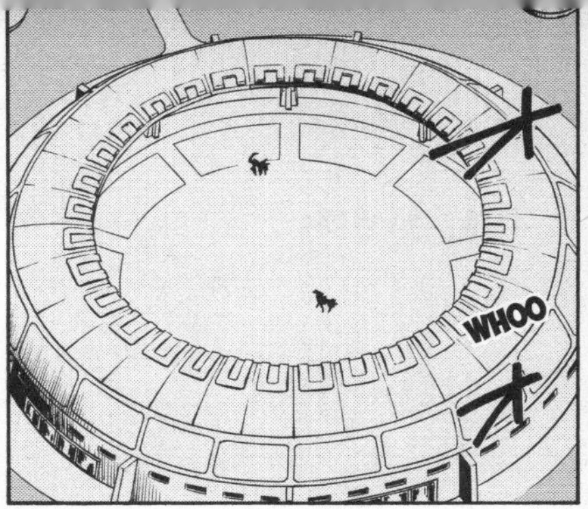
WHOO

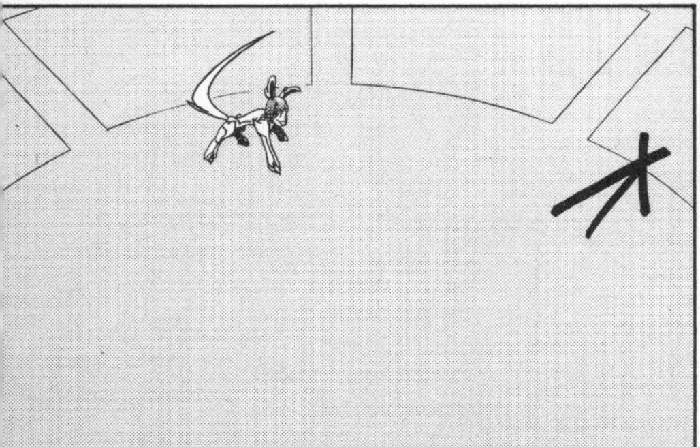
OOO

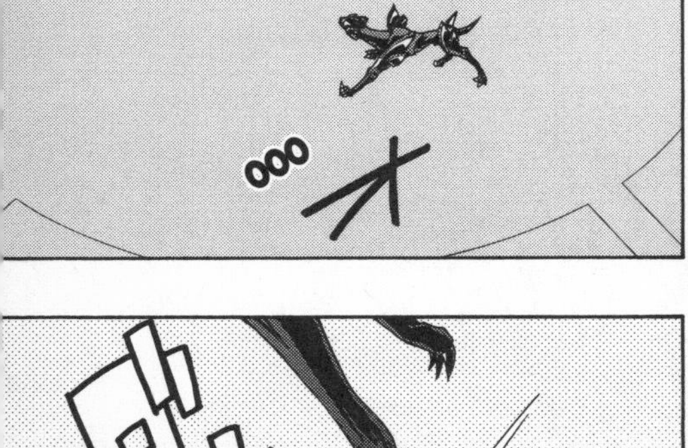
KICK

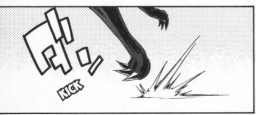

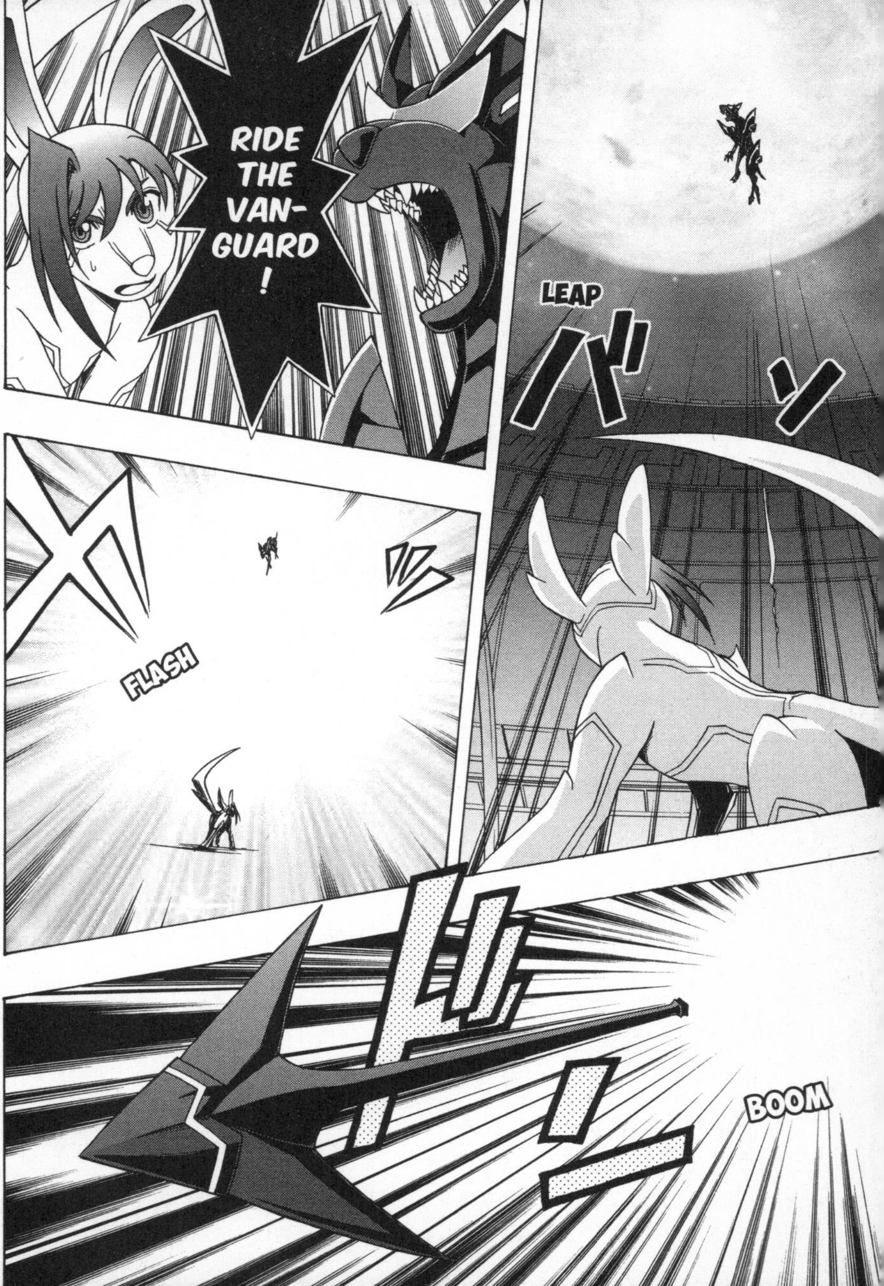
LEAP
バッ
RIDE THE VAN-GUARD!
FLASH
BOOM

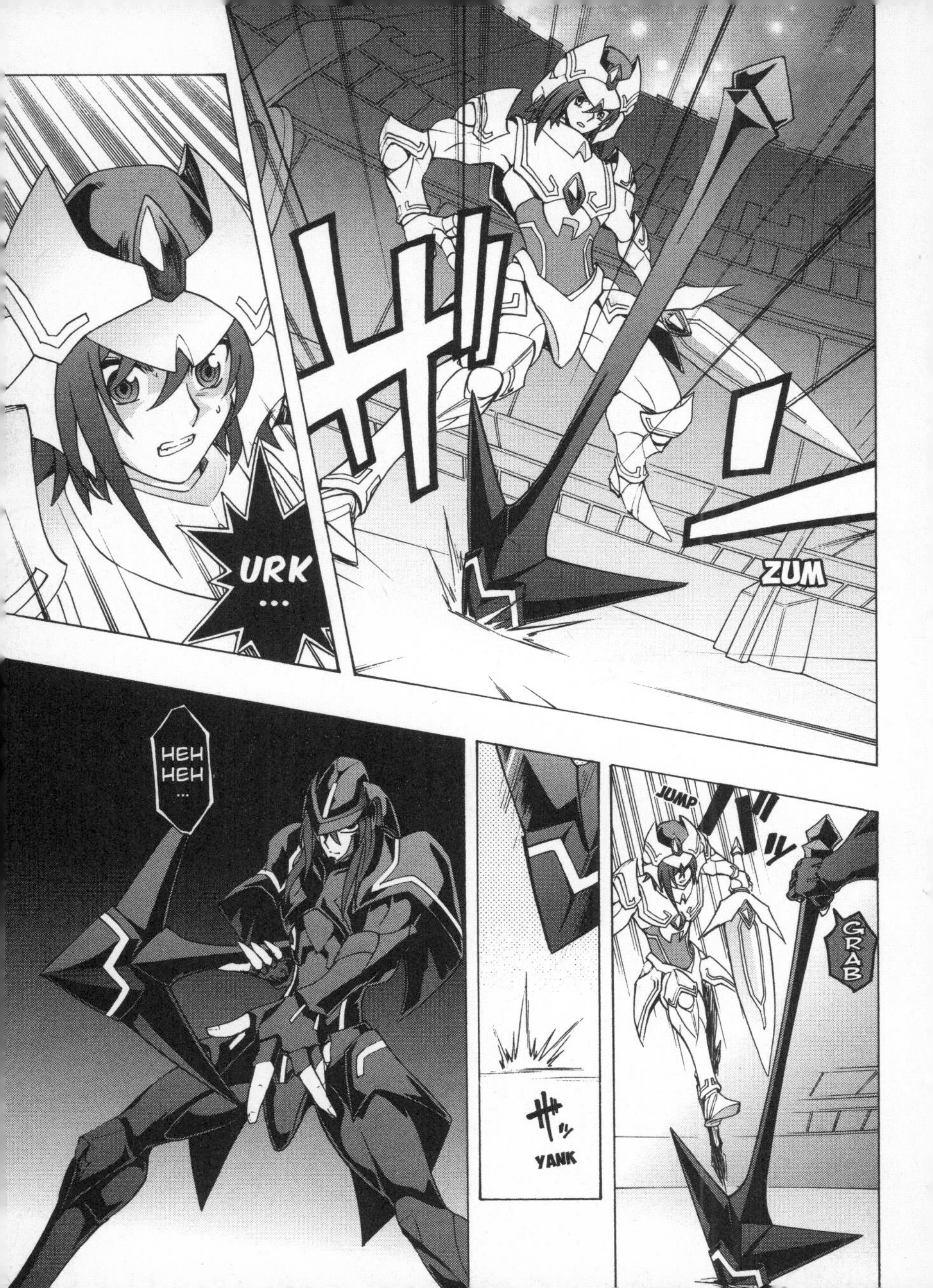
ZUM
URK
...
JUMP
GRAB
YANK
HEH
HEH
...

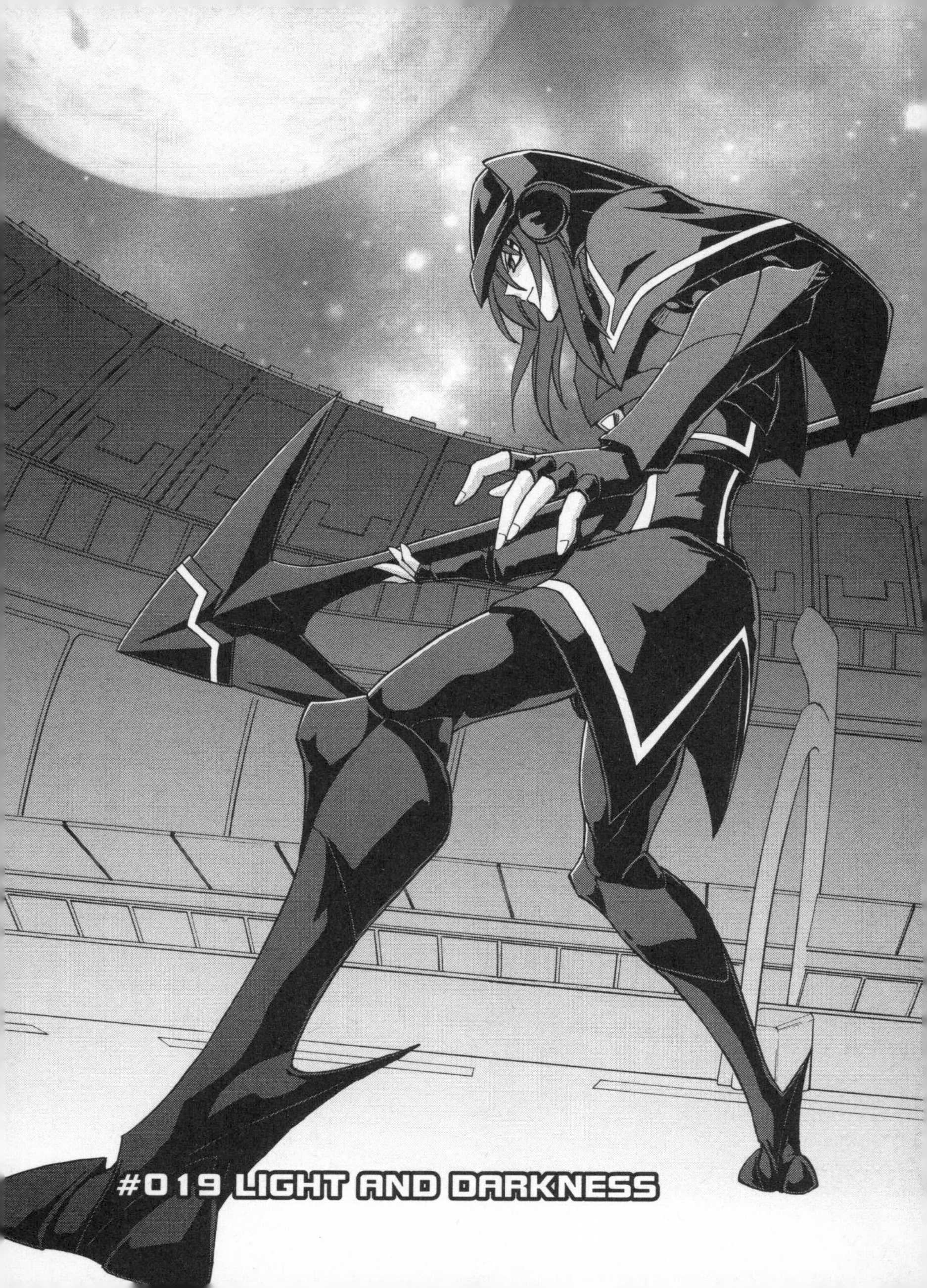
#019 LIGHT AND DARKNESS

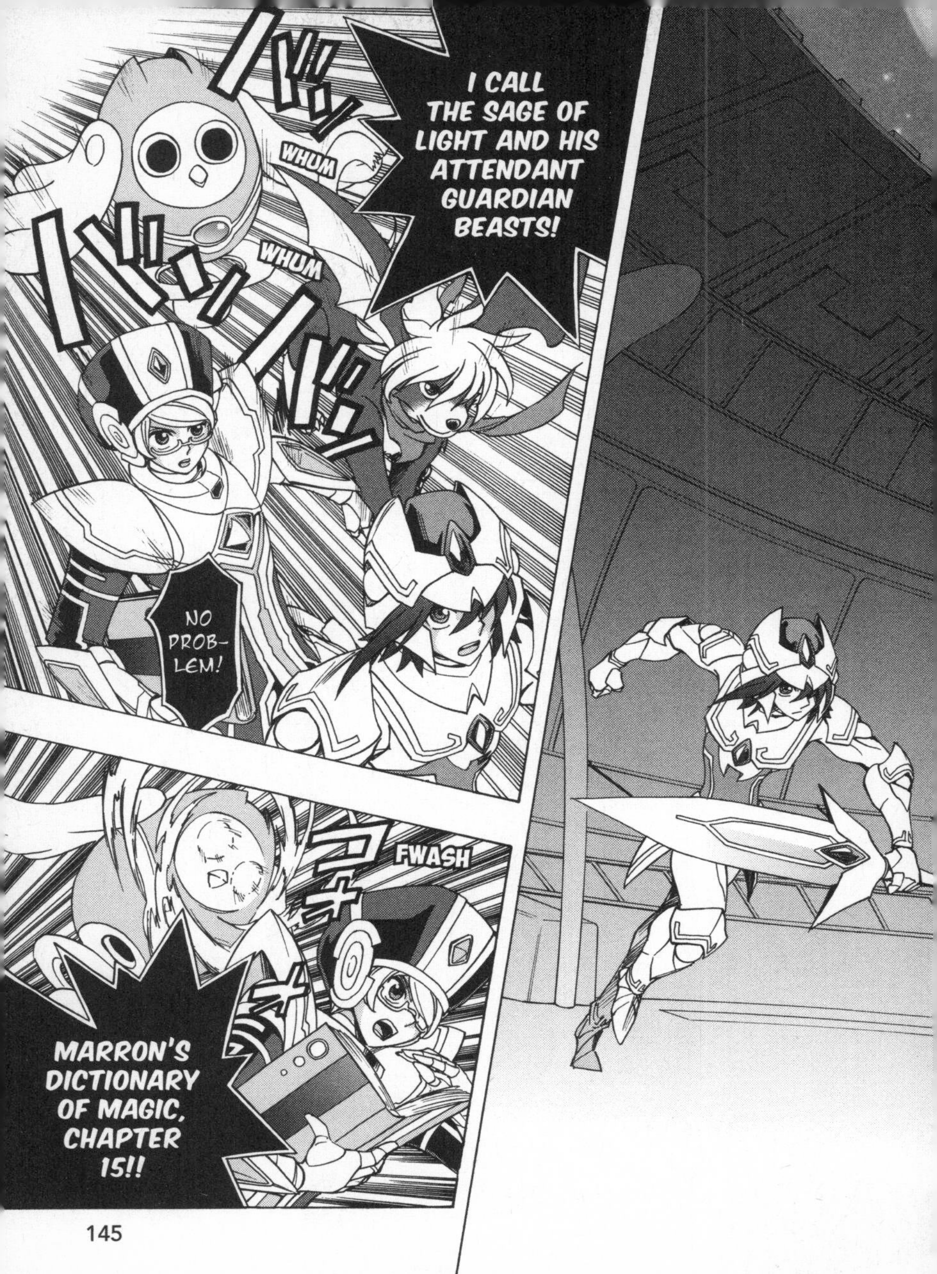
I CALL THE SAGE OF LIGHT AND HIS ATTENDANT GUARDIAN BEASTS!
WHUM
WHUM
NO PROB-LEM!
FWASH
MARRON'S DICTIONARY OF MAGIC, CHAPTER 15!!

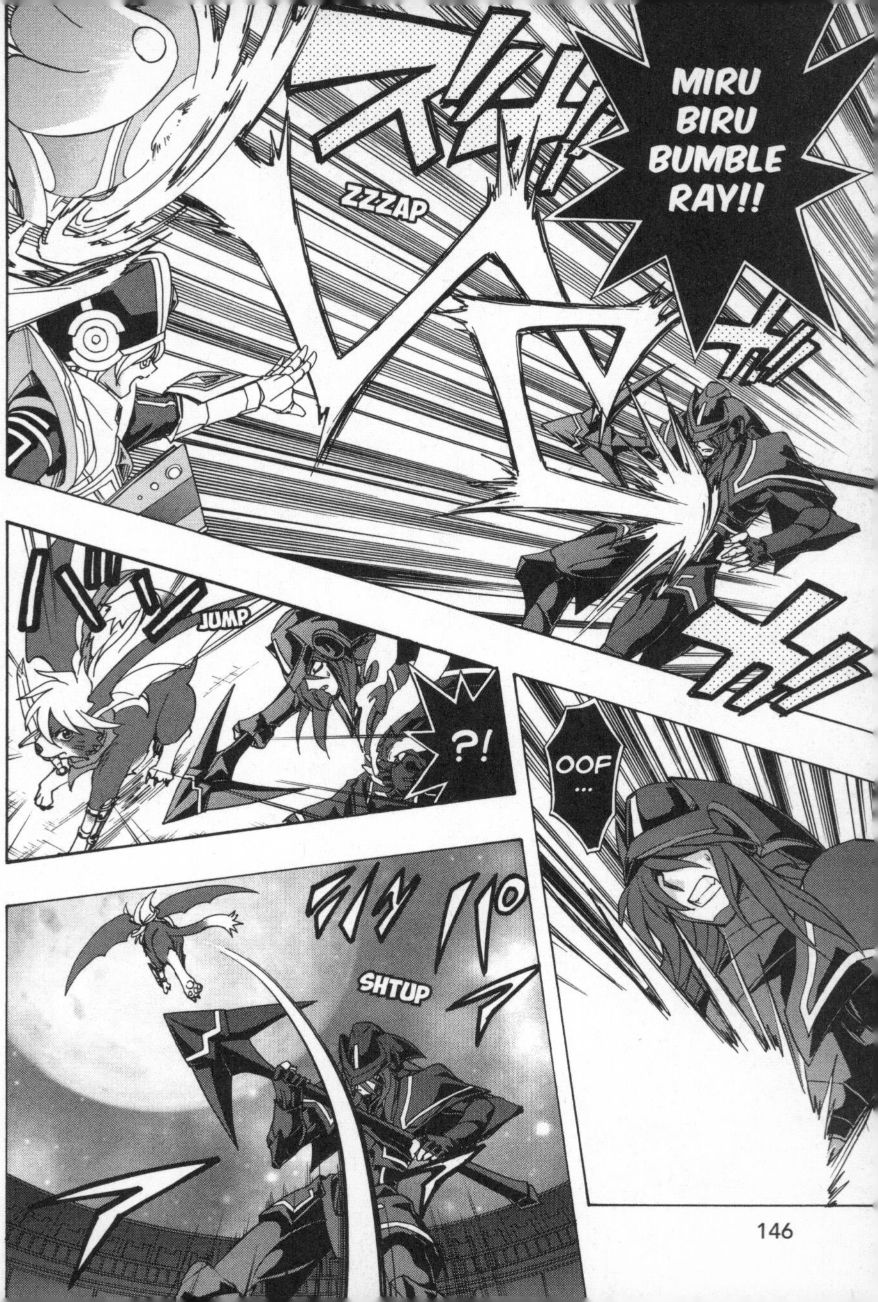
MIRU BIRU BUMBLE RAY!!
ZZZAP
OOF ...
?!
JUMP
SHTUP

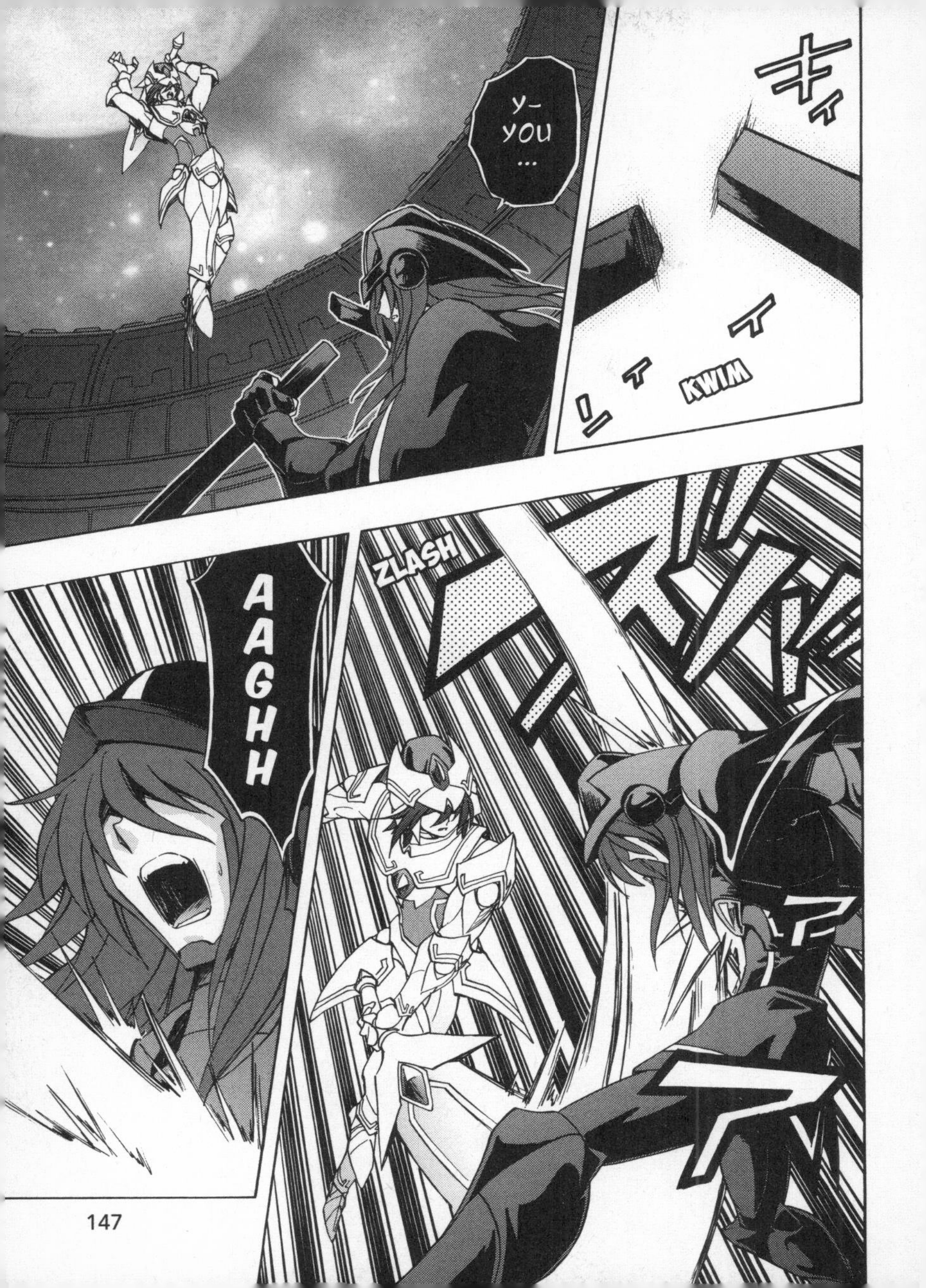
KWIM
Y-YOU ...
ZLASH
AAGHH

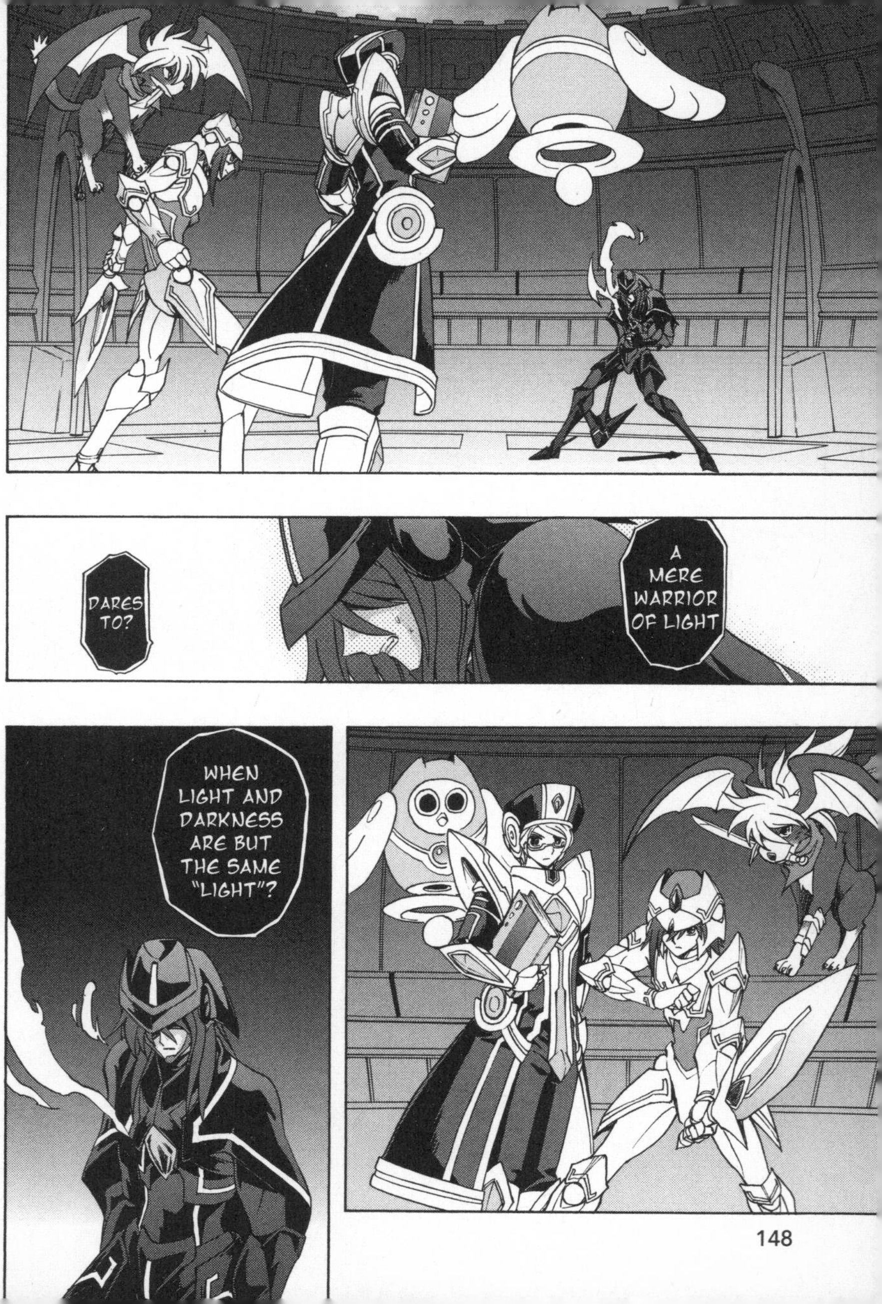
A MERE WARRIOR OF LIGHT
DARES TO?
WHEN LIGHT AND DARKNESS ARE BUT THE SAME "LIGHT"?

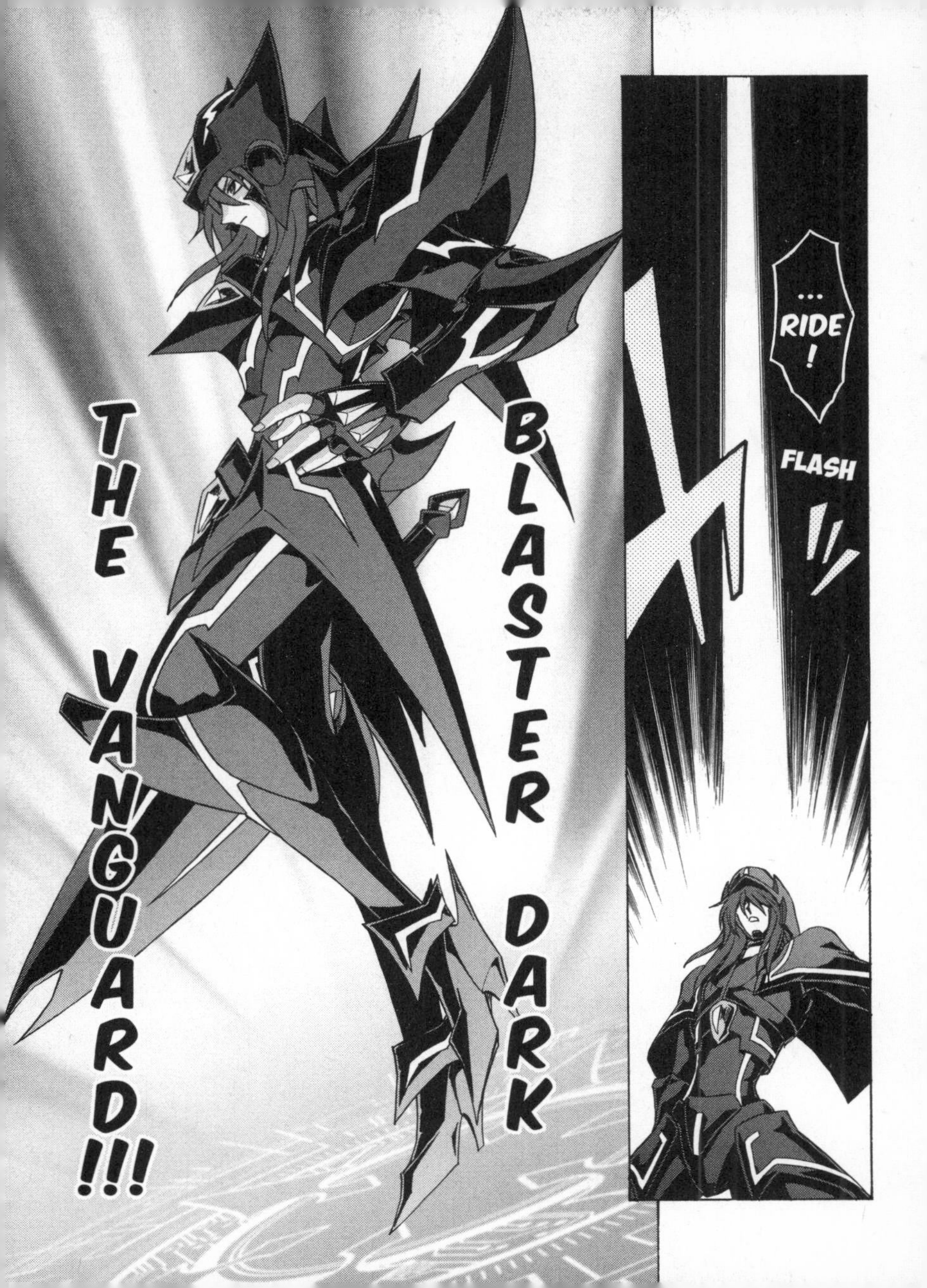
...RIDE!
FLASH
BLASTER DARK
THE VANGUARD!!!

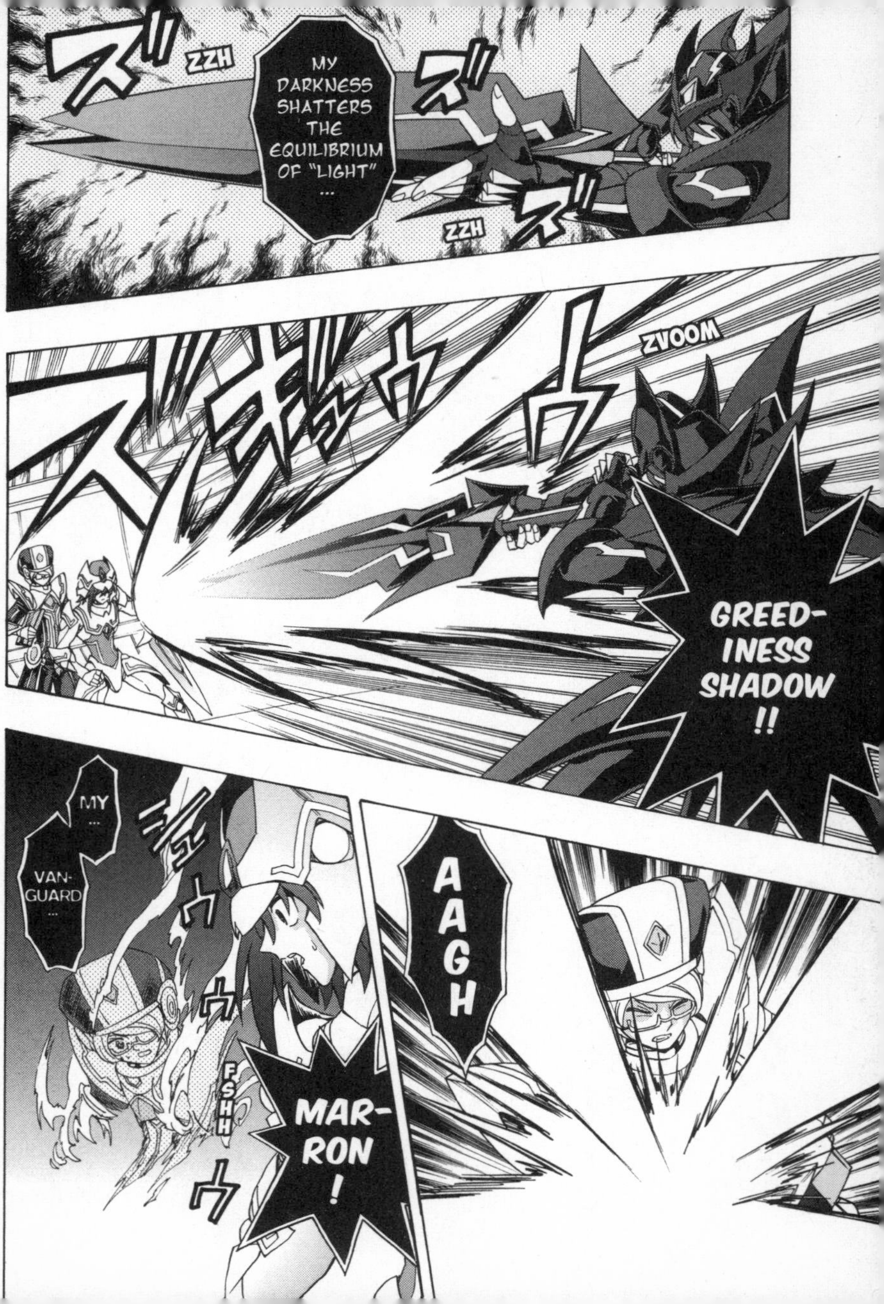
ZZH
MY DARKNESS SHATTERS THE EQUILIBRIUM OF "LIGHT" ...
ZZH
ZVOOM
GREED-INESS SHADOW !!
MAR-RON !
AAGH
MY ... VAN-GUARD ...
FSHH

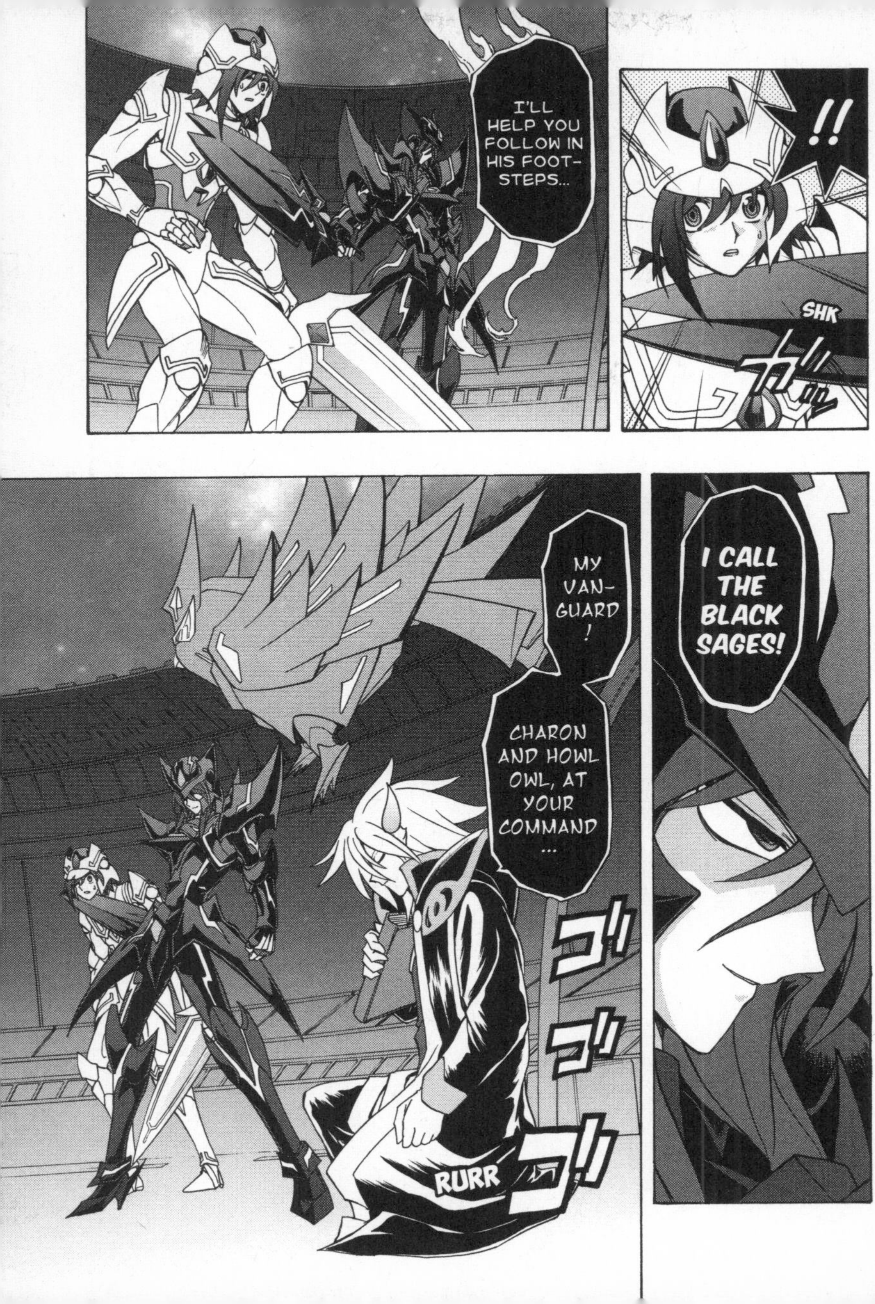
!!
SHK
I'LL HELP YOU FOLLOW IN HIS FOOT-STEPS...
I CALL THE BLACK SAGES!
MY VAN-GUARD!
CHARON AND HOWL OWL, AT YOUR COMMAND...
RURR

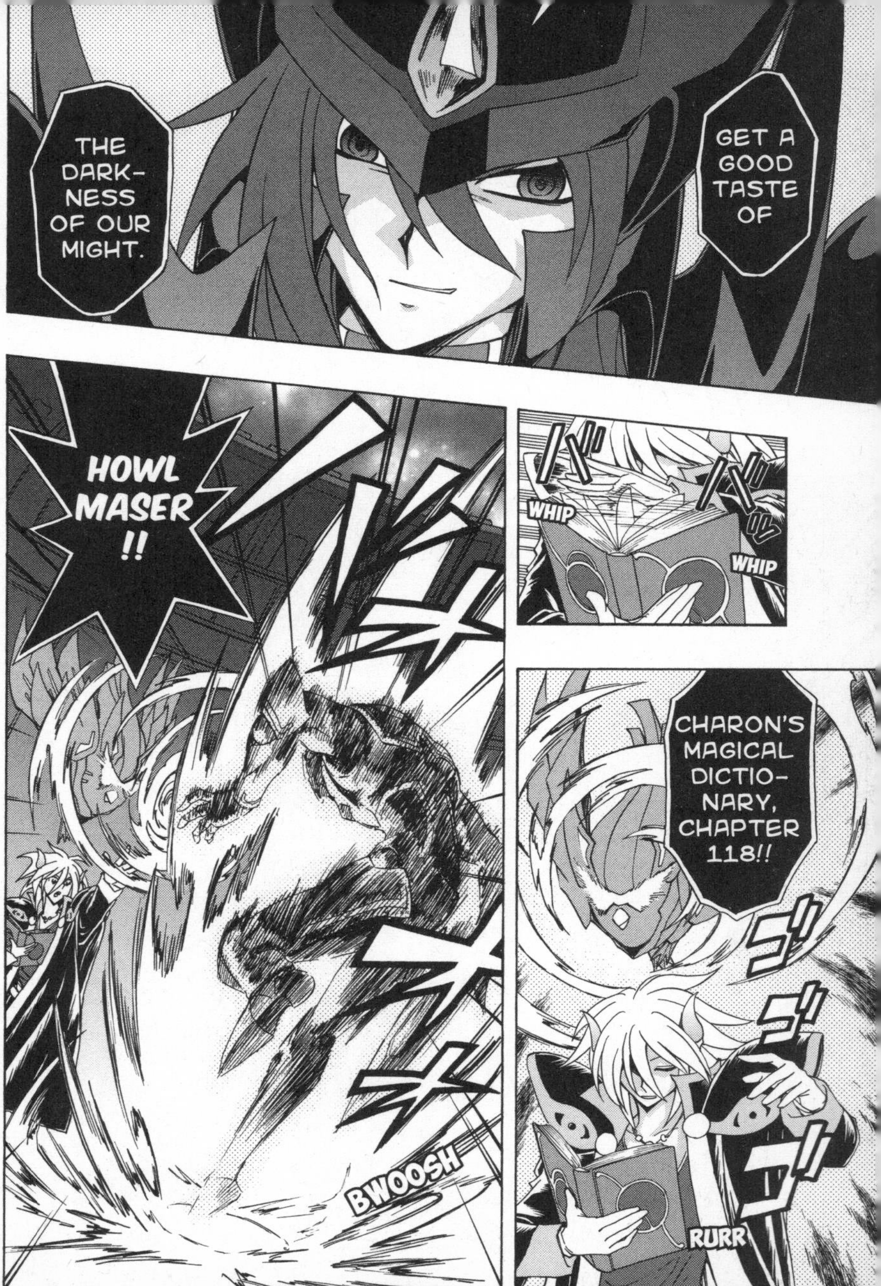
GET A GOOD TASTE OF
THE DARK-NESS OF OUR MIGHT.
WHIP
WHIP
CHARON'S MAGICAL DICTIO-NARY, CHAPTER 118!!
RURR
HOWL MASER !!
BWOOSH

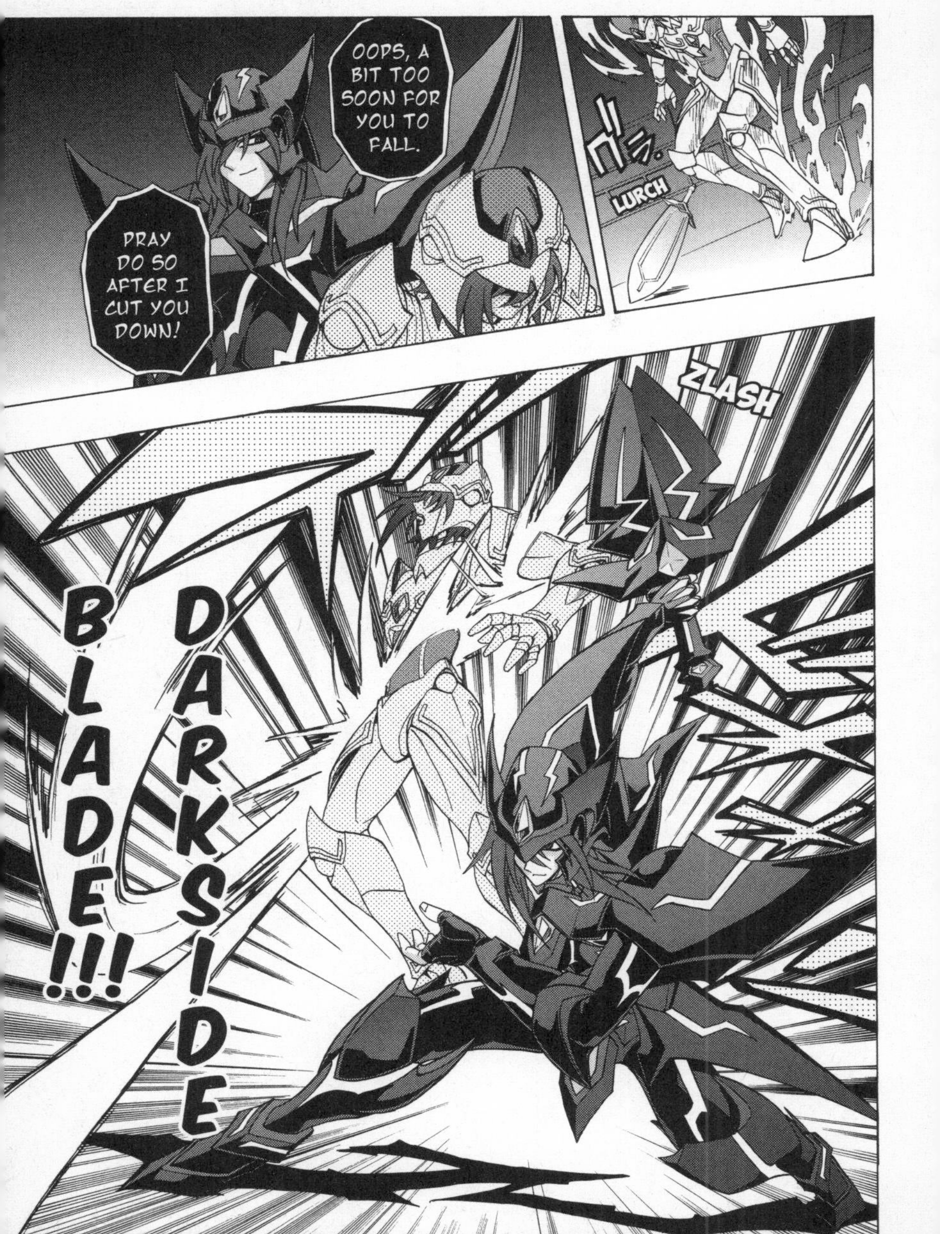
LURCH
OOPS, A BIT TOO SOON FOR YOU TO FALL.
PRAY DO SO AFTER I CUT YOU DOWN!
ZLASH
DARKSIDE
BLADE!!!

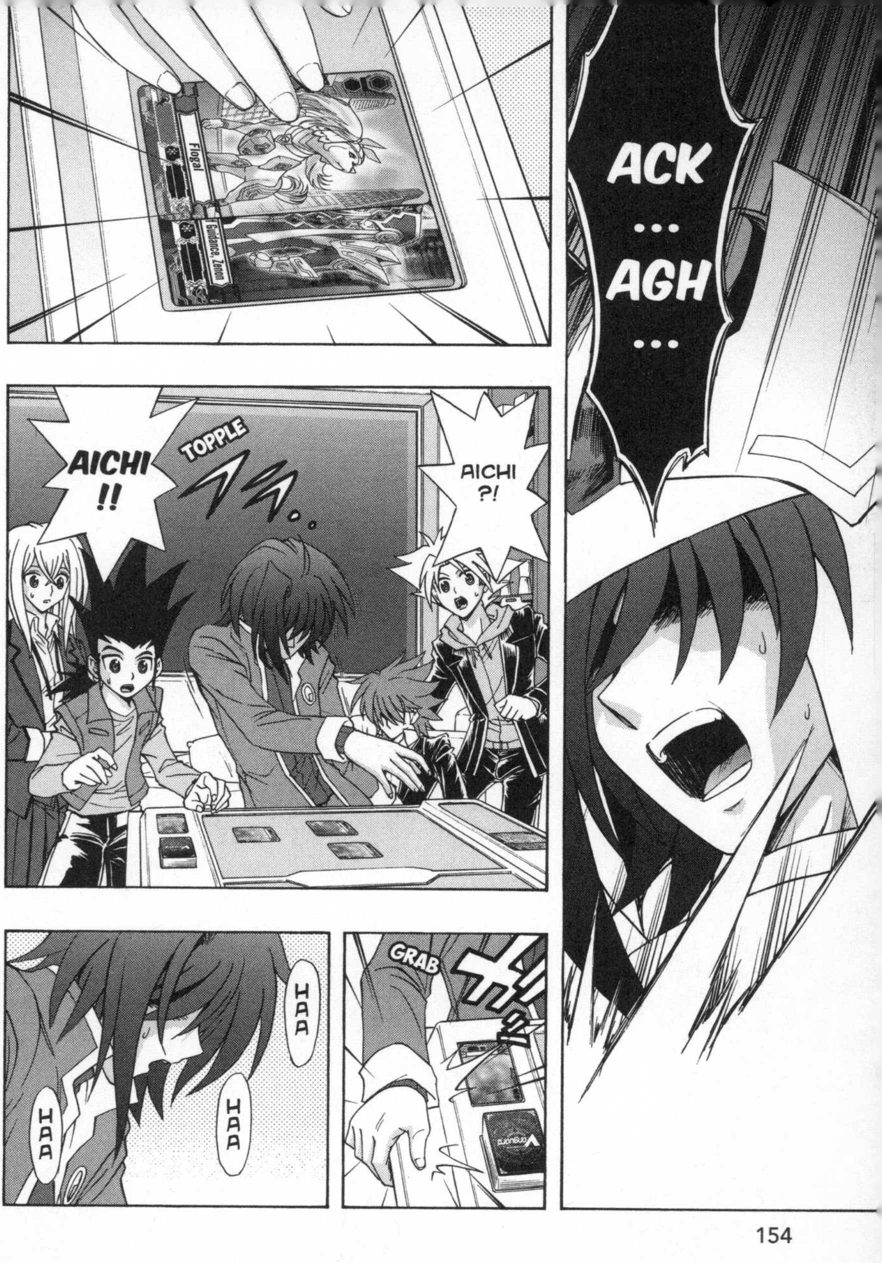
ACK ... AGH ...
Flogal
Guidance, Zenon
AICHI ?!
TOPPLE
AICHI !!
GRAB
HAA
HAA
HAA

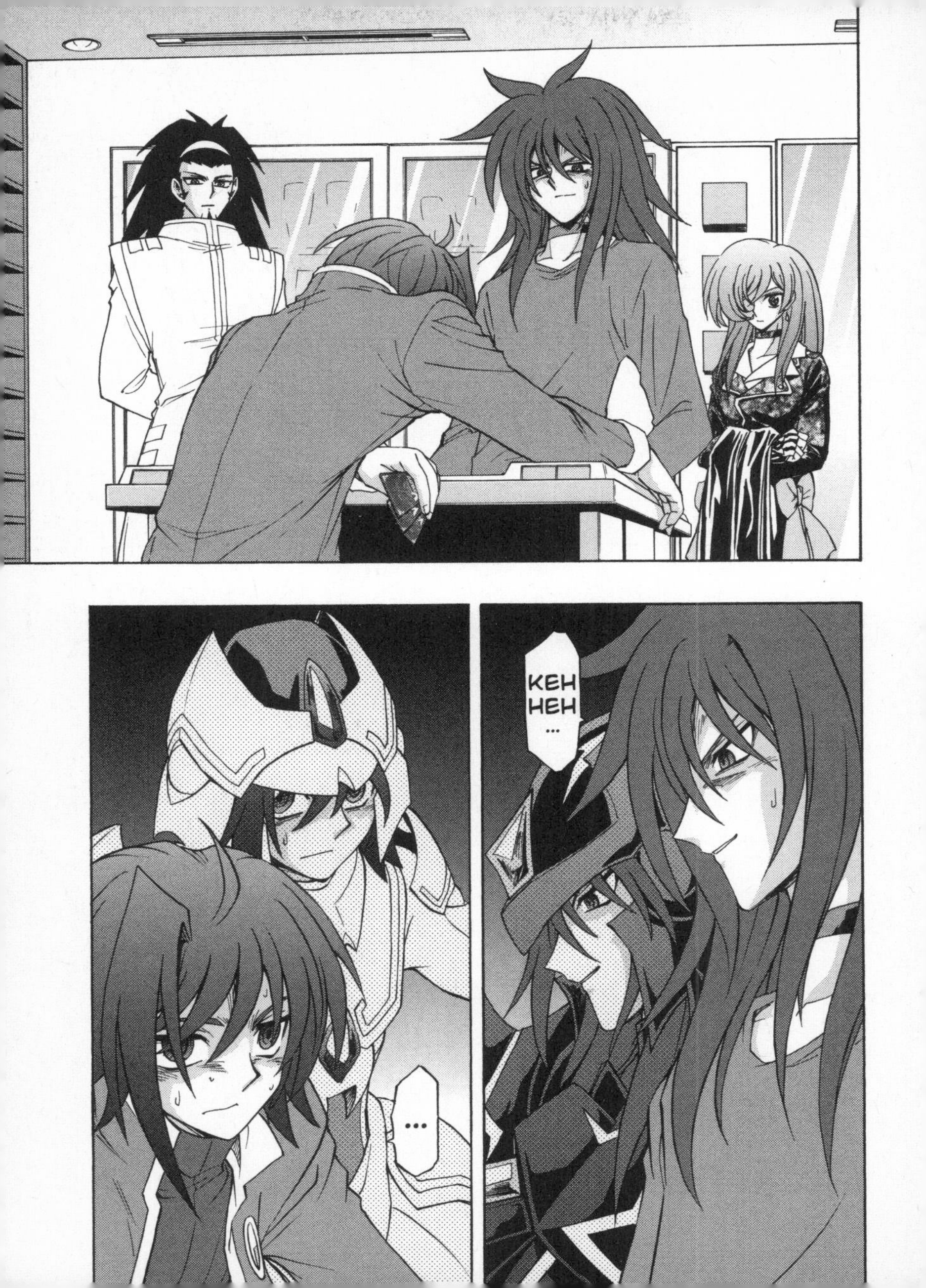
KEH HEH ...
...

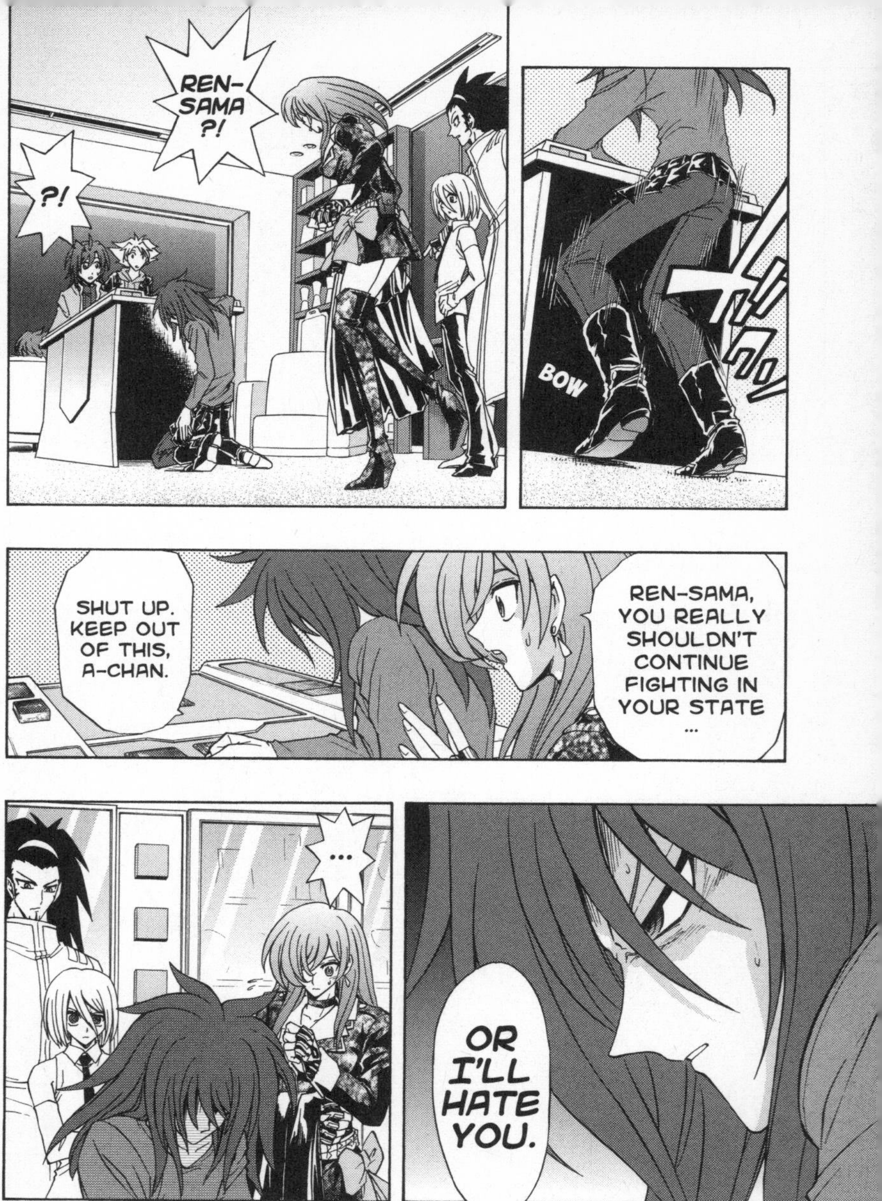
BOW
REN-SAMA ?!
?!
REN-SAMA, YOU REALLY SHOULDN'T CONTINUE FIGHTING IN YOUR STATE ...
SHUT UP. KEEP OUT OF THIS, A-CHAN.
OR I'LL HATE YOU.
...

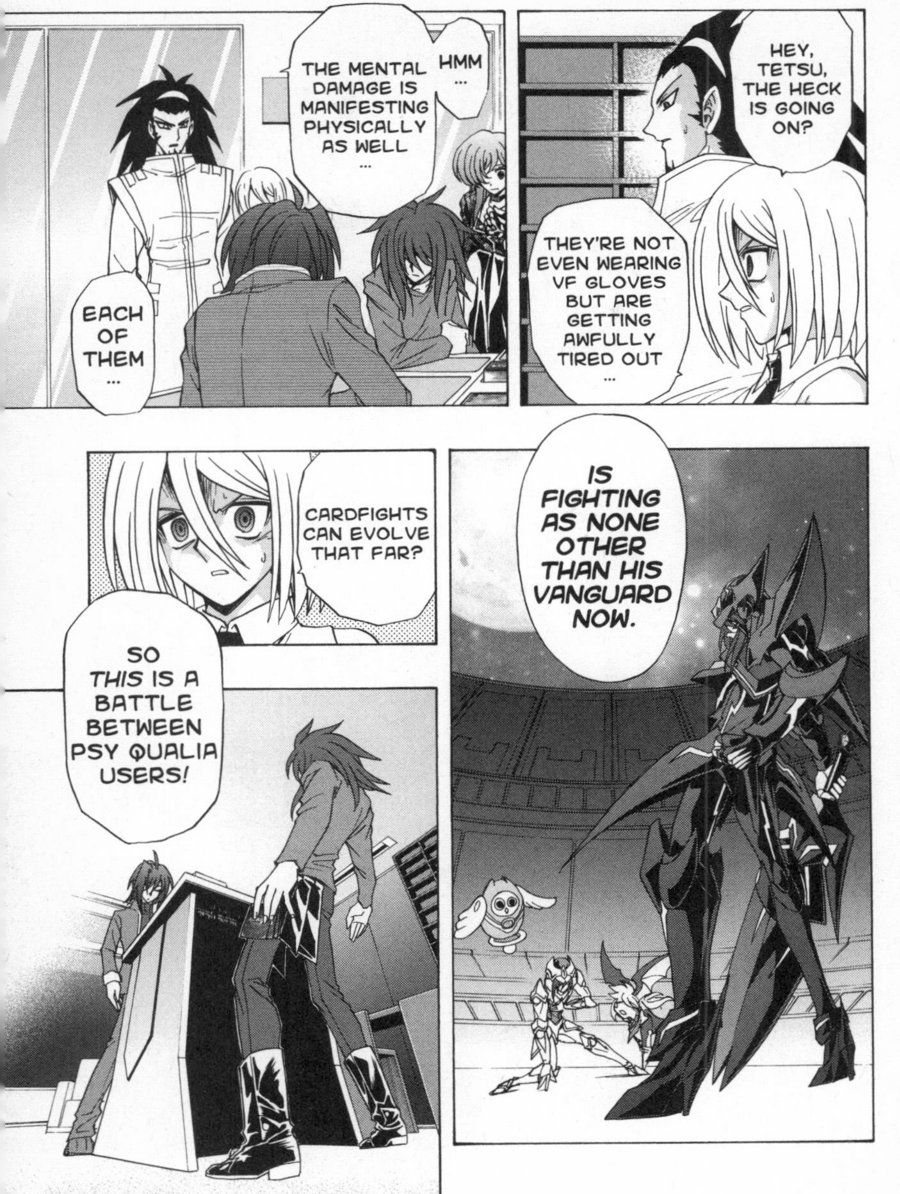
HEY, TETSU, THE HECK IS GOING ON?
THEY'RE NOT EVEN WEARING VF GLOVES BUT ARE GETTING AWFULLY TIRED OUT ...
HMM ...
THE MENTAL DAMAGE IS MANIFESTING PHYSICALLY AS WELL ...
EACH OF THEM ...
IS FIGHTING AS NONE OTHER THAN HIS VANGUARD NOW.
CARDFIGHTS CAN EVOLVE THAT FAR?
SO *THIS* IS A BATTLE BETWEEN PSY QUALIA USERS!

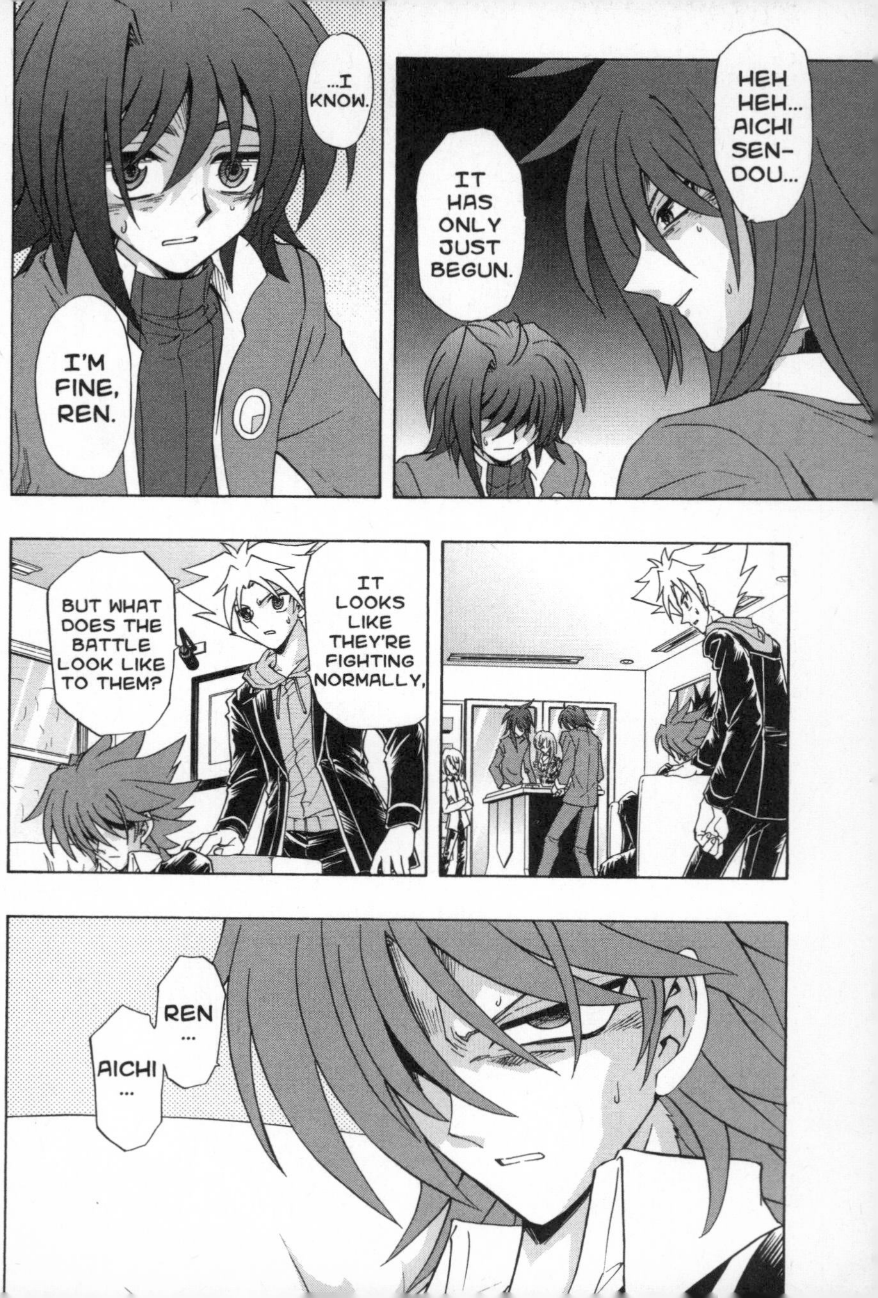
HEH HEH... AICHI SEN-DOU...
IT HAS ONLY JUST BEGUN.
...I KNOW.
I'M FINE, REN.
IT LOOKS LIKE THEY'RE FIGHTING NORMALLY,
BUT WHAT DOES THE BATTLE LOOK LIKE TO THEM?
REN...
AICHI...

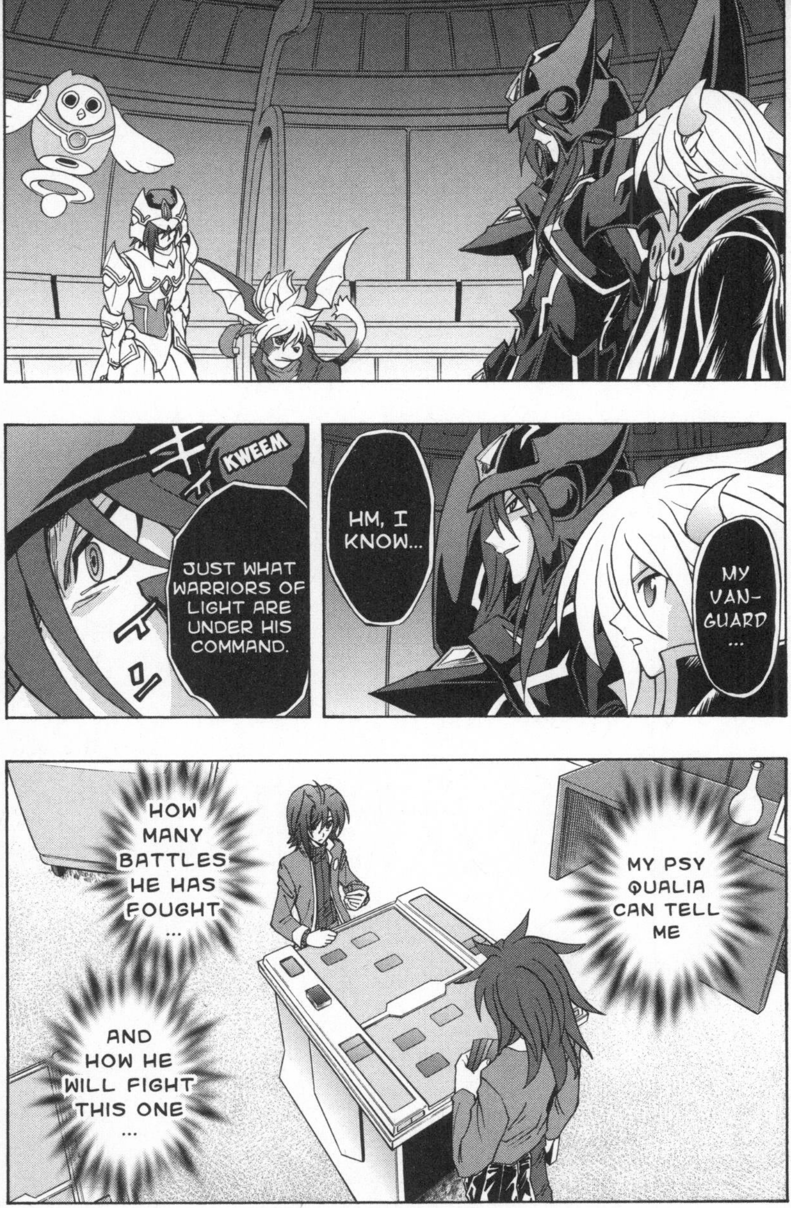
MY VAN-GUARD ...
HM, I KNOW...
KWEEM
JUST WHAT WARRIORS OF LIGHT ARE UNDER HIS COMMAND.
MY PSY QUALIA CAN TELL ME
HOW MANY BATTLES HE HAS FOUGHT ...
AND HOW HE WILL FIGHT THIS ONE ...

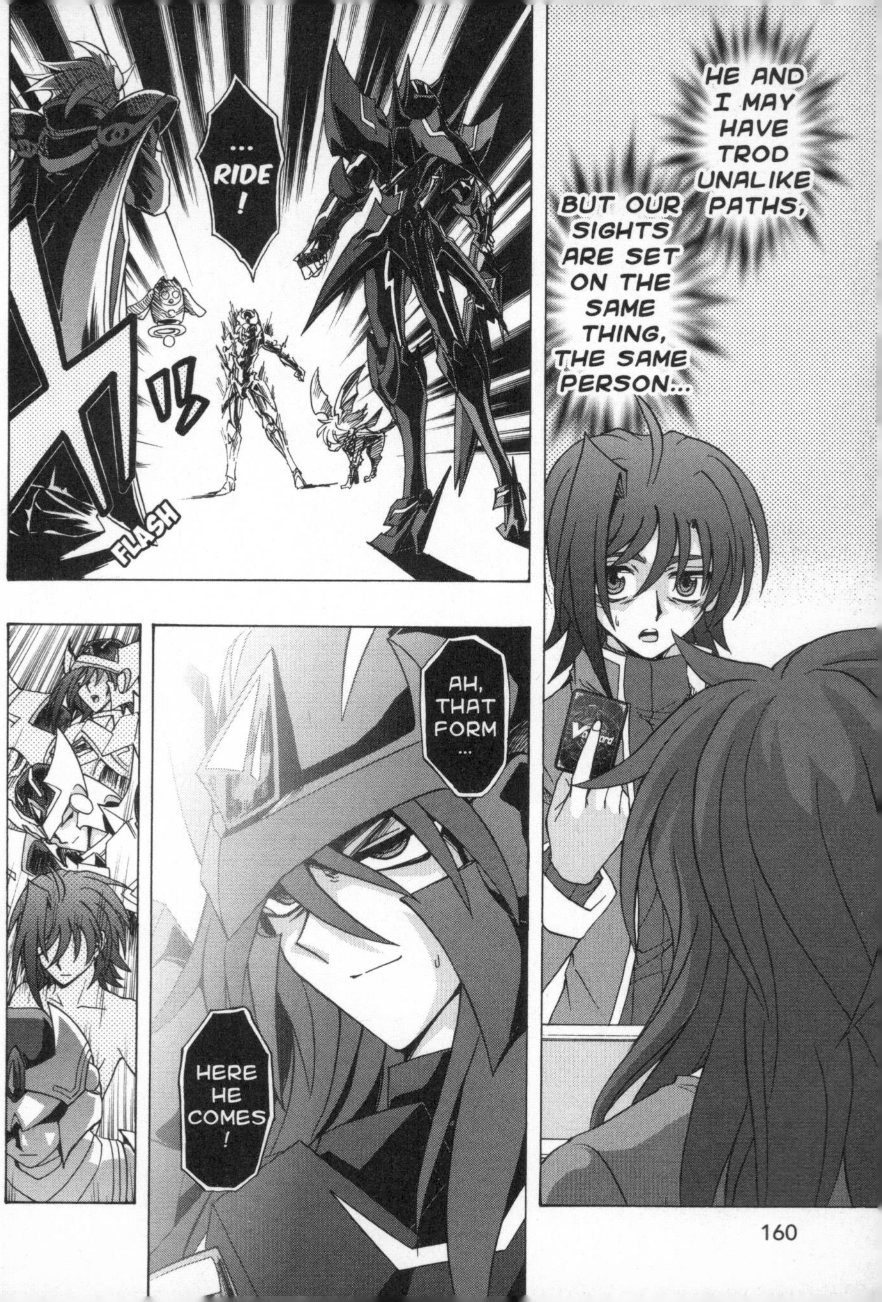
HE AND I MAY HAVE TROD UNALIKE PATHS,
BUT OUR SIGHTS ARE SET ON THE SAME THING, THE SAME PERSON...
... RIDE!
FLASH
AH, THAT FORM...
HERE HE COMES!

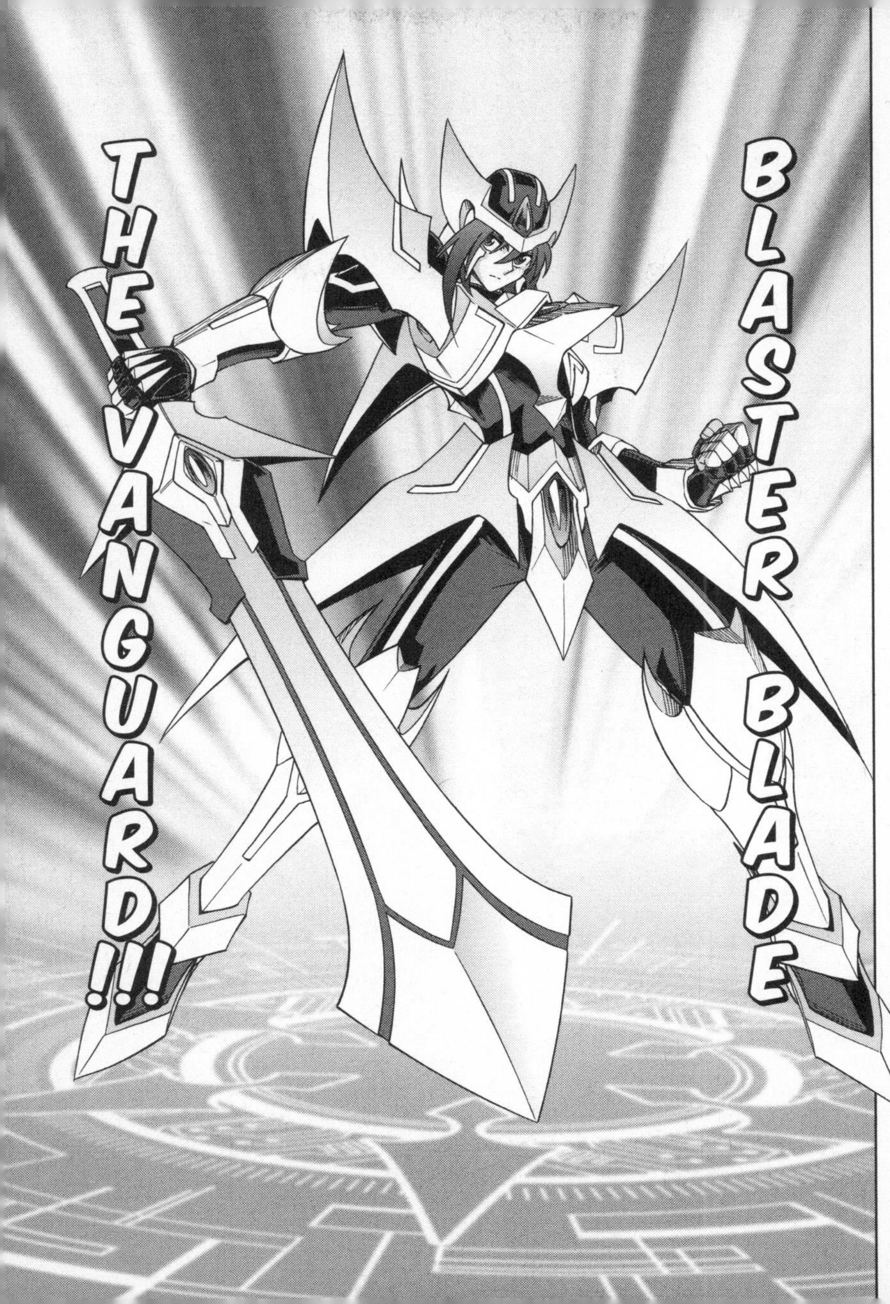
BLASTER BLADE
THE VANGUARD!!!

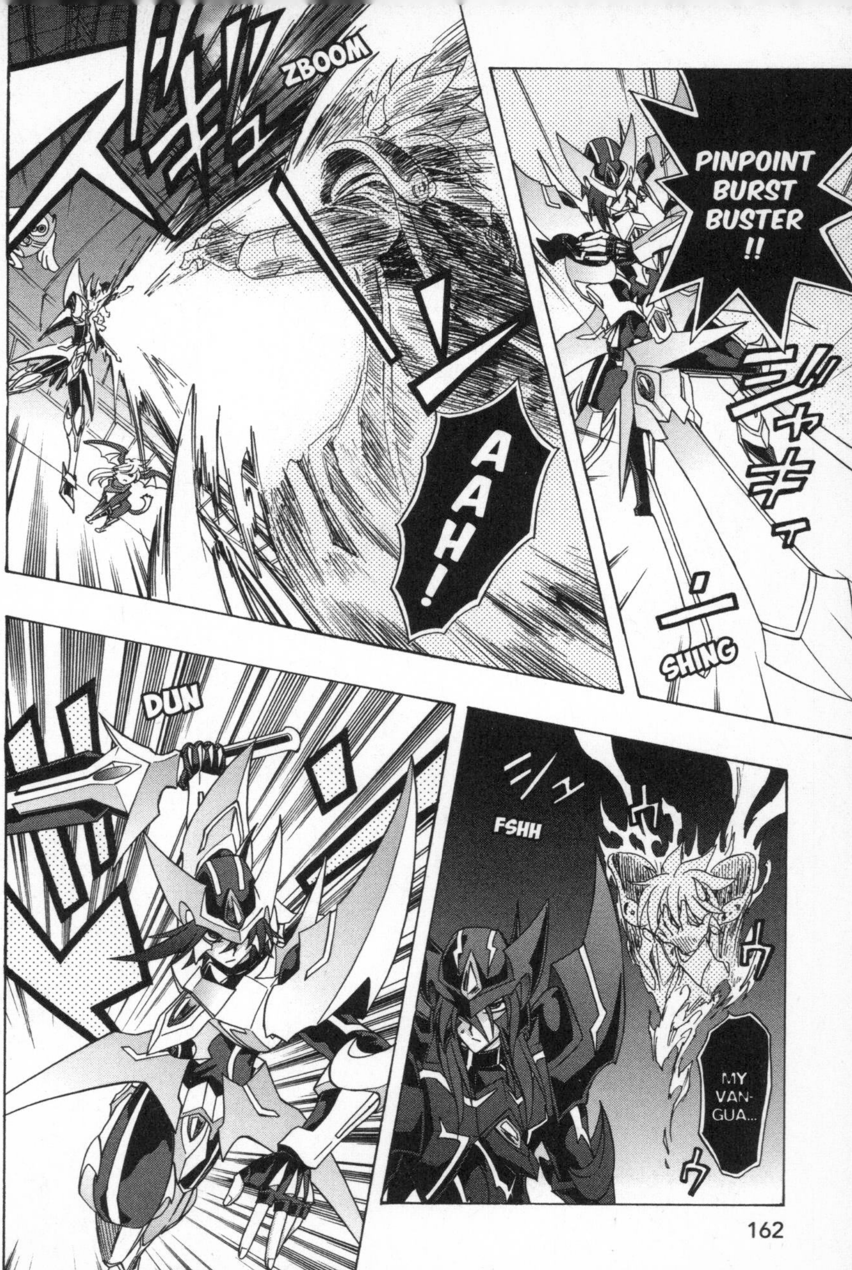
PINPOINT BURST BUSTER !!
SHING
ZBOOM
AAAH!
FSHH
MY VAN-GUA...
DUN

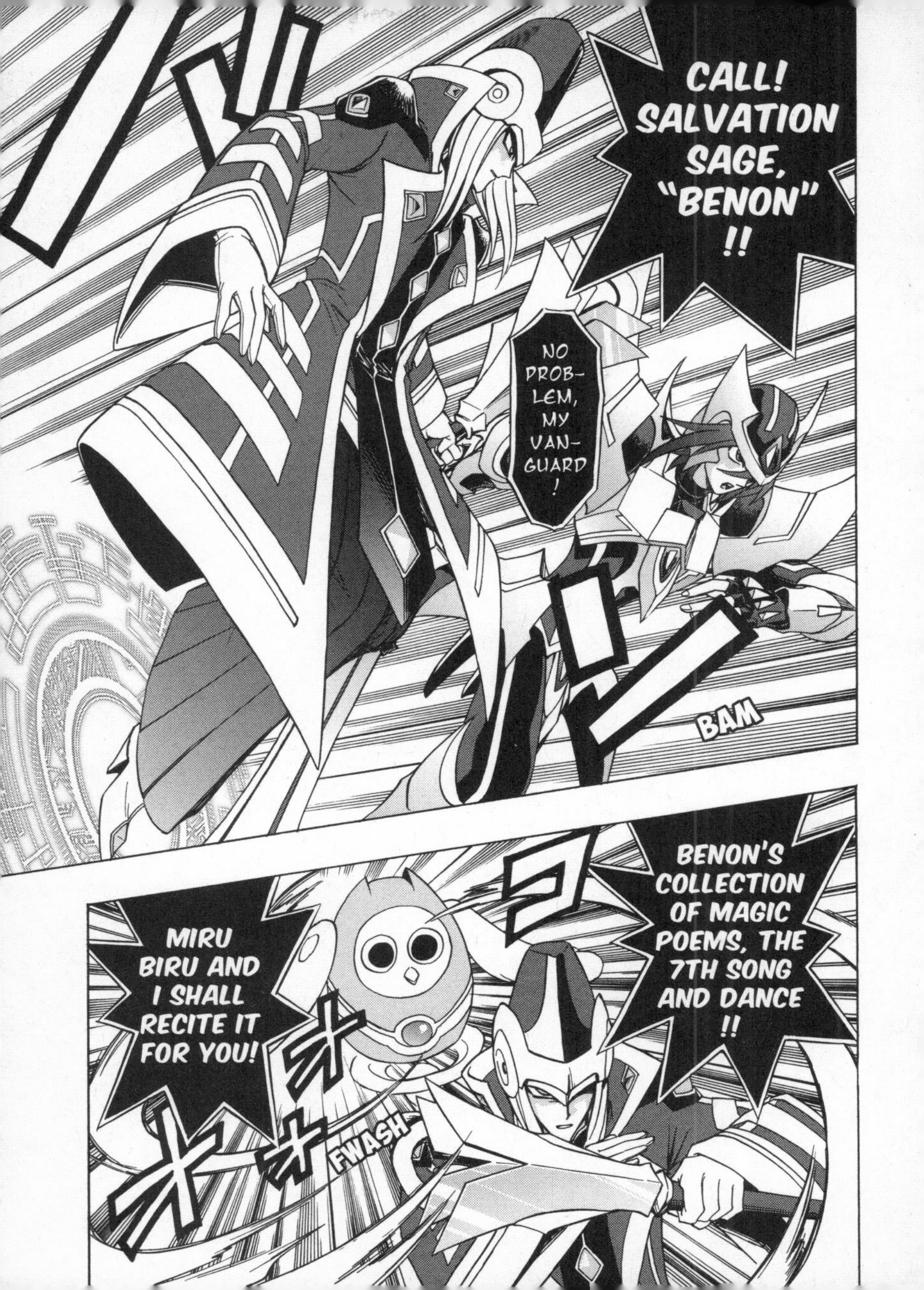
CALL! SALVATION SAGE, "BENON" !!
NO PROB-LEM, MY VAN-GUARD!
BAM
BENON'S COLLECTION OF MAGIC POEMS, THE 7TH SONG AND DANCE !!
MIRU BIRU AND I SHALL RECITE IT FOR YOU!
FWASH

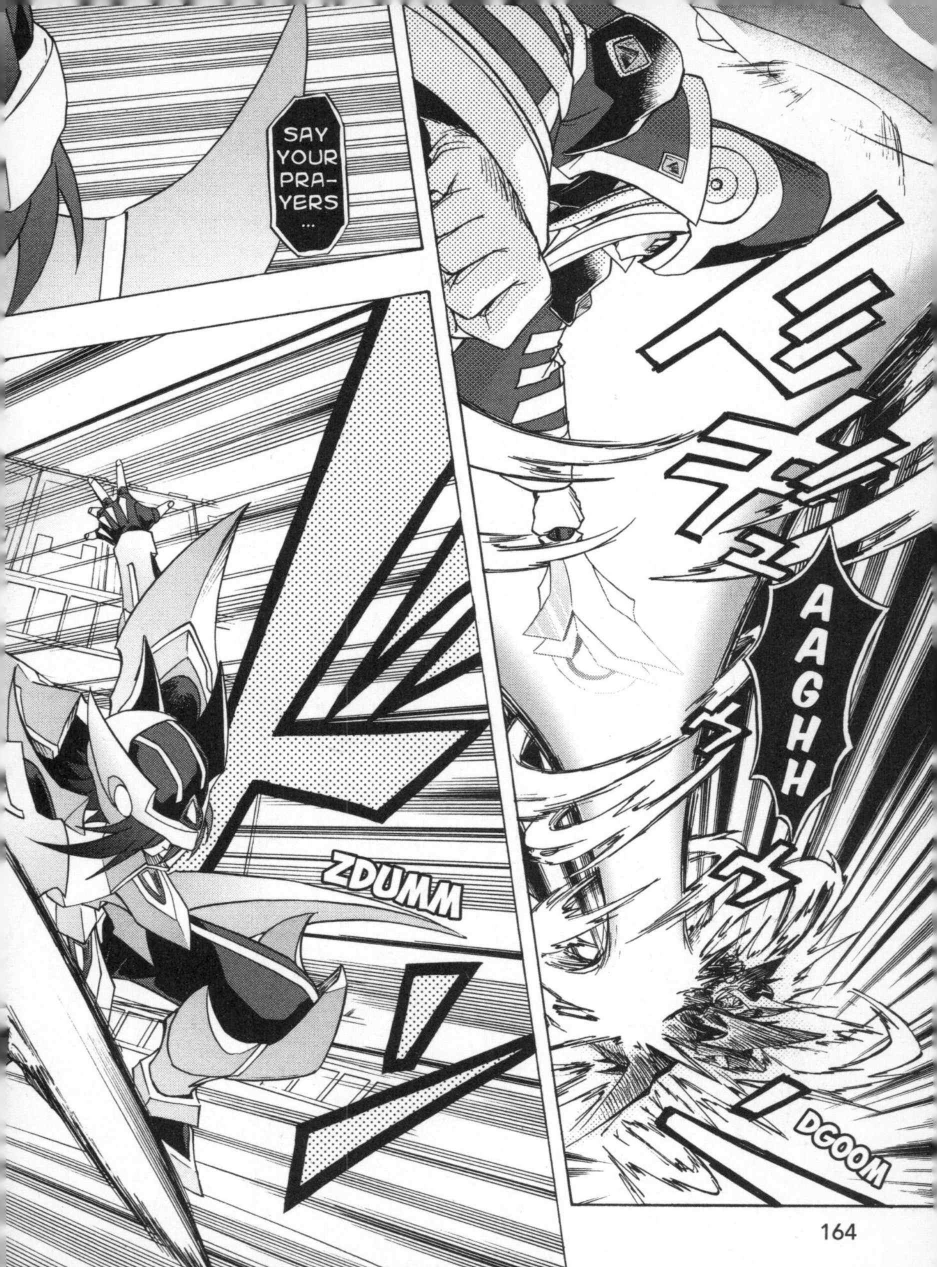
AAAGHH
DGOOM
SAY YOUR PRA-YERS...
ZDUMM

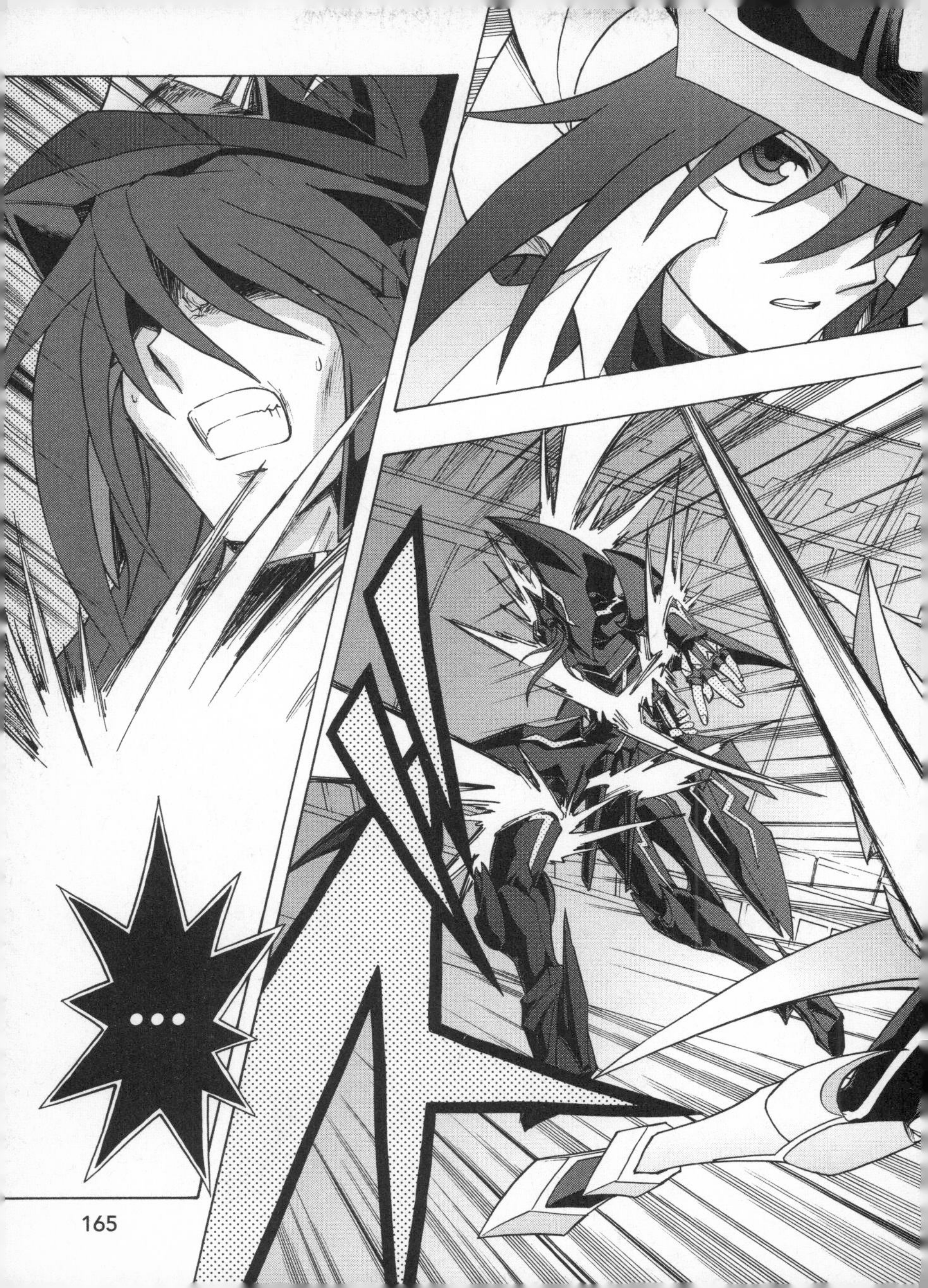
...

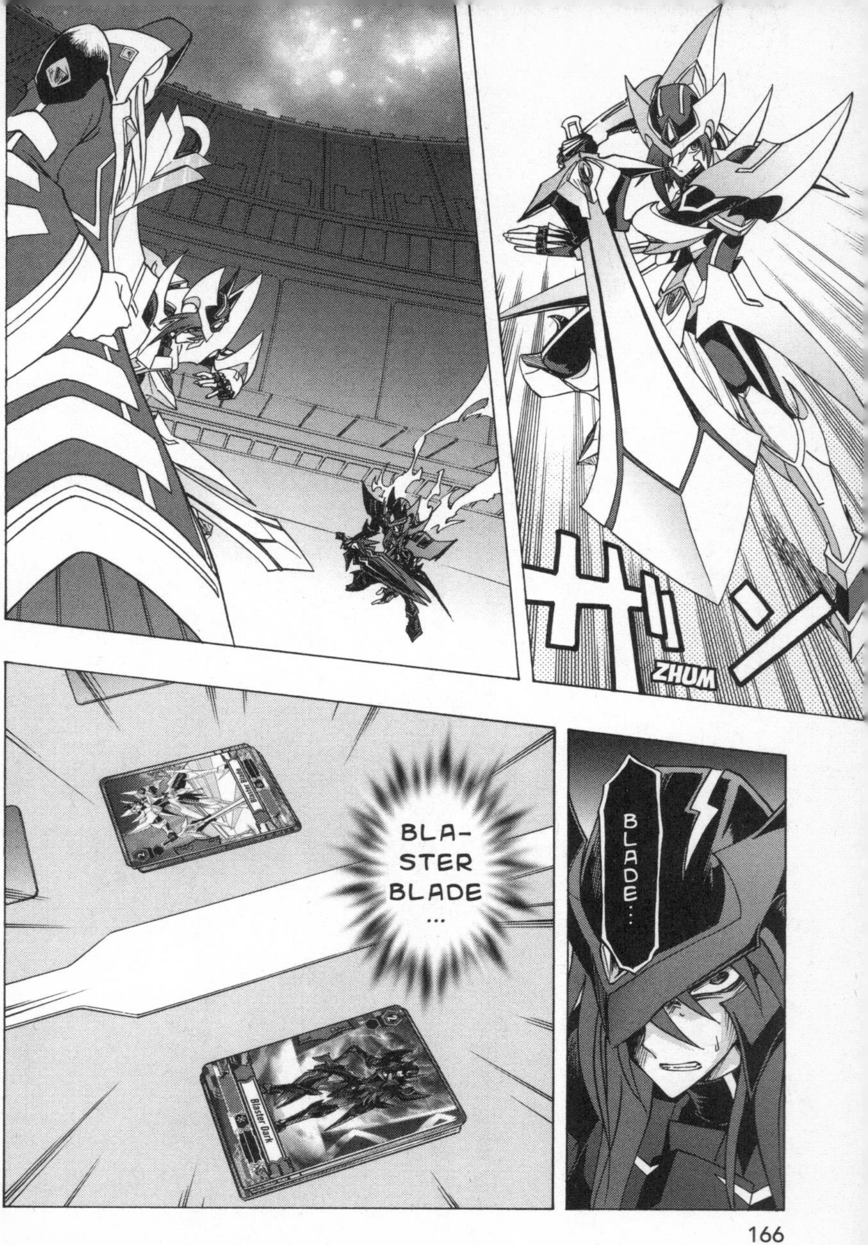
ZHUM
BLADE...
Blaster Blade
BLA-STER BLADE ...
Blaster Dark

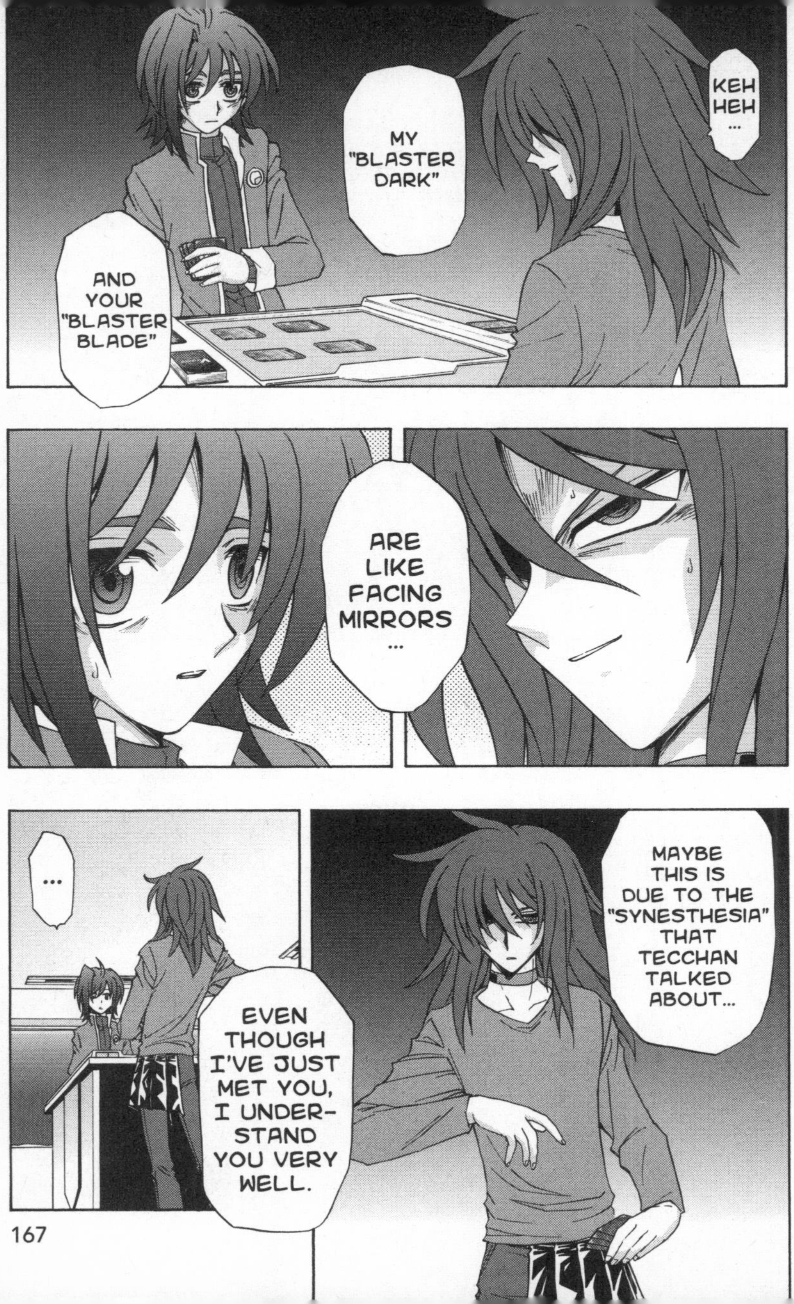
KEH HEH ...
MY "BLASTER DARK"
AND YOUR "BLASTER BLADE"
ARE LIKE FACING MIRRORS ...
MAYBE THIS IS DUE TO THE "SYNESTHESIA" THAT TECCHAN TALKED ABOUT...
EVEN THOUGH I'VE JUST MET YOU, I UNDER-STAND YOU VERY WELL.
...

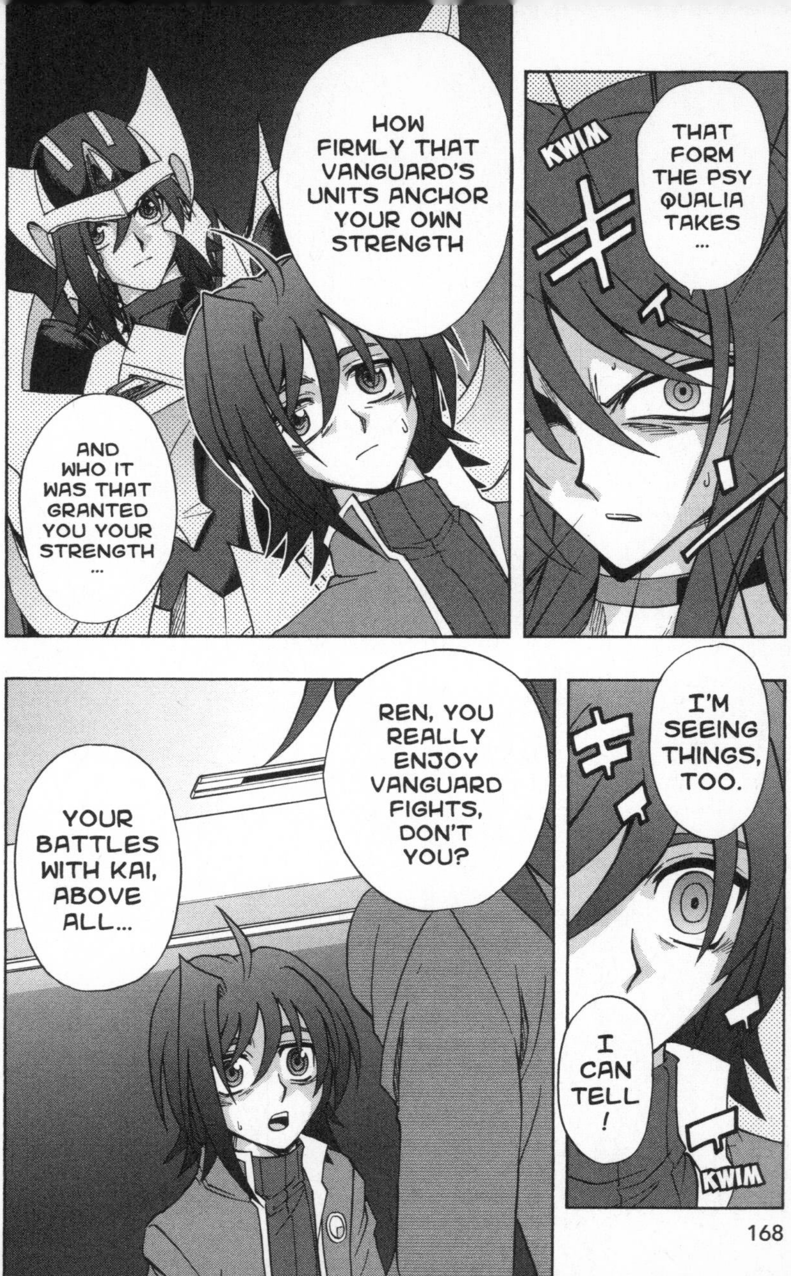
KWIM
THAT FORM THE PSY QUALIA TAKES ...
HOW FIRMLY THAT VANGUARD'S UNITS ANCHOR YOUR OWN STRENGTH
AND WHO IT WAS THAT GRANTED YOU YOUR STRENGTH ...
I'M SEEING THINGS, TOO.
I CAN TELL!
KWIM
REN, YOU REALLY ENJOY VANGUARD FIGHTS, DON'T YOU?
YOUR BATTLES WITH KAI, ABOVE ALL...

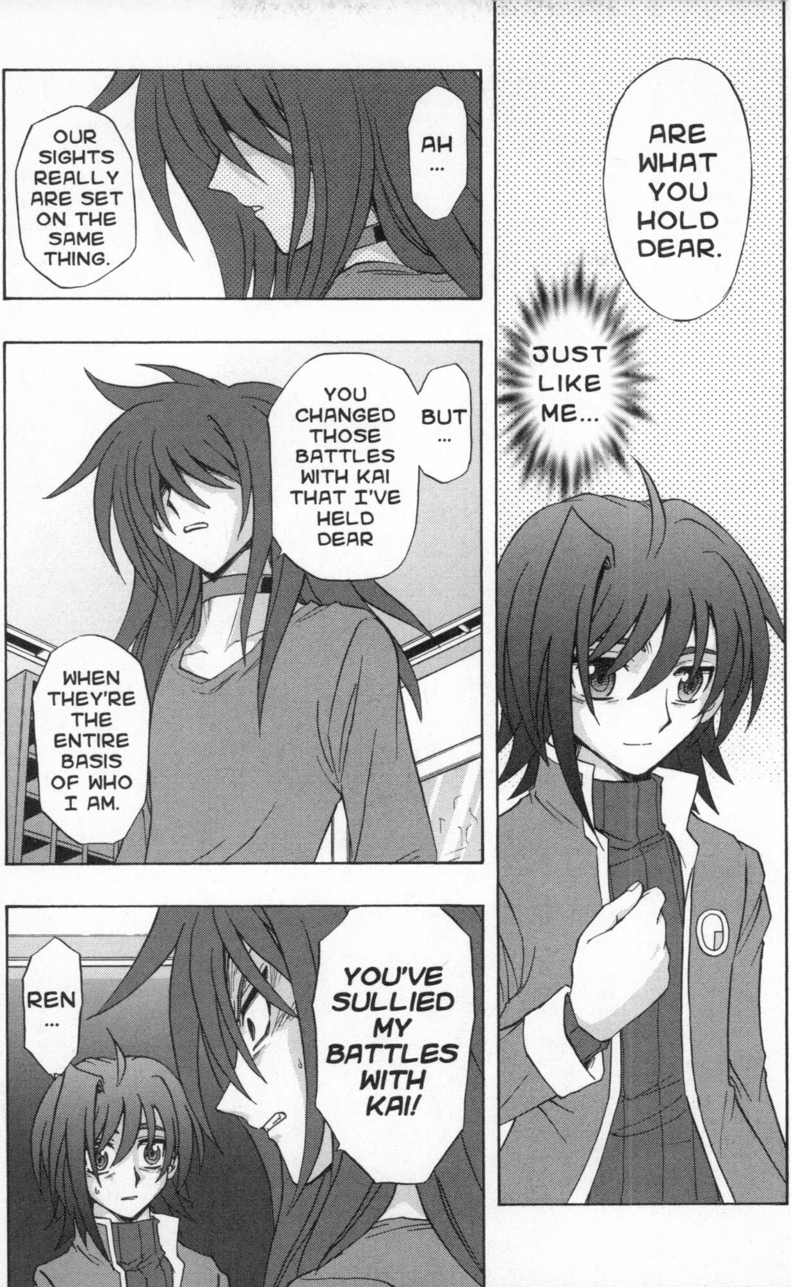
ARE WHAT YOU HOLD DEAR.
JUST LIKE ME...
AH ...
OUR SIGHTS REALLY ARE SET ON THE SAME THING.
BUT ...
YOU CHANGED THOSE BATTLES WITH KAI THAT I'VE HELD DEAR
WHEN THEY'RE THE ENTIRE BASIS OF WHO I AM.
YOU'VE SULLIED MY BATTLES WITH KAI!
REN ...

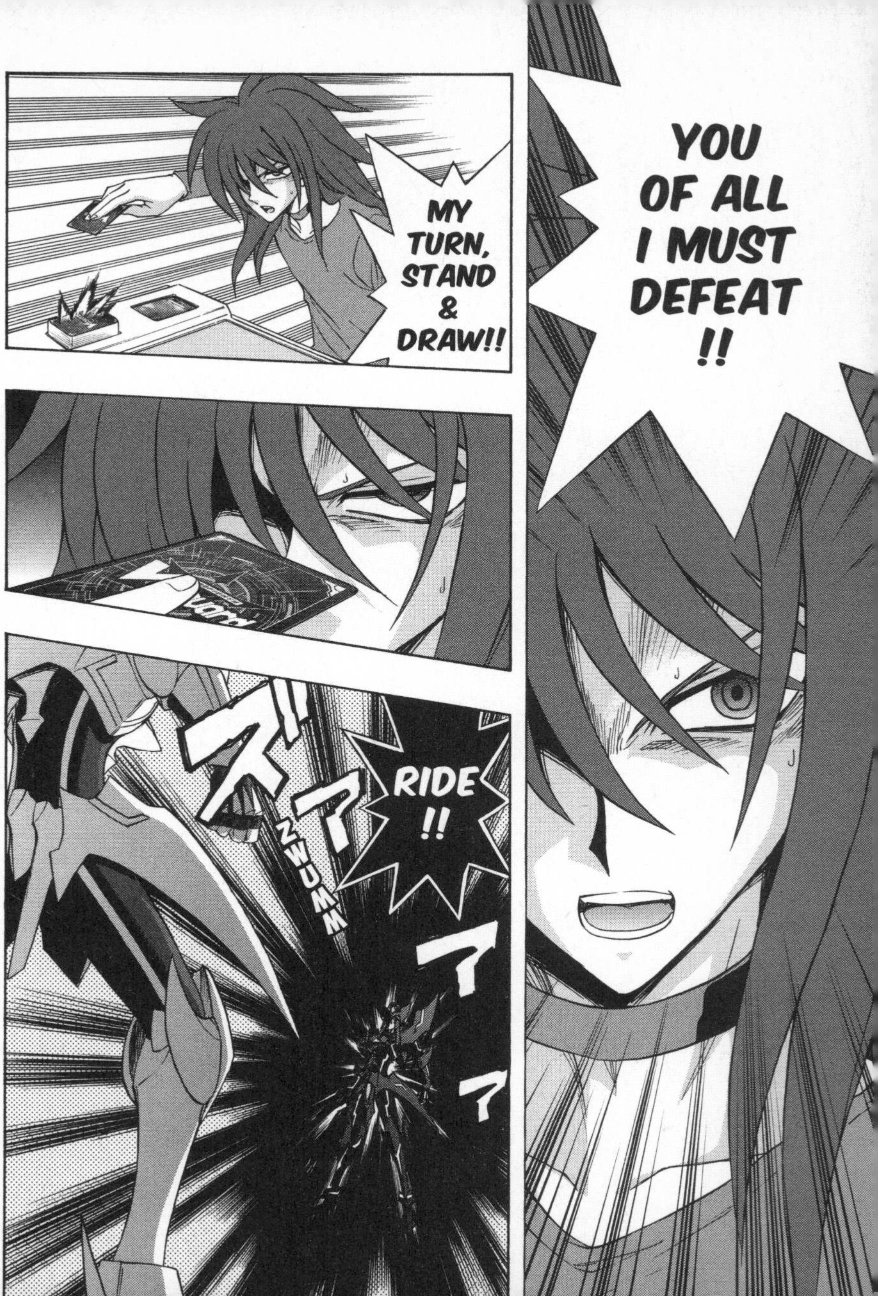
YOU OF ALL I MUST DEFEAT!!
MY TURN, STAND & DRAW!!
RIDE!!
ZWUMM

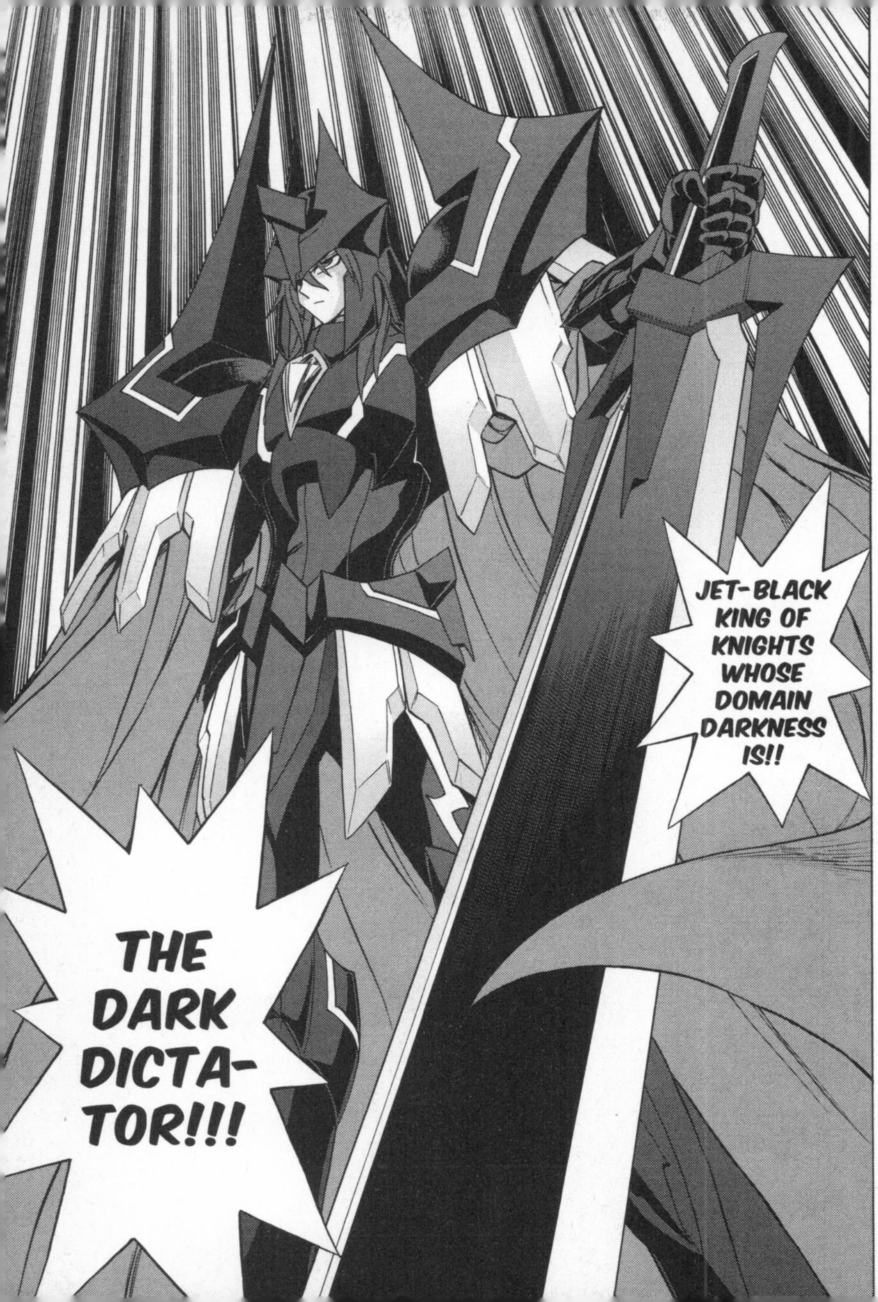
JET-BLACK KING OF KNIGHTS WHOSE DOMAIN DARKNESS IS!!
THE DARK DICTA-TOR!!!

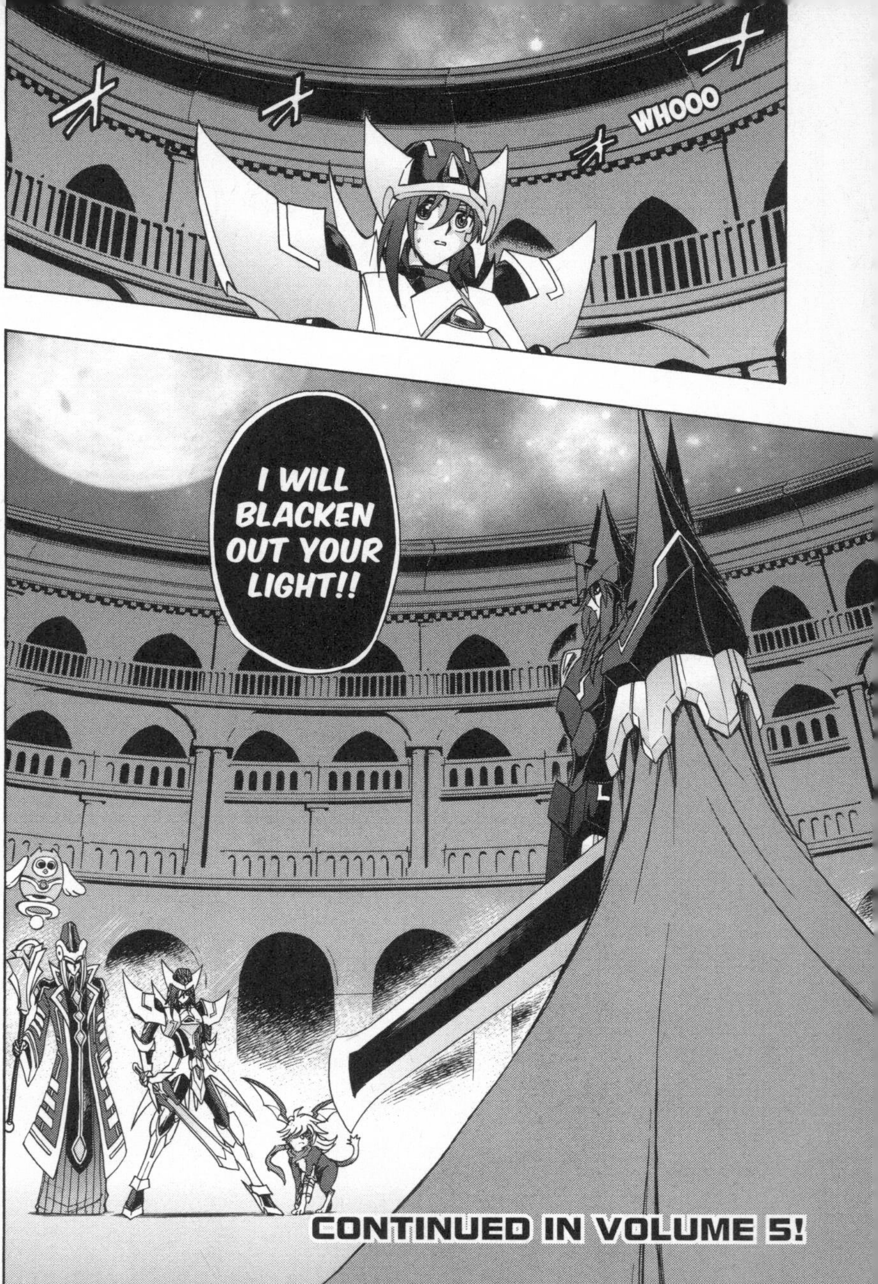
WHOOO
I WILL BLACKEN OUT YOUR LIGHT!!
CONTINUED IN VOLUME 5!

BONUS!

CARDFIGHT!!
Vanguard

NEVER-
BEFORE-
SEEN IMAGE
BOARDS

CHAR-
ACTERS

**Miyaji Academy High
School Summer Uniform**

**Hitsue High School
Summer Uniform**

Kai
doesn't
wear
a tie.

Sleeves
are split

A slit
on this
one too

skin

AK
2011.4

BONUS! CARDFIGHT!! Vanguard

NEVER-BEFORE-SEEN IMAGE BOARDS

CHAR-ACTERS

Fall Semester Casual Clothes

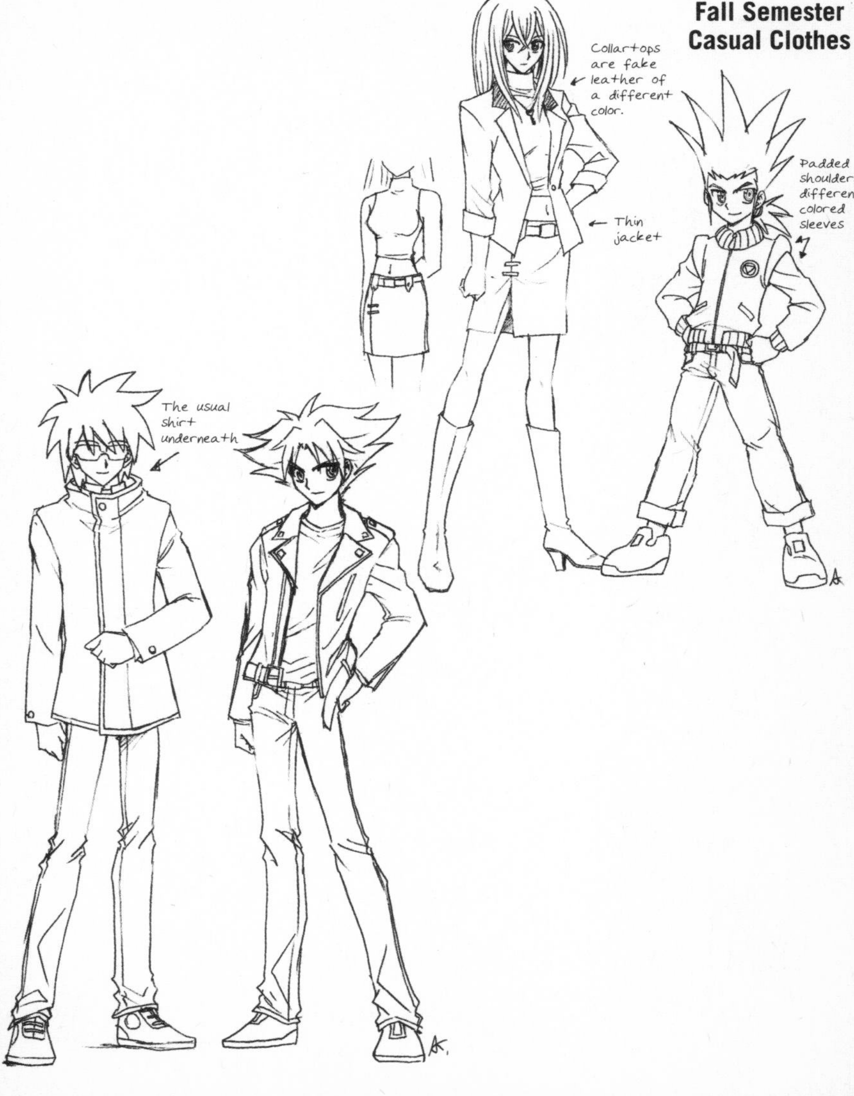

Collartops are fake leather of a different color.
Thin jacket
Padded shoulders, different-colored sleeves
The usual shirt underneath

**Fall Semester
Casual Clothes**

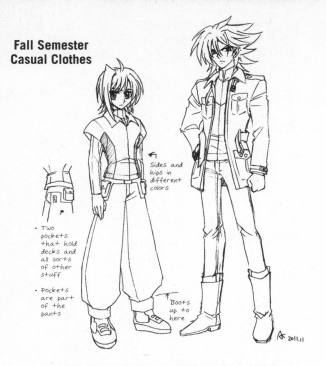

Sides and hips in different colors

• Two pockets that hold decks and all sorts of other stuff

• Pockets are part of the pants

Boots up to here

AK 2011.11

CARDFIGHT!! VANGUARD VOL. 4
ORIGINAL DESIGNS OF THE FEATURED UNITS

CHAPTER 16
Lizard Runner, Undeux / 安達洋介 (Yosuke Adachi)
Embodiment of Armor, Bahr / 安達洋介 (Yosuke Adachi)
Death Feather Eagle / Daisuke Izuka
Lizard Solider, Raopia / タイキ (taiki)
Nightmare Painter / 田所哲平 (Teppei Tadokoro)
Black Sage, Charon / KEI

CHAPTER 17
Lizard Runner, Nafd / Eel
Red Gem Carbuncle / 叶之明 (Akira Kano)

All Other Units / Akira Itou

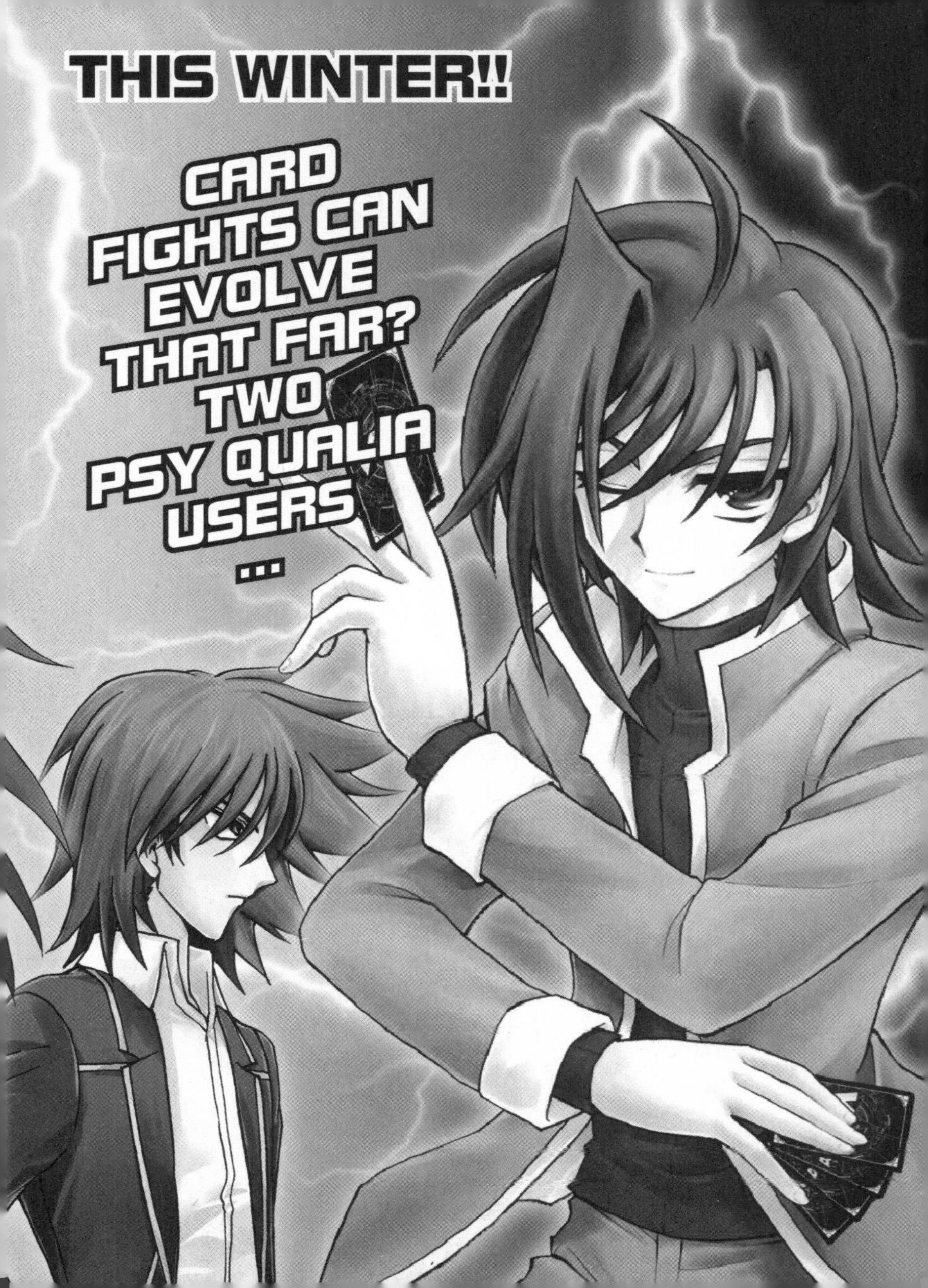
THIS WINTER!!
CARD FIGHTS CAN EVOLVE THAT FAR? TWO PSY QUALIA USERS ...

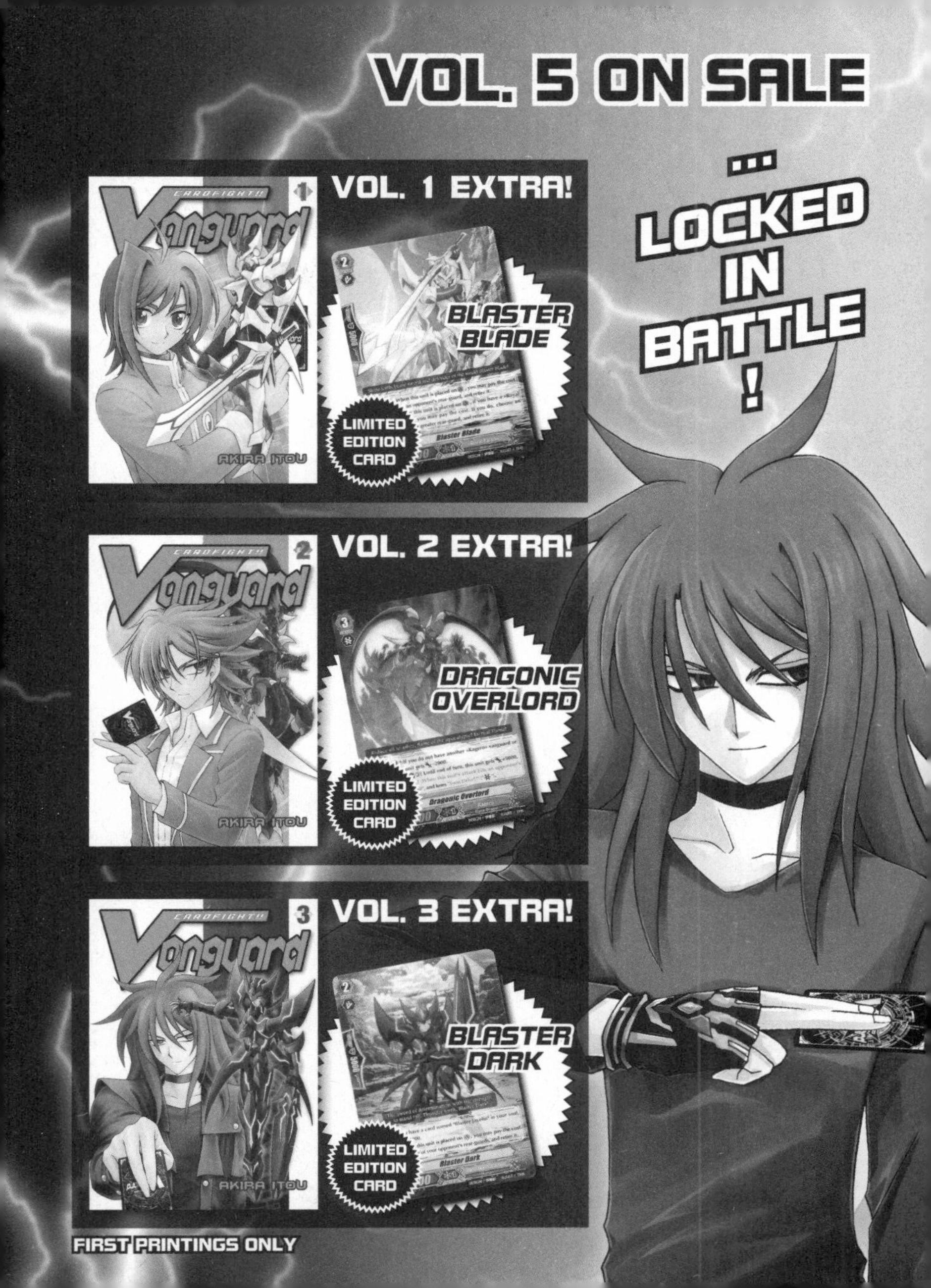
VOL. 5 ON SALE
... LOCKED IN BATTLE !
CARDFIGHT!! Vanguard 1
AKIRA ITOU
VOL. 1 EXTRA!
BLASTER BLADE
LIMITED EDITION CARD
CARDFIGHT!! Vanguard 2
AKIRA ITOU
VOL. 2 EXTRA!
DRAGONIC OVERLORD
LIMITED EDITION CARD
CARDFIGHT!! Vanguard 3
AKIRA ITOU
VOL. 3 EXTRA!
BLASTER DARK
LIMITED EDITION CARD
FIRST PRINTINGS ONLY

CARDFIGHT! VANGUARD
VOLUME 4

Production: Grace Lu
           Anthony Quintessenza

Copyright © Akira ITOU 2012
           © bushiroad All Rights Reserved.
Edited by KADOKAWA SHOTEN
First published in Japan in 2012 by KADOKAWA CORPORATION, Tokyo.
English translation rights arranged with KADOKAWA CORPORATION, Tokyo
through TUTTLE-MORI AGENCY, INC., Tokyo.
English language version produced by Vertical, Inc.

Translation provided by Vertical, Inc., 2014
Published by Vertical, Inc., New York

Originally published in Japanese as *Kaadofaito!! Vangaado 4* by KADOKAWA
CORPORATION
Kaadofaito!! Vangaado first serialized in *Young Ace*, 2011-

This is a work of fiction.

ISBN: 978-1-939130-65-5

Manufactured in Canada

First Edition

Vertical, Inc.
451 Park Avenue South
7th Floor
New York, NY 10016
www.vertical-inc.com

DEC 2 1 2014